JAPAN

THE SYSTEM THAT SOURED

JAPAN
THE SYSTEM THAT SOURED

The Rise and Fall
of the
Japanese Economic
Miracle

RICHARD KATZ

An East Gate Book

M.E. Sharpe
Armonk, New York
London, England

An East Gate Book

Prior Publication: Some material in this book was previously published in
Japan Economic Studies, March–April 1996, and the *Washington Quarterly*,
Vol. 20, No. 2, Spring 1997

Library of Congress Cataloging-in-Publication Data

Katz, Richard, 1951–
Japan: the system that soured—the rise and fall of the Japanese
economic miracle / Richard Katz.
p. cm.
"An east gate book."
Includes bibliographical references and index.
ISBN 0-7656-0309-8 (cloth : alk. paper). —
ISBN 0-7656-0310-1 (pbk. : alk. paper)
1. Japan—Commercial policy. 2. Industrial policy—Japan.
3. Japan—Economic conditions—1989– I. Title.
HF1601.K29 1998
338.952—DC21   98-11091
CIP

Printed in the United States of America

MV (c)   10   9   8   7   6   5   4   3   2
MV (p)   10   9   8   7   6   5   4

To Linda and Laura

Contents

Part Four: The Road Ahead

Appendices

Acknowledgments

Without the help and encouragement of many people in the U.S. and Japan, this book could not have been written.

There is scarcely a major idea in this book that I have not talked over with my friend and journalistic colleague Peter Ennis, the U.S. correspondent for the Japanese business magazine *Toyo Keizai* and the editor-in-chief of its English-language publication, *The Oriental Economist Report*. Peter and I have been talking about Japan for nearly a quarter of a century. If not for him, the ideas in this book would have been less clear, less accurate, and less interesting.

At a key point in my work, I received sage advice from Daniel Sneider, another friend and journalistic colleague. Dan is a former Tokyo correspondent for the *Christian Science Monitor*. Without his advice, the research project that led to this book might never have been undertaken.

Many people gave support and encouragement along the way, but the following individuals provided special assistance that helped the ideas in this book see the light of day: Kent Calder, Merit Janow, Takao Toshikawa, Yuji Aso, Wakako Otsubo, Takashi Kiuchi, James Kilpatrick, and Motoya Kitamura.

Several people from the assorted "analytical camps" surrounding Japan-related issues, as well as some other individuals, read various parts of the manuscript and offered comments, criticism and suggestions. They include: Walter Hatch, Ira Wolf, Clyde Prestowitz, Hugh Patrick, David Asher, Edwin Marks, and Peter Rush.

Meanwhile, the Japan Economic Seminar, a quarterly gathering of economists, provided me with the opportunity to get professional feedback on the thesis of this book. The Seminar's leaders are: Professors James Nakamura, Hugh Patrick, Kazuo Sato (who took the trouble to write a long critique), and, at the time, Fumio Hayashi. The discussant for the paper was Sumiye Okubo.

The original research for this book came out of work for my Masters

Degree in Economics at New York University. My thanks to my readers, Professors Bernard Wasow and Edward Wolff, and the departmental secretary, Marjorie Lesser.

At JETRO New York, Hiro Sato and Katsuhiko Masubuchi, tirelessly located critical data for me. The same is true of Tonya Kemp and some of the other staff at the Japan Economic Institute in Washington, DC, as well as Mali Quintana at the New York Office of Deutsche Morgan Grenfell. I thank them all wholeheartedly.

My thanks to all who provided feedback and assistance. As usual, the help people gave me should not be taken to imply endorsement of my views. Any errors of fact or judgment are my sole responsibility.

At M.E. Sharpe, editor Doug Merwin was very supportive. He readily endorsed the unusual notion of a "crossover" book that would address a general audience in the main section and have more technical appendices in the back for textbook use. He also made sure the book would get out quickly enough to address a rapidly changing situation. In Angela Piliouras I was given a production editor who worked harder and was more tolerant of all my changes and updates than I had any right to expect.

None of the words in this book have been as hard to find as ones sufficient to express my infinite gratitude to my wife, Linda, and my daughter, Laura, who turned 3 years old while this book was being written. Linda has been my partner, adviser and confidante throughout this project. She took on far more than her share of household and parental responsibilities, and delayed some of her own work-related projects, in order to give me time to write. Laura exhibited unbelievable patience with my inability to play with her as much as I used to, and she kept reassuring me that, "The publisher will say it's a beautiful book." This book is dedicated to them.

List of Figures

List of Tables

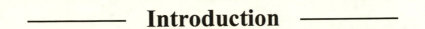

Introduction

What Happened to the Miracle?

Chapter 1

Mainframe Economics in a PC World

The ideas of economists and political philosophers, both when they are right and when they are wrong, are more powerful than is commonly understood. Indeed the world is ruled by little else. Practical men, who believe themselves to be quite exempt from any intellectual influences, are usually the slaves of some defunct economist. Madmen in authority, who hear voices in the air, are distilling their frenzy from some academic scribbler of a few years back. . . . Soon or late, it is ideas, not vested interests, which are dangerous for good or evil.

—John Maynard Keynes, 1936[1]

If Japan fails to end industrial policy, its postwar developmentalism may be judged a failure.

—Yasusuke Murakami, 1996[2]

What Happened to the "Japanese Juggernaut"?

Generals, they say, are trained to fight the last war; that is why they lose the next one.

That, in a nutshell, is why the high-flying Japanese economic miracle tumbled to earth. The ideas and strategies that worked so brilliantly in the era of industrial takeoff had outlived their usefulness once Japan's economy matured. And yet Japan could not bring itself to leave them behind. Over time, past strengths became the source of current weakness.

As a result, the nation once predicted to dominate the world economy now struggles to keep up. The world's greatest growth machine spent much of the 1990s hardly growing at all. The economic system once seen as a model for the world is now viewed as the country's biggest ball and chain.

Even some of the bureaucracies that managed Japan for so long seem shell-shocked. "[T]he economic system that has supported the fifty years of economic development following World War II is ill-suited for future growth" is how Japan's Ministry of International Trade and Industry (MITI) put it in a belated recognition of the problem. "Structural reform is a race against time and Japan is clearly falling behind in that race," the Economic Planning Agency warned in December of 1996. Many of Japan's once-vaunted economic practices, says the EPA, "are now nothing more than obstacles to future economic development."[3]

Without sweeping structural reforms, Japan will continue to stagnate. Japan's productivity growth is so dismal these days that, even if it operated at full capacity, economists say the fastest it could grow is around 2 percent or so. That's half the 4 percent rate it averaged from 1975 to 1990. And yet, because of Japan's myriad macroeconomic problems, Japan has commonly been unable to operate at full capacity. In four out of the six years since fiscal 1992, Japan has grown less than 1 percent, and in three of those four years less than 0.5 percent. Japan grew less over the entire five-year period from mid-1992 through mid-1997 than it did in the single year of 1990. Unless there is massive budgetary stimulus, this negligible growth is expected to continue through at least 1998 and 1999 (see Figure 1.1). By the dawn of the new millennium, Japan will have spent an entire decade growing more slowly than the United States, the nation it was supposedly "on track to overtake by the year 2000."[4]

Nor is this a temporary slump. According to official forecasts, without reforms, even at full capacity, the fastest growth Japan could sustain between now and 2010 is only 1.8 percent a year. After 2010, says the normally optimistic MITI, the combination of poor productivity and a declining labor force means it will get worse. Japan's growth potential will plunge to only 0.8 percent a year.[5]

How did this happen? How could the world's most acclaimed economic miracle have stumbled so badly?

The root of the problem is that Japan is still mired in the structures, policies and mental habits that prevailed in the 1950s-60s. What we have come to think of as the "Japanese economic system" was a marvelous system to help a backward Japan catch up to the West. But it turned into a terrible system once Japan had in fact caught up. Korea's current trevails are a more tumultuous example of the same phenomenon.

In the "last war," the battle to industrialize Japan in the 1950s-60s, the "developmental state"[6] policies that gave rise to the nickname "Japan Inc." worked brilliantly. But that was so only because the country was in the "catch-up" phase of its economic evolution. All along the economic horizon

Figure 1.1 **What Happened to the Miracle?**

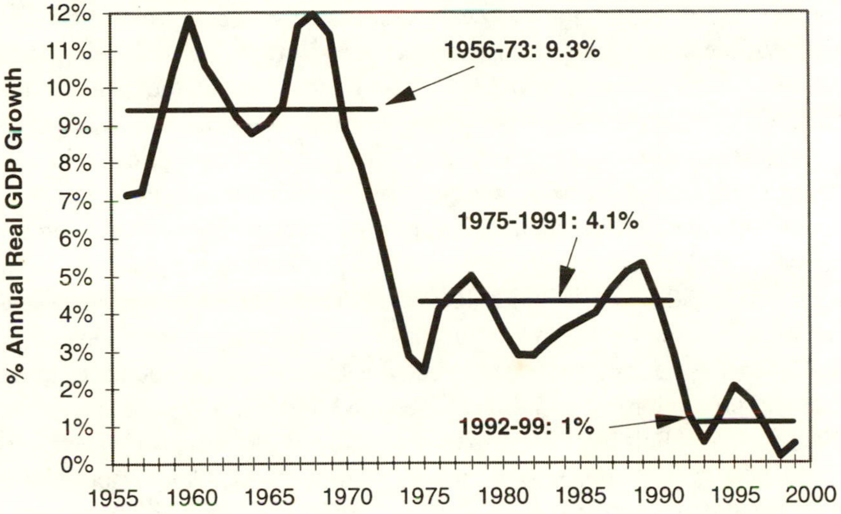

Source: EPA (1977) for 1956–96. 1977–99 are consensus estimates as of March 1998.
Note: All are fiscal years. The line depicts a 3-year moving average.

were a host of infant industries, from autos to electronics, with the potential to become world-class competitors. However, these industries needed a jump-start to get over the initial hurdle. They had not yet acquired either the economies of scale or the learning-by-doing efficiencies to be competitive. Without protection, they might have been strangled in their cradles. The auto industry, for example, was almost wiped out by a flood of European imports during a brief interlude of free trade in 1953. And yet, these were industries that, if given an initial boost, could become powerful exporters able to compete without further aid. Indeed, as each grew, the ripple effects stimulated the others. The growth of steel lowered steel prices, which in turn lowered car costs, leading to more car sales, hence more demand for steel. The same kind of economies of scale and inter-industry synergy applied to TVs and semiconductors. Hence, when Tokyo applied promotional policies in the catch-up era—from stiff import quotas, to massive subsidies, to authorization of export cartels— it fostered an industrial takeoff the likes of which the world had never seen.

Admittedly, even in the catch-up era, Tokyo also aided many industries with no potential to become exporters, from aviation to chemicals. And when it did, the measures flopped.

Yet, the very nature of an economy in the state of catch-up is that it contains a plethora of true infant industries. Consequently, on balance, Japan's promotional policies well deserved the label "economic miracle." Would Japan have industrialized even without such developmental policies? Undoubtedly. Would it have done it anywhere near as fast? Hardly.

Unfortunately, at the very point in Japan's evolution when the "developmentalist" policies should have been loosened, they were reinforced. By the 1970s, when Japan had matured economically, "catch-up economics" had turned counterproductive. There were no more infant industries needing an initial push. "Developmental state" policies make sense only for an economy still in the "state of development."

Nonetheless, Japan continued to use the same economic tactics of protection and promotion in the 1970s and beyond. Indeed, when the oil crises of 1973 and 1979 hurt basic industries, protection of these industries was intensified. The "Japanese economic model" that we see today is not, as some have suggested, a different *kind* of capitalism. It is rather a holdover from an earlier *stage* of capitalism. It is the spectacle of a country vainly trying to carry into maturity economic patterns better suited to its adolescence.

For Japan, this turned into a recipe for debilitation. Instead of turning infant industries into export stars, the same tools amounted to a cocoon that protected inefficient—but politically connected—industries from competition, domestic as well as foreign.

If industrial policy is a matter of "picking winners and losers," then the essence of Japan's malaise is that it gradually shifted from promoting winners to protecting losers.

As this happened, Japan turned into a deformed dual economy—a dysfunctional hybrid of super-strong exporting industries and super-weak domestic sectors. Under the pressure of stiff competition overseas, exporters like autos and machinery learned to offer some of the best technology and highest productivity in the world. Just as Washington overestimated the strength of the Soviet Union by extrapolating from its mighty nuclear arsenal, so many Americans, who were exposed only to the exporting sectors, naturally presumed that all of Japan was as efficient as the exporters. Within Japan, however, the picture was quite different. Domestic manufacturing sectors from food processing to textiles, which were protected from competition, let themselves become woefully backward by international standards. In food processing, for example, Japan's productivity is one-third of U.S. levels and falling further behind. And yet, more people work in food processing than in autos and steel combined.[7]

Gradually, over the course of the 1970s and 1980s, Japan's unique dual economy worsened. Slowly, almost imperceptibly, the country's economic arteries became increasingly clogged and rigid.

Even worse, the dual economy was gradually sowing the seeds of its own destruction. The dual economy was sustainable only so long as efficient exporters earned enough to prop up weak domestic sectors. The high prices Toyota paid for glass, rubber, basic steel, and so forth were, in effect, subsidies to these suppliers. But, by the late 1980s, the exporters found it harder to bear the burden. They were caught in a squeeze between high costs at home and a rising yen, which made it harder to pass on those costs in export markets. As a result, more and more of the efficient exporters were being driven overseas. They were investing in offshore markets rather than in Japan itself. Step by step, Japan's efficient export sectors were being "hollowed out." As this happened, the productivity of the entire economy started being dragged down to the level of the stagnant sectors.

Precisely because the process was so gradual, no alarm bells went off.

Sure, a few productivity experts spoke of the dual economy and of the dangers of "hollowing out." Most people, however, were so bedazzled by Japan's trade performance that the dry rot eating away at the nation's domestic foundations went virtually unnoticed.

At the end of 1989, when Japan's "bubble economy" was at its height, the country felt on top of the world. The crippling heart attack was but a few months away, but Japan felt stronger than ever.

Japan's exporting industries had conquered one piece of economic terrain after another: from TVs and steel, to cars and computer memory chips. Year after year, the country racked up the world's largest trade surpluses.

Not only that, Japan's GDP expanded more quickly than that of any other industrialized country. Later on, some economists would discover that the apparent high growth of the 1980s was achieved by methods that were unsustainable. Japan compensated for its domestic inefficiencies—and thereby temporarily hid them—by pouring on tons and tons of investment. Japan by that time was so unproductive that it needed to invest 35 percent of GDP just to get the same growth that a typical country could have gotten with 25 percent. This was the opposite of the situation in the 1950s-60s, when Japan truly did achieve a growth miracle.[8]

This path to growth, unfortunately, had clear diminishing returns. Japan had to run ever faster just to stay in place. That is, unless Japan devoted ever-larger portions of its national income to investment, its growth would inevitably slow. Japan's extraordinary savings and investment rates were not a sign of vigor, but a response to weakness. At the time, however, they were the envy of the world.[9]

By the late 1980s, Japan seemed on the verge of doing in finance what it had previously done in manufacturing. Its banks, the world's largest, were spreading out internationally. At one point, they accounted for 17 percent of new loans in the U.S. True, profits were razor thin. Sure, these banks dispensed with the creditworthiness screening that is elementary in the U.S. No matter, they were growing bigger every year. To some, it seemed as if Japan could, and did, influence a U.S. presidential election by either dispensing or withholding its money so as to influence American interest rates. The claim was dubious, but even some well-connected people believed it at the time.

Most wondrous of all was Japan's high-flying stock market. It seemed to defy all the laws of valuation that constrained prices elsewhere. It gave America's Japanese competitors access to money far, far cheaper than anything U.S. firms could obtain. For a while, the cost of capital was effectively zero. Borrowers using so-called convertible bonds could repay their lenders in their own stock rather than cash. Since stock prices didn't seem limited by these companies' own earnings performance, it was almost as if these companies had a license to print money.[10] No wonder Toyota, Matsushita and others could afford to put factories all over the world, thereby gaining even more market share. No wonder Japan, with only half of America's population, was investing more than the U.S.

As it turned out, much of this investment had no more economic value than the fabled pyramids of Egypt. At least the latter brings in tourist dollars. But in Japan it was a pyramid of bad debt that was being constructed. Only a few years later, the Japanese landscape would be dotted with empty office buildings and unused factory space. Still, while the party lasted, the economy boomed.

All along there was an Achilles' Heel. If the stock market ever fell—or even stopped rising—the boom would end. Japan's companies would be forced to repay all their loans in real money, not paper shares. They would be burdened with a mountain of debt that could threaten both them and their banks. No need to worry about that, however. Study groups composed of the nation's "best and brightest" patiently "explained" to skeptics that stock prices unthinkable elsewhere reflected the "unique" character of Japanese finance.[11]

Not only in Japan, but also in the U.S., some analysts began to speak of a "Japanese economic system" that had gone "beyond capitalism."[12] Journalist James Fallows, in support of his view that Japan's trade threat needed to be "contained," conjured up the image of a peculiar nation with an unbeatable economic model, a hybrid of Confucius and Friedrich List.[13] As late as 1992, Lester Thurow, who as Dean of MIT's business school was responsible for training hundreds of America's future business leaders, wrote of a Japanese system of "producer economics" that was far superior to the "free-market consumer economics" prevalent in the U.S.[14]

To some in the U.S., particularly the so-called revisionists, Japan's supposed superiority loomed as a dark threat. In Asia, Japan was said to be positioning itself as the "brain" and "headquarters country" of the world's fastest-growing economic region. In the U.S., "Japan"—never this or that Japanese company, but "Japan"—was using its cheap money to buy up America's property, its companies, its movie studios, and even its government officials.

Warnings were sounded that "the Japanese" were using their money to buy up America's best high-tech companies. If Japan weren't "contained,"[15] it would soon become unstoppable. "The fear was palpable," recalls a State Department official. He remembers examining one proposed Japanese buyout of an American firm when he served on the inter-agency Committee on Foreign Investment in the U.S. (CIFIUS). The committee was originally set up to prevent adversaries from surreptitiously investing in defense contractors. In the late 1980s, it turned its attention to Japanese investment in U.S. high-tech firms. In this particular case, the man from State suggested that the Japanese investment was innocuous and should not be barred. Suddenly, he heard the epithet "traitor" being hurled at him from across the table by his Commerce Department counterpart.

So great was the illusion and the hysteria that even one of America's most highly regarded economists, Lawrence Summers, was taken in. In December of 1989, he wrote:

> Today, Japan is the world's second largest economy. . . . Furthermore, an Asian economic bloc with Japan at its apex . . . is clearly in the making. This all raises the possibility that the majority of American people who now feel that *Japan is a greater threat to the U.S. than the Soviet Union* are right [emphasis added].[16]

That comment stands as a monument to bad timing. Only a month later, Japan's roof caved in. It began with a crash of the stock market and real estate that wiped out hundreds of billions of dollars of wealth overnight. Soon, the collapse spread to the rest of the economy. The nation that had defined growth suddenly seemed incapable of growing. This was no ordinary recession. This was a downshifting of the whole economic trajectory compounded by a financial crisis. For three years, from the beginning of 1992 to the beginning of 1995, Japan barely grew at all. As of early 1998—eight years after the stock market crash—the economy has yet to recover.

The banks' huge assets quickly turned into a liability. In the colorful metaphor of Ken Courtis, chief economist at the Tokyo office of Deutsche Bank, the banks had "Himalayan balance sheets and Saharian returns." The mountain of bad debt dwarfed America's S&L disaster. While the government let a few banks go under, most were kept alive. Some survive only through hundreds of billions of dollars of government bailout money.[17]

Even the pride of Japan—the mighty manufacturing industry—was caught up in the malaise. As of late 1997, industrial production was barely higher than in 1990. One million manufacturing jobs disappeared between 1992 and 1996 and another 1.25 million were expected to evaporate by decade's end. This would stretch out over a decade's time a loss comparable in percentage terms to the abrupt loss the U.S. rust belt suffered in the 1979–83 recession.[18]

A decade ago, U.S. forecasters had warned Japan would leverage its dominance in computer memory chips to capture leadership in computers themselves. Today, however, the world's biggest chipmaker is not NEC or Toshiba, but Intel. The world's biggest memory chipmaker is no longer Japanese, but Korean. IBM was humbled, not by Fujitsu or Hitachi (which were too busy trying to be like IBM), but by Microsoft and Intel.

For a while, the illusion of recovery seemed to emerge in 1995–96. But that was only due to artificial props that could not be sustained indefinitely. One prop was a massive campaign of public works that sent the budget deficit to 6 percent of GDP—far higher than American deficits during the worst of the 1980s. The second prop was an export drive propelled by the tailwind of a cheapening yen. Unfortunately, the illusory recovery allowed Japan's leaders to delude themselves that they could muddle through without undertaking the deep reforms needed to overcome the economy's structural ossification. Tokyo completely underestimated the depths of Japan's problems. Hence, when the government removed its fiscal prop by cutting back public works and then, in the spring of 1997, hiking the consumption tax, the economy plunged once again.

The economist who had so worried about the Japanese "threat," Lawrence Summers, was now Deputy Treasury Secretary of the U.S. He had to acknowledge that neither he nor others had foreseen the shaky reality behind Japan's imposing facade:

> Four years ago . . . few would have forecast the range of difficulties that Japan has encountered. . . . Financial problems, deflation, structural rigidities and difficulties in innovation have held back Japan's economic growth. In 1993, the IMF forecast long term growth for Japan of 4 percent; today, the figure is half that.[19]

To be sure, all economies are subject to shocks. And some analysts suggest that Japan's travails are nothing more than a temporary reaction to the excesses of the late 1980s financial bubble. But a seemingly healthy economy does not either experience such an extreme bubble, nor descend into years of malaise, unless something is very rotten at the core. The bubble was not merely an aberration caused by misguided monetary policy; it was the last hurrah of a faltering system trying to pump itself up. It was as much a symptom of Japan's deep-seated problems as a cause.

By the late 1990s, few in Japan still denied that the economy was in deep trouble and in need of big change. Even the Japanese government has said that, unless Japan reduces high costs at home, its most efficient exporters will continue to drift overseas. Matsushita will continue exporting air conditioners from Malaysia instead of Japan. The key, says MITI, is to end the regulatory and other practices that shield its domestic sectors from the pressure of competition:

> The Japanese economy is characterized by the existence of a dual structure in which efficient manufacturers and inefficient service-related sectors coexist. This is one of the main reasons for the high-cost structure.
>
> In particular, productivity is low in such key sectors as transportation, telecommunications, finance, energy, and distribution. . . . Furthermore, low productivity in the aforementioned sectors acts as a drag on manufacturing and other service sectors, preventing their development and lessening their international competitiveness. This is the thing which feeds the *hollowing out phenomenon of the manufacturing sectors,* and the replacement of non-manufacturing sectors by foreign service companies [emphasis added].
>
> As a result, within the sectors that are not exposed to international competition, there is an urgent need to forcefully move ahead with deregulation and competition promotion policy in order to increase productivity and competitiveness.[20]

The Economic Planning Agency has finally acknowledged that Japan's pervasive import barriers are part of the problem, and increased imports a necessary part of the solution. In its 1996 *Economic White Paper*, it declared, "An increase in imports would stimulate incentives to raise productivity of domestic industries."[21]

The rapid aging of Japan's population makes the whole situation particularly dire. Japan's labor force is now declining, and it will keep on shrinking in coming years. In part because of the long work hours that keep husbands away from home, many Japanese women are now delaying marriage until late in their 20s and are reluctant to have more than one child. As the years go on, there will be fewer workers for each retired person. Unless the remaining workers can produce a big rebound in productivity growth, warns Robert Feldman, Salomon Brothers' Tokyo economist, eking out any increase in living standards over the next 20 years is going to be tough.[22]

Actually, Japan has two problems hindering growth: a supply-side problem and a demand-side problem. The supply-side problem is low productivity growth. This is caused by a system that protects the inefficient sectors at the expense of the efficient sectors. Even if Japan were to run at full capacity, it could not grow at more than 2 percent a year on average.

The demand-side problem is that Japan finds it difficult to run at full capacity. The dual economy has so distorted the normal economic mechanisms that Japan is chronically unable to consume all that it produces. On the one hand, with economic maturity, the country's investment needs have slowed down. And yet, unlike in other mature economies, personal consumption has not risen to take up the slack. Consumption as a share of GDP is lower than in other advanced economies. The consequence is that Japan suffers from a kind of economic anorexia—a chronic deficiency of purchasing power.

The only way Japan avoids chronic recession is by artificially stimulating demand. One method to stimulate demand is for Japan to export the excess production by running huge trade surpluses with the rest of the world. A second method is for the government to run mammoth budget deficits sometimes as high as 6 percent of GDP. However, whenever the financial strains of big budget deficits and the political strains of huge trade surpluses cut off those routes to growth, then Japan is stuck.

This anorexia is the ultimate reason why the bubble was launched. The 1985 Plaza Accords, which sent the yen soaring, cut off the trade surplus route to growth and the economy began to slow. Tokyo responded by artificially pumping up real estate, stocks and capital investment with monetary steroids. Since much of even the physical investment had little real economic value, the bubble collapsed and banks are loaded with mountains of bad debt. The bubble was not a mere mistake; it was a false solution to a real problem.

Once the bubble collapsed and investment fell, anorexia returned. Despite budget deficits that hit 6 percent of GDP in 1997 and a rebounding trade surplus, Japan has found it very difficult to dig itself out of its economic hole. As of early 1998 the economy was still limping along.

Japan's economic anorexia did not exist in the high-growth era when rapid investment drove growth. As with much else in the dual economy syndrome, it began to emerge in the 1970s and 1980s.

Japan now finds itself in the same turning point as other industrial economies before it. No industrial economy can progress beyond a certain point without becoming a mass consumption economy. America faced this problem in the 1930s and successfully responded with the New Deal. The Soviet Union was unable to meet this challenge and collapsed. The famous Maekawa Commission Report of 1986 pointed out the need for the same transformation in Japan. Instead, Japan launched the bubble. Now, ten years later, the pressing need to make the transformation is back again, but with the economy in far worse shape.

Japan won't sink into the Pacific, of course. And its multinational firms will remain formidable competitors. Still, increasing portions of the exports of these multinationals are from overseas plants. "What's good for Toyota" is no longer necessarily "what's good for Japan."

Thorough Reform or Just Muddling Through?

There are some analysts who say that, once Japan finally gets past this patch of bad growth and recovers to a long-term growth rate of about 2 percent, then it can "muddle through." After all, the U.S. doesn't grow much faster. But, for a nation whose corporate debt loads, social security needs, and political institutions are geared to higher growth, such mediocre expansion is a recipe for lingering financial fragility and political instability.

For one thing, warns MITI, by 2020 such low growth would leave Japan unable to meet its social security obligations unless it took 60 percent of every worker's salary in taxes and ran a budget deficit at 20 percent of GDP. That's four times as high as the U.S. peak in the mid-1980s—a clear financial impossibility.[23]

At 4 percent growth, Japan's workers had no fear of a trade-off between job security and growing wages; at 2 percent, they do. At 4 percent growth, businesses could readily pay their debts; at 2 percent many cannot. College graduates used to have no fear of finding jobs with room for advancement; at lower growth, many have trouble finding jobs at all. At 4 percent growth, nearly everyone in Japan enjoyed a steady improvement in living standards. At 2 percent or less, some people will gain; others will not. At higher growth, there was enough wealth for Japan's efficient sectors to subsidize its inefficient sectors via high prices. With lower growth, the burden of those high prices becomes intolerable.

Even under the best of circumstances, Japan will not return to 4 percent growth. Its economy is too mature. Still, with sweeping reforms, economists say Japan could grow at 3 percent a year between 1996 and 2010 instead of 2 percent. In that case, its GDP would be $850 billion larger. That's enough to pay not only for all the investment Japan does every year but for all the houses it builds as well.

Unfortunately, if there are millions who would benefit from reform, there are also millions who would temporarily lose out. The big losers would be all the people in the inefficient sectors who have been protected from competition all these years. According to economist Iwao Nakatani, thorough reform would eliminate 10 million jobs. It would also eventually create 11 million new jobs. But those whose jobs are in jeopardy are not likely to be mollified. And that—not simply the resistance of hidebound bureaucrats—is why reform is so hard to achieve. How many politicians want to risk putting their voter base through wrenching changes that dwarf what the U.S. Midwest experienced in the 1980s?

This is what worries one of the foremost reformers among Japanese business leaders, Fuji-Xerox chieftain Yotaro Kobayashi. Speaking to an audience at the New York Japan Society, Kobayashi was quite candid about his frustrating experience on the Hiraiwa Commission. This was a blue-ribbon panel that, like so many before it, had produced vague proposals for study rather than calls for concrete action. "Maybe growth at 1.75 percent over the next decade is not scary enough for the Japanese people," he wondered. Too many of Japan's voters might prefer stability to the risks that reform entails. If so, then Japan could be stuck in the worst possible situation: growth so low as to preclude vitality, but not low enough to compel reform. The nation that was supposed to dominate the 21st century would be reduced to trying to "muddle through."

Kobayashi may be right. And yet the momentum for reform has taken on a life of its own. Already, the strains produced by lower growth and need for reform have shattered the former consensus of Japanese politics. For almost four decades, the Liberal-Democratic Party (LDP) held power continuously as a catchall coalition of the efficient and inefficient. But, as the economic strains turned into political division, the LDP split and fell from power. Although the LDP has since regained the Prime Minister's post, it has a shadow of its former power.

More importantly, even LDP Prime Minister Ryutaro Hashimoto, a lifelong benefactor of the protected vested interests, has had to rule by offering up reform programs like the proposed "Big Bang" reforms in finance. A debate rages over whether this will really prove to be a "Big Bang" or just a "Wee Whimper." The fact remains: neither Hashimoto nor anyone else can any longer rule by openly opposing reform. Even reform's bitterest opponents are compelled to pay it lip service, at least in public.[24]

As of early 1998, Japan seems to be caught in a tug of war between two eras. The Old Regime has collapsed and its defenders are surreptitiously trying to resuscitate it; yet, not even the reformers are quite sure what should replace it. While the old mandarins, like the once-exalted Finance Ministry, have been discredited, no new respected institutions, leaders or clear visions have arisen to take their place. The opposition parties, divided by both lack of ideas and personal squabbles, have been amazingly ineffective. The country is floundering and could take years to find its bearings.

So far, real reform is still hard to come by. Even when concrete actions are taken, reform has all too often been reduced to a narrow issue of deregulation that ignores widespread private anti-competitive activities. What is needed is not simply less bureaucratic meddling, but an overhaul of all the *private* anticompetitive activities that stifle Japan's cartelized dual economy.

Nonetheless, Humpty-Dumpty cannot be put back together again, either economically or politically. That simple reality means that the fight over reform will continue to dominate Japan's economic and political life for years to come.

It is certainly true that Japan's current political leaders prefer to patch up the cracks in the system rather than change it. Indeed, once the LDP finally regained its majority in the Lower House of the Diet in the summer of 1997, the arrogance of the party machine returned, as did its desire to protect the vested interests backing the party. The dinosaurs in the LDP put huge roadblocks in the way of even the weak-kneed reforms that Hashimoto had offered. In private, the LDP former chief cabinet secretary Seiroku Kajiyama lashed out at both reform and opposition leader Ichiro Ozawa, the man whose defection led to the downfall of the LDP in 1993. "Ozawa's always talking change, change, we have to change. But why do we have to change? Our system has been working well for 100 years."

Such attitudes have led some analysts to suggest that Japan's elite will somehow find a way to muddle through to recovery without any fundamental overhaul. While the current leaders will no doubt make such an attempt, it is getting harder and harder for them to succeed. Their options are narrowing. The reason is that there is a genuine and growing conflict of interests among the different sections of Japan Inc. These can no longer be smoothed over as easily as before because growth is so low. As a result, Japan's elite is neither leading reform nor completely stonewalling. Instead, it is wavering. It is indecisive. One day it resists change and the next day it scurries to catch up to processes it can no longer control. This indecisiveness is the classic sign of a regime in trouble.

Every time Tokyo plugs one hole in the dike, that action just causes another one to appear. For example, the Bank of Japan has lowered interest rates to almost nothing (0.5 percent) in an effort to shore up the banks. Yet, this is decimating the regulated insurance companies, who can no longer earn enough interest to pay off their pension obligations. As a result, Nissan Life has gone bankrupt and there are rumors of other bankruptcies waiting in the wings. Meanwhile, in the Nissan Life failure, the policyholders were left holding the bag. People counting on insurance annuities for their retirement lost much of their life savings. As a result of that, many Japanese policyholders are now withdrawing their policies or not renewing their insurance policies. For the first time since World War II, in 1997 the insurance premiums paid into insurance companies actually decreased. That pushes weaker insurance companies even closer to failure.

The bottom line is that the current system is not tenable and cannot be sustained. There are too many cracks in the webs of mutual support that previously underpinned Japan's political economy. Until Japan undertakes sweeping reforms, it will lurch from crisis to crisis — in politics, in finance and in economics.

No one can predict *how* new realignments will come about —just as no one predicted in January of 1993 that the LDP was about to fall. But one can confidently say that sooner or later there will be another shakeup, and then another, until finally—probably years from now—fundamental reform is achieved.

The Need for Countervailing Institutions

When we ask why the Japanese miracle soured, the fundamental cause was neither a power-hungry bureaucracy nor vested interests. The ultimate cause was that too many of Japan's practical men remained the slaves of defunct ideas.

Blinded by the glare of past triumphs, Japan continued to adhere to obsolete policies just because they used to work. As Bowman Cutter, a management consultant who served as deputy director of the National Economic Council (NEC) during Clinton's first two years, put it:

> I analogize Japan to a big corporation like IBM or GM that has had a very successful business model for a long time. But now that business model is obsolescent.
>
> Many in Japan say that, as soon as they get past this bad patch of low growth, they can return to an economic structure of export-led growth with low personal consumption. I disagree. Given Japan's size, its structure of export-led growth is not sustainable in the world today, politically or economically.[25]

The caterpillar, not believing it had turned into a butterfly, refused to leave the cocoon. No wonder it couldn't fly.

In one sense, Japan is not unique. All over the world, institutions, whether in government or business, hold onto strategies long after they have outlived their usefulness. The mistakes born of success are often the most stubborn, the most difficult to correct.

Consider IBM's unrequited love affair with the mainframe computer. In the 1960s-70s, "Big Iron" had brought IBM to the pinnacle of world technological and business leadership. IBM just couldn't bring itself to shift gears during the 1980s, when the personal computer started to change the very nature of computing. The great irony is that IBM itself was the first to widely commercialize the PC.

In a way, IBM's viewpoint was understandable. As long as computers and mainframes were synonymous, IBM would remain on top of the world. Like bureaucracies elsewhere, it had learned to become very efficient at operating within a given environment and was reluctant to see that environment change.

There were warnings, of course. As far back as 1987, a study commissioned by then-Chairman John Akers showed that the mainframe was losing steam. And IBM's stock started to slip. But neither Akers nor other IBM execs ever acted on these warnings. On the contrary, IBM repeatedly put other promising technologies on the shelf because they seemed to undermine the mainframe.

How could any maverick inside IBM challenge the dogma? Look at our profits, the Old Guard could, and did, answer. Indeed, just as Japan's stock prices were hitting their highest point in 1989, so were IBM's profits. It earned more money than almost any other firm in corporate history. Three years later, the firm lost more money than almost any other in U.S. corporate history. It had to lay off 200,000 workers and its very survival was in question.

Still, there is one big difference between the IBM story and the Japan story: the absence of countervailing institutions. While individual institutions almost always suffer from excessive conservatism, a country can still prosper as long as it is hospitable to new institutions that introduce new ideas.

In the U.S., as IBM dug in its heels, Microsoft and Intel rose to take its place. What keeps Microsoft on its toes is Bill Gates' fear that there is some bright, brash 18-year-old out there gunning for him—and knowing that the American financial system will provide the money to try. When the American Big Three automakers started wasting man-hours putting out defect-ridden gas guzzlers, the American political economy let in their Japanese competitors. Today, no one doubts that, precisely due to the competition, the Big Three's productivity and quality are way up.

In Japan, unfortunately, such countervailing institutions are harder to find.

One corruption-ridden party, the Liberal-Democratic Party, has ruled the country almost continuously for the past four decades. Japan still lacks an effective opposition with a realistic chance of taking power.

In the Japanese corporate world, there are few analogues to American upstarts like MCI, Home Depot, or Wal-Mart. It's not that individual Japanese are any less imaginative or ambitious or entrepreneurial than people elsewhere. It's that a corporate setup dominated by collusive oligopolies and cartels makes it difficult for new companies—whether foreign or domestic—to break into the club.

The corporate "old boys club" is reinforced by a bank-dominated financial system in which a dozen large banks own, and are owned by, their biggest customers. Would-be challengers often find it hard to get the necessary financing. Japan's stock market is not a free-wheeling vehicle for shifting capital out of declining firms and into promising new ones. Instead, it's an anti-takeover device in which 60 percent of the shares are held by each corporation's own corporate allies, customers, suppliers, and banks—and sometimes even competitors. Instead of new companies arising to start new industries, large companies in mature industries use their huge retained earnings to diversify into new fields in which they are often ill-equipped: Nippon Steel going into amusements parks; Komatsu Construction into computers; Matsushita Electric into Hollywood. When these ventures fail, no heads seem to roll.[26]

Japan's exporters do, of course, face stiff competition in the overseas markets; that is what has compelled them to become so efficient. But at home, companies are not forced to pay the price for holding onto obsolete practices—until it is too late. Hence, Japan's unique dual economy: super strong exporters and astonishingly inefficient domestic sectors.

Unfortunately, once companies and their labor forces have learned how to make money in a certain institutional framework—whether it's making the world's best car or forming cartels to rip off consumers—they have a stake in keeping things as they are. They find politicians willing to support them; develop ideologies that rationalize their behavior; and discover professors willing to give those ideologies a respectable veneer. If, in addition to all this, countervailing institutions are few and far between, institutional change becomes very hard.[27]

This is why in Japan, as in so many other countries, trade opening is the *sine qua non* of overall economic reform. It takes imports from companies which are not part of the club to shake up all the collusive arrangements that prevent competition at home. Imports, in effect, provide a powerful countervailing institution. They substitute for the competitive political and economic mechanisms that are missing within Japan.

It's not that trade opening is more important than domestic deregulation and trust-busting at home. It's that the necessary domestic reforms are more likely to occur if competition from imports is increased. Analysts have long talked of *gaiatsu* (literally, foreign pressure) in political terms. Reformers in Japan have often surreptitiously used U.S. pressure to create changes that Japan's one-party state was unable to achieve on its own. *Gaiatsu* has been so important that the U.S. is sometimes called Japan's unofficial opposition party. Imports are, in effect, economic *gaiatsu*. It's unfortunate that economic *gaiatsu* is necessary, but it does seem unavoidable.

One of the best examples of economic *gaiatsu* is the explosive growth in Japan's cellular phone industry. Today, it seems that everyone in Japan walks around with a handyphone. It wasn't that way a few years back, when high prices suppressed demand. Motorola's pressure to open the market and change regulations and practices created a revolution. Companies sold phones cheaply instead of leasing them at high rates. Phone call rates tumbled. And, in response, demand soared. Motorola had always contended that the measures it asked for would help its competitors. It may have sounded disingenuous, but it has been proven right — in spades. From January 1994 to June 1997, the number of cell phone subscribers increased from 500,000 to 24 million. In fact, according to Takashi Kiuchi, chief economist at the Long-Term Credit Bank (LTCB), the purchase of cell phones and use of them increased GDP by about ¥1 trillion, or 0.2 percent of GDP, during that period. For an economy struggling to achieve 1 percent growth, that's nothing to sneeze at.

The potential of trade opening was particularly seen in the early 1990s when a sharp rise in the yen drew in more imports. These imports unleashed a wave of "price destruction" that weakened the power of domestic cartels, brought down monopolistic prices in a host of industries, and helped spur support for reform among exporters. Unfortunately, once the yen reversed course in 1995 and became cheaper, the flow of imports slowed and so did the momentum for reform. Without significant trade opening, it is hard to see how the forces of reform will be strong enough to defeat the power of entrenched interests.

In countries without strong countervailing institutions, it usually takes a crisis to force change. That's what began to happen to Japan when the bubble popped. That led at least some of the nation's leaders to reexamine all their long-held myths. Sakura Shiga, the former director of the Economic Planning Agency's Planning Division, described the shock effect:

> All of our long-cherished assumptions—that the Japanese economy will always grow, that asset prices always rise, that full employment is virtually guaranteed, that financial institutions are invulnerable, that Japan has the safest society in the world—are now being overturned. People in Japan are losing self-confidence and wondering what has gone wrong. In short, we are aware that we are in crisis for the first time in these fifty years of postwar prosperity, and we know we have to revamp our society and economy. . . .
>
> Although experts had long recognized these . . . structural problems, the problems were unfortunately obscured by the euphoria of the economic

bubble period. The bursting of the bubble revealed the problems to have worsened considerably.[28]

Rethinking has occurred in the political world as well. In 1996, Yukio Hatoyama, the grandson of one LDP Prime Minister and the son of an LDP Dietman, quit the LDP to help form a new opposition party, the Democratic Party. As of 1997, it was the third largest party in the Diet. Calling for thorough reform, Hatoyama declared:

> Until the seventies, the Japanese bureaucracy had performed well in the goal of helping the economy catch up with the West. Once it had achieved this goal, however, the bureaucracy lost its sense of purpose. Self-preservation and self-aggrandizement became its goals. . . . This *ancien regime* has put political decision-making beyond the reach of citizens and driven innovative industries out of Japan. The vaunted industrial policy, which had nurtured many infant industries in the fifties and sixties, degenerated into the protection of sunset industries and never-do-well industries at the consumers' expense.[29]

And, of course, the economic storms hitting most of East Asia at the end of 1997, punctured much of the hubris surrounding the so-called Japan model or Asian model of economics. In a sense, Japan was lucky. After years of disguised sclerosis, it finally received an unmistakable wake-up call. Without a crisis, as Mancur Olson writes in *The Rise and Decline of Nations*, the sclerosis induced by cartel-like activities can persist indefinitely.[30]

"The System That Soured": Toward a New Paradigm about Japan

If new ideas are needed in Japan, then new thinking about Japan is needed in America.

For two decades, American policymaking about Japan has been polarized around an increasingly bitter and sterile debate. Guided more by contentious issues of U.S. trade policy than by a dispassionate look at Japan itself, the debate has produced both flawed analysis and ineffective policies.

At one pole, there are those—epitomized by some of the so-called revisionists— who insist that Japan still benefits from its protectionism. For example, in a 1996 letter to *Orbis*, Chalmers Johnson accused the journal of spreading Japanese "disinformation" after it printed an article by David Asher analyzing Japan's bubble and bust. Johnson even resigned from the *Orbis* board over this matter. The financial frenzy of the late 1980s, Johnson insisted, was "not a bubble; this is governmental policy." The bubble and the high yen were really "a wonderful political cover" for a Finance Ministry scheme to "recreate the Greater East Asian Co-Prosperity Sphere." Any accounts of post-bubble economic difficulties are just part of a deliberate "deception" campaign from Tokyo:

> Japan's policy in the world today is to buy a little more time—to milk the Americans a little longer and wait for conditions in East Asia to ripen. Within a few years they will either offer their own leadership in Asia or else guide their people into accepting Chinese hegemony. In order to buy time, Japan sends out messages of change, disarray, or catastrophe whenever it looks like the Americans might be about to take action.[31]

Eammon Fingleton's *Blindside* (1995) is a book-length rendition of the same "deception" thesis.[32]

At the other pole, many orthodox economists argue on the basis of neoclassical theory that any Japanese interference in the market, even in the 1950s and 1960s, had to have been either inconsequential or outright detrimental. Hugh Patrick contends that accounts of the role of government in Japan's development are "exaggerated," insisting that "quite free markets for commodities and labor" produced the high growth era. Yet, for much of that period, no imports could get in without government approval while government-authorized cartels controlled 30 percent of manufacturing.[33] David Weinstein and Richard Beason argue that "Japanese industrial policy seems to have transferred resources out of high growth sectors and into low growth sectors." The critical role of industrial policy in the promotion of such export superstars as autos, steel, and electronics is discounted.[34]

However, if we deny the reality of what so many Japanese leaders experienced firsthand, then it is hard to understand why such policies continue to retain a grip on the minds of those leaders.

Many neoclassical economists and traditional political-military experts act as if merely conceding the existence of Japanese trade barriers might somehow give too much ammunition to the trade hawks. In 1994, economist Jagdish Bhagwati recruited dozens of economists to sign a letter denouncing the Clinton Administration for a "crude and simplistic view that Japan is importing too few manufactures owing to structural barriers."[35] But such assertions deny the reality of what so many American and other non-Japanese companies have repeatedly experienced. As a result, these economists unwittingly and unnecessarily undermine the credibility of a free trade response to Japan's barriers. In any case, perfectly respectable neoclassical economists have long since disproved Bhagwati's claim.[36]

Neither the "revisionist" nor "traditionalist" paradigms have been good guides to policy.

The "revisionist" view treats Japan as a monolith that will respond only to pressure. When this analysis influenced policy in the first two years of the Clinton Administration, the policy backfired. It elicited a nationalist defensiveness that pushed Japanese reformers into bed with conservatives. Tokyo became, if anything, even more intransigent.

The "traditionalist" view has fared no better. In the attempt to maintain strong U.S.–Japan ties, traditionalists have often minimized trade issues as a mere irritant in an otherwise sound relationship. They have limited their own conceptual options by accepting the notion of a trade-off between security and trade issues. "Is it really worth jeopardizing American F-16 bases in Japan just so Florida can sell some more oranges?" traditionalist security officials have, in effect, argued.

Such a view, however, fails to appreciate how the same mindset responsible for Japan's closed market also leads to Japan's insularity on security matters. As Peter Ennis, editor of *The Oriental Economist Report*, puts it, these two problems are "two sides of the same coin." Moreover, the ineffective trade policies resulting from the traditionalist view created a dangerous vacuum often filled by revisionists, protectionists and other trade hawks. The very posture that traditionalists adopted to maintain good U.S.–Japan ties helped lead instead to their corrosion.

Clearly, we need a different paradigm to analyze Japan and guide policy. This paradigm would understand Japan as a case of a "once-successful system that soured."

This is not a new notion, but one that has been tragically overlooked. Back in 1982, University of Washington Professor Kozo Yamamura published an essay on this topic entitled "Success That Soured." In that essay, Yamamura pointed out that Japan was still dominated by legal and illegal cartels, import restrictions, and other vestiges of the high-growth era, but that any positive role had run out of steam. A similarly balanced and evolutionary view was presented in a 1985 book called *The Competition*, by three analysts from the Hudson Institute, Thomas Pepper, Merit Janow and Jimmy Wheeler. On the one hand, it critiqued Patrick and his cothinkers for limiting their discussion of government's role to a paradigm of government *versus* the market. Then, commenting on Johnson, it pointed out that, since industrial policy was best used as a device to help "late industrializers" catch up, its vestiges were becoming "increasingly costly to the domestic economy" as Japan matured.[37]

In Japan, too, analysts warned that carrying on a once-successful industrial policy for too long was a policy fraught with peril. As early as 1975, Professor Hiroya Ueno, of Seikei University, sounded the alarm:

> One might say that this [the late 1960s] was a period in which Japan was drunk with the spectacular results of its industrialization plan and its industrial policy.... We should have recognized that industrial policy, which had been justified until then, and systems adopted on its behalf, had already finished their roles....
>
> [T]he collusive oligopoly system prevailing in heavy and chemical industries ... may ... become even more prolonged and troublesome after-effects [of industrial policy] for the Japanese economy. The reason is that, as a general political rule, a system, once established, cannot be dissolved or reformed until a revolutionary event or considerable abuse takes place. It means that groups and organizations that were artificially created to meet the need of a specific system tend to grow with this system into powerful champions or political pressure groups that can no longer be controlled by this system.[38]

Unfortunately, in the heat of the 1980s ideological wars between "revisionists" and "traditionalists," these more nuanced views of Japan fell by the wayside.

Now, however, as people try to understand why the Japanese miracle failed, new analysts are picking up the trail. We will discuss these new analysts in Chapter 13.

A policy guided by the "system that soured" paradigm would appreciate that Japan does still differ from most other capitalist nations, but that Japan is crippled by many of its differences. It would recognize that this situation gives rise to internal political pressures for change, including more openness to imports and foreign investment. It would understand that the change in mindset needed to revitalize the economy would engender a more cosmopolitan attitude in Tokyo on all kinds of topics, including security. It would seek to further those changes, or at least take them into account, in designing policies. No one should expect or desire Japan to become a carbon copy of America, no more than Europe or the Asian NICs are. But, certainly, Japan can become a lot more open and, in its own interests, it now needs to be.

Trade negotiators have long recognized that America has enjoyed the most success in negotiating with Japan when its trade agenda coincided with the needs of internal forces in Japan, and therefore when it could find implicit allies in Japan. Because Japan cannot solve its problems without greater trade openness, the current crisis in Japan is likely to produce a lot more allies. As Undersecretary of Commerce Everett Ehrlich put it in a recent report:

> The structural opening of Japan's economy is inevitable. When it happens, not only will U.S. exports find a new and welcome home, but then and only then will Japan's economy finally find the basis for the new and sustained round of growth that has eluded it in this decade. . . . We have too often thought of these policies [the U.S. trade agenda] as unilateral concessions we demand of the Japanese. It is time to think of them instead as tonics for what ails Japan.[39]

None of this implies that Japan is about to "embrace the American model." America has its own problems, some of them more difficult to solve than Japan's. How, for example, does America, with its huge "education gap," find a new job for a 50-year-old autoworker with a 10th-grade education?

In America, especially since the Reagan era, the dominant philosophy has been: Let the train of economic efficiency roll on as fast as possible regardless of who gets crushed in the wheels. That is hardly a compelling model for a country with a communitarian social ethic. Nor is Europe an attractive alternative. There, the social safety net is so thick that employers are reluctant to hire, the unemployed are content to remain so, unemployment hovers at or near double digits, and right-wing demagogues exploit the situation to win electoral gains.

Japan will have to find its own path, one that combines the need for efficiency with its own social values. Certainly, Japan needs to improve productivity. And to do this, it will have to allow more competition, including competition from imports. It also needs a financial system that can direct money to its most efficient use and screen companies for their ability to pay back. Assuredly, it needs competitive elections. But nothing dictates that Japan has to accomplish these tasks in the same way that America does.

Saying that Japan is embracing the American model because it gives the market more sway is like saying Franklin Roosevelt adopted the Japanese model because he created the New Deal. In fact, like the 1930s Marxists who claimed capitalism could not reform itself, it is the oppo-

nents of reform in Japan who claim that reform means Americaniza-
tion. Twenty years from now, Japan will look very different, but it will
still be Japan.

While nothing dictates that reform will succeed, it's hard to imagine
that a nation as intelligent and resourceful as Japan could let itself fail. At
the same time, it's difficult to chart the path that will let Japan overcome
its institutional roadblocks in the near future. In all likelihood, Japan will
not reform within five years; within twenty, it almost certainly will.

Part One

The Two Japans

——————— **Chapter 2** ———————

Japan's Deformed Dual Economy

The Two Japans

Nowhere do we see more sharply the obsolete and self-defeating nature of the Japanese system—and what happens when countervailing institutions are missing—than in the field of international trade. Japan remains entangled in a thicket of informal barriers that keeps imports, indeed overall trade, inordinately low. The result is a deformed "dual economy" unique in the industrial world. The secret of the economy's tribulations is that there is not one Japan, but two.

The bright side of Japan's economy is its exporting sector—industries like autos, consumer electronics, semiconductors, and machinery. This is the Japan that Americans see. Almost all the images of a rich, powerful, efficient Japan stem from these exporting industries.

In most cases, these export stars owe their initial takeoff to the "developmentalist" policies applied in the 1950s-60s. For example, an initially uncompetitive auto industry was rescued from oblivion by aggressive protection against cheaper European imports. Until the early 1960s, anyone wishing to import had to seek foreign exchange from MITI. In the case of autos, MITI refused to grant foreign currency for any imports beyond minimal quotas until 1965 when the industry was competitive on world markets. Even then, the quota was replaced by a prohibitive tariff. Similarly, the TV industry was not only given import protection, but it operated both legal and illegal cartels in which the industry charged high prices at home to subsidize lower-priced exports.

As these industries became export superstars, they drove the rapid industrialization of the rest of the economy. This success is what gave Japanese neomercantilism its legendary reputation.

But what the Old Guard in Japan and its U.S. admirers forget is that— as we'll detail in Chapter 6—promotion and protection succeeded only when used for genuine infant industries. That is, industries which had the

Table 2.1

Japanese Output per Hour by Industry Compared to the U.S. (U.S. = 100)

	1950	1965	1973	1979	1990	%of 1992 Mfg. Jobs	Germany 1990
Machinery and equipment	8	24	51	80	114	39	88
Basic and fabricated metal products	13	23	61	84	96	12	99
Chemicals and allied products	13	32	60	78	84	5	77
Other manufacturing	10	20	34	40	55	24	80
Textiles, apparel and leather	25	38	53	55	48	10	88
Food, beverages and tobacco	27	26	40	40	37	11	76
Total manufacturing	17	27	49	63	78	100	86

Source: van Ark (1995), pp. 56–73

intrinsic potential to become self-sufficient exporters, but which had not yet gained the economies of scale or learning-by-doing efficiencies to be competitive. They needed an initial jump-start.

Precisely because these exporters faced international competition, they could not permanently rest on government aid. They either had to hone their competitive edge or die. And so, they did. In many of these exporting sectors, Japan leads the world in productivity and technology (e.g., see machinery in Table 2.1). Japanese labor productivity is 24 percent ahead of the U.S. in automaking, and 15 percent ahead in consumer electronics. Japanese firms have often been the first in the world to introduce new products, from VCRs to oil supertankers, or to apply new processes, from solid-state TV to the continuous casting of steel.

Unfortunately, most Japanese live and work in quite another Japan—a Japan that neither exports nor imports and is therefore unknown to most Americans. This Japan is the product of the dark side of Japanese neomercantilism, the side that increasingly dominated in the 1970s and 1980s.

As Japan matured, it naturally ran out of "infant industries." Protection was now superfluous and should have been abandoned. But Tokyo nonetheless applied a whole new round of widespread protection.

The initial impetus for the new protectionism was the deep industrial slump that followed the 1973 oil shock. Growth halved. Once-prosperous industries were suddenly plagued by chronic excess capacity. For many, this was not just a temporary shock. Aluminum, petrochemicals, shipbuilding, textiles, basic steel, and many others were now permanently priced out of the market: not just by the oil shock, but by the rise of the Asian NICs, the elevation of Japanese wages, and other fundamental trends. The troubled industries accounted for at least half of Japan's manufacturing output, and a third of its factory workers.

Unwilling or unable to endure the pain of downsizing, companies and workers cried out. And the bureaucracy, often spurred on by the Liberal-Democratic Party *zoku* (caucuses), granted them relief. After all, the ruling Liberal-Democratic Party (LDP) depended for money and votes on some of the sectors that would be most hurt by the economic shakeup. And so, industrial policy degenerated into little more than po-litical pork barreling and logrolling.

All of this belies the myth that, at the heart of the "Japanese economic model," lies a bureaucracy that is immune to political pressure and there-fore free to make decisions in the national interest. Now, it is certainly true that many industrial policy decisions were based on Japan's genuine economic needs. But, it is equally true that ministries are often captives of the industries they are supposedly guiding.

A classic case involves the years of struggle by former MITI official Morihisa Naito to end restrictions on gasoline imports as well as the ban on self-service gas stations. Success finally came in 1996–1998. The restrictions had subsidized Japan's notoriously inefficient refiners, led to rampant price-fixing, and provided a cushion for 60,000 gas stations, twice what a free market would support. When word of Naito's efforts got out, gas station owners distributed a "Wanted" poster with his photo. Meanwhile, his colleagues at MITI accosted him, demanding to know why he was jeopardizing their future job prospects. Like most officials in Japan, these bureaucrats expected to retire in their mid-50s and get a cushy position at the very companies they are overseeing. No wonder they didn't want any feathers ruffled.

Multiply such stories hundreds of times and one can easily see why so many moribund sectors won protection.

MITI and other agencies claimed that their protective measures were designed to smooth the downsizing, provide a social safety net, and ease the transition to Japan's next industrial phase. In reality, measures like the famed "recession cartels" of the 1970s and 1980s[1] did precisely the oppo-site. They tried to resist the decline, slow it down, or even shift the burden to other countries (i.e., by exporting at "dumping" prices, which forced companies in other countries to take a greater share of global cutbacks).

In the end, a trade pattern that had begun as a way of promoting genuine infant industries was increasingly reduced to a crude protection racket for a host of "has-been" and "never-was" sectors. From cement, paper, and glass, to petroleum refining and petrochemicals, and even the formerly competitive basic steel, it seemed that almost no one was denied insulation from market competition.

Like a permanent crutch that leaves the muscles atrophied, protection left whole sections of the Japanese economy ossified and backward. As a 1995 report of the United Nations Industrial Development Organization (UNIDO) put it:

> A major feature of the Japanese economy is the dislocation between the domestic market and the rest of the world. While the former is served by the *uchi* ["inside" companies —rk], which are among the most *in*efficient companies, the latter is served by the *soto* ["outside" companies —rk], which are among the most efficient in the world. Traditionally, the *uchi* have been subjected to a plethora of governmental regulations designed to protect them from foreign competition or newcomers at home. Under these very favorable conditions, the *uchi* have not been motivated to reduce their fixed costs and improve their competitiveness vis-à-vis foreign producers [emphasis added].[2]

Look, for example, at food processing and textiles in Table 2.1. Japanese productivity in food processing is an astonishing *one-third* of U.S. performance and *losing ground*. In textiles, it's almost as bad. Yet, almost 2 million people work in food processing alone, more than in auto, auto parts, steel and metalworking combined. And another 1 million work in textiles.

The weak sectors so far outweigh the strong that, when it comes to overall manufacturing productivity, Japan still lags behind even the Europeans, let alone the U.S. (see Table 2.2).

Only half of the overall gap in manufacturing productivity between Japan and the U.S. can be accounted for by such tangible factors as education of the labor force, capital–labor ratios, plant size, age of equipment, composition of manufacturing, and so forth. The other half, say experts, is caused by management practices, and those practices in turn highly depend on whether or not managers face competitive pressures forcing them to improve. In the export market, those pressures are intense; in the domestic sectors, they are often absent.[3]

Japan's handling of its petroleum refining industry shows the system at

Table 2.2

Manufacturing Real Value-Added per Hour, Percent of U.S. Level

	1970	1975	1980	1985	1990	1993
France	73.3	78.5	89.8	89.8	91.3	87.8
Germany	78.7	87.3	95.2	90.5	85.9	82.5
Japan	44.5	54.1	66.2	69.9	77.9	76.2
UK	51.3	53.0	52.3	58.3	66.0	69.8

Source: See Table 2.1

its worst. In the interests of "energy independence" Japan insisted on developing its own indigenous refiners rather than either importing refined oil or relying on the foreign refiners already ensconced in Japan, such as Exxon. As Hugh Patrick has explained:

> The greatest MITI failure, however, has been in the way it handled scale and entry in the petroleum refining industry. In order to reduce the large foreign share in Japanese oil refining, MITI promoted the entry—under pressure from a number of business groups each of which wanted a piece of the action—of a large number of too-small refining plants and companies with inadequate capacities to upgrade facilities to optimum scale. . . . These mistaken policies and programs have carried over into some petrochemical products as well.[4]

Having let new domestic companies into the petroleum refining business, MITI felt obliged to shield them not only from foreign competition but even from a Darwinian shakeout at home. In order to avoid excess capacity and "excess competition," the 1962 Petroleum Industry Law liberalized imports of crude, but retained MITI control over imports of refined petroleum products. Moreover, the law required firms to get MITI approval before investing in new capacity.[5]

Despite attempts to shift the costs onto consumers instead of industry, Japanese inefficiency in petroleum was so great that even industrial consumers of petroleum products had to pay prices much higher than world levels.[6] This created a domino effect. Because protection of the refining sector made petrochemicals inefficient, the latter too required unusual assistance. MITI's right hand (the Energy Agency protecting petroleum refining) and its left hand (the Basic Industries Bureau promoting petrochemicals) were working at cross purposes. Unlike steel, which started off as a ward of the state but eventually stood on its own and became an export superpower, petrochemicals never really did.

Even with this protection, petroleum refining still could not compete. Even worse, the U.S. and Europe were pressuring Japan to liberalize imports. Tokyo did so its way. In 1986, MITI had a law passed which liberalized imports of industrial products, but allowed only Japanese refiners to import consumer-oriented petroleum products like gasoline. Behind the protection of this law, MITI officials organized a secret and illegal cartel among six Japanese refining companies to raise prices by restricting supply. Although high-priced consumer products supplied the brunt of refinery profits, the system ended up raising all prices, even on industrial users. Industry protested the high prices, as did MITI sections with industry clients. Still, the protesters had to wait until 1996 when this 10-year law finally expired. When it did, gasoline prices fell 25 percent even before the first gallon of imports arrived.[7]

The non-manufacturing sectors that make up more and more of Japan's economy have even less exposure to international competition. Hence, productivity in these sectors is particularly backward.

Consider wholesale and retail trade, where productivity is only 44 percent of U.S. levels. This sector employs 11 million people—more than a fifth of Japan's entire workforce and almost as many people as in all of manufacturing. It accounts for 12 percent of GDP. Shielded from both foreign direct investment and local competition, it provides "disguised unemployment" for hordes of mom-and-pop shops, cushy profits for layer upon layer of middlemen, and a huge voting bloc for the LDP. Former MITI official Taichi Sakaiya reports:

> One widely heard aphorism is that, while America needs two people to build a car and one to sell it, Japan requires one person to build a car and two to sell it. The average retail price in America is 1.7 times the factory invoice price; in Europe, it is also less than 2 times the factory price. Only in Japan does it hit an incredible 3 times the factory price. It costs Japan 2 to 3 times as much to sell a car as it does for Europe and America.[8]

Then there's construction, where the Economic Planning Agency found that Japanese firms bid up to 45 percent higher than American firms for the same contract.[9]

Costs are so high because the industry is pervaded by an illegal, but protected, system called *dango* in which bidders agree ahead of time on who will get the winning bid. As one of Japan's biggest industries—10 percent of its GDP and of its workforce—construction lies at the heart of Japan's daisy-chain of inefficiency.

This industry can charge high prices because *half* of its output goes to public works projects. An incredible 90 percent of these public works contracts involve *dango*. This industry, in turn, is a transmission belt to the taxpayer of the excessive prices charged by many of Japan's other moribund sectors. It is one of the biggest purchasers of materials, from cement to glass to steel. Half of all Japanese steel is bought by the construction firms. These materials industries comprise about a fifth of Japanese manufacturing.[10]

Yet, the industry and its suppliers are politically untouchable since the construction cartel provides much of the under-the-table money that feeds Japan's politics. Gavan McCormack reports:

> When sudden light was cast on the inner workings of the system in 1993 and 1994, it was learned that 1 percent of all public works contracts of up to ¥2 to 3 billion [$16 to 24 million] and 0.5 percent in cases of contracts for sums of more than ¥10 billion, had been going in gifts to politicians. . . . Given the scale of the public-works budget, this means that more than ¥300 billion annually [*$2.4 billion a year* —rk] was being diverted from the public to political or private ends.[11]

In 1994, says McCormack, 111 out of 511 former Ministry of Construction bureaucrats were found to have moved from the bureaucracy either to the big construction firms they formerly supervised or else into related semipublic entities.

That kind of money and connection buys a lot of protection. No wonder U.S. efforts to pry open the construction industry have proved futile. So have efforts to pry open some of construction's suppliers like glass and cement where cartel-like activities are equally prominent and productivity equally terrible.

In 1997, a senior MITI official said it was politically imperative to cut public works spending, not so much to reduce Japan's astronomical budget deficit, but to cut off the money flow to the construction industry's parliamentary caucus (*zoku*) inside the LDP.[12]

Poor productivity is not limited to traditional industries. It afflicts even telecommunications, another shielded sector that is a make-or-break industry for Japanese ambitions in high tech. Due to the near-monopoly of the quasi-state-owned Nippon Telephone and Telegraph (NTT), labor productivity is only 77 percent of U.S. levels while the productivity of capital is a dismal half of U.S. standards.[13]

It is often said that sectors like retail trade and construction are "non-tradables." But, in most countries there is plenty of international competition via foreign direct investment. Foreign-owned firms are a big part of the U.S. retail scene as are foreign-based contractors. There is no reason these sectors could not be subject to international competition—if only Tokyo wanted them to be. But in Japan, foreigners account for only 0.1 percent of total direct investment (i.e., setting up companies rather than buying stocks). This compares to 4 percent for France, 7 percent for the U.S. and 13 percent for Britain.[14]

Japan's dual economy was not always so extreme. The syndrome emerged in the 1970s in the aftermath of the oil shock and other fundamental trends. The real problem was not the external shocks *per se*, but Japan's poor response.

As the dual economy syndrome grew, it fed on itself. The weaker the lagging sectors got, the more protection they demanded—and got. That just rendered them even weaker.

In the terms of analyst David Asher, the archetype "developmental state" had transformed itself into an "*anti*-developmental state."[15]

Unless Japan overcomes its dualism, warns Michael Porter in *The Competitive Advantage of Nations*, its future is in danger:

> While domestic rivalry is intense in every industry in which Japan is internationally successful, however, it is *all but absent in large sectors of the economy*. In fields such as construction, agriculture, food, paper, commodity chemicals, and fibers, there are cartels and other restrictions on competition, some sanctioned by the government. Almost none of these (and other similar) industries have ever achieved international success. . . . The absence of effective competition in large sectors of the economy is a danger signal and represents a serious challenge to continued Japanese economic advancement . . . [emphasis in original].
>
> Most importantly, government policies in a range of industries has had the effect of undermining competition and sheltering inefficient competitors, lowering the overall productivity of the economy. . .
>
> Limits on competition in one form or another have also led to inefficiency in a wide range of other fields. . . . MITI-sanctioned "recession" and "rationalization" cartels, which suspend rivalry and involved *de facto* protection, have preserved unproductive firms in dozens of other industries. Only a handful of the more than sixty industries involved have subsequently achieved international success.
>
> Japan, then, is characterized by some of the fiercest domestic rivalry of

any nation juxtaposed with large areas of little or no rivalry. . . . [This is a] danger signal for the future.[16]

Import Barriers: The Bodyguard of Domestic Cartels

Japan's trade patterns are the linchpin of the entire dual economy (Figure 2.1). The country's best performers are the industries that face world competition through either exports or imports or both. These industries come closest to matching or beating their U.S. competitors. By contrast, the industries shielded from world competition, i.e., with low exports and low imports, are horribly inefficient by world standards. Japan's exporters are efficient *because* they face world competition; Japan's domestic sectors are inefficient because they do not. In fact, an industry's relative openness to trade can explain about two-thirds of how its productivity stacks up compared to its U.S. counterpart (that is the meaning of R^2 = 0.64 percent in Figure 2.1).

Figure 2.1 **More Exports *and Imports* Mean Higher Productivity**

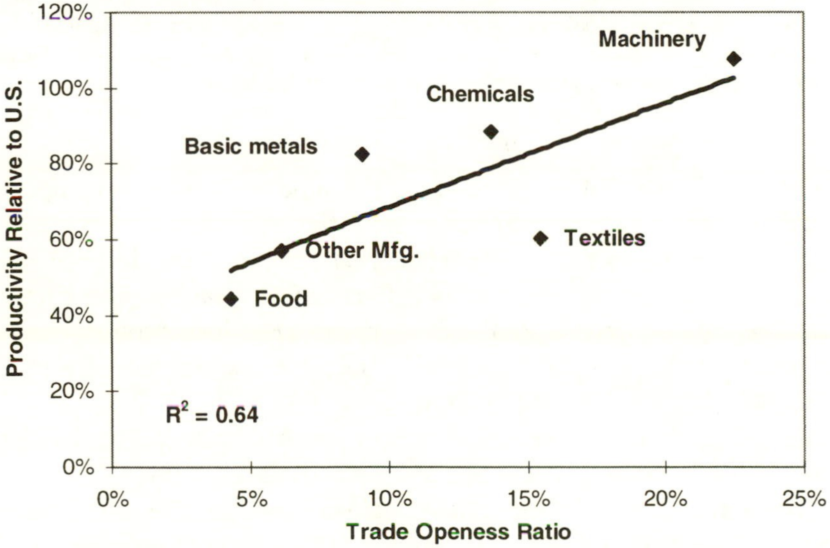

Source: EPA (1995a), van Ark and Pilat (1993)
Note: The data is for Japan in 1987. Trade Openness = Exports as % of Output, plus Imports as % of Consumption. Productivity = Total Factor Productivity (productivity of capital plus labor) of each industry relative to the U.S. level. R^2 = 0.64 means that 64% of the difference in each sector's relative productivity can be explained by the trade openness ratio.

Figure 2.2 **Japan Has the Industrial World's Worst Dual Economy**

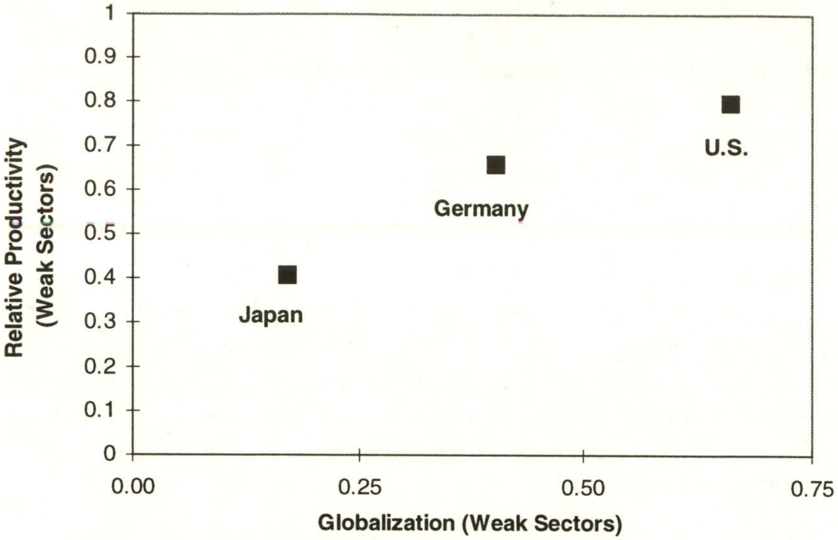

Source: McKinsey Global Institute (1993), Exhibit S-4 after Pg. 4.
Note: Globalization refers to McKinsey Index for exposure to international competition. The number is average globalization of the sectors in which a country's industry lags behind world leaders. Relative Productivity refers to the average productivity of each countries' lagging sectors relative to the international productivity leader in their industry (e.g. Japanese processed food at 30% of U.S. level). Japan's weak sectors had the lowest globalization and the worst relative productivity.

Goldman Sachs' Tokyo office found the same result when it compared a series of exporting versus domestic industries. In a typical example, the internationally exposed shipping industry *cut* its fixed costs during 1984–94. In the same period, the sheltered food and beverage industry let its fixed costs almost *double*. Productivity expert Dale Jorgenson picked up the pattern in his comparison of U.S. and Japanese productivity in 28 different industries. Over the period from 1960 to 1970, Japan largely closed the productivity gap in nine export-oriented manufacturing industries while it failed to close the gap in the rest of the economy.[17]

To a limited degree, trade-related dualism exists in other countries as well. McKinsey Global Institute has found that, in all countries, those sectors facing world competition are a lot closer to matching the world's benchmark leader than sheltered sectors. But, in no other country is the gap between international and domestic sectors so great as to give rise to an extreme "dual economy" (see Figure 2.2).[18]

Germany may not have any broad sectors that outshine the U.S. in efficiency, but neither does it have any broad sectors that lag far behind world standards. On average, its manufacturing productivity is higher than that of Japan (right-hand column of Table 2.1).

The claim to fame of Japan's industrial policy is that it is supposed to accelerate an economy's shift of jobs, output and investment from low-productivity sectors to high-productivity sectors. There's plenty of evidence that Japan's industrial policy did just that in the 1950s-60s, as we'll explore in Chapter 6. However, in the past decade or so, Japan's protectionism has done just the opposite.

Compare how the U.S. and Japan have responded to the forces of globalization and rising currency rates. The U.S. response has made it stronger; the Japanese response made it weaker. In the U.S., when the dollar rose, both exporting industries and import-competing industries were forced to improve their productivity in order to compete. In Japan, by contrast, only the exporters have faced that pressure. Indeed, Japan's dual economy is so distorted by its protectionism that, under the pressure of a rising yen, Japanese workers actually shifted *from* the efficient sectors *into* the inefficient, exactly the opposite of the U.S.

This effect is seen in Table 2.3. In the early 1980s, the rising dollar forced exporters to raise their prices, thereby undercutting sales. Meanwhile, foreign imports into the U.S. were now cheaper, making it harder for American firms to sell unless they lowered prices and hence profits. In order to stay in the game, both exporters and import-competing sectors had to improve their productivity. And both sectors did, almost to the same degree.

In Japan, by contrast, when the yen rose in the late 1980s, only high-export industries felt the pressure and they showed good productivity growth. The low-export industries, shielded from competition from imports, performed very poorly.

In the early 1990s, another ratcheting upward of the yen coincided with Japan's recession. As is typical of recessions, reported productivity is negative. Once again, the low-export, low-import sectors performed much worse than the exporters. But notice that, while high-export sectors shed workers to restore competitiveness (while raising the wages of those workers who remained), the low-export sectors shielded from competition hardly downsized at all. In relative terms, there has been a shift of workers from high-productivity to low-productivity sectors! The opposite pattern took place in the U.S.: low-productivity, low-export sectors shed the most workers.

Table 2.3

Dualism in Japan; No Dualism in the U.S.

	Annual rates of growth in:				
Type of Good	Output	Labor Productivity	Total Factor Productivity	Number of Employees	Wages
U.S. 1980–85					
All manufacturing	2.2	3.3	2.3	–1.1	6.5
High-export mfg.	3.3	3.6	2.5	–0.3	7.1
Low-export mfg.	1.7	3.2	2.1	–1.5	6.0
Non-manufacturing	3.6	0.9	0.4	2.7	5.9
Japan 1985–88					
All manufacturing	3.6	3.5	0.8	0.1	3.3
High-export mfg.	7.0	7.0	3.5	–0.1	3.5
Low-export mfg.	1.8	1.6	–0.8	0.2	3.1
Non-manufacturing	5.1	3.7	0.3	1.4	3.7
Japan 1993–94					
All manufacturing	–2.6	–1.2	–3.3	–1.5	2.1
High-export mfg.	–2.7	0.7	–2.1	–3.4	2.6
Low-export mfg.	–2.6	–2.4	–3.9	–0.2	1.9
Non-manufacturing	1.0	1.1	2.4	2.2	0.5

Source: EPA (1996a), pp. 200–201

Note: In both countries, the high-exports sectors are: general machinery, electrical machinery, transportation equipment and precision machinery. The low-export sectors are all the rest of manufacturing. Labor Productivity = increase in output per worker. Total Factor Productivity = increase in output per unit of labor time plus capital.

Figure 2.3 **Japan's Dual Economy Worsens; Germany's Eases**

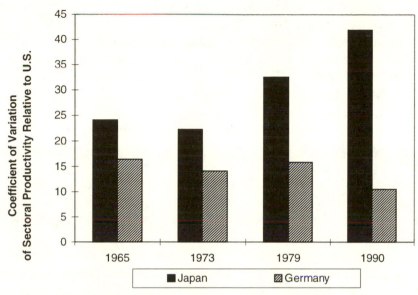

Source: van Ark and Pilat (1993), pg. 17; Tilton (1996), pg. 205-206
Note: Dualism is measured by a statistic called the "coefficient of variation." When this
number is small, it means that all industries are clustered around the average; when it is
large, it means there is a wide variation in performance from industry to industry. As a
country modernizes, this coefficient should get smaller. In both Japan and Germany, the
dualism decreased from 1965 through 1973. While it kept decreasing in Germany, it
rebounded smartly in Japan. Japan went off the tracks in the 1970s.

Normally, the kind of dualism found in Japan is seen only in newly
industrializing countries as some sectors modernize before others. But as
modernization spreads throughout the economy, dualism usually declines.
Indeed, this is exactly what happened in both Germany and Japan in their
initial catch-up period through the early 1970s. And then, as Germany
continued to modernize, its dualism decreased even further. But in Japan,
alone of all industrialized countries, dualism revived after the 1973 oil
shock (Figure 2.3).

Even worse, there was a fundamental change in the characteristic of
Japan's dualism. In the high-growth catch-up period, the inefficient traditional sectors tended to "subsidize" the modern sectors (e.g., low prices
for farm goods compared to industrial goods). But in the post-1973 period, the opposite occurred: the efficient were subsidizing the inefficient
(e.g., lower prices for the output of efficient industries and higher prices
for the output of farms and inefficient industries like glass, cement, food

processing, and so forth). This has not only sapped Japan's overall vigor, but, as we'll see in Chapter 3, is driving Japan's most efficient industries to leave the country and invest offshore.

Low imports do not directly create Japan's inefficiencies. That, as we shall see, is created by domestic collusion, cartels and other anti-competitive practices. But there is no way domestic industries could get away with these slipshod practices if imports were free to come in and seize the markets.

If imports were freely available, how could Japanese producers manage to charge domestic customers 60 percent more than world prices for steel, 70 percent more for cement, and 64 percent more for petrochemicals? Not surprisingly, in each of these industries, repeatedly organized into cartels by MITI, imports as of 1992 remained negligible: only 1.2 percent of consumption in cement, 7 percent in steel, and 8 percent in petrochemicals.[19]

Import barriers are the indispensable bodyguard of domestic cartels.

True, Japan restricted imports during the high-growth era. But over time the targets of protection shifted from infant industries to senile industries, from protecting the future to protecting the past.

It is not the case, as is so often assumed, that Japan has always protected everything in sight. The degree of protection has always varied widely from sector to sector. In the high-growth era, it was the "strategic" or "developmental" sectors that received the most protection. In 1963, the highest effective rates of tariff protection were accorded to sectors that were either currently high exporters (textiles, steel, and the shipbuilding portion of transport machinery) or would become export superstars in the future (like electrical machinery, the automotive portion of transport machinery)—in other words, sectors that either already enjoyed international competitiveness ("comparative advantage" in the economics jargon), or were gaining it (see Table 2.4).

In fact, as export strength increased in the machinery sector, protection became increasingly superfluous and was steadily reduced. The more exports rose as a share of output, the smaller the tariffs became (Figure 2.4). On the whole, formal protection steadily fell in the high-growth era as tariff rates halved from 32 percent in 1963 to 14 percent in 1973.

Had this pattern continued, perhaps Japan would have become a liberal trading partner.

Then came the 1973 oil shock. Once again protectionism reared its head. But now the targets were very different. By 1978, sectors getting

Table 2.4

Effective Rates of Protection by Industry (%)

	1963	1968	1973	1978
Manufacturing	32	24	14	22
Textiles	54	28	18	38
Wood products	14	25	16	18
Paper and pulp	10	18	11	9
Leather and rubber products	31	22	12	14
Chemicals	33	18	15	12
Petroleum and coal products	19	14	7	19
Iron and steel	30	30	17	19
Nonferrous metals	30	34	22	21
Metal products	14	20	10	6
Machinery	37	20	8	6
General machinery	23	14	9	6
Electrical machinery	31	16	5	7
Transport equipment	61	31	9	3
Precision instruments	35	23	10	6

Source: Itoh and Kiyono (1988) pg. 161

Figure 2.4 **As Exports Go Up, Tariffs Come Down, 1960-80**

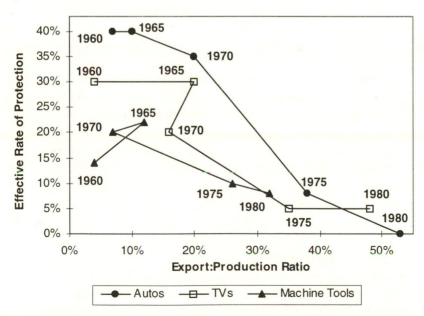

Source: Adapted by author from Itoh and Kiyono (1988), Pg. 162

Figure 2.5 **Protecting the Future Vs. Protecting the Past**

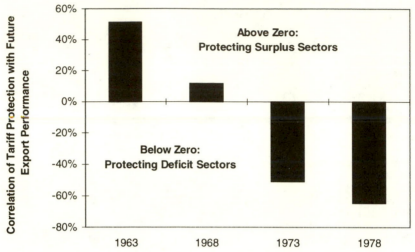

Source: Table 2:4 for ERP, for Net Exports:Output Ratio, Tilton (1996), pg. 11
Note: For explanation, see text.

the most protection were either ones where Japan's former competitiveness was eroding (textiles, metals) or ones where Japan never had competitiveness in the first place (wood products, paper, leather, chemicals).

This shift is illustrated more precisely in Figure 2.5. For various years, we measured the correlation between the tariffs for each sector for a given year and the trade performance by that sector in *future* years.

In 1963, the sectors getting the biggest tariff protection were those that had the biggest trade surpluses 20 years later. There is a positive 51 percent correlation between the size of a sector's tariff protection in 1963 and the size of the sector's trade surplus in 1982. But as time went on, the link between tariff protection and future export prowess steadily dropped. By 1978, the biggest tariffs were now going to sectors that showed a trade *deficit* a decade and a half later. That is shown in Figure 2.5 by the 64 percent *negative* correlation between tariff protection and the size of the sector's net exports. Japan was now protecting its uncompetitive "has-been" and "never-was" sectors.

The Industrial Cartels: Enforcers of Import Barriers

The Japanese government has claimed that all the import barriers are gone. Tariffs are now low. And yet the numbers show a nation that uniquely imports very little in the way of competing goods. Where are the "invisible barriers"? Is the government pulling strings behind the scenes?

In a few cases, government involvement is still operating. Formal barriers (like petroleum restrictions through 1996) and/or informal "administrative guidance" (warnings to importers of textiles not to overdo it) provide the "visible hand." But, most often these days, the government just provides a tolerant, or even supportive, environment. The key enforcers are in the private sector.

"To see how it works, check out the industry associations," one Japanese banker told me. Under the shelter of legal cartels in the 1970s and 1980s, and, these days, a blind eye by the Japan Fair Trade Commission (JFTC), associations of producers and users regularly collude. They agree on a price and boycott those who don't go along. This process is detailed in an illuminating new book by Mark Tilton, *Restrained Trade*.[20]

In the cement industry, where five companies control about 60 percent of sales, Tilton reports:

> Construction trade associations agreed to buy only from members of the domestic cement trade association, while members of the cement association agree to sell only to construction association members that abide by the agreement. If a construction company buys imported cement, domestic [cement] companies will no longer sell to that company. . . .
>
> [In] Kobe, the dock workers union formally refused to unload the cement [that one construction company tried to import]. . . . The longshoring company said it could not do the work because Japanese cement companies had told it they would no longer give the company work if it handled foreign cement.[21]

The same applies in steel, where five firms control about 70 percent of sales, and where Nippon Steel and Toyota get together every year and negotiate the "big buyer price." Even the powerful Mitsubishi Heavy Industries (MHI) was threatened with a cutoff of supplies and other retaliation when it wanted to buy a bit of steel from Korea's Pohang, whose prices were a third less than the Japanese cartel's price. Despite prices 60 percent above world levels, the much-vaunted opening of Japan's steel industry was a meager rise from 1 percent of consumption in 1980 to only 7 percent in 1992.[22]

Fear of retaliation is only one factor in this mutual protection scheme. Equally important is the fact that each sector, including exporters like autos and electronics, desires its own protection from imports. So, up to now, no one has wanted to knock over the chessboard.

Now, as we shall see in the next chapter, exporters in autos and electronics and other sectors face a dilemma: the costs are outweighing the benefits.

Chapter 3

"Hollowing Out": Driving Away the Geese That Lay the Golden Eggs

If current trends continue, in ten years, our company won't export a single item from Japan. Half of our sales will be overseas—even more than the 30 percent overseas sales we have today. But what we sell overseas, we will have to make overseas.
—Consumer electronics executive, 1995[1]

Back in 1988, Matsushita assembled VCRs in a brand new plant outside of Osaka. An assembly line that seemed to snake around forever was filled with hundreds of robots. Each one did only one simple task. In combination, they added up to an incredibly impressive feat of organization. Its simplicity was its cleverness. The assembly line was built because the rise of the yen since 1985 had compelled Matsushita to double its productivity quickly. Today, that plant no longer exists. It's been moved to Southeast Asia. As the yen kept soaring, productivity hikes at home just could not keep up.

In the last ten years, that story has been replicated a hundredfold. By 1994, half of all Japanese VCRs were made outside of Japan, up from a negligible 6 percent ten years earlier. Already, more TVs and microwaves are made outside of Japan than back home. Refrigerators are almost at that point. More than a third of all passenger cars are made outside of Japan (Figure 3.1).

All of these absent plants are the victims of Japan's dual economy. Ultimately, there is no free lunch. If Japan's inefficient sectors are to be coddled, someone has to pay the bill. As long as the sheep being fleeced were mainly consumers and taxpayers, the system was sustainable, even if inequitable. But, over time, Japan's efficient exporters also began suffering higher and higher penalties due to Japan's protectionist system. As a result, the system is starting to kill the geese that lay the golden eggs. That, in the end, is why the system cannot continue.

Figure 3.1 **Offshore Production Replacing Domestic Output**

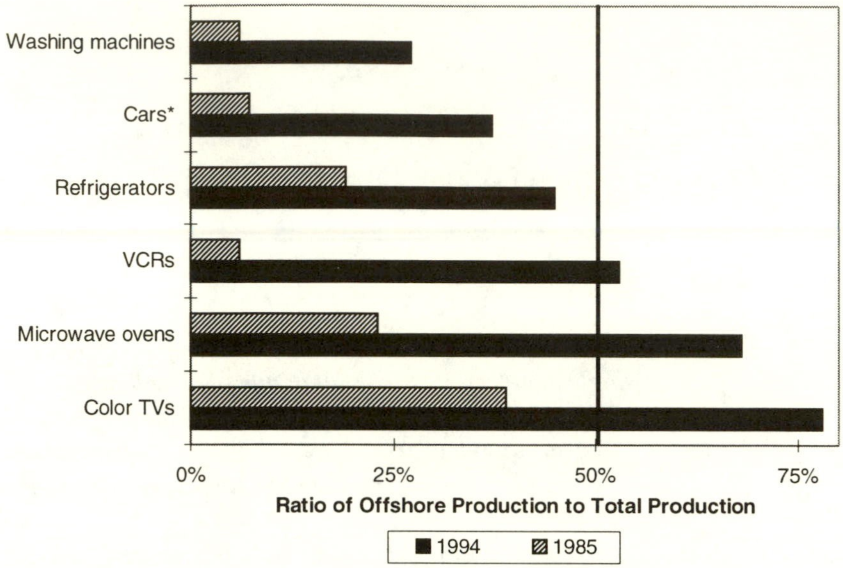

Ratio of Offshore Production to Total Production

■ 1994   ▨ 1985

Source: Nakajima (1996); Japan Automobile Manufacturers Association
Note: When the bar crosses the 50% line, the majority of output is produced overseas and has become larger than domestic output. *Figure for passenger cars is 1996.

Every time Toyota builds or operates a factory in Japan, it pays more than its foreign competitors for the cement in the building, for all the steel, rubber, plastic and glass that go into its cars, even the electricity to run the plant. Utility rates a third higher than those in the U.S. subsidize domestic oil refiners and construction firms.[2] It has to pay 50 percent more than its American competitors to ship its cars and its showrooms are paying 60 percent higher commercial rents. It also has to pay higher wages because food and other consumer items cost twice as much as in the U.S. (Figure 3.2).

The higher input prices paid by Japan's exporters are a hidden subsidy, a transfer of income to Japan's inefficient sectors. A full 30 percent of the input costs to manufacturing come from just four inefficient and shielded sectors where Japanese prices are far above world levels: energy, distribution, transport and communication.[3]

For a long time, the strong sectors could afford to pay the higher prices to subsidize the weak. But no more.

The very process of shielding paper and cement from imports ends up making it harder for Japanese companies to export autos and elec-

Figure 3.2 **Dual Economy Imposes Huge Costs on Exporters**

(Japanese Price Index of Intermediate Inputs to Industry, 1994, U.S.=1)

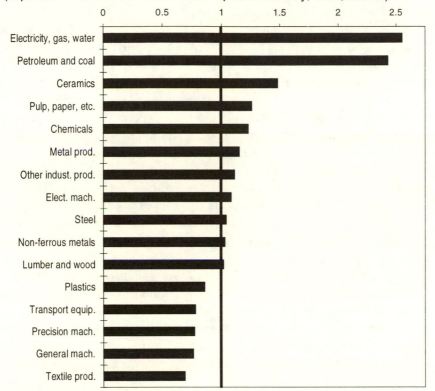

Source: MITI (1994a), pg. 72

Note: The approximate 2.5 figure for electricity, water and gas means that users in Japan must pay more than 2.5 times what U.S. users would pay.

tronics from Japan. That's why the Panasonic air conditioner at your local store was made in Malaysia instead of Osaka.

Here's how it works. If a country imports too little, but its exports keep expanding, its trade surplus will tend to rise beyond a sustainable level. As this happens, its currency will have to rise. That means Japan's exporters cannot recoup their costs unless they raise their prices overseas. But raising prices cuts down on sales. And so, by pricing exports out the market, the rising yen reduces the surplus. This process is the reason that the Japanese yen has seen a stunning secular rise over the past 25 years. That's why it is a staple of economics that barriers to imports usually end up being barriers to exports as well.

The result of all this is that Japan not only imports too little, it also exports too little! To see why: suppose that internal and external constraints limit Japan's trade surplus to 2 percent of GDP (usually, Japan's surplus fluctuates between 1 percent and 3 percent of GDP). This can be attained with imports at 10 percent of GDP and exports at 12 percent. Or it can be done with imports at 20 percent and exports at 22 percent. The point is: if Japan won't import more than 10 percent of GDP, then it *cannot* export more than 12 percent of GDP no matter how competitive its exporters are. On the other hand, if Japan were willing to let imports rise to 20 percent of GDP, then it could have exports equal to 22 percent of GDP. Once imports are limited, being more competitive is no more than a temporary help to the exporters. In fact, the more competitive Japan's exports are, the higher the yen will have to go to restrain them. A dip in the yen may raise the trade surplus and help exporters for a while, but ultimately the low level of imports will cause the yen to rise again.[4]

The only way Japan can export more is by importing more. The biggest obstacle to Japanese exports is not American protectionism, but Japanese protectionism.

And so Japan's exporters are increasingly caught in a squeeze play: forced to pay higher and higher input prices at home but no longer able to pass these costs along to customers overseas.

The irony is that, while the Japanese state is often lionized as the rational, monolithic mobilizer of the strategic industries, in reality the state is schizoid. One set of measures boosts dynamic industries, while another set sacrifices them to preserve their weaker cousins. As reform economist Yukio Noguchi has pointed out:

> [Many non-Japanese experts] consider the main object of government to be large corporations in strategic industries while I see it to be the low-productivity sectors. . . . [Many policies] transfer income from the first sector [the efficient exporting industries] to the second sector [the inefficient domestic industries]. . . . [One] important factor is government action to protect the second sector from competing pressures through import restrictions, limits on market entry, and price controls . . . .Unless agriculture and small companies are forced to rationalize and their markets opened up to foreign competition, living standards are unlikely to improve much henceforth.[5]

Slowly but surely, enlightened sections of Japan's bureaucracy are coming to understand that it is in Japan's interest to start dismantling the protection behind its dual economy rather than to continue pretending it does not exist. In 1996, the Economic Planning Agency even called for more imports:

> An increase in imports would stimulate incentives to raise productivity of domestic industries and reduce the current surplus, which would lessen pressure on the appreciation of the yen.[6]

This new recognition is one reason why, in 1996, MITI finally abolished the law that had restricted imports of petroleum products.[7] This is also the reason why MITI pushed through the cabinet a mandate to lower costs to international levels in four key sectors by 2001.

For example, MITI has mandated that regulated electric utilities lower their rates by 20 percent in order to meet German levels. Given the key role utilities have played both as a source of high costs for industrial customers, but also as a cost-absorber for weak sectors like construction, lower rates will have ripple effects throughout the dual economy.[8]

Still, when it comes to action, the "clientelism" dominating both the political world and MITI's "vertical" bureaus—those responsible for particular industries—makes real change an uphill climb.

Consider the Ministry's response in early 1997 when Japan's trade surplus with the U.S. began rebounding. MITI Minister Shinji Sato called in Japan's automakers and told them to export less; they were causing trouble.[9]

But why should Japan export fewer cars? It's very good at making cars. Why didn't Sato call in the beer makers and tell them to import more foreign containers, bottles or cans? Why didn't he call in the publishers and tell them to import more paper? Or the construction companies to import more cement, glass and lumber? Why, instead, is MITI becoming even more intransigent on market access issues in paper and glass? To answer this is to go to the dualism at the heart of the post-1973 Japanese political economy.

Speaking in confidence, a career official at MITI said he agreed that Sato should have promoted more imports in the interests of Japan's competitiveness. This in itself was surprising because, in the past, MITI officials have usually denied there was any need to increase imports or that any forces were suppressing them. Asked why Sato didn't take that step, he replied, "He took the path of least resistance. It's always been easier in Japan to restrain exports than to increase imports."[10]

Driving the Exporters Away to Asia

Now comes the end of the road. Squeezed between the anvil of sky-high prices at home and the hammer of the secularly rising yen, many of Japan's best companies in its strongest sectors have been compelled to go offshore.

In 1996, for the first time ever, Japan's multinationals sold more through overseas affiliates than through exports from Japan. In the early 1990s, exports accounted for 25 percent of the total sales of Japan's top 1,000 companies; by 1996, it was down to 20 percent.

In this "era when companies can choose their country" (as MITI put it in a 1996 "Long-Term Vision" Report), many of Japan's best manufacturers are choosing some place other than Japan. Over the past eight years, Matsushita doubled its workforce from 131,000 to 266,000, but only 6,000 of the new hires were in Japan. Hitachi also doubled its workforce, from 171,000 to 332,000, but actually decreased its Japanese payroll by 1,000.

In many cases, the hollowing out has gone so far that there has been an absolute decline in domestic output. Take cars, for example. On a global basis, Japanese automakers produced almost as many cars in 1996 as in 1990, almost 17 million. But only 10 million of these cars were produced within Japan itself, down from 13.5 million six years earlier. The missing 3 million units were now being made overseas, as overseas production doubled from 3 million to 6 million. By 1998, according to Goldman Sachs estimates, Japanese production at home was expected to decline even further to 8 million units as still more capacity is shipped abroad. At that point, Japanese companies could be producing more cars abroad than at home.[11]

As Japan's efficient sectors flee, the domestic economy's manufacturing job base sinks and the economy becomes more and more dominated by its low-productivity sectors. This lowers overall productivity even more. By the year 2000, according to MITI, Japan was expected to have 15 percent fewer factory jobs than in 1992.

Japan is operating by a kind of comparative *dis*advantage. The efforts it makes to preserve its weaker sectors are driving its best away.

The sectors investing abroad are the very ones that used to be Japan's top exporters. Autos and electronics lead the pack (Figure 3.3). By the mid-1990s, *half* of all capital investment by the auto and electrical machinery industries was made *outside* Japan. In steel, the proportion was one-third. As Keith Henry of MIT's Japan program so pithily expressed it: "Made in Japan is being replaced by Made by Japan in Asia."[12]

By 1996, Toshiba no longer exported a single TV or video deck or PC

Figure 3.3 **The Most Efficient Leave; the Weakest Stay at Home**

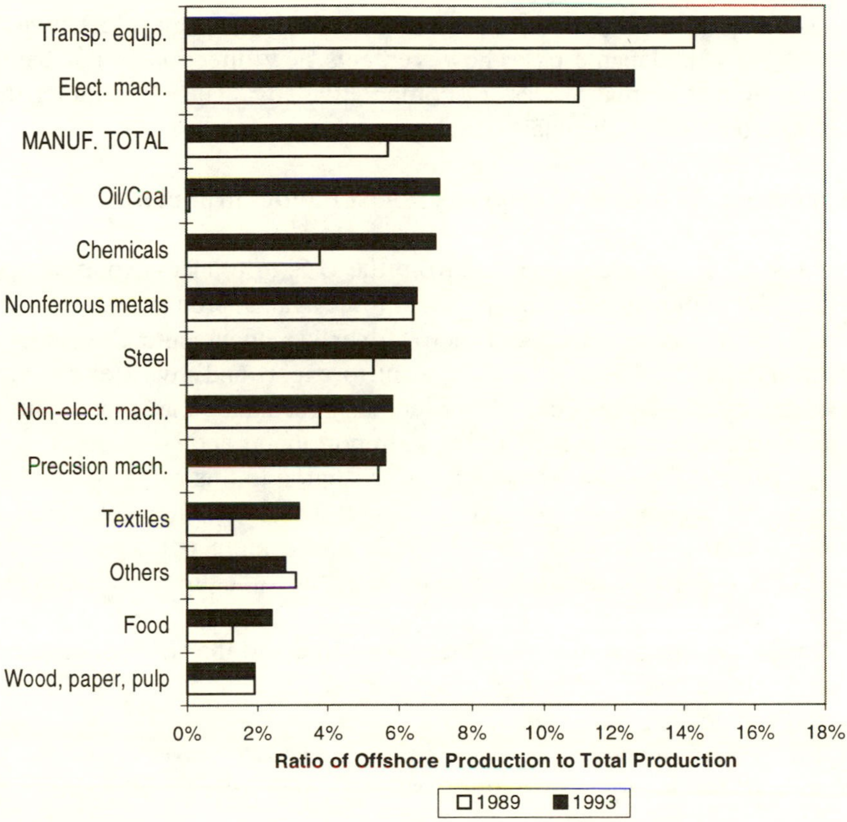

Ratio of Offshore Production to Total Production

□ 1989   ■ 1993

Source: MITI (1994b)

from Japan. All its overseas sales were being supplied from offshore production platforms. In 1995, Sony announced it would soon stop making TVs for exports.

Who then will be left in Japan? Under the current setup, Malaysia gets to produce computer chips just so Japan can keep paper.

Initially the impact of "hollowing out" was hidden because investment in Southeast Asia actually stimulated production in Japan. Japanese exports had to supply the new plants with equipment and supplies. In 1995, 25 percent of all Japanese exports were sent to the offshore affiliates. However, by 1996 or so, the replacement of exports from Japan itself by exports from Japanese affiliates in Southeast Asia was starting to dampen manufacturing back home. This effect was magnified as Japan increased imports of textiles, cheap TVs, and so forth from its overseas affiliates rather than making these at home.

Mature economies do, of course, increase their foreign direct investment (FDI). In Japan's case, however, this new direction is not being driven by that normal process of comparative advantage. It is rather the ultimate outcome of the dual economy.

Exporters: A Force for Antiprotectionist Politics in Japan?

In most every advanced country, from the U.S. to France, exporters and especially multinationals are a political force against protectionist politics within their own country. As Helen Milner has documented, eventually multinationals realize that, if they want to export and invest elsewhere, they must reciprocate. They also eventually recognize that protection in their host country limits their ability to import inputs and raises costs.[13]

Up to now, Japan has remained the exception to this rule. Yet, just as bureaucratic France—a country to which Japan is often compared—moved from protectionism in the 1920s and a more open policy after World War II, so Japan will have to move in the same direction if it hopes to revive.

Indeed, if Japanese multinationals hope to avoid the squeeze on them that we have discussed in this chapter, they have no choice but to end Japan's protectionism.

So far, unfortunately, they have found it easier to leave Japan than to change it. In the jargon of political science, they have found it easier to exercise "exit" than "voice."[14]

And perhaps until now, they have not realized how much Japan's protectionism was hurting them. But the costs are becoming higher with every passing year.

In the end, Japan's powerful exporters cannot entirely escape the damage inflicted by Japan's protection of the inefficient by going offshore. They still depend heavily on the domestic market and, given Japan's social contract, have to retain hosts of redundant workers. In the long run, their prosperity requires reform within Japan itself.

Sooner or later, Japan's multinationals, in their own interest, will have to reckon with this reality.

Chapter 4

From Growth Superstar to Economic Laggard

Still Struggling to Catch Up

It's no news that Japan has faced some rough economic times during the 1990s. However, the notion that Japan's troubles go back two decades and that, unremedied, they will continue for many more years surely goes against the grain of what most of us—including this author—have always believed. After all, Japan grew faster than America, Germany or any other industrial country during the 1980s. It must have been doing something right—or so it would seem. Some will even argue that, once Japan gets past its patch of bad growth, it will resume its supposed trajectory to "owning" the twenty-first century.

Well, there is no such trajectory.

Japan did have a growth "miracle" during the 1955–73 "high-growth era." That is undeniable. In less than a generation, Japan raised itself from a poor agricultural country to a Newly Industrializing Country (NIC), from the income level of 1990 India to nearly that of 1990 Korea. Japan *quadrupled* its GDP per worker from $3,500 to $13,500 in only 18 years. No other major country, before or since, has managed this all-important development task in such a short time. And that includes the Asian tigers.

Had Japan continued at that pace it might indeed have become the world's richest country. But, the miracle ran out of juice more than 20 years ago. During 1973–90, Japan's growth in GDP per worker tumbled from the 8.4 percent level of the 1960s to only 3 percent.

Japan's drastic deceleration cannot be blamed on the oil shocks, as is so often assumed. While the first oil shock undoubtedly helped trigger Japan's fall from the sky, it was only a trigger, not the cause. According to renowned growth economist Angus Maddison, higher oil prices lowered Japan's growth by only 0.2 percent a year over the course of 1973–84.[1] The underlying cause for Japan's problems was not the oil shock *per se*, but Japan's poor *response* to it, as well as to other fundamental trends, from rising wages to the emergence of the Asian Newly Industrializing Countries (NICs).

The fall in growth was farther and longer than economists—even those writing after the oil shock—expected. Writing in 1975, economists Denison and Chung projected 6 percent growth in GDP through 1990, on the way to a gradual descent of the potential growth rate down to 3.25 percent by the year 2002. This is far higher than what actually occurred (Figure 4.1). As late as 1978, i.e., five years *after* the first oil shock, MITI still assumed 6 percent growth rates through the year 2000.[2]

The reality is that, far from getting ready to surpass the rest of the world, Japan still has a long way to go just to catch up. In a list of 23 European, North American and Asian countries, ranked by real GDP per worker, Japan was still 17th in 1990. No one would deny that Japan's progress in catching up to the world leaders has been remarkable—especially considering how far back it started. Back in 1955, Japan's output per worker was only 30 percent of European levels and now it's at 80 percent. But the fact remains: Japan has a way to go before it equals Germany or France or even Italy and Spain (Table 4.1).

The idea that Japan is behind even Italy in output per worker will no doubt be met with skepticism. But that's only because people tend to presume that the entire economy is as productive as the export sectors. Once one considers the great inefficiency of the domestic sectors, the overall inefficiency of the Japanese economy is readily understandable. Japanese sources agree. The Japan Productivity Center for Socio-Economic Development ranks Japan 9th among 11 industrial countries. With Japan at a scale of 100, the U.S. comes in first at 138, and Italy ranks third at 123.[3]

This is shocking only because we have been told so many times that, at present currency values, Japan is among the richest countries in the world. In 1996, with the yen at 108, Japan's nominal GDP per person was $35,000 compared to only $29,000 for the U.S.

However, such figures represent a "money illusion" rather than reality. Did Japan really become twice as wealthy between early 1990 and early 1995 when the yen doubled in value but real GDP barely moved? Did Japan then abruptly become 60 percent poorer when the yen dropped back again? If your wages are twice mine, but the prices you pay are three times higher, who has the higher living standard?

To eliminate such "money illusions," economists adjust currencies to

Figure 4.1 **Japan's Growth Decelerates Much More Than Expected**

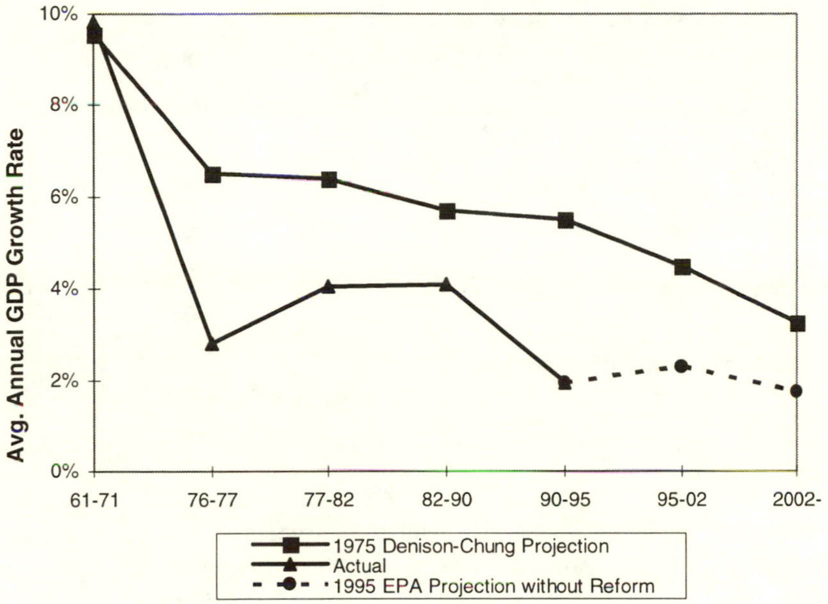

Source: Denison and Chung (1976) pg. 139-151, EPA (1995a, 1995b)

Table 4.1

Real GDP per Worker, Percent of U.S. Level

	1955	1960	1970	1973	1980	1990
U.S.	100	100	100	100	100	100
Italy	36	45	64	65	85	84
France	46	55	71	74	85	83
West Germany	47	57	70	74	86	80
UK	57	60	61	63	67	73
Spain	29	34	54	61	68	72
JAPAN	15	20	38	42	51	62
South Korea	11	11	15	17	25	44

Source: Summers and Heston (1995)
Note: This relationship is measured on a Purchasing Power Parity (PPP) basis. See text
for explanation.

Table 4.2

Real GDP per Capita, Percent of U.S. Level

	1955	1960	1970	1980	1990
U.S.	100	100	100	100	100
Canada	72	73	78	92	95
Germany	53	66	73	78	79
JAPAN	21	30	56	66	79
France	49	59	71	77	77
UK	64	69	66	66	73
Italy	37	46	58	67	69
Spain	27	32	45	48	53
Korea	9	9	13	20	37

Source: Summers and Heston (1995)

Note: This relationship is measured on a Purchasing Power Parity (PPP) basis. See text for explanation.

reach what is called the "Purchasing Power Parity" (PPP) basis. PPP means that a basket of goods costs the same in the U.S. or Japan or Malaysia. That way, one can judge: how many hours of work does it take the average American, or Japanese or Malaysian to buy a shirt or a car?

Table 4.1 incorporates the PPP correction. Now it is true that, even on a PPP basis, Japan does appear to have equaled Germany and France by some other measures, e.g., the commonly used GDP per capita, that is, per person (Table 4.2).

However, this result is more a product of demographics than productivity. Due to the postwar baby boom, Japan's working age population grew much faster than the total population, rising from 60 percent of the total population to 70 percent. So, even if workers had shown zero increase in productivity, GDP per capita would still have risen. This gives the illusion of a better performance than is sustainable. In the long run, a nation can only consume as much as it produces. GDP per capita is a measure of how much wealth is available to be consumed each year, while GDP per worker measures how much a country can produce.

The long run is now about to hit Japan. Due to the baby dearth, its labor force is now shrinking even as its total population continues to grow. So, even if GDP per worker remains the same, GDP per capita will fall. Robert Feldman of Salomon Brothers has examined the aging dilemma in detail.[4] He says that, without a sharp recovery of productivity, GDP per capita could actually fall for the next 20 years.

For this reason, PPP-adjusted GDP *per worker* is the best measure of a country's comparative income and sustainable growth.

Why Japan Used to Grow Faster Than the U.S.

Many people have the impression that Japan had superlative growth in the 1980s, because it grew faster than countries like the U.S., Germany or France. Yet, no one suggests that Japan's growth was slow because it could not match the breakneck clip of Korea or Taiwan or even the recent speed of India. Japan grew faster than the U.S. and Germany for exactly the same reason that it grew more slowly than Korea, Taiwan or India. This is exactly what growth theory, and decades of data, tell us to expect. Countries start off growing slowly, reach their highest rate of growth during the industrial "takeoff," and then slow down. After the industrial takeoff is completed, the richer you get, the slower you grow.

There are two reasons for this growth pattern. One is the famous "law of diminishing returns." Give a farmer his first tractor and his output will zoom. Give him a tractor, plus irrigation, plus fertilizer, plus storage facilities and his output will zoom even more. But, once a farmer has 10 tractors, adding one more will not do all that much. Rich countries are those with more capital per worker (see Figure 4.7 below on page 66), so they grow more slowly.

The second reason is technology. The very poorest countries grow slowly because they are unable to absorb the most modern technology due to low educational levels and other causes. Meanwhile, the most advanced countries that are on the frontier of technology can raise their efficiency only as fast as global technology frontiers expand. The NICs, by contrast, enjoy one of the "advantages of backwardness." They do not have to reinvent the wheel. They can leapfrog in mere years into modern technologies that it took more advanced countries several decades to develop. And so, when they take off, they grow very fast. In economic theory, the NICs' extra burst of growth is called the "catch-up effect." In fact, among a group of 22 rich and industrializing countries, the "catch-up effect" alone can account for 70–80 percent of the difference in their growth rates.

Taking this "catch-up effect" into account, we find that Japan's growth performance is divided into two periods. During the 1960s high-growth era, Japan truly did experience miraculous growth. Its growth was far higher than one would expect for a country at its stage of development. But, during the 1970s-80s, Japan was right on the trend line for the catch-up effect. It grew faster than the U.S. and Germany and France simply because it was poorer than they—not because it had found some growth elixir (Figure 4.2).

Notice the analogous roles of Korea and Japan. Both were stars at more or less the same stage of development. Japan was the "miracle economy" from 1960–73, when it made the transition from about $5,000 GDP per worker to about $14,000. Korea was the fastest grower (6.1 percent a year) during 1973–90 when it made the transition from about $6,000 GDP per worker to about $16,000 (compare top and bottom panels in Figure 4.2).[5]

If we compare Japan just to the other industrialized countries in the Group of Seven (Figure 4.3), we can see that, during the 1970s and 1980s, Japan grew no faster than the trend line predicts. It grew faster than the others simply because it was poorer than they were.

To properly compare Japan's performance to that of other countries, we have to look at them during the same stage of development. During 1955–73, Japan's GDP per worker leaped from $3,500 to $13,500. Its growth in that era, 8.4 percent, was far higher than that of any other major country during the same stage of development, including the Asian NICs (Figure 4.4).

But, once Japan matured, its performance fell off considerably. Its rate of growth from 1975 to 1990, when it went from $13,500 to $22,500 per worker GDP, was 3.5 percent. That was below Italy, which achieved 4.0 percent, and considerably below France and Germany, which achieved 4.5 percent at a comparable stage.

From Growth Superstar to Economic Underachiever

While the stage of development is an extremely important factor in determining how fast a country grows, it is by no means the only one.

One of the most important other factors is investment rates. Among countries at the same stage of development, the ones that invest more grow faster (Figure 4.5).

In addition, growth will be fastest in countries that give their people more education. That's because more educated people can better adopt the most modern technology. Growth will also be higher in countries that are more open to trade with other countries, that have more stable politics and macroeconomic policies, and so forth.

When we add in some of these other factors, the real question is why

Figure 4.2 **Japan: Growth Superstar in 1960s, Also-Ran in 1973-90**

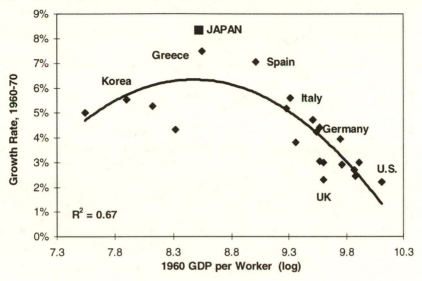

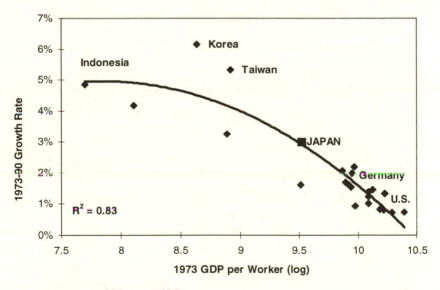

Source: Summers and Heston (1995)

Note: In this chart, the *growth rate* of each country's GDP per worker is plotted against its initial *level* of GDP per worker (in logarithm form). $R^2 = 0.83$ in the bottom panel means that 83% of the difference in the growth rates among these countries can be explained by the single factor of its initial GDP per worker.

Figure 4.3 **Japan Grew Fastest of the G7 Because It Was the Poorest**

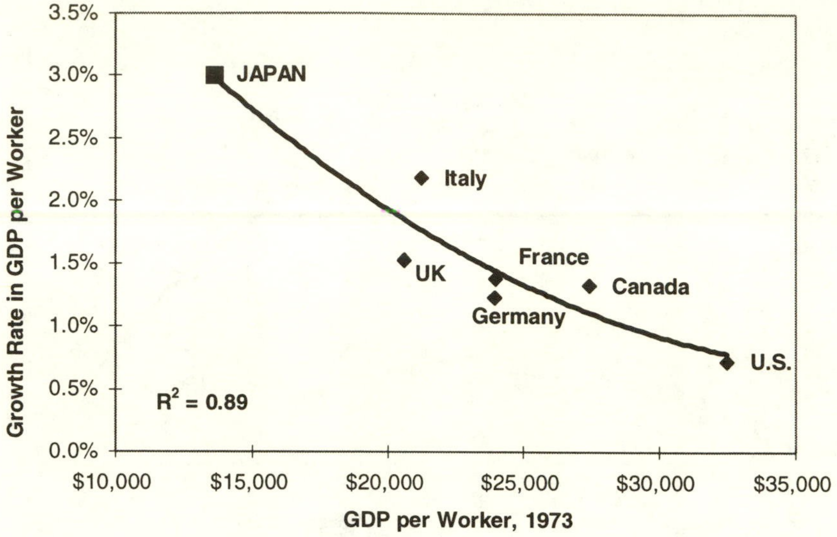

Source: Summers and Heston (1995)
Note: G7 refers to the seven rich countries known as the Group of Seven. $R^2 = 0.89$ means 89 percent of the variation in the growth rates of the countries can be explained by the difference in their 1973 GDP per worker.

Japan didn't do a lot better after 1973. Consider how much Japan was investing in the post-1973 period—an incredible 35 percent of GDP, far more than any other industrialized country. It's hard to think of an industrialized country outside the Soviet Union that invested so much and had so little growth to show for it.

We can evaluate how well Japan really did compared to other countries through the use of a technique known as econometric modeling. If we plug some of the key growth factors—the catch-up effect, the rate of investment, openness to trade, population size and education levels—into an equation, we can explain about 90 percent of the difference in growth rates among countries. We can then see if Japan was getting the same "bang for the buck" from these key growth factors as a typical country.[6]

This growth model confirms the popular impression that Japan was indeed a miracle economy during the 1960s. The model projects that Japan's GDP per worker should have grown "only" 7 percent a year if it got no more benefit from the "catch-up" factor, investment, education, trade and so forth than other countries. Instead, it grew much faster, at 8.4 percent (Figure 4.6). Its growth was 1.4 percent *above* the model projection.

Figure 4.4 **Japan Leads Pack during Takeoff Era, Lags Afterward**

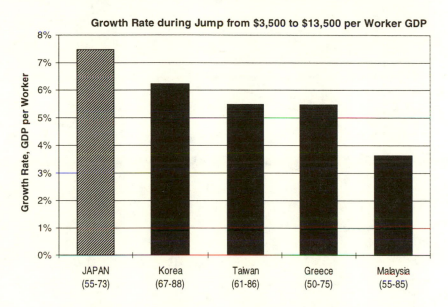

Growth Rate during Jump from $3,500 to $13,500 per Worker GDP

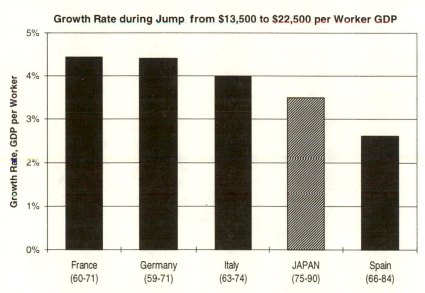

Growth Rate during Jump from $13,500 to $22,500 per Worker GDP

Source: Summers and Heston (1995)

Figure 4.5 **Higher Investment Rates Mean Faster Growth**

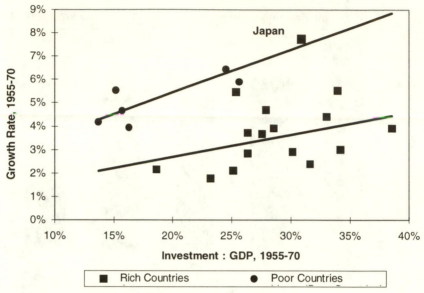

Source: Summers and Heston (1995)
Note: Japan was a poor country at the time.

Figure 4.6 **Growth Exceeds Forecast in 1960s; Falls Short After 1973**

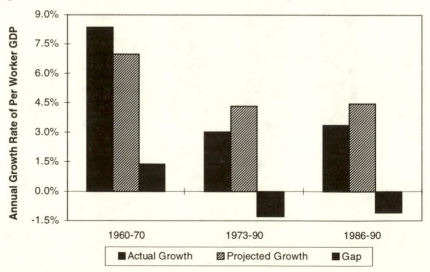

Source: Author's calculations as described in footnote 6 and Appendix D

By contrast, according to the model, Japan should have grown at 4.3 percent a year during 1973–90. Instead it only grew 3 percent. Its growth was 1.3 percent *below* the model projection. Even during the 1986–90 bubble, Japan was an underperformer, growing at 3.4 percent a year compared to the model projection of 4.4 percent. Clearly, Japan's economic arteries were clogging long before the 1990 heart attack.

Moreover, Japan's differences from the model projection are far greater than just the usual variation that countries have. Something very special about Japan's economic policies and economic patterns made it a growth superstar in the 1950s-60s and an economic underachiever during 1973–90. Explaining that "something special" is the task of this book.

The Need to Leap to Innovation-Driven Growth

One of the most important tasks in a country's development is to make the transition from the "investment-driven" stage of growth to the "innovation-driven" stage.[7] According to competitiveness expert Michael Porter, in the investment-driven stage, the stage of a Newly Industrializing Country, how much a country invests is the most important factor in growth. But once a country matures, how much it innovates is the key. In the first stage, building cement plants is key; in the latter, it's engendering Intel's and Wal-Mart's.

In the innovation-driven stage, what counts most is not only how much a country invests, but what it gets in return for that investment—in other words, not just how many bucks, but how much bang per buck.

Japan and the Soviet Union are both cases of countries that grew very fast during the investment-driven stage, yet failed to make a successful transition to the innovation-driven stage. One would not think this, judging by Japan's exporters. They are among the most innovative companies in the world. But in the domestic side of Japan's dual economy, where competition has been stifled, the leap to the innovation-driven stage failed to occur.

Initially, as a country moves from poverty to become a NIC, development is driven primarily by pure investment. The more tools a worker has to work with, i.e., more infrastructure, factories and equipment, the more he can produce (Figure 4.7). To a large extent, "throwing money at the problem" goes a long way.

Naturally, the more a country invests, the faster it can accumulate more capital per worker. One reason for Japan's miracle in the high-growth era is that Japan accumulated capital far faster than other countries. Even as a

Figure 4.7 **Countries Get Rich by Accumulating Capital**

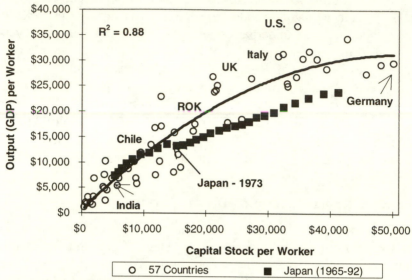

Source: Summers and Heston (1995)

Note: During 1965-1973, Japan kept pace with other countries. But after 1973, it gained far less additional GDP for its increases in capital stock. Data prior to 1965 are not available. $R^2 = 88$ means that 88 percent of the difference in GDP per worker can be explained by differences in capital per worker.

poor country in 1950, with a per capita income no higher than Pakistan's was in 1990, Japan invested 17 percent of GDP, compared to 10 percent for a typical country at that level. From that level, investment zoomed, finally reaching an astronomical peak of 41 percent in 1973 (Figure 4.8).

This phenomenon created a very powerful "virtuous cycle." That is, high investment rates led to high levels of capital stock per worker, which in turn led to higher GDP per worker. Since people with higher living standards can afford to save more, that increased wealth led to higher investment rates, and thus even greater levels of capital stock per worker, and so on. This reciprocal feedback between investment and growth created an explosion into very rapid growth. As a result of this process, during the high-growth era, the capital stock per worker grew much faster in Japan than in other countries at the same stage of development (Figure 4.9).

However, as a country matures, diminishing returns set in. Returns to capital investment will automatically drop unless this trend is countered by improved technology. At that point, further growth is driven less by

Figure 4.8 **Japan Invests Much More than Others**

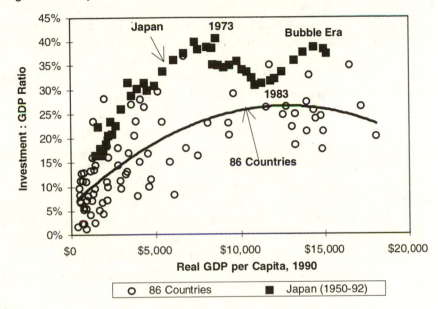

Figure 4.9 **Hence Its Capital Stock Grows Faster**

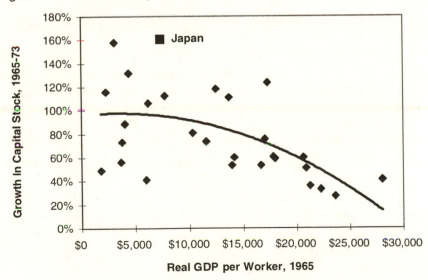

Source: Summers and Heston (1995)

how much a country invests than by how efficiently it invests. To progress further, it must shift to innovation-based growth. What matters is not how many steel mills a country builds, but whether it is adding continuous casting techniques and minimills; not how many 486-generation PCs its businesses buy, but the move from 486 PCs to Pentiums.

If we compare a broad range of countries, capital stock per worker explains about 88 percent of the reason why rich countries are rich and poor countries are poor (Figure 4.7). But once a country becomes mature, capital stock per worker only explains about 25 percent of the differences in wealth (Figure 4.10). Efficiency of investment is more important.[8]

For mature countries, what counts is not just how many dollars a country is investing, but how much additional GDP it gets for each dollar invested. This is where we see the big difference between the results for Japan in the high-growth period and in the post-1973 era. In the late 1960s, for every $1 that Japan added to its stock of capital, i.e., the value of all the infrastructure, factories, and equipment, Japan's GDP grew by $1.22. But, by the 1980s, for every $1 in added capital stock, Japan's GDP grew only $0.43 (Figure 4.11).

Of course, all nations face diminishing returns as they grow richer. But Japan's case is different. In the high-growth era, Japan not only invested more than other countries, it got a much bigger bang for the buck than other countries at comparable stages of development (top panel of Figure 4.12). It is this combination of both extremely high investment and very efficient investment that made Japan's industrial takeoff a true miracle.

This efficiency did not continue in the post-1973 era. Japan continued to pour on the investment. But it gained far less from this investment than comparable countries (bottom panel of Figure 4.12, also see Figure 4.7).

By the 1970s-80s, Japan's high investment rates were not a mark of strength, but of weakness. They were simply a Sisyphus-like effort to make up for increasing inefficiency: more perspiration to make up for less inspiration.

Japan uses capital more inefficiently than almost any other advanced country. According to the McKinsey Global Institute, Japan's productivity of capital is one-third less than that of the U.S. In 1992, Japan used 22 percent more capital per person and 40 percent more labor than the U.S. and yet its output per person was 23 percent *less*.[9]

In the late 1950s, Japan obtained a bigger boost to GDP from every addition to capital stock—higher "marginal productivity of capital" in the

Figure 4.10 **In Mature Economies, Efficiency of Investment Is Key**

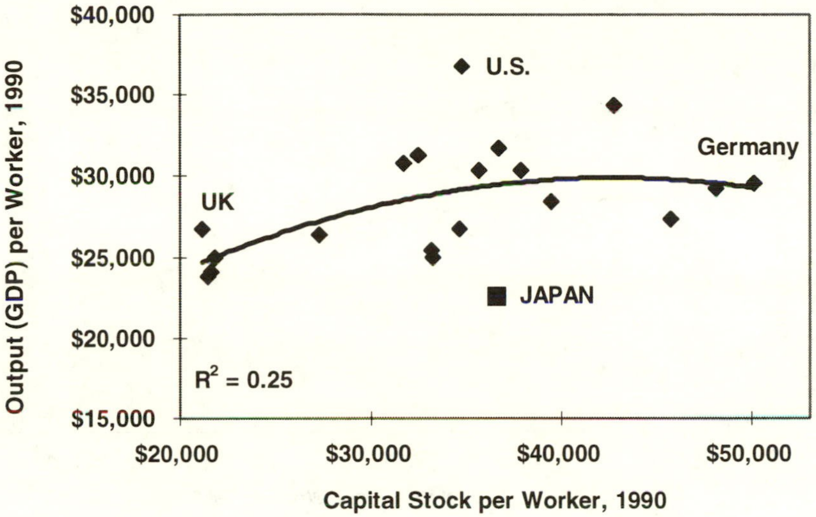

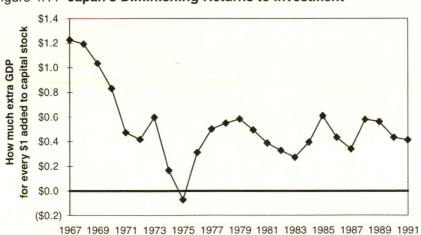

Capital Stock per Worker, 1990

Source: Summers and Heston (1995)
Note: Japan's GDP per worker is the lowest among these 19 rich countries despite capital per worker in the middle range. $R^2 = 0.25$ means that 25 percent of the difference in a country's GDP per worker can be explained by its capital per worker.

Figure 4.11 **Japan's Diminishing Returns to Investment**

Source: Summers and Heston (1995)
Note: This chart shows how much Japan's GDP grew for every $1 increase in its stock of capital. This is a 2-year moving average.

Figure 4.12 **Extra Bang for the Buck in 1960s; Below Par after 1973**

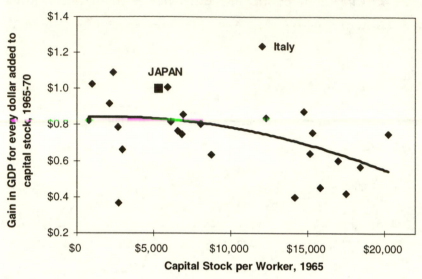

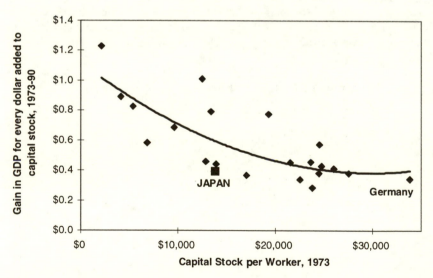

Source: Summers and Heston (1995)
Note: This chart shows how much GDP increases for every $1 added to capital stock, a
measure known as the IOCR (Incremental Output:Capital Ratio)

Table 4.3

Japan Moves from Best to Worst Rate of Return on Capital

	Japan	U.S.	UK	Germany	France
1955	34	16			
1960	28	14	23	24	24
1970	18	12	15	14	18
1980	8	9	11	9	11
1990	4	6	8	5	6

Source: Alexander (1997), p. 8.
Note: The information in the table is the real aggregate rate of return on gross nonresidential fixed capital stock.

economics jargon—than France, Germany, the UK, and the U.S. But that's exactly what we should expect to find. As a poorer country, Japan should have a higher marginal productivity of capital. By 1990, its marginal productivity of capital had fallen behind both the Europeans and the U.S. although it still remained poorer (Table 4.3).[10]

Japan's use of capital during 1973–90 was so unproductive that, according to the "growth model" discussed above, Japan had to invest 35 percent of GDP just to get the same rate of growth that a typical country could have obtained with only 25 percent of GDP. Japan was depriving its people of an awful lot of consumption—an amount equal to 10 percent of GDP—without giving them enough in return. This is the economics behind the common saying: "Rich Japan, poor Japanese."

In the end, Japan's attempt at investment-led growth when it should have focused on innovation-led growth is an effort in futility. As time goes on and returns from investment sink even further, Japan would have to invest more and more of its GDP just to keep the same rate of growth. This simply cannot be done.

The issue of efficiency explains why countries that trade more grow faster (as we will detail in Chapter 9). By applying competitive pressure and forcing companies to match world standards, trade adds to the efficiency of investment. In essence, countries that trade more grow faster for the same reason that industries that trade more show better productivity. Trade breaks down local monopolies and oligopolies and forces companies to match world standards upon pain of extinction.

In the 1970s and 1980s, Japan had one of highest rates of investment:GDP and lowest rates of trade:GDP among all advanced countries and NICs. By contrast, the Asian NICs emphasized trade rather than sheer investment as the path to growth. Japan's low trade dependence lies at the heart of both its dual economy and the consequent inefficiency of its investment.

A Japanese Model?

During the 1980s, a host of books suggested that the U.S. and other advanced countries model themselves after Japan, from its high savings rates to its manufacturing techniques to its industrial policies.

It is certainly true that the U.S. could afford to save more (while Japan should save less and trade more). And it is also true that many U.S. factories learned a great deal by watching the methods of Japan's manufacturing exporters. However, any advanced country that imported Japan's ways of doing things wholesale would have lowered, not raised, its growth. Japan's practices in the high-growth era may provide some guides for NICs and would-be NICs. But the mature Japan is an object lesson in what to avoid.

Part Two

The Success and the Souring

Chapter 5

The Politics of
Japanese Economic Policy

The Drive for National Autonomy

Japan's history poses a mystery. It seems clear that Japan's perpetuation of obsolete practices, particularly its import barriers, has exacted a terrible cost. But, if that is so, then why does protectionist thinking remain so tenacious in Japan?

The easy answer is that powerful vested interests like the farm and construction lobbies have politicians in their hip pocket. And clearly there is some truth to that. But, if that were the whole story, then why do so many of Japan's most brilliant economists defend Japan's crass protectionism—usually by denying that it even exists?

Part of the answer is that Japan's neomercantilist ideas worked. At least they worked *temporarily* and *under very specific conditions* associated with the catch-up process. That gave them a hard-to-shake credibility.

But why did these ideas continue to retain their iron grip for so many years after they had turned counterproductive? Why was it not until the crisis of the 1990s that even a few leading economists, business leaders and bureaucrats began to question them?

The answer, we think, lies in a passage that economists Jeffrey Sachs and Andrew Warner wrote about developing countries, but which fits Japan like a glove:

> [M]ercantilist trade and industrial policies were a crucial mechanism by which new nation states consolidated their political power both relative to competing domestic interest groups . . . and other nations. . . . [I]t is no accident that Alexander Hamilton championed trade protection in his "Report on the Subject of Manufactures," . . . or that Friedrich List [an intellectual hero in Japan —rk] championed industrial policy in the period just before German unification. Both men saw such policies as part of state building. . . .

> Most recent models of trade policy have been based on interest-group politics. Trade policy is viewed as the outcome of the relative political strengths of various factional, class, or sectoral interests. Such political considerations have surely played an important role in the SLI (state-led industrialization) strategies of developing countries, but more often in the perpetuation of policies than in their origin. . . . [I]n Egypt, India, Mexico and Turkey . . . ideology, state building, and geopolitics, rather than domestic interest groups, were the fundamental forces that initially led to SLI. Once SLI policies had built up a protected sector, however, powerful interest groups developed to defend them.[1]

Upon reading this, one can't help reflecting on the role of the Japanese state in promoting industrialization as a means of preserving national autonomy. Japan's modernization began in the late nineteenth century as a forced march under the slogan "Rich Country, Strong Army." In the postwar era, the government's industrial policy was led by many of the same men who organized the prewar economic mobilization.

In the century-old Japanese economic ideology, economic development was not an end in itself, but a means. The goal was *autonomy*. Indeed, the very first Five-Year Plan adopted by the Cabinet during the high-growth era was called, "A Five-Year Plan for Economic Autonomy." In 1952, MITI Minister Ryutaro Takahashi declared:

> The essence of economic policy in peace-time Japan is the speedy attainment of economic independence. To that end, hastening the rationalization of industry is vital.[2]

If autonomy was the goal, then catching up to the West economically— and nurturing on Japanese soil the full panoply of modern industries— was seen as the way to achieve that goal.

Very little of Japan's current economic structure and policies can be understood without grasping the ideological power of this drive for autonomy. Why, for example, won't Japan relinquish even dismally uncompetitive industries like oil refining? The answer, according to economist Mitsuhiro Seki, is because the autonomy mentality demands that Japan be self-sufficient in every important industry:

> [T]he full-set industrial structure, which sees a single nation incorporate within itself all the industrial and technological functions required for preeminence [is] something that Japan has unflaggingly pursued since it began its industrial modernization in the Meiji Era of the nineteenth century. . . .

In contrast, the European style of industrial structure ... seemed to embody the benefits of the theory of comparative production costs ... that is, each nation seemed to have its own field of expertise within a system of mutual interdependence. ... To have all industrial structure within one's own borders was considered natural in the Soviet Union, China, and other socialist powers. ... Among the developed countries, *only Japan* possesses a full-set industrial structure comprising all industries at a relatively high level of sophistication [emphasis added].[3]

The Birth of a Nationalist Economic Ideology

The drive for autonomy emerged from centuries of Japanese history. Only a little more than a century ago, Japan was a country almost completely closed off from the outside world, a country where the penalty for leaving was death. Japan had once been open to the world, but early in the 1600s, a new group of rulers, called the Tokugawa Shogunate, took over Japan. Ostensibly fearing a takeover by Europeans, who had already made inroads into the Philippines and China, these new rulers executed Christian missionaries en masse and walled off the country. Ships were burned, trade was almost completely halted, and Japan turned inward.

Then, in the 1840s, came troubling rumors that China—the Middle Kingdom—was being humbled by opium and gunships at the hands of "barbarians" from Europe. If even China could not resist, what if the Westerners turned their eyes to Japan?

In 1854 the long-feared danger came to pass. Black gunships led by U.S. Commodore Matthew Perry appeared off the coast of Japan. For the first time in history—but certainly not the last—an American demanded Japan open itself to trade with the West. Within a few years, the weak Shogun had been forced to submit to treaties in which Japan not only agreed to trade but even lost control over its own tariffs. It took until 1911 for Japan to regain tariff autonomy.[4] To this very day, whenever foreigners want to buy a Japanese company or ask that Japan import rice, "black ships" have a good chance of showing up in a newspaper headline.

Finally, in 1868, a group of modernizers took over Japan in a revolutionary event known as the Meiji Restoration.[5] No xenophobes, these new rulers heartily embraced many Western ideas—from economics, technology and politics to clothing, food and music. Nonetheless, their purpose remained autonomy. Under the slogan "Rich Country, Strong Army," they resolved to make Japan so strong economically and militarily that Japan could never again be forced to submit to a foreign power. They established a Bureau of Industrial Promotion to propel economic development; that's where MITI got its start.

While the state has played a strong role in many "late industrializers," its role was particularly strong in Japan's emergence. During the first part of the Meiji era, from 1868 to about 1900, the state supplied more than a third of all capital to private industry. It helped promote modern industries like railways, shipping, steel, paper, brickmaking, and, for the export market, silk and cotton textiles. While Japan welcomed foreign technology and advisers, the government restricted foreign investments or loans that might make it overly dependent.

The state had to take the lead because business was so weak. In 1868, Japan had neither modern business institutions like commercial banks and the joint-stock company, nor a true business class. While a few pre-Meiji merchants, notably Mitsui and Sumitomo, became great *zaibatsu* (corporate groups), government officials complained that most merchants shied away from modern industry. Mitsui was far more partial to trade and banking than to manufacturing. The Meiji elite had both to establish modern capitalist institutions and recruit a new industrialist class. The latter came mostly from the former nobility, the *samurai*, rather than the pre-Meiji merchants. Some of the new zaibatsu, like Mitsubishi, gained their prominence as a direct result of state support:

> In 1875, the government handed over thirty ships free of charge to Iwasaki Yotaro's Mitsubishi Company, along with an operating subsidy of over ¥200,000 per year [this evolved into the NYK line—rk]. This measure too was prompted by internal security considerations and anxiety to eliminate foreign shipping companies, the American Pacific Mail Line and the British P&O Steamship Company, which had captured the coastal trade between treaty ports. Within a year the foreign shipping companies were convinced that their role was over.[6]

As Japan developed, the new business class increasingly took the helm and the state receded. So did excessive fear of foreign domination. By the early twentieth century, foreign loans were being welcomed. Giants like Toshiba formed joint ventures with firms like General Electric. In the 1920s era of "Taisho democracy," universal manhood suffrage was finally enacted. Prime ministers were designated by the leading political party in the Diet (parliament) rather than named by a handful of the country's unelected "elders." Who knows where all this would have gone had tragedy not struck? Rodney Clark writes, "The organization of Japanese and Western industry was probably more similar in 1910 than in 1970."[7]

But tragedy did strike. The Depression came early to Japan, beginning with a devastating banking crisis in 1927. Starvation among farmers, protectionist measures by the West against Japanese exports, and a military influenced by Japan's cult-like "secret societies" all combined to fuel a nationalist paranoia. Japan had to resist being deliberately suffocated by the "ABCD powers" (America, Britain, China and the Dutch), the nationalists proclaimed.

A still-fragile democracy was unable to resist—especially after terrorists assassinated a Prime Minister, cabinet ministers, and the head of the Mitsui *zaibatsu*. In 1931, the renegade Kwangtung Army seized power in Manchuria, renaming it Manchukuo. There, so-called reform bureaucrats proceeded to build an industrial state that they hoped would serve as a "proving ground" for a statist economic model in Japan itself. It's remarkable how many of the leading MITI officials of the 1950s got their start in making industrial policy in Manchukuo, including the career MITI official and late 1950s Prime Minister Nobosuke Kishi.[8]

In the process of fighting the Depression and mobilizing for war, Japan gradually ushered in many of the institutions and practices that guided the postwar high-growth era.

Just one month before the takeover of Manchuria, the government passed the important Industries Control Law.[9] In an important precedent that set the pattern for the postwar era, the law did not create direct state control over industry, but rather *"self-control"* by industry associations. Enterprises within a given industry were to form cartels to fix levels of production, establish prices, limit new entrants and control marketing. Still, the Ministry of Commerce and Industry (MCI), MITI's predecessor, had veto power over major investments and price-control measures. As a result of this law, cartels were organized in 26 designated important industries—from silk thread (Japan's biggest export) to paper, cement, iron and steel, shipbuilding, and electrical machinery.

Another law gave the MCI control over allocation of all foreign exchange, which meant power to decide what could and could not be imported. MITI would retain this power until 1964.

Over the course of the 1930s, various laws were passed to promote specific industries, such as petroleum, machine tools, aircraft, light metals, iron and steel, and automobiles. By 1939, Ford and GM, who had dominated the market, were out of business in Japan.

State allocation of credit was created by the 1937 Temporary Funds Adjustment Law, passed just two months after Japan invaded China. Banks had to obtain permission from the Ministry of Finance (MOF) for any loans above ¥100,000. The MOF categorized loans as either "favored," "permitted," or "proscribed." The law created a system of formal state guidance over private credit allocation that would remain in existence up until 1963.

Finally, three months before the bombing of Pearl Harbor, Japan passed the Important Industries Association Ordinance. It organized Mussolini-style "control associations" in each important industry to cartelize the industry. Once again, state priorities were implemented through the mechanism of "self-control" rather than direct state control. Many of today's industry associations in sectors from banking to cement are direct lineal descendants of these prewar control associations.[10]

There is no question that these efforts speeded up Japan's move to heavy industry—moving it from 35 percent of manufacturing in 1930 to 65 percent by 1940. But they also created a pattern of industrial organization, government–business relations, and attitudes that remain powerful even today. Indeed, reform economist Yukio Noguchi calls today's setup the "1940 system" in reference to its prewar origins.[11]

Postwar Dualism: Strategy versus Compensation

Japan's prewar history has set the stage for a big debate among American observers of postwar Japan. Some, like political scientist Chalmers Johnson, stress continuity between the two eras. Others say the postwar Occupation-era reforms created a big break with the past. This issue is only one facet of a much bigger debate that has polarized American discussion for the past two decades: What is the nature of Japan's political economy? Both sides in this debate seem to have taken categorical positions that miss the "shades of grey" in the Japanese setup.

One view, championed by economists like Hugh Patrick, portrays Japan as essentially a free market economy, not unlike the U.S.:

> I am of the school which interprets Japanese economic performance as due primarily to the actions and efforts of private individuals and enterprises responding to the opportunities provided in quite free markets for commodities and labor. While the government has been supportive and indeed has done much to create the environment for growth, its role has often been exaggerated.[12]

At the opposite pole stands Chalmers Johnson. He sees postwar Japan, like its prewar predecessor, as a "developmental state" in which the bureaucrats rule and all other interests are subordinated to national economic development. It is a state in which:

> Most of the ideas for economic growth came from the bureaucracy and the business community reacted with an attitude of what one scholar called "responsive dependence."[13]

Perhaps neither Patrick nor Johnson would have taken as categorical a stance except that they felt the pendulum had gone too far in the other direction.[14] And, as we will detail in Chapter 13, perhaps the debate would not have become so polarized except that, amidst the trade battles of the 1970s and 1980s, there were important ramifications of the analysis. Trade hawks and proponents of industrial policy felt justified by the Johnson view while the Patrick analysis seemed to vindicate the free traders.

But in fact, as so many scholars of the 1970s and 1980s have documented, Japan was neither a free market paragon nor a bureaucratic authoritarian developmental state. Rather, it was a highly *politicized* economy. Particularly in the high-growth era, major decisions about what industries existed, what companies were in those industries, investment levels, and even prices were all influenced by *negotiations* and *lobbying* rather than being determined by either the market or bureaucratic edict. Indeed, in 1987, John Haley wrote an essay entitled "Governance by Negotiation."[15]

This circumstance should not be surprising. How else other than negotiations and lobbying could a "developmental state" resolve the central political problem of rapid development: that it creates losers as well as winners? In a free market economy, leaders can lay the blame on impersonal market forces. But, the very nature of state-promoted development is that individuals are making decisions that influence who receives what benefits at whose expense. If so, then why does rapid growth have a higher value than social equity? Why are steel company profits more deserving than coal miners' jobs?

In a democratic state, the claims of the "losers" cannot be denied by government edict. If worse comes to worst, voters could always vote for the Socialists and Communists. And if the Liberal-Democrats (LDP) were to fall from power, what would become of all the officials' developmental plans?

This was no idle threat. In the early 1970s, with the rise of urbanization, and Left victories in several cities, an extrapolation of trends showed the Socialists and Communists eventually displacing the LDP. To stay in power, the LDP had, in Kent Calder's term, to "compensate" the losers.[16]

One of those loser sectors was small business, a traditional LDP bastion twice as large as the vital farm vote. During the late 1950s and 1960s, when the LDP majority seemed secure, the government had favored larger modern companies over small businesses. Big companies received the tax breaks, subsidies and government loans. Banks charged big companies interest rates one-third lower than small firms. Supermarket chains started edging out small stores. In response, owners of many small businesses slowly started turning to the Socialists and Communists. By 1971, owners of one-sixth of all small businesses were involved with the Communist-affiliated small business federation, *Minsho*, and even more were voting for the Left.[17]

The LDP had to act to avoid losing power. It responded with a crass payoff—a redistribution of income worth billions of dollars—disguised as no-collateral government "loans" to over half the nation's small businesses. At the same time, the Finance Ministry overlooked large-scale tax evasion by small businesses on as much as 60 percent of their income.[18]

On the legislative front, the LDP executed a policy turn that later had international repercussions. In 1973, the LDP passed the famous Large-Scale Retail Store Law, which officially allowed small businesses to obstruct the expansion of supermarkets and department and chain stores, and unofficially made it possible for them to cartelize their neighborhoods and thereby raise prices. The LDP even passed an outright prohibition against pharmacies opening up branch stores. When the Supreme Court declared this unconstitutional, the Health and Welfare Ministry—the bailiwick of Ryutaro Hashimoto, a future Prime Minister and, earlier, of Hashimoto's father—issued a *sub rosa* directive for the drug producers not to sell to any such pharmacies. Drug companies that didn't wish to see their license approvals drag on for years obliged.[19]

The LDP need was so great, it even turned down lobbying by one of its biggest contributors, the banks. Due to lobbying by small shopkeepers, the LDP delayed for almost two decades efforts by the banks to issue revolving credit cards. The reason was not to suppress consumption and raise savings, as is often argued. Rather, giving banks the business would have undercut the credit facilities already being run by small stores.[20]

From the LDP's standpoint, it worked beautifully: *Minsho* membership declined after 1973.[21]

Meanwhile, to retain the farm base, the LDP bought votes with billions of dollars of subsidies. By the 1980s, more than *75 percent of all farm income came from subsidies and price support programs*—a percentage far higher than in any other industrial state, including France. The LDP repeatedly turned down requests by the big business federation, *Keidanren*, to lift restrictions on agricultural imports, despite the fact that these restrictions ended up indirectly penalizing Japan's exports.[22]

The bottom line is this: even if all sections of the Japanese state had been single-mindedly devoted to development as their highest priority—which was not the case—nonetheless, it could not have acted solely on that priority. In order to keep the government's party in power, it would still have often had to sacrifice developmental concerns to the electoral needs of the LDP. Throughout the high-growth period, government policy was continually confronted with the trade-off between promoting winners and compensating losers, between the politics of "strategy" to promote growth and the politics of "distribution" to spread the fruits of growth, or, in American parlance, between the general public interest and the special interests.

The government didn't choose between these two options. It did both. As James Vestal documents, Tokyo's "pro-growth" measures gave aid to such key export industries as shipbuilding, steel, synthetic fibers, and autos. Meanwhile, its "anti-growth" policies handed out heavy subsidies to preserve employment in such flagging sectors as coal mining, sake breweries, and small business.[23]

Most importantly, over time, as Vestal points out, the balance shifted. During the high-growth era, the lion's share of aid went to promoting winners; after the 1973 oil shock, when growth plummeted, the number of losers needing compensation rose abruptly. Meanwhile, the winners needed less help. And so, the brunt of policy shifted from promoting winners to propping up losers.

The dualism between strategy and compensation, stresses Kent Calder, is built into the very character of both the LDP and the bureaucracy. Japan's bureaucracy is divided between "strategic ministries" like MITI and "regulatory ministries" like Posts and Telecommunications, Health and Welfare, Construction, and Transport, and part of the Ministry of Finance, such as the Banking Bureau. This structure is paralleled by the various divisions of the LDP's Policy Affairs Research Council (PARC), a group that serves as a kind of "rump parliament" in Japan's one-party state.[24]

The clients of the "regulatory" side of the government include several internationally important industries, such as pharmaceuticals, airlines, and telecommunications. And yet, while many of MITI's clients have become export superpowers, almost none of the clients of the regulatory agencies have. (The main exception was the shipbuilding industry, which was under the jurisdiction of the Transport Ministry and was successful in the 1950s and 1960s.) Through both direct lobbying and through their LDP representatives, weaker industries have "clientelized" the regulatory Ministries to such a degree that:

> Most of these industries receive substantial government assistance, but not in any strategic fashion. *None of these industries is competitive internationally* [emphasis added]. . . .
>
> "In our search for the dynamic center of the Japanese political economy . . . we have found fragmentation and clear internal split between "strategists" and "regulators."[25]

The dualism was also built into the government's lending program to private industry. Initially, capital was so scarce and new industries so risky that private capital could not do the job alone. In the very early days, government loans financed a third or more of all capital investment, for such critical areas as steel, machinery, coal, electric power and agriculture. Initially, coal and farming received huge loans because coal was a key energy source and farm loans helped agricultural modernization and reform. Later these loans became a pure bailout. As time went on and industries became stronger, a division of labor developed. Private banking took over the role of financier to strategic industries, albeit influenced by industrial policy. Government loans were increasingly devoted to compensation sectors (Table 5.1). After 1965, ever-larger shares of government loans were devoted to housing and small business.[26]

Managing the trade-off between strategy and compensation is not just a matter of government budgets and laws. It permeates the operations of Japanese business on such core matters as investment, purchases, and even price.

Just consider one example of this "reciprocal consent" process from the energy industry, as documented by Richard Samuels.[27] By the 1950s and early 1960s, imported oil had become much cheaper than domestic coal. The heavy industries being promoted by MITI had a great desire to make the switch. And yet, this would mean severe dislocation for several hundred thousand coal miners who knew how to make their displeasure felt. In 1959–61, a long and violent strike by a Socialist-led coal miners union coincided with riots over renewal of Japan's security treaty with the U.S. and weakened the government during that crucial period.

Table 5.1

Government Funds Key Boost to Industry Investment

Government Funds as a Percent of Capital Investment	1952	1955	1956	1965
Marine transportation	33	50	33	65
Coal	33	33	47	61
Agriculture	70	48	55	53
Electricity	50	43	24	21
Land transportation	19	9	15	20
Textiles	46	20	13	15
Machinery	33	18	6	8
Chemicals	35	11	6	6
Iron and steel	32	4	4	3
Total		30	16	16

Source: Vestal (1993), p. 100

The political pressure was so strong that, for a while, MITI had to reverse the program it had begun in 1952 to promote heavy oil use. In 1955, MITI pushed through a law that *restricted the number of oil-fired plants the utilities could build.* And this occurred at a time when other branches of MITI were trying to promote a domestic petroleum refinery industry!

MITI's strongest leverage in forcing the two sides to negotiate was the 1949 Foreign Exchange Law, under which, *until as late as 1964,* all imports needed MITI approval. At various points, MITI's price for granting foreign exchange to steelmakers and utilities was their purchase of domestic coal at high prices. Over and over again, one reads in Richard Samuels' analysis passages like:

> Direct negotiations between large mine owners and large coal consumers were the basis for computation of standard prices [agreements on standard prices were part of the 1955 law—rk]. . . . In 1957, the coal industry . . . insisted on a price increase for ¥550 per ton for large consumers. . . . Heavy industry called upon MITI to admonish producers to show better self-control, and in June the producers announced an exceptional ¥50 per ton price reduction. It was the first time that MITI, intervening on behalf of heavy industry, succeeded in disciplining the coal industry. . . .
>
> [In 1961] the electric power industry used [a recent agreement with the Coal Association] to gain *additional exemptions from the [1955] Boiler Law so as to build new oil-fired thermal plants* . . . [emphasis added].[28]

As time went on, the users rebelled and the costs to Japan's industrial development became just too severe. Direct state subsidies had to replace pressure on consumers. While MITI claimed its program was aimed at "easing" the downsizing of coal, the "easing out" subsidies lasted until 1986![29]

The coal case may sound particularly extreme, but for large sections of the economy, this pattern of lobbying and negotiations over prices, investments and so forth was the rule, not the exception. In the 1970s and 1980s, while one division of MITI was protecting Japan's inefficient oil refiners, the petrochemical industry had to lobby another division of MITI for either the right to buy cheaper foreign feedstock or else lower prices for the domestic product. A similar story took place as late as the 1990s, when heavy machinery makers wanted to import much cheaper steel from Korea. Strong-arm tactics by the Japanese steel cartel forced the machinery makers to negotiate on how much they could import while the steel cartel had to agree to somewhat lower prices.[30]

Sometimes, negotiations and lobbying even determined whether companies could enter a business in the first place. One of the most famous cases was the attempt in 1950 by then-tiny Kawasaki Steel to build Japan's first modern integrated steel facility. It would produce the kind of steel sheet needed by the emerging auto and consumer electronics industries rather than the heavy plate still produced by Japan's Big Three: Yawata and Fuji (later to be merged into Nippon Steel) and Nippon Kokkan.[31]

To build such a facility, Kawasaki needed huge loans, and in the high-growth era, the allocation of credit was not a market issue but a highly charged matter of policy and politics. Capital was so scarce that the government provided a third of all loans to the steel industry.[32] Moreover, even private loans were influenced by politics.

Japan's financial structure had become highly centralized during the prewar mobilization. Hence, during the high-growth era, almost all external financing for big business came from a dozen or so large commercial banks (the so-called city banks) and three long-term trust banks. Stocks amounted to less than 4 percent of company funds as late as 1968 while bonds played a similarly negligible role. If companies were dependent on banks, the banks in turn were dependent for their loan expansion on repeated injections of funds from the Bank of Japan (BOJ).[33]

This chain of dependence gave both government bodies and the Bankers Federation great influence over private bank loans. Added to this was the fact that government backing of an industry was, as Hiroya Ueno put it, "tantamount to a governmental guarantee."[34] For risk-averse bankers, the combination of carrot and stick was hard to resist. As Ueno writes:

[T]he significance of selective allocation of public funds is found in offic- ially designating certain industries as key or growth industries and in guid- ing private financial institutions to extend credit actively to these industries. . . . [I]nterest rates were artificially regulated by the MOF, and private funds were allocated, under the guidance of public financial institu- tions, by city banks which competed for market shares.[35]

Until 1963, the BOJ officially listed industries in order of priority for receiving, or *not* receiving, funds and exercised unofficial "window guid- ance" thereafter. MITI had its own priority list for credit allocation. And to complicate matters, so did the Bankers Capital Adjustment Committee of the Federation of Bankers Associations, whose representative sat on MITI's Industrial Structure Deliberation Council. Calder reports:

[Until 1968] this committee made regular judgments on the major lending decisions of its members—declaring in 1965, for example, that both steel and automobile industry capital investment needed to be stretched out to avoid the emerging dangers of excess capacity [the same recommendation MITI was making at the time —rk].[36]

These different bodies did not always agree. While MITI was partial to the emerging capital-intensive heavy industries, like auto and steel, that would be *future* earners of valuable foreign exchange, the more cautious BOJ preferred that scarce credit be reserved to light labor-intensive indus- tries like textiles that were *current* exporters. For two years, from 1949 to 1951, the BOJ fiercely resisted MITI's efforts to promote the auto indus- try. And sometimes, who received credit had less to do with grand policy than with simply having ties to the right people.[37]

It was in this charged atmosphere that Kawasaki sought the huge fund- ing its plans would require. Well-connected forces lined up on each side of the battle.

Over at the Bank of Japan, Governor Naoto Ichimada—nicknamed "The Pope"—was outraged that upstart Kawasaki wanted to "waste" Japan's scarce capital. And the banks, dependent on BOJ money, were not inclined to defy the powerful Ichimada—not even Kawasaki's main bank, Dai-Ichi. Moreover, over at MITI, officials close to the entrenched Big Three steelmakers had no desire to see them undercut by new compe- tition from Kawasaki.

Yet others at MITI welcomed Kawasaki's plans because it would mod- ernize the steel industry as well as promote the auto industry. Meanwhile, over at the government's Japan Development Bank (JDB), Kawasaki received support from two of the most influential business leaders and power brokers in postwar Japan. They were JDB Chairman Ataru Kobayashi, and Sohei Nakayama, a future chief of the powerful Industrial Bank of Japan (IBJ) who was then serving as JDB Vice Chairman. Nakayama personally lobbied both private banks and even the World Bank to provide the funds. Another key ally was Finance Minister—and future Prime Minister—Hayato Ikeda, who helped Kawasaki get funding from the securities industry.

It took a few years, but Kawasaki Steel eventually gained enough financing from the JDB, the World Bank, and some securities firms to build its plant. It became a huge success. But, given the BOJ's opposition, only a few private banks participated. The bottom line was that Kawasaki did not get its funds as it would have in the U.S., simply by going to banks and the bond markets and being subject to their private judgment. Nor did a unified and strategically oriented "developmental state" grant Kawasaki the money because it knew this would upgrade Japan's technological capacity. Instead, tumultuous politics, lobbying, and negotiations determined the outcome.

Not all industries functioned in this manner, of course. But enough did to shape the character of the economy throughout the high-growth era, and sometimes beyond.

In an essay aptly entitled "Governance by Negotiation," John Haley wrote:

> This process of negotiation with bureaucratic accommodation to interests with access to the Diet or other sources of power is, I believe, an accurate paradigm of the Japanese patterns of governance. Consensus was necessary to achieve compliance and compromise was necessary to achieve consensus.[38]

The Cartelized Economy

While Japan's industrial policy was an immense success in the high-growth era, at its core lay a fundamental contradiction, one that would end up cartelizing Japan's corporate world.

The contradiction was this: the very fact that the government was supporting a risky industry lured more companies than the industry could support. Having embraced an industry or company, the government could be counted on not to let it fail. Small firms failed all the time, but big ones almost never did. Bankruptcy, far from being regarded as a cleansing shakeout of the inefficient, as "creative destruction," was considered a violation of an implicit social contract, a source of disorder and confusion. The healthy force of risk had been so neutralized that companies were overeager to borrow and bankers overeager to lend. Ueno comments:

> Once a decision was made by public financial institutions to finance an industry or an enterprise, private financial institutions competed with one another in financing them with almost no investigation.[39]

Added to all this was the herd instinct engendered by the "full-set" mentality. If one *keiretsu* had a chemical company or petroleum refiner, others wanted one too; if one built ships, the others did too.

The entry of so many firms defeated the very purpose of the initial support. The original rationale for industrial policy was that Japanese firms were too small to be competitive against imports; they needed help until they were large enough to compete on their own. But, if too many companies entered and none were allowed to fail, how could any of them achieve economies of scale? Petroleum refining was only the worst instance of this endemic problem.

There seemed to be only one solution. MITI and the initial companies in an industry had to exclude unwanted intruders—not just foreign firms, but also domestic ones as well. Barriers to entry were the *sine qua non* of the entire industrial policy system.[40]

But how to limit entry? The key lever was once again MITI's power to allocate scarce foreign exchange under the Foreign Exchange Control Law of 1949. Because the need for foreign exchange was so pervasive, the leverage was enormous. As of 1971, 40 percent of all industrial output consisted of products—from color TVs to petrochemicals to air conditioners—which didn't even exist in the Japanese market in 1951.[41] In almost all cases, these new products required the import of foreign technology, and that meant foreign exchange for royalty payments. Between 1950 and 1960, 28 percent of all investment by importing firms consisted of technology imports; indeed, technology imports accounted for 9 percent of all investment in the entire economy.[42]

Hence, until the system ended in 1964, the power to allocate or deny foreign exchange was the power to determine which industries, and even which companies, could get off the ground.

It took Sony six months to convince skeptical MITI officials that it wasn't wasting $25,000 by licensing the transistor. MITI officials said they didn't know why an upstart company deserved scarce foreign exchange when even the product's American inventor, Western Electric, thought it had little commercial value. MITI did ultimately give in, but it was lobbying, not the individual decisions of risk-taking entrepreneurs and investors, that determined whether or not Sony got into the game in the first place.[43]

While Sony's case is the one best known in the U.S.—because it is so beloved by U.S. critics of industrial policy—it was only one case among many. Initially, MITI allowed only four new firms to enter the auto industry in the 1950s. Similar limitations applied to the new TV industry. When nylon came on the scene in 1951, MITI at first granted a license to import the new technology to only one company, Toyo Rayon. As the market expanded, a second license went to Nippon Rayon in 1954, and then additional firms in the 1960s. For polyethylene, the first four licenses for importing technology went to three of the big *zaibatsu*—Sumitomo in 1958, Mitsubishi in 1960, and Mitsui in 1962. By the end of the decade, 10 firms were involved.[44]

Attaining the initial approval was critical because, in Japan's corporate setup—where financing and distribution ties were often locked in—initial industry leaders often had the capacity to block latecomers. Consider consumer electronics. Hardly a single new firm has entered and become a power in the consumer electronics industry since 1960. No new electronics firm has been able to establish a full production and distribution *keiretsu* since Sanyo entered in 1947.[45]

To be sure, this was not an iron vice. Quite a few firms have been able to enter lucrative industries against the resistance of both MITI and the entrenched companies. These include such household names as Sony, Honda, and Mitsubishi Motors. Yet, it is notable that upstarts like Sony in consumer electronics and Honda in cars first made their big breakthroughs by selling in the U.S. and then using that position to make headway back in Japan itself. Moreover, the very fact that such examples are celebrated shows that entry is far from automatic.

Since the choice was so often between getting in on the ground floor or missing the boat altogether, it is not surprising, as in the case of Kawasaki Steel, that the lobbying was so intensely political.

Even when entry was limited, that did not end the contradiction. The economies of scale led to an inherently unstable situation that antitrust expert Eleanor Hadley has labeled "cut-throat oligopoly."[46]

Economies of scale mean that the bigger a firm gets, the more efficient it becomes. In that case, the best route to long-run profits is to maximize sales by grabbing market share. This is quite the opposite of the normal situation without economies of scale. Normally, there is a trade-off between maximizing profits and maximizing share. If a firm cuts price to gain share, it may lose more profits on the price drop than it gains on the sales increase. But, when economies of scale prevail, even if a firm loses money to gain sales, it will make it up later in lower costs. In that situation, the best way for a rational firm to maximize long-run profits is to maximize sales.

In the high-growth era, most Japanese manufacturing firms in the plethora of new emerging industries did enjoy economies of scale. And so, as Murakami and Yamamura point out, the well-known drive of Japanese firms for maximizing sales rather than profits originated as a rational strategy; it was not some strange artifact of Japanese business culture. The problem lies in continuing to practice share-maximizing strategies when the firm no longer enjoys economies of scale.[47]

But what is rational for one firm may not work out so well when all firms try to do it—especially when those firms are not restrained by fear of bankruptcy. If every firm is hell-bent on increasing its output and sales, even at the cost of initial losses, then as sure as night follows the day, excess supply is going to result.

And when excess supply occurs, prices in Japan are going to fall and the surplus is going to be exported at prices way below cost.

This is what MITI called "excessive competition." Under a free market, the solution would be simple: a Darwinian shakeout with the survival of the fittest. But in Japan that was not allowed.

And so, "excess competition" became simultaneously MITI's *bête noir* and its *raison d'être*. MITI's own policy helped create the excessive competition in the first place. The worst excess supply problems almost always occurred in the very industries MITI was promoting. And then the excess competition required MITI's further intervention to address it. MITI was both the hurricane and the Red Cross.[48]

Some analysts have mistakenly concluded from industry's refusal to restrain themselves at MITI behest that MITI's industrial policy was irrelevant. This is a misreading of the situation. The underwriting of an industry by MITI and the BOJ created the context within corporate managers operated—a low-risk environment. It did not give MITI or the BOJ fingertip control, but had the industrial policy not existed, and therefore the risk–reward ratio higher, corporate managers would have operated in a very different fashion.

The initial strategy adopted by MITI, other Ministries, and business leaders against "excess competition" was pressure on firms to merge. In 1967, a powerhouse business committee (known as Sanken), led by the same Sohei Nakayama who had helped out Kawasaki Steel, came up with a proposal for wholesale mergers in seven industries: steel, automobiles, machine tools, computers, petroleum refining, petrochemicals, and synthetic textiles. Sanken's most spectacular success of this policy came with the creation of Nippon Steel in 1970, but that was because the two firms involved, Yawata Steel and Fuji Steel, both wanted the merger. In other cases where firms were small, weak and dependent on government largesse—such as in the auto parts and machine tool sectors—the merger policy also succeeded.[49]

Usually, however, companies rebelled. The same executives who sought government intervention when it meant subsidies or keeping out new competitors suddenly discovered the virtues of free enterprise when their firms were about to be merged out of existence. The failure of the Transport Ministry to merge crisis-wracked shipping firms in the 1960s was typical. In autos, the rebellion against MITI was spectacular, as we'll detail below.[50]

With mergers reduced to an exception, the government authorized industry cartels, and this became the norm. As in the 1930s, "self-control" rather than "state control" was the *modus operandi*. As Yamamura explains:

> If the largest firms were to grow rapidly by adopting new technology that was usually larger in scale than what it replaced, it had to produce more. . . . The problem was that an increase in productive capacity often tended to exceed the domestic demand and increase in export did not occur swiftly enough. . . . To overcome such a *temporary gap* in supply and demand, the firms, if they were to be motivated to grow, needed "freedom" to fix prices and/or limit output until domestic and international demand could increase. If the rapidly growing firms were allowed to engage in temporary "cooperative action" to fix prices or limit output, no potentially ruinous price-cutting competition would occur, threatening bankruptcies and no loss in profits would result, reducing the internal reserves needed to the next round of expansion enabling the firms to adopt even more advanced technology [emphasis added].[51]

In times of slack, the cartels were given power to impose limits on capacity and output of their members, to *coordinate prices*, and to even

Table 5.2

Government-Authorized Cartels Control a Third of Manufacturing

% of Shipments Controlled by Authorized Cartels	1960	1970
Textiles	78	69
Apparel	65	67
Nonferrous metals	51	30
Publishing and printing	47	18
Stone, clay and glass	41	41
Iron and steel	35	59
Food	34	18
Pulp, paper and products	27	9
Precision instruments	26	56
Chemicals	23	23
Nonelectrical machinery	16	28
Rubber products	13	43
Lumber and wood	10	74
Electrical machinery	8	26
Leather and products	7	13
Metal products	7	20
Other	7	7
Furniture and fixtures	6	
Transport equipment	2	32
TOTAL MFG.	28	31

Source: Imai (1980), p. 111

control a firm's investment in new capacity. Since, during downturns, limitations were assigned *pro rata* based on market share, every time the industry recovered, the capacity race to enlarge market share became even more fierce. That would create yet another cycle of overcapacity and the need for yet another cartel. Industries like shipbuilding, cement, steel, chemicals, machinery, electronics, textiles and others formed cartels over and over again as the industry oscillated between collusion and fierce competition.

The number of cartels kept rising. In 1955, there were 162 legal cartels. From 1965 through 1973 the number of officially authorized cartels averaged 1,000 each year. Throughout the 1960s, *about 30 percent of all industry was controlled by cartels* (Table 5.2).[52]

Once cartels became the norm, and antitrust enforcement evaporated, illegal cartels also proliferated. In the late 1960s, Japan's Fair Trade Commission found that prices of 2 percent of all goods sold in Japan were set under *legalized* price resale maintenance agreements (a practice illegal under

Table 5.3

In Half of Industry, Prices Shaped by Regulation or Cartels

Wholesale level	% Controlled Prices	Consumer level	% Controlled Prices
Petroleum and coal products	100	Fuel and light	100
Textiles	87	Miscellaneous	77
Nonfood farm products	83	Clothing	70
Iron and steel	62	Food	37
Perishable foods	60	Housing	29
Lumber and wood	59		
Chemicals	46	TOTAL	54
Food	41		
Ceramic products	38		
Metallic minerals	33		
Housing	29		
Electrical machinery	28		
Nonelectrical machinery	22		
Other	20		
Metal products	4		
TOTAL MFG.	41		

Source: Ueno (1980), pp. 428–429.

Note: No date is given but the data appear to apply to some time in the early 1970s. The table includes cases where prices are influenced by government regulation or industry cartels.

U.S. antitrust law) while another *20 percent* were set by *covert and illegal* upstream control of retail prices by manufacturers and/or distributors.[53]

Since so much of the economy was either regulated by government, or controlled by official cartels, or subject to oligopolies, it is not surprising that in as much as *half of manufacturing, market-determined prices did not prevail* (Table 5.3).

Instead of responding flexibly to market supply and demands, prices were heavily influenced by cartels or other intervention. In industries where prices had once been flexible and had fallen with productivity growth, suddenly prices were flexible only upward. They were rigid downward. Not surprisingly, it was in the most heavily cartelized industries that prices were least responsive to normal market signals.[54]

In some oligopolistic industries like urea, bearing steel, rails, rubber and others, collusion was further cemented when leading firms bought stocks of their own *competitors*. Caves and Uekasa comment:

These shareholdings could tip the balance when a firm must choose between an action expected to increase profits on an industrywide basis and one designed to raise its own net revenues at the expense of its rivals.[55]

Since the whole purpose of cartels and collusion was to keep prices and profits high, imports had to be restricted. Otherwise, cheap imports would add to supply, undercut cartel prices and destroy the entire system.[56]

Often industries were cohesive enough—or an industry leader was dominant enough—for "self-control" through cartels to be sufficient. But as anyone witnessing OPEC can observe, the great Achilles Heel of cartels is that the more a cartel raises prices, the greater the temptation of members to cheat. Under such circumstances industries often brought the government in to enforce the setup on its own members—at the expense of mavericks, newcomers, consumers, and foreign competitors.

This whole issue became a public controversy when Sumitomo Metals rebelled in the mid-1960s. Cartels to enforce production cutbacks and price controls had been created in the steel industry during the 1958 recession:

> Each manufacturer was to carry out sales at the "list price" that it had previously reported to MITI ... and *when manufacturers violated their own "list prices"* [i.e., sold at a lower price] *MITI was to undertake administrative guidance accompanied by strong penalties.* . . . [F]or the 10 years following the institution of the list-price system in 1959, the system continued in place. . . .
>
> From 1967, [the MITI-led] Steel Committee ... drew up annual and long-term supply and demand forecasts ... and calculated the new capacity on which construction would need to be begun each year. *The detailed allocation of investment among the firms*, based on the results of the Council studies, was to depend in the first instance on the *autonomous coordination of the firms themselves* and in instances in which coordination could not be obtained, decisions were to be made under the *administrative guidance of MITI* [emphasis added].[57]

Initially, 33 steelmakers signed up. The system worked for a few years and prices firmed. Indeed, when demand recovered in the early 1960s, MITI had to stop the steel cartel from gouging customers in auto and other priority industries.

But eventually, the temptation to cheat became too big. By 1965, the system of self-control had broken down and the threat of bankruptcy loomed due to overcapacity during a downturn. MITI "recommended" a

10 percent cutback in output and all of the "Big Six" went along. When MITI ordered a second cutback, Sumitomo Metals refused, claiming MITI's system was biased in favor of older steel firms at the expense of newer, more efficient ones. MITI threatened to deny Sumitomo the foreign exchange needed to import coking coal. Initially Sumitomo executives called a press conference to protest. But they eventually had to back down.[58]

From Sumitomo's standpoint, MITI was an officious bureaucracy acting as the hired gun of Sumitomo's inefficient competitors. From the standpoint of the steel cartel, MITI was the "long arm of the law," enforcing community discipline on a self-centered Sumitomo. In their view, Sumitomo was a selfish "free rider." It was quite willing to enjoy the high prices created by the self-restraint of the other cartel members, but was unwilling to make any sacrifices of its own. Seeing cases like the Sumitomo example as an issue of government *versus* industry misses the point, as Robert Uriu points out:

> Because cutbacks in production or capacity require short-term sacrifices, firms will only cooperate if they know that other producers are similarly bound. In all of these cases [that Uriu examined —rk] industry actors first tried to manage competition on their own but usually found that effective enforcement was beyond their capabilities. They thus sought government regulation as a necessary outside enforcement mechanism.[59]

Given the difficulties of enforcing cartel discipline, it's easy to see why entrenched firms felt it necessary to keep out newcomers who might cause "confusion in the market." Especially foreigners who would certainly not be as willing as Japanese firms to play by the rules of the game.[60]

During the high-growth era, the rationale for the cartels was to promote growth in rising sectors. But once the economy was cartelized, it remained so. As late as 1989, 276 legal cartels remained in force. Of the cartels in place in the early 1980s, almost half had been in place for 25 years and over two-thirds for more than 20 years.[61]

By no means were all sectors of the economy heavily cartelized to the same degree. In 1970, 30 percent of manufacturing was under the control of legal cartels. But in textiles, the cartelized share was 70 percent, and in electrical machinery "only" 26 percent (Table 5.2).[62]

According to Daniel Okimoto, by the 1980s, competitiveness and technological progress became a key dividing line between the sectors with and without heavy collusion and cartelization. In semiconductors and consumer electronics, where new products were constantly being unveiled, changes in market share and company rankings were continuous. But, in old-line mature industries with high fixed costs, weak international competitiveness, undifferentiated product lines and/or one or two dominant companies, government-supported collusion and cartels have been rife. The extreme case is the inefficient flat glass industry, where three companies have divided the industry in an unyielding 50:30:20 split for three decades.[63]

Thus did the cartelized economy turn into the "dual economy."

Industrial Policy: The Politics of Scarcity

Ultimately, industrial policy is the politics of scarcity. It is rationing. All the tools that give a "developmental state" leverage are artifacts of scarcity. Once scarcity disappears, influence may remain, but not power.

Take for example the 1949 Foreign Exchange Law, rightly called by Chalmers Johnson MITI's single most powerful tool.[64] MITI was rationing a scarce commodity, foreign exchange. Suppose Japan had not acceded to foreign pressure to end the allocation system in 1964. The fact is, once Japan began running chronic trade surpluses in the mid-1960s, companies and banks were flush with hard currency. MITI would have lost its leverage over them, whether or not the currency allocation scheme remained on the books.

The event that certified this lost power was Mitsubishi's determination to enter the auto industry in defiance of MITI. In the interests of economies of scale, MITI had been trying to merge Japan's several auto firms into essentially two groups, built around Toyota and Nissan. Prince allowed itself to be absorbed into Nissan, but all the other firms successfully resisted. Moreover, the Mitsubishi *keiretsu*, which had no auto firm yet, wanted to enter and resented the whole MITI scheme. On May 12, 1969, Mitsubishi abruptly announced it had reached a deal with Chrysler to form a new company in which Chrysler would have a 35 percent share. It didn't even warn MITI in advance. This, reports Chalmers Johnson, was:

> the biggest shock MITI ever received in its history . . . The fallout from the Mitsubishi-Chrysler deal was enormous. The politicians and businessmen immediately read it as a declaration of independence by some big businessmen from MITI.[65]

Unlike Sumitomo Metals a few years earlier, Mitsubishi did not need to be in MITI's good graces to obtain foreign exchange.

The same principle applies to the allocation of private credit as an industrial policy tool. Normally, when capital is scarce, interest rates rise. That deters borrowing and therefore reduces *market demand* to equal *market supply*. In Japan, however, the monetary authorities deliberately maintained a low-interest-rate policy, particularly for favored big businesses. As a result, there was an artificial scarcity: companies were willing to borrow much more than the funds available. While this gap could have been made up with foreign borrowing, the government restricted that. With demand outstripping supply, companies, in effect, stood in line for funds. That gave the monetary authorities, MITI and the banks the power to ration out credit to the favored.

By the mid-1960s, however, Japan was no longer capital-scarce. On the contrary, savings had risen so fast relative to investment that Japan was exporting the excess capital. Credit rationing was no longer possible. Indeed, the bankers' Capital Adjustment Committee disbanded itself in 1968.

If the tools of governmental industrial policy lost their force once the age of scarcity passed, what then remained? The cartelized economy. Sometimes this was backed up by the active encouragement of the state, as in the "recession cartels" of the 1970s and 1980s. At other times, it was extralegal collusion made possible by the MITI's "wink of the eye" and the Japan Fair Trade Commission's "blind eye."

"Self-control" rather than "state control" was the dominant mechanism of the post-scarcity era.

Tanaka's "Money Politics": Third World Politics in a First World Economy

External circumstances, i.e., the oil shocks of the 1970s, merely set the stage for the shift in the balance from "strategy" to "compensation." But external circumstances don't explain *why* Japan's response was so poor. For that we must look to the electoral needs of the LDP and especially to the distortion of Japanese policymaking by Kakuei Tanaka's notorious "money politics."

When Tanaka became Prime Minister in 1972—over the objections of big business—it marked a sea change in Japanese politics.

Prior to Tanaka, "compensation" of the special interests was seen as the price that the system had to pay in order to keep the party of "strategy"—the party of big business and the bureaucracy—in power. Men like Tanaka were looked down on as mere machine politicians whose job it was to manage that compensation and win the votes. Uneducated provincials like Tanaka were never intended to become Prime Minister. And yet that is exactly what Tanaka did. And that meant the LDP was now headed by a faction far more interested in political compensation—especially compensating themselves—than in developmental strategy.

As long as the vested interests were willing to provide money and votes, then the Tanaka faction was quite willing to reciprocate. It would supply all the pork, subsidies, loans, cartels, import restrictions and whatever else it took to gain the interest groups' support—all the while taking their cut. And that cut could be enormous, with Tanaka's personal take adding up to 3 percent of the gross amount on some construction projects, according to Johnson.[66] Tanaka *major domo* Shin Kanemaru would later be arrested with millions of dollars' worth of solid gold bars in his home.

Consequently, at the very time when the *demands* for compensation were rising, so was the willingness of the Japanese state to *supply* that compensation.

Tanaka and his allies spent little energy worrying that their policies might be reducing Japan's efficiency and thereby reducing the resources for future payoffs. They just presumed the economy would remain an unending horn of plenty.

Little of Tanaka's grip was diluted either by his fall from power in 1974 over one bribery scandal or by his indictment and jailing (and eventual conviction) over another in 1985. For the next two decades, Tanaka was the kingmaker, the "shadow shogun."[67] His faction remained the largest in the LDP, he and his cronies continued to extract payoffs, and he had a virtual veto over who could become Prime Minister. Yasuhiro Nakasone's cabinet was ridiculed as the "TaNakasone" cabinet. Today, aside from Democratic party leader Naoto Kan, most every powerful politician today—reformer or conservative—is a scion of the Tanaka faction: from Prime Minister Ryutaro Hashimoto, to Liberal leader Ichiro Ozawa, to former Prime Minister and current Minseito leader Tsutomo Hata and, finally, Democratic Party co-leader Yukio Hatoyama.

All of this begs the question: how did a faction whose leader combined the corruption of a Ferdinand Marcos with the interest-based machine politics of a Richard Daley and a kind of Japanese populism come to power in the first place? How, despite its leader's disgrace, did it manage to dominate Japanese politics and Japanese policy for so long? How is it that three Prime Ministers at the beginning of this decade had to resign over corruption scandals? In short, how do we explain how a First World economy came to be ruled by a Third World regime? Certainly, the Tanaka faction was corrupt, but if corruption were all his faction amounted to, it's hard to see how it could have ruled Japan for so long. It must have filled some need. What was it?

The answer to these questions is rooted in how the LDP has maintained a monopoly on power for most of the postwar era.[68]

Throughout the postwar era, the voting system in Japan has acted to promote the special interests ("compensation") over the general interest ("strategy"). However, as with so much of the Japanese political economy, what was tolerable in the high-growth era became a recipe for disaster in the slow-growth period.

Up until the 1995 electoral reform, Japan had a unique electoral system. Instead of a single Diet member representing an entire district, each district in Japan elected three to five members of the Diet with every voter getting one vote. That means a Diet member can win an election with only 15–20 percent of the vote instead of 51 percent as in most countries. Because this system splinters the Opposition, it has contributed to the LDP's monopoly on power. In a five-member district, the LDP might win three seats, the Socialists one and another party one.[69]

The downside of this system is that it promotes parochial thinking and vested interests. The key to winning with such a narrow slice of the vote is not addressing national issues, but rather assembling organizations of personal support groups, called *koenkai*. The *koenkai* are based on local vested interests that benefit from state largesse, such as farmers, retailers, doctors, construction firms, local banks, or even social groups. Individual Dietmen may have dozens of different *koenkai* in their district. Leonard Schoppa comments:

> Such clientelism, not uncommon in democracies of all types, might not have been a large problem had it been pursued only by a few politicians in a few sectors. When such strategies were pursued by hundreds of Dietmen in a wide range of issue areas over an extended period of time, however, they created a system that was extraordinarily biased toward private goods [i.e., special interests—rk]. Over time, whole Ministries were sucked into this particularistic system.[70]

In every country, there is a need to balance general and special interests. Both kinds of interests are valid. Sometimes, however, very small groups can hold the entire nation in gridlock. Everyone knows about the power of the sugar lobby or the ethanol lobby in the U.S. But, in Japan, the electoral system makes that sort of thing more the rule than the exception. Japan's embargo on rice imports is a classic case. This, suggests Schoppa, is one reason why crises and foreign pressure (*gaiatsu*) are often needed to move Japan off the dime. It also explains why Japan is so often resistant even to those parts of the American trade agenda that would seem to coincide with the interests of Japan as a whole.

Koenkai are held together not only by the Diet members' ability to win special favors through the bureaucracy, but by money. As Tanaka was wont to put it, "electoral power comes from numbers and numbers come from money." Dietmen go to dozens of weddings and funerals passing out white envelopes full of cash. An average Diet member can spend up to $1 million each year on activities in his district to keep up *koenkai* support. No wonder so many Dietmen are so eager for kickbacks and bribes.[71]

While individual Diet members may come and go, the *koenkai* live on. Just as India's Nehru passed on the Prime Minister's post to his daughter and she passed it to her son, so the *koenkai* avoid nasty succession struggles by passing a Diet seat to a member's son or protégé. Nearly half of the LDP Dietmen elected in 1990 were sons of previous Diet members. Prime Minister Hashimoto inherited his Diet seat from his father as did Opposition leader Ichiro Ozawa, while reform leaders Yukio Hatoyama and Morihiro Hosokawa both had grandfathers who were Prime Ministers.[72]

As long as the LDP held a stable majority in the 1950s and 1960s, the *koenkai* merely had seats at the table of power. Those with broader concerns sat at the head. The real policymakers in the LDP were mostly aristocratic former bureaucrats. Until the ascension of Tanaka, Japan's Prime Minister had almost always been a former bureaucrat chosen by the other Diet members and local LDP chiefs. Most senior party leaders, committee chairmen and key cabinet ministers were also former bureaucrats. In the cabinets of the 1950s and 1960s, former bureaucrats held 50 percent of the cabinet posts. They almost always headed MITI, MOF and the Foreign Ministry. These men consulted with their former ministerial colleagues on matters of state policy while professional politicians like Tanaka were handed the dirty work of doing whatever it took to win elections.[73]

With the arrival of Tanaka, the *koenkai* suddenly moved to the head of the table. The number of cabinet posts held by former bureaucrats declined from 50 percent to 30 percent. In addition, more and more of the ex-bureaucrats serving in the Diet came from compensatory Ministries like Posts and Telecommunications, Construction and Agriculture instead of the elite MITI, MOF and Foreign Ministry, as in the old days.[74]

The ascendance of Tanaka did not mean a complete takeover by the *koenkai*. Tanaka had been at the center of politics too long to forget who was needed to create the wealth he wanted to redistribute. However, if Japanese politics was a battle fought between the 40-yard lines of strategy and compensation, the *koenkai* had just gained a lot of yardage.

Why, then, did the LDP Diet members hand their party, and the nation, over to Tanaka? Because the very success of the "developmental state" in promoting growth had undercut the demographic basis of electoral support for the government's party. LDP rule had always depended on solid support from the farmers—along with gerrymandered districts that gave farmers in, for example, Hyogo Prefecture *five times* as many Diet seats per capita as urban voters in Osaka. Of all the LDP Dietmen elected in 1972, 60 percent came from rural districts; only 10 percent came from the metropolitan areas of Tokyo, Osaka, Kobe, Nagoya and Fukuoka. Among the Tanaka faction, 80 percent came from farm districts.[75]

Urbanization, however, was gradually eliminating the farmers and hence the farm vote. At the same time, the government's favoritism toward big business was undermining support among small businesses. The LDP's vote steadily descended from 60 percent in the late 1950s to an even split with the Opposition by 1969 and *less* than the combined votes of the splintered opposition during the entire 1970s.[76]

The LDP had to find a way to shore up its existing base while searching for a way to appeal to the new white-collar urban electorate.

The turning point came in the fight for the Prime Minister's post in 1972. The fight came down to yet another former Finance Ministry bureaucrat or else Tanaka, a man who knew how to use money to get votes. The LDP Diet members, who select the Prime Minister, had to go for Tanaka. In the end the shift worked. In 1955, almost 70 percent of the party's vote had come from farmers and merchants; by 1980, their share was down to less than 40 percent. Meanwhile, the share of urban white- and blue-collar workers in the LDP vote total doubled from 30 percent to 60 percent (Table 5.4).

To grab the new base without losing the old one, Tanaka spent the government's money like water. To shore up the traditional base, Tanaka and his heirs devoted money to government loans to small business, farm price supports, construction projects and so forth. At the same time, new programs were introduced to satisfy the demands of the urban middle class. These urban voters were not organized into *koenkai* and their demands were more welfare- and consumer-oriented than producer-oriented. Hence,

Table 5.4

The Changing Base of LDP Support

Share of Total LDP Vote (%)	1955	1962	1965	1975	1980
Managers and salaried workers	14	18	24	26	29
Laborers in retail and manufacturing	16	18	20	25	28
Small business owners	25	27	28	25	23
Farmers	43	34	29	19	15

% of Group Voting for LDP	1955	1962	1965	1975	1980
Salaried workers	36	42	41	34	43
Managers	*	*	56	48	54
Laborers in manufacturing	32	31	27	32	40
Laborers in retail	*	*	40	38	45
Small business owners	59	61	61	59	62
Farmers	52	53	64	62	70

Source: Ramseyer and Rosenbluth (1997), p. 40

Note: In 1955 and 1962, laborers in retail are included with laborers in manufacturing, and managers are included in salaried workers. The top panel omits 1972, thereby missing the drop in the small-owner vote.

money was spent on expensive programs for health insurance, social security and education.

Actually, the LDP had already begun its new appeal to the new urban "middle mass" as it was called, even before Tanaka became Prime Minister. In 1970, the Diet session was called the anti-pollution Diet since it passed so many laws aimed at the same constituency.

Tanaka, however, took the LDP shift to new heights. Not content to spend real money, he even pressured the BOJ to print more. This set off a round of 30 percent inflation known as "crazy prices." As Alex Kinmont of Morgan Stanley's Tokyo office pointed out, "the bubble of the late 1980s was Japan's second bubble. Tanaka's bubble was the first."[77]

With all this money being spent, the budget deficit ballooned. From a small surplus in 1973, the budget swung into a deficit equal to 5.5 percent of GDP by 1978. Since the deficit also filled a need for Keynesian stimulus in the post-oil-shock slump, big business did not call a halt until the early 1980s. By that time the LDP had successfully won enough of the urban vote to end the danger of a leftist takeover. Moreover, a growing trade surplus was providing enough economic stimulus to dispense with fiscal steroids.[78]

Table 5.5

Small Business Cartels Proliferate

Year	Total Cartels	Cartels for Small and Medium Businesses
1964	970	588
1965	999	587
1966	1,079	652
1967	1,040	634
1968	1,003	582
1969	948	522
1970	898	609
1971	844	439
1972	976	604
1973	985	607

Source: Caves and Uekasa (1976), p. 487

Note: The data show the number of legal cartels granted exemption from the Anti-Monopoly Act. For small businesses, enforcing collusion was difficult without the legal force of a cartel.

Cartels: Japanese-Style Redistribution

Over time, budget constraints required a major shift in the mechanism of the payoff to the *koenkai*. This in turn had big repercussions for the economy. Over time, more and more of the budgetary payoffs, be it on spending or tax breaks, went to support the LDP's new urban base rather than its old farmer–retail base. As Ramseyer and Rosenbluth point out, the portion of money going to programs of interest to the urban white-collar voter, like health insurance, pensions and education, increased from a quarter of the budget in 1970 to a third by 1975. Old-fashioned *koenkai* pork, like public works, and programs for small business and farmers, declined from 41 percent of the budget in 1975 to 26 percent in 1987. When the budget cuts put in place after 1980 are considered, the *koenkai* were getting a smaller share of a shrinking pie.[79]

If the LDP was increasingly limited in using the budget and taxes to support the *koenkai*, how did it do it? Through high prices in the private market. Cartels had always been prolific in small business, allowing these businesses to charge high prices (Table 5.5). Now this was stepped up.

Regulations like the Large-Scale Retail Store Law, a proliferation of "recession cartels" in the materials industries, and *dango* (bid-rigging) in construction, among others, all allowed Japan's inefficient sectors to charge monopolistic prices and maintain employment far above market levels. Japan's notorious high prices are a disguised income transfer mechanism as well as a vehicle for disguised unemployment. Consumers pay high prices to producers, both efficient and inefficient, and efficient producers in turn pay high prices to the inefficient. High prices, the collusion that high prices require, and the import barriers that the cartels require are all "off-budget" LDP support for the *koenkai*.

During the high-growth era, it could be argued, the *koenkai* served a useful political and economic function. The overall system was so partial to big business that the latter were getting too large a share of national income. The *koenkai*, in effect, reset the balance. They made sure that the fruits of Japan's high growth were spread among all of society's members. Consequently, Japan has one of the most equal distributions of income and wealth in the world.

In a sense, the LDP acted like "conservative socialists." They provided in hidden form, through cartels and high prices, the same sort of social safety net and redistribution that European Social Democrats openly provided through tax breaks and budgets. The very fact that the safety net is hidden and built into the structure of the private political economy is what makes it so hard to dismantle this system today. As long as growth was good, then the combination of full employment and equal distribution of income worked. The tide was rising and it did lift almost all boats. This three-legged stool of growth, full employment and equal distribution of income is part of what T. J. Pempel has called Japan's "creative conservatism."[80]

At the same time, by keeping the party of growth in power, the *koenkai* provided a useful political benefit that outweighed its costs. To use Calder's terminology, compensation was the price for keeping strategy in power.

As time passed, however, and Japan's inefficient sectors became increasingly cartelized in the low-growth era, the *koenkai* exacted the price that most "distributional coalitions" exact.[81] They weren't just redistributing income; they were lowering total social wealth.

When the government uses taxes and the budget to redistribute income from the wealthy to the poor, it is pretty much a zero-sum game. GDP as a whole is neither raised nor lowered to any significant degree, just shifted around. However, when high prices are used as a disguised form of redistribution, society is doing more than just robbing Peter to pay Paul. That method of wealth distribution undermines wealth production. Resources are so misallocated that redistribution becomes a negative-sum game. GDP is lowered.

This concept is well known in the case of import protection. During the 1980s, it was estimated that it cost American consumers up to $200,000 for every autoworker job saved by the restraints on Japanese auto shipments to the U.S. Neither autoworkers nor auto companies saw more than a fraction of that money. On net, there was a sizable "deadweight loss" to American GDP.

Multiply this pattern thousands of times and one gets a picture of the effect on Japanese GDP of its redistribution cartels. In the long run, the cartels were undermining the resources needed to pay them off. The growth leg of the three-legged stool was being continually shortened. In 1990, the stool tipped over.

Chapter 6

1955–73: The System Succeeds in the Era of Catch-Up

The Paradox of "Market-Conforming Industrial Policy"

"Market-conforming industrial policy"? Isn't that a contradiction in terms? On both sides of the barricade that divides "revisionists" from neoclassical economists, many observers of Japan act as if it were. The economists scorn the notion of bureaucrats and politicians thinking they can replace market prices in "picking winners and losers." Meanwhile, revisionist James Fallows finds virtue in bureaucrats deliberately "getting the prices wrong."[1]

In reality, there is no inherent contradiction. The economy is a kind of organism that normally evolves on its own via standard market forces. But markets require market institutions, such as modern finance, and in a developing country those institutions may be weak. That's when industrial policy can fill a gap.

When industrial policy does succeed, it does so either because it *accelerates* the normal market evolution in a developing country, or because it makes up for systemic glitches in the market ("market failures" in the academic jargon). On the other hand, when industrial policy tries to defy normal market evolution, when it tries to *preserve* industries and jobs doomed to decline, then it fails. "Accelerationism" versus "preservationism" is the big divide between successful and unsuccessful industrial policy.

In the case of Japan, industrial policy succeeded in those cases where it accelerated the normal "virtuous cycle" between *growth* and *development*. By growth, I simply mean that an economy's GDP ten, twenty or thirty years from now is two or three times bigger than it is today. By development, I mean all the changes in the composition of the economy that happen as it evolves. Early on, farming is the biggest economic sector; later it is manufacturing; still later, services. At first, manufacturing is characterized by textiles and footwear; later on, by cars and PCs. In

Table 6.1

As Japan Grew Richer, Spending Shifted to New Manufactured Goods

	Percentage of total spending spent on:			
	Food	Clothing	Housing, Lighting and Fuel	Others
1950	56	12	10	22
1970	34	10	9	47
1987	26	7	11	56

Source: Minami (1994), p. 299
Note: Based on 7-year moving averages.

poor countries, investment rates are low; as countries get richer, invest-ment rates rise; as they get richer still, investment rates recede again.

Neither growth nor development can occur without the other.

Aside from the lucky few who hit the petroleum jackpot, no poor country can grow rich without industrializing. It is the shift of workers from low-productivity farming and textiles to higher-productivity indus-trial sectors that creates higher income per worker.

At the same time, it is growth that engenders development. As a coun-try gets a little richer, people invariably spend a smaller share of their income on food and a larger portion on manufactured goods (Table 6.1). Without this shift in demand, manufacturers would lack sales and indus-trialization would stop dead in its tracks. Moreover, this shift in demand lures still more farmers to move to the factory, thereby propelling further industrialization.

From this standpoint, anything that accelerates development will ac-celerate growth, while anything that accelerates *sustainable* growth will accelerate development. That is why Japan's industrial policies succeeded in the catch-up era. They did not cause Japan to industrialize, but they did cause it to industrialize *faster*, and therefore to grow faster.

Even where there is no accelerationist industrial policy, the virtuous cycle of development and growth occurs naturally through organic market forces. If it didn't, the industrialization process would not be so wide-spread throughout the world. When TVs are new, spending on them grows much faster than income; once the market is saturated, demand shifts to other commodities. When petroleum becomes sufficiently cheaper than coal, factories switch. Over time, the "invisible hand" stead-ily shifts the economy from buggy whips to memory chips.

This market mechanism is so wondrous that *if* all the conditions were right—including, among other things, perfectly competitive markets—then no human intervention could allocate resources more efficiently. Industrial policy would be at best superfluous and more likely detrimental.[2]

In the real world, however, the preconditions for markets to work perfectly are often missing. When that happens, the invisible hand needs a helping hand.

Modern economics readily acknowledges that the market is not entirely self-regulating when it comes to business cycles, inflation, recessions, depressions and unemployment. Daily monitoring and intervention by the Federal Reserve is needed to avoid overheating inflationary booms and consequent depression-sized busts. Even as the International Monetary Fund and the U.S. Treasury have correctly urged the countries of Asia to adopt more market-oriented financial systems, they have also correctly recognized that financial markets can panic. When that happens, they are not entirely self-correcting. As Treasury Secretary Robert Rubin put it in his January 21, 1998, speech:

> Anyone who has spent substantial time enmeshed in markets, as I have, appreciates that financial markets tend to go to extremes, including the market for bank credit extension — and when they reverse, they sometimes do so with great force. . . . Some say that doing nothing [in the Asian financial crisis] would be best, because markets would ultimately solve the problem on their own. Let me say as someone who spent 26 years on Wall Street and who has an enormous belief in markets, there are problems that markets alone simply cannot solve. In this country, we recognized that long ago, with measures such as the Federal Reserve System, the Securities and Exchange Commission and deposit insurance. There is simply too much risk that markets alone will not resolve these problems of financial instability, and therefore given our stakes in Asia we must try to help get these countries back on track.[3]

Neoclassical economics also recognizes patterns of market failures in the "microeconomy."

A classic case is the problem of research and development (R&D). When a company performs R&D, the spillover benefits—"externalities"—for that company's customers, suppliers and even its competitors are so large that the company actually doing the R&D can capture only a small part of the resulting social profits. If society relied on the market alone, there would be far too little R&D. Hence, orthodox economics endorses tax credits and other incentives to promote R&D.

Another, more contentious, case is connected with the issue of free trade. When a rich country like the U.S. trades with a poorer country like Mexico, the GDP of both countries is increased. For the two countries as a whole, therefore, free trade is a win-win proposition. Within each country, however, some people gain while others lose. The reason is that, with increased trade, each country shifts its production base to what it does best. The U.S. will stress capital-intensive, technology-intensive goods, while Mexico will import those and increase output of labor-intensive goods. That, in turn, means that, within the U.S., the demand for capital, technology and highly skilled white-collar labor will increase, thereby increasing the income of owners of capital and the salaries of skilled labor. In contrast, the demand for unskilled and semiskilled labor has decreased and so the wages of these laborers will decrease. Economists estimate that globalization is responsible for about 10–20 percent of the growing wage inequality in the U.S. in recent years. Not surprisingly, blue-collar unions oppose free trade. (However, the reality is that the vast majority of the growth in wage inequality is caused by differences in education, with the college-educated getting a much higher wage premium over less educated workers. That's because recent increases in technology have increased demand for educated workers.)

Under these conditions, the market does not pass the economists' usual criterion for maximizing welfare even though it increases GDP. There is a solution to this dilemma. The gains to the winners so outweigh the harm to the losers that the former can compensate the latter. Suppose the winners gain $2,000 for every $1,000 taken from the losers. In that case, tax and budget policies could be used to redistribute $1,500 from each of the winners to all the losers. Everyone would be $500 better off after free trade than before. Or, if $1,000 were redistributed from the winners to the losers, then the winners would be $1,000 better off and the losers would be no better or worse off than before. The market itself is incapable either of such redistribution or of deciding how big it should be; it must be supplemented by politics. The need for such compensation to supplement the market—for reasons of equity as well as to reduce political opposition to free trade—has been recognized by orthodox economics ever since John Stuart Mill first proposed it in 1825.[4]

The systematic failure addressed by Japan's industrial policy is the dilemma caused when economies of scale or learning-by-doing efficiencies prevail. In these circumstances, the bigger a firm gets, and the more experience it has, the more efficient it becomes. Just look at Microsoft. It costs it the same to develop Windows 95 whether it sells one copy or 50 million. So, the more copies it can sell, the lower the cost per copy. Moreover, as customers learn to use it, they don't want to switch and have to learn another system. So, once a company enjoying economies of scale takes off, it can easily lock in a lead.

These are the conditions where the unrestricted market regularly produces oligopolies and monopolies, from Intel to Boeing. But, in most industries, monopolies and oligopolies reduce economic efficiency—as we saw in the case of the "American Big Three" automakers before Japanese competitors came in. They also produce arrogance. Hence, when economies of scale prevail, allowing the market to proceed on its own would paradoxically undermine the very conditions upon which market efficiency depends: vibrant competition.

The normal antidote for this problem is either strong antitrust action or else regulation of "natural" monopolies. But what happens if the economies of scale occur, not within a single country, but across countries? If economies of scale prevail, then the nation first out of the starting block could lock in a lead. Just ask Airbus about Boeing, or Fujitsu and Hitachi about IBM back in the heyday of mainframe computers.

For this reason, it was not only nationalist economists like Alexander Hamilton and Friedrich List who advocated protection and subsidies for "infant industries." Ever since John Stuart Mill, classical economics too has recognized the so-called infant industry argument for *temporary* protection. In Mill's famous passage:

> The only case in which, on mere principles of political economy, protecting duties can be defensible, is when they are imposed temporarily (especially in a young and rising nation) in hopes of naturalizing a foreign industry in itself perfectly suitable to the circumstances of the country. The superiority of one country over another in a branch of production often arises only from having begun it sooner. . . . But the protection should be confined to cases in which there is good ground of assurance that the industry which it fosters will after a time be able to dispense with it; nor should the domestic producers ever be allowed to expect that it will be continued to them beyond the time necessary for a fair trial of what they are capable of accomplishing.[5]

And that is what Japan's industrial policy amounted to when it was successful: infant industry protection and promotion on a grand scale.

The classic case is cars. Japan had some initial experience in automaking before World War II,[6] and the industry certainly had the potential to become competitive, but in the ashes of the war it was not yet able to stand on its own. In fact, during a brief interlude of liberalized trade in 1953, some 30,000 inexpensive European cars flooded in—15 times the 1950 figure— overwhelming domestic output, then only about 5,000. Without intervention, the Japanese industry might have been suffocated in its cradle.[7]

Like so many other industries in Japan at that time, autos faced a "Catch-22." Because of economies of scale, Japanese automakers couldn't become competitive until they got big. However, under normal free trade conditions, they couldn't get big until they became competitive.

For this reason, in a struggle lasting for two years between 1949 and 1951, the Bank of Japan tried to stop MITI's plan to promote a domestic auto industry, saying Japan should depend on imports instead. The BOJ, along with economists in the World Bank, reasoned that autos were too capital-intensive an industry for capital-scarce Japan. Given its plenitude of cheap labor Japan should instead concentrate on labor-intensive items like toys and textiles, they argued.[8]

But MITI persevered. In response to the European threat, MITI simply slammed on the brakes—real hard. In those days, under the 1949 Foreign Exchange Law, anyone needing foreign exchange for any import whatsoever had to get it from MITI, and so MITI simply refused to allocate foreign exchange for the import of foreign cars beyond a minimal quota. Not until 1965, when the industry had become competitive, with almost 10 percent of its output being exported, was the import of passenger cars "liberalized," i.e., changed from a quota system to a tariff. Even so, the effective rate of tariff protection (ERP) was put at a prohibitively high 40 percent.

Beyond import protection, the industry also received enormous subsidies helping it to engage in the enormous investment required. These included not only huge tax breaks and low interest loans to the automakers themselves, but critical aid to key supplier industries, from auto parts and machine tools to steel. For 15 years, from 1956 to 1972, 15 percent of all loans to the auto *parts* industry came from the government, and for some priority parts producers, the figure sometimes reached as high as 50 percent (!)—usually at interest rates 3–4 percent below market rates.[9] This is rarely mentioned when some writers claim that Toyota, Nissan et al. received little governmental financial aid. Moreover, since the government had designated the industry a priority, bankers were no longer afraid to lend to an industry previously seen as too risky.

Once the auto industry overcame the initial hurdles, it turned into

Japan's greatest success story without the need for additional aid. With great perseverance, it came back from a failed attempt at exporting to the U.S. market. It even developed entirely new techniques of manufacturing, e.g., Toyota's famed just-in-time system. These techniques revolutionized manufacturing just as the Ford system had a half-century earlier.

In the end, an industry emerged that, by 1985, was the world's largest. It exported the majority (54 percent) of its output, accounted for 26 percent of all Japanese exports, 21 percent of all manufacturing investment, and 11 percent of all manufacturing output, and was one of the largest customers for such other priority industries as steel, machinery and electronics.[10]

And it owed its start to MITI's shield and sword. As Hiromichi Mutoh commented:

> [T]he rationalization efforts of the firms in the [automotive] industry were of course crucial, but if the increasing share during 1951–53 of European cars, which were able to overcome the tariff barrier despite its height, is noted, then the important role played by import restrictions policies cannot be ignored.[11]

It should go without saying that, if Japan's automakers had not had the intrinsic potential to become competitive, Japan's promotion of autos would have been no more effective than efforts in other countries where the landscape is littered with "white elephants" from steel to petrochemicals to autos. Nor, if the auto industry's initial takeoff had not been limited by the hurdle of economies of scale, would industrial policy have been necessary. In the case of Japanese autos and other success stories, both protection/promotion measures and intrinsic competitiveness were necessary; neither alone was sufficient.

Most American economists are skeptical of infant industry protection and promotion. Their reasons stem from political judgments, not economic theory. They rightly worry that infant industry arguments are often used as a cover for crass protectionism of uncompetitive industries. Protection should only be used as a temporary aid to industries that have the potential of eventually meeting world prices and becoming exporters. When applied as a permanent policy of import-substitution, as in much of Latin America, protection has proven to be a disaster.

Japan was certainly not exempt from this pattern. The most egregious case was the bungled effort to nurture the petrochemical industry. MITI applied all the usual tools. It not only protected and promoted the industry itself. It also tried to boost petrochemical sales by helping one of the industry's key customers, synthetic fibers, which also happened to be a targeted industry. The government extended JDB loans, bought tons of synthetic fiber material and exempted all export income from taxes during 1953–61.[12]

Unfortunately, while MITI's Basic Industries Bureau was promoting petrochemicals, its Energy and Natural Resources Agency was protecting Japan's inefficient petroleum refiners. Consequently, Japan's petrochemical firms were forced to pay sky-high prices to Japanese refiners for petroleum-based feedstocks, and so were foredoomed from becoming competitive.[13]

As competitiveness expert Michael Porter underscores, there is a clear distinction between industries where industrial policy is advisable and where it will fail:

> In the early Japanese successes, such as steel, shipbuilding, and sewing machines, this sort of government role [protection and promotion —rk] was constructive. Price was important to competitive position in the segments in which Japanese firms competed. Many of the industries were capital intensive. Competitive advantage depended on having modern, large-scale facilities. Government's levers at this stage were powerful ones. . . .
>
> In these early successes, however, government was not working in isolation. Japan also had advantages in other determinants such as demand conditions (ships, steel and motorcycles) or related and supporting industries (sewing machines) that contributed to success. . . .
>
> It is also important to recognize that in other large and significant industries such as chemicals and plastics, aerospace, aircraft and software, *in which Japan brought no other advantages to the industry*, aggressive efforts by government to develop the industry have largely failed to produce true international competitors [emphasis added].[14]

Economists also worry that limiting imports will stifle competition. That, too, is a legitimate worry. Hence, successful industrial policy requires that there be enough domestic companies in any industry to ensure competition. A policy of a single "national champion" as often was practiced in Europe has proved to be a failure. Fortunately, populous Japan had a large enough domestic market to support several competing firms in the strategic industries. Moreover, it was MITI policy to encourage such domestic competition. However, in many other less populous countries, too small to support several large-scale firms in the same industry, following this aspect of the Japanese model is not possible. In such countries, systematic protection might prove to be a bust rather than a boon.

The bottom line is this: not every industry in Japan that received aid went on to become a competitive exporter, but most industries that did become export superstars received critical protection and promotion during their initial stages.

Breaking the Balance of Payments Bottleneck

Suppose Japan had not boosted the auto industry. If Toyota, Nissan et al. really had the potential to be competitive, many economists would argue, then the industry would have eventually developed anyway—just a little later and a little slower with less bureaucratization of the economy. Perhaps they are right—assuming the industry could have gotten the necessary financing. But consider the consequences of a slower pace for Japan's overall industrialization drive.

In Japan, industrial policy changed the country's export mix, thereby helping to break one of the chief bottlenecks to growth faced by any developing country and one we see in Asia today: recurrent balance of payments crises. Had Japan not solved this problem, high growth could never have gotten off the ground.

In order for Japan to industrialize, it had to import indispensable capital goods and raw materials. In addition, without import controls, imports of consumer goods would also rise with income growth. Under normal conditions, rapid growth would cause imports to race ahead of exports. For a while, Japan could borrow. Indeed, developing countries can, and often should, run significant trade deficits for quite a while. But unless lenders see sufficient export growth on the horizon, they will stop lending—sometimes abruptly. Then comes the inevitable payments or debt crisis. Latin America's endemic crises, and the 1997 currency crises throughout Asia, shows how powerful and pervasive this bottleneck is.

It is hard to remember, but Japan too once suffered from this classic problem. Up through 1955, its trade deficits were so huge that there were fears that Japan might not even be able to finance basic imports of food and raw materials. Even after 1955, there were still several occasions (1954, 1957, 1961 and 1963) when the Bank of Japan had to tighten money to slow down growth: not because of any internal strain, but purely because high growth at home was causing imports to mushroom far beyond the ability of exports to pay for them.[15]

Some economists contend that trade was not all that important to Japanese growth since imports amounted to only 10 percent of GDP. But

Figure 6.1 **Manufacturing Growth Needed Proportional Imports**

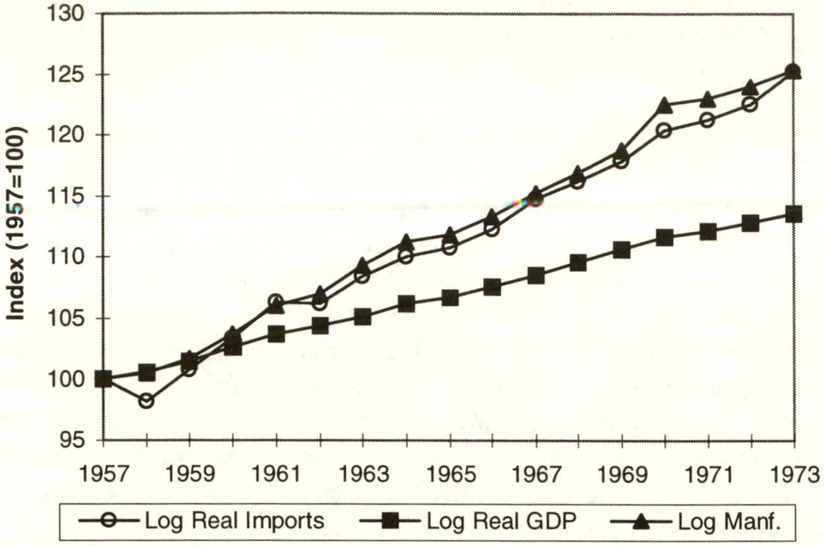

Source: EPA (1995a)

Note: This chart shows the growth of inflation-adjusted imports, GDP and manufacturing. It is an index with 1957 = 100 and is on a logarithmic scale. See text for explanation.

some matters are an all or nothing situation. What does it matter if Japan had the world's most modern steel plants if it couldn't pay for iron ore, coking coal and fuel? During the high-growth era, manufacturing growth marched in lockstep with imports (Figure 6.1). Had imports not been able to grow as fast, then manufacturing could not have grown as fast either.

For this very reason, when Prime Minister Hayato Ikeda announced in 1960 a plan to double Japanese GDP in only ten years, many economists were skeptical. Japanese exports could never grow fast enough to pay for the imports required by that kind of growth, they protested.[16]

Consider what it would take to surmount this problem. From 1955 to 1965, Japan grew at more than 9 percent a year. On the other hand, its biggest customer and supplier, the U.S., was growing at only 3.5 percent a year. Suppose that, in both countries, every time GDP grew 1 percent, then imports grew 1 percent. In that case, Japan's imports from the U.S. would grow at 9 percent a year while its exports to the U.S. would grow only one-third as fast.

What if, somehow, this pattern changed? Suppose America's imports from Japan could grow 3 percent with every 1 percent hike in American

GDP. In that case, Japan's exports and imports would grow at the same 9 percent rate and there would be no balance of payments crisis to stifle growth.

This is where Japan's market-conforming industrial policies entered the story. Japan needed to rapidly change the product mix of its exports.

Japan's single largest export in the 1950s through the early 1960s was textiles. That is a classic kind of good where spending grows more slowly than GDP. During the 1960s, for every 1 percent increase in GDP of Japan's trading partners, Japan's textile exports rose only 0.5 percent. Since growth in demand is not all that responsive to growth in income, such goods are said to have "low income elasticity (responsiveness) of demand." Japan needed to export goods where world demand would grow much faster than GDP (i.e., goods with a "high income elasticity of demand"), goods like consumer appliances and cars, the steel to make them, and the ships to transport them. For every 1 percent increase in the GDP of Japan's trading partners, Japan's steel exports would go up 3 percent—i.e., Japan's steel exports could be expected to grow three times as fast as world income (Table 6.2).

Added to this was another problem. Even if Japan strove mightily to raise its productivity, the payoff in sales varied widely from product to product.

In the case of goods like textiles, if improved competitiveness allowed the price of Japanese exports to drop by 10 percent from $100 to $90, other countries bought only 6 percent more. In that case, the amount of money Japan earned on that good actually *dropped* ($90 × 1.06 = $95). This is the same dilemma faced by farmers. The more productive they become, the smaller their revenue. On the other hand, in the case of automobiles, whenever Japan's export price dropped by 10 percent, foreign consumers bought 26 percent more cars (Table 6.2). In that case, sales rose ($90 × 1.26 = $112). This is typically the case with new goods until the market becomes saturated. Currently, as the price of a PC drops, sales rise even faster. Items where a price drop increases sales revenue are said to have a "high price elasticity of demand."[17]

Unfortunately, back in 1955, 60 percent of Japan's exports were items for which growth in world demand was "stagnant." Only 20 percent of Japan's exports belonged to the group of industries in which income and price elasticity were rapidly raising global import demand. By contrast, in West Germany, UK and Italy, about half of exports were in the fast-growing industries.[18]

Table 6.2

Market-Conforming Strategy: Targeting Growth Industries

	Income Elasticity (% increase in sales for every 1% increase in GDP)	Price Elasticity (% increase in sales for every 1% fall in price)
Domestic consumption		
Textiles	0.6	0.8
Food	0.4	0.7
Consumer durables	1.5	1.4
Exports		
Textiles	0.5	0.6
Metal products	1.4	2.2
Machinery	1.4	1.5
Automobiles	1.9	2.6
Chemicals	3.0	
Iron and steel	3.2	1.2

Source: Ueno (1980), p. 398

Note: The data cover 1960–71. In case of domestic consumption, the income elasticity is the percentage increase in sales for every 1 percent increase in Japan's GDP. In the case of exports, income elasticity is the percentage increase for every 1 percent increase in the GDP of Japan's trading partners. Price elasticity means the percentage *increase* in sales for every 1 percent *fall* in price, or the percentage fall in sales for every 1 percent rise in price. Japan tried to target industries where rapid productivity gains at home would be rewarded with big sales gains due to high income and price elasticities.

And so, as the 1960 "Income Doubling Plan" and various MITI "Visions" explained, Japan needed to rapidly shift its export mix. It had to ship products where Japan got a triple whammy: i.e., where it could expect rapid productivity hikes so it could charge lower prices; where the price drops would produce the biggest hike in sales; and where world demand was expected to rise even faster than overall GDP growth. Through this process, Japan hoped to emulate the export structure of more advanced nations like Germany. It wanted to ship fewer labor-intensive items like textiles and more capital- and knowledge-intensive items from steel to autos and machinery (Figure 6.2).[19]

Having the goal of an upgraded industrial structure is one thing; achieving it is quite another. What made Japan's efforts successful in the high-growth era was that, for the most part, they intersected with market evolution. They exploited, rather than defied, the powerful organic forces of economies of scale, inter-industry spillovers, and price/income elasticities of demand.

Figure 6.2 **The "Diamond of Development": Emulating Germany**

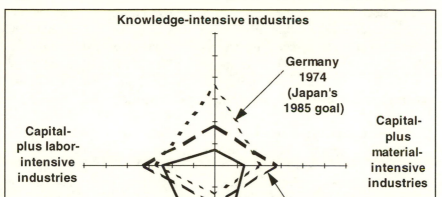

Source: Zysman (1983), pg. 239

Note: This "diamond of development" shows how Japan's export mix changed as it developed. In 1959, most of its exports were in labor-intensive industries. By 1974, the majority were either in capital- and material-intensive sectors like steel, plastics and fibers, or else capital- and labor-intensive sectors like light machinery and cars. In a 1974 vision, the Economic Planning Agency proposed that, by 1985, Japan move to the export mix which Germany had already achieved in 1974. In this export mix, the biggest exports were in knowledge-intensive products like computers, instruments and heavy machinery.

Consider steel and shipbuilding, two of the biggest priorities in the upgrade plan. By 1975, these two industries, together with autos, would account for 40 percent of Japan's total exports, up from 11 percent in 1950. Equally important, steel was a vital input to other exporters, from autos to machinery, as well as being essential to domestic output.

While both steel and shipbuilding had the potential to become competitive, in the early 1950s, both faced the same Catch-22 as autos. Ships suffered a 10–15 percent price disadvantage vis-à-vis British and German competitors. In fact, one of the shipbuilder's biggest hurdles was that they, like automakers, were compelled to buy protected Japanese steel at prices up to 40 percent above world levels.[20]

The traditional free trade solution would have been for Japan to import cheaper steel. However, the steel industry enjoyed tremendous economies of scale. If steel sales could grow—due to orders from the shipbuilders, automakers and others receiving protection—then steel costs could drop. Indeed, by the early 1960s, due to a subsidized "rationalization plan" utilizing the most modern technology and much larger plants, steel costs had dropped to a level below the American competition.

> Investment in larger plants undoubtedly helped lower production costs, contributing to the 35 percent decline in labor and raw materials costs in Japanese steel production between 1956 and 1970. . . . At least at the plant level, there were substantial scale economies, with larger plants able to produce steel more cheaply than small ones.[21]

Because the industry enjoyed high price elasticities, as prices dropped, sales accelerated. This led to even greater scale economies, and thus further price drops.

Then, the inter-industry spillovers—"external economies" in the economics jargon—kicked in. The drop in steel prices cut costs for shipbuilding, leading to greater ship exports and thus, through economies of scale, lower costs in that industry. Soon, the ripple effects spread throughout the economy. Increased ship exports produced more orders for steel, leading to still more economies of scale in steel, and, as a result, lower costs for the *auto* industry, all of which stimulated more demand in the machine tool industry! This cross-industry ripple effect is exactly what the government's 1960 Economic White Paper had predicted.[22]

All three industries—ships, steel and autos—eventually became supremely competitive but it was not the actions of "private individuals and enterprises responding to the opportunities provided in quite free markets for commodities and labor" that initially made them world class players.[23] It was protection and promotion.

Like the automotive sector, both steel and shipbuilding received the benefits of import protection. Except for one year when emergency imports were needed (1957), steel imports never topped 3 percent of consumption throughout the 1950s, and never exceeded 1 percent from 1962 through 1977. Virtually no ships were imported in this era.[24]

Both industries also received heavy government subsidies. During the mid-1950s, the government's Japan Development Bank provided 36 percent of all the investment funds for shipbuilding and 10 percent of steelmakers' investment (at half of market interest rates).[25] They also received hefty tax breaks. In 1957, for example, a special tax break for exporters amounted to a full 12 percent of all steel profits. In addition, there was a special depreciation allowance for the industry equal to another 13 percent of income.[26]

Moreover, in shipbuilding, government policy took an unusually heavy hand. Well into the 1970s, report Trezise and Suzuki, the Transport Ministry consulted with the industry and each year:

> decide[d] on the tonnage of ships to be built, by type (tankers, ore carriers, liners, and so on) and allocate[d] production contracts and the ships among the applicant domestic shipbuilders and shipowners. The selected shipping lines receive[d] preferential financing and in turn [were] subject to close government supervision.[27]

Both steel and shipbuilding used the initial aid to great advantage and became powerful competitors. Japanese shipbuilders were pioneers in the development of supertankers. Japanese steelmakers built new "greenfield" plants with the latest electric arc furnace technology which their U.S. counterparts were still resisting. They learned how to make steel with less iron ore, less coking coal, and less energy than others did. Had these innovations not occurred, protection would have failed.

Through these protection/promotion policies—and similar ones in virtually every major Japanese exporting industry from machine tools to TVs—the campaign to shift Japan's export mix was amazingly successful. In 1950, textiles made up nearly half of Japan's exports while machinery exports were negligible; by 1975, the reverse was true (Figure 6.3). By 1964, Japan stood fourth behind the U.S., West Germany and Britain in the percentage of exports based in industries enjoying a rapidly growing world demand.

Nor was this an issue of propping up export industries permanently unable to stand on their own. From 1964 until the 1973 oil shock, the shipbuilding industry's profitability was often 25–30 percent above the manufacturing average and it paid wages far above the norm. In the 1960s, Japan had the most efficient shipbuilders in the world. Automakers often earned rates of return on assets as much as 60–80 percent above the manufacturing average and it also paid high wages. Indeed, as these industries' competitiveness improved and protection became superfluous, tariffs were reduced.[28]

The export shift broke the balance of payments bottleneck. During the period of 1955–65, every time Japan's GDP went up 1 percent, its imports went up 1.2 percent but its exports went up 3.5 percent—just as the architect of the income doubling plan, Osamu Shimamura, had promised.[29]

Figure 6.3 **Reversal of Fortune: Textiles and Machinery**

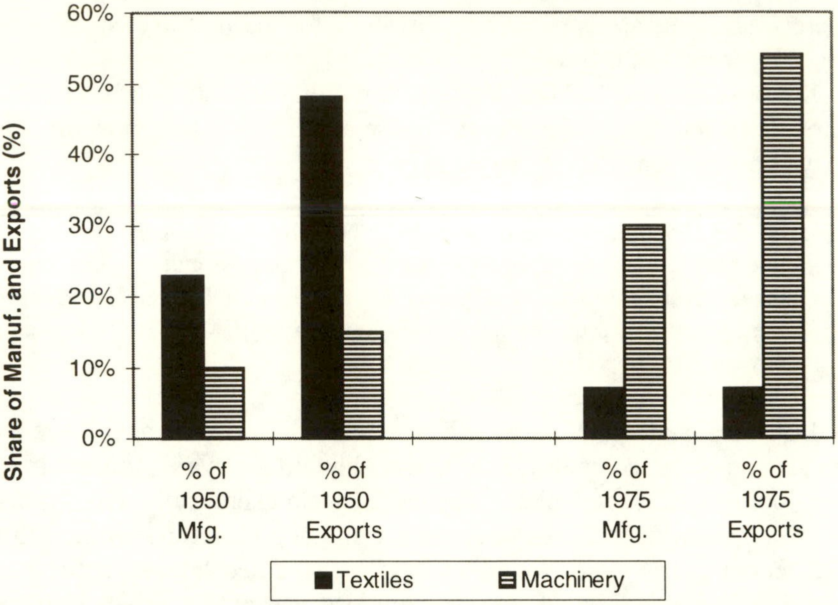

Source: Itoh and Kiyono (1988), pg. 156

By the mid-1960s, the era of balance of payments deficits was over. Never again would the need to rein in a trade deficit force policymakers to rein in growth. The income-doubling plan, far from being overly ambitious with its forecast of 7.5 percent annual growth, proved to be too cautious by far. Growth was actually 9.3 percent a year.

Had Japan not rapidly shifted its export composition, however, the income-doubling plan might have been stillborn. A full third of Japan's export growth in the 1960s came not from improved competitiveness or the growth of world GDP but solely because Japan changed its menu of export items. By 1971, some 33 percent of Japan's exports consisted of products that it had not exported at all ten years earlier.[30] Given the more or less constant relation between GDP and imports, if exports had been one-third lower, and, hence, imports one-third lower, so might have GDP growth. There would have been industrialization, but no high-growth miracle. As economist Hisao Kanamori, one of the titans of the era, wrote in 1968, during the peak of the high-growth takeoff:

In terms of the world demand pattern, the composition of Japanese exports was, at the outset, unfavorable for growth, but Japan's success in transforming the commodity composition accounts to a large extent for its subsequent export expansion. If it had persisted in exporting more traditional items, with stagnant demand, export prices would have had to be drastically lowered, leading to a deterioration of the terms of trade. That may have led to the "immiserizing growth" that the advocates of domestic development feared.[31]

Economists who oppose industrial policy would argue that, even without policy intervention, the upgrade in Japan's export mix would have occurred naturally. The market forces of productivity growth, "income elasticity," and "price elasticity" would have gradually shifted domestic industrial structure and export mix, as such forces do elsewhere. But that's exactly the point. To the extent that industrial policy was market-conforming, it did more or less what the market would have done, but it did it *faster*. It accelerated the process by cutting through the Catch-22 dilemmas faced by infant industries. And the consequences were enormous. Suppose Japan had grown only 6 percent a year during 1953–71 instead of its actual 9 percent growth. By 1971, its GDP would have been 40 percent smaller!

We by no means claim that Japan's industrial protection/promotion policies were always limited to the industries that deserved them: genuine infant industries characterized by economies of scale, rapid productivity hikes, inter-industry ripple effects, and rapid growth in world demand. In fact, many industries with no future export potential were aided for all kinds of reasons: because advanced industrial countries had them and so Japan wanted them also; because they would help Japan become more self-sufficient; because they had powerful political supporters; and because of fear of social unrest in declining industries. What we are claiming is that the measures succeeded only where the proper infant industry productivity and demand criteria were met; they failed when applied elsewhere.

The bottom line, however, is this: because of the nature of a developing economy during the era of industrial takeoff, there were a host of genuine infant industries—enough to make the policy a brilliant success.

Why Industrial Policy Works Only in the Era of Catch-Up

Even economists who acknowledge the validity of infant industry promotion point out another problem: even when infant industry promotion is legitimate, the system of protection is usually carried on long after the infants have grown up.

That, in fact, is the heart of Japan's post-1973 problems. Some of the same industries getting big government loans in the 1950s—steel, marine transport, electric power—were still (or once again) the biggest recipients three decades later.[32]

The great danger of industrial policy is not that it sometimes aids the wrong industries during the catch-up era. That does happen, as we have seen. But there are so many worthy recipients that the benefits of developing the right industries outweigh the costs of helping the wrong ones. The greatest danger, as Yasusuke Murakami, one of Japan's foremost proponents of "developmentalism," points out, is that the whole system persists long after it has become self-defeating.

The key to successful industrial policy, as we have stressed, is economies of scale, learning-by-doing efficiencies, rapid technological change, extensive inter-industry spillovers and so forth. Those are the conditions in which industries require—and can benefit from—state aid to overcome the initial hurdle. Murakami argues:

> Industrial policy is effective only vis-à-vis promising industries in a phase of decreasing cost [i.e., with economies of scale —rk]. Thus the key of industrial policy is to limit its application.[33]

Takatoshi Ito summarized the issue thusly:

> In general, industrial policies succeeded for industries with scale economies, such as steel, and failed for industries without scale economies, such as coal.[34]

The point is: it is only during the transitional period of the industrial takeoff that these conditions proliferate throughout the economy. That's when so many industries are new and small. Once an economy becomes mature, these conditions are the exception rather than the rule. And by that time, financial markets are well enough developed to deal with the exceptions.

In the late 1950s, Japan had such increasing returns to scale that, on average, a 100 percent increase in inputs yielded a 140 percent increase in output. This was a far higher level than Europe or the U.S., which also enjoyed some economies of scale, but which were already more mature. As Japan matured, the returns to scale steadily descended and by the late 1970s, Japan no longer enjoyed economies of scale. In fact, by 1990, measured returns to scale for Japan were *lower* than those of France, Germany, UK, and the U.S.[35]

Since the erosion of these advantages is so gradual, it's impossible to pinpoint exactly when the net benefits from industrial policy ran out. By some measures, says Japanese economist Hiroya Ueno, the benefits ran out as early as 1965 and by other measures as late as 1970.[36]

Once an economy becomes mature, so-called industrial policy is nothing more than rank protectionism, applied to formerly competitive industries like steel and shipbuilding, or even to industries that were never internationally competitive in the first place, like paper, glass and cement. The very policies that had been the country's most potent medicine now become its most dangerous poison. This, says Murakami, is what happened to Japan:

> The difficulty with industrial policy, though, is not so much in designating priority industries as in revoking this designation—that is, in having an effective "sunset" provision in the policy. When technological innovation comes to an end of a cycle and the rate of increase in product demand decelerates, the period of decreasing cost [through economies of scale, learning curve effects, etc. —rk] comes to an end. At this point, industrial policy no longer has a *raison d'être*. Once established, however, the relationship between industry and government becomes difficult to terminate; thus industrial policy continues, becoming nothing more than protectionism, and maybe even hampering the development of a competitive environment in the economy as a whole. The greater danger of industrial policy is this inertia in the relationship between industry and bureaucracy. . . .
>
> In postwar Japan . . . the symbiotic relationship between individual industries and the ministries in charge of them has grown stronger; thus there is a chance that the industrial policy implemented for a growing industry may, with the slowing of growth in that industry, become a protectionist policy for a stagnant industry. . . . Changes in industrial structure . . . have made industrial policy toward the leading postwar industries unnecessary and impossible to implement. . . .
>
> *If Japan fails to end industrial policy, its postwar developmentalism may be judged a failure.* . . . The Japanese experience provides a valuable lesson for future developmentalist countries. Industrial policy must include in advance a rule for bringing itself to an end [emphasis added].[37]

As early as 1975, Hiroya Ueno had warned about the dangers of the cartelized and oligopolistic corporate structure created by Japan's industrial policy. Though this corporate structure had promoted growth in the catch-up era, it had already turned into a force for stagnation by the time of his writing. Ueno noted that, in the earlier period, the system had led to falling prices; later, it led to high and rigid prices:

> Producer and export prices decreased in about the same way as the average cost but started to rise in 1967. Therefore, 1967 seems to have marked a clear end to the effectiveness of industrial policy. . . .
>
> [Industrial policy] gave rise to the formation of an oligopolistic system in these [heavy and chemical] industries. However, initially, economies of scale brought about price reduction. These called forth competition in investment. . . . Therefore, during this period [the high-growth era], workable competition prevailed. This oligopolistic system was growth-oriented and competitive. In this sense, industrial policy had more merits than demerits until about 1965. . . .
>
> [However] as growth slows down, this tendency [of collusion among oligopolists on price and investment] becomes stronger and the oligopolistic system becomes stagnant and collusive. . . .
>
> A stagnant and collusive oligopoly system in the slow growth period tends to curtail competitive and efficient investment activity.[38]

The same issue has been tackled from a slightly different vantage point by Michael Porter. He argues that industrial policy can be successful when the source of a country's competitive advantage is investment-driven growth. But, it does not succeed in what he calls the innovation-driven stage. That's the stage when the ability to nurture a Microsoft is more important than capital formation:

> The investment-driven stage, as the name implies, is one where the ability and willingness to invest is the principal advantage rather than the ability to offer unique products or produce with unique processes. . . .
>
> The investment-driven route to competitive advantage is only possible in a certain class of industries: those with significant scale economies and capital requirements but still a large labor cost component, standardized products, low service content, technology that is readily transferable. . . . [At that stage], government's role can be substantial. It can be important in such areas as channeling scarce capital into particular industries, promoting risk taking, providing temporary protection to encourage the entry of domestic rivals and the construction of efficient scale facilities, stimulating and influencing the acquisition of foreign technology and encouraging exports.[39]

But, once a country has matured and innovation, rather than capital, is the source of competitive advantage, there is no longer room for industrial policy:

> Allocation of capital, protection, licensing controls, export subsidy and other forms of direct [government] intervention lose relevance or effectiveness in innovation-based competition.[40]

The high-growth era was Japan's era of investment-driven advantage, the era of big capital-intensive industries like steel. That, as we saw in Chapter 4, was when Japan got the biggest improvement in output for its investment.

By the early 1970s, developmentalism had hit the end of the road.

Japan's Secret: Accelerating the "Arc of Catch-Up"

Japan is often held in awe for its remarkable record of catching up to the U.S. As late as 1955—when the economy had finally recovered its prewar peak—Japan's GDP per worker was a meager 15 percent of U.S. levels and far below European standards. By 1990, it had risen to 60 percent of American levels and was nearly reaching European levels. In per capita terms, the catch-up seems even more remarkable, from only a fifth of U.S. levels to nearly 80 percent.

But the fact is: catching up to the leaders is quite widespread. Over the course of the postwar period, dozens of countries, from Brazil to Germany and from Pakistan to France, have been catching up to the U.S.

The most rapid catch-up has been among the two dozen members of the "rich countries club," the Organization for Economic Cooperation and Development (OECD). Forty years ago, most of these countries had only half the income per worker as the U.S.; now they're up to almost 80 percent (Figure 6.4).

Among another two dozen Third World countries *not* including the Asian NICs, GDP per worker more than doubled, bringing their average from 16 percent of U.S. levels in 1960 to 24 percent in 1990. As we will discuss in Chapter 9, among countries that trade a great deal, the catch-up process is nearly universal.

Sheer arithmetic dictates that, if those further behind are to catch up, they have to grow faster than the leader. And, as we can see in Figure 6.5, the further behind the U.S. that a country was in 1955, the faster it grew.

Figure 6.4 **"Catch Up" Is Normal: Japan Did It More Quickly**

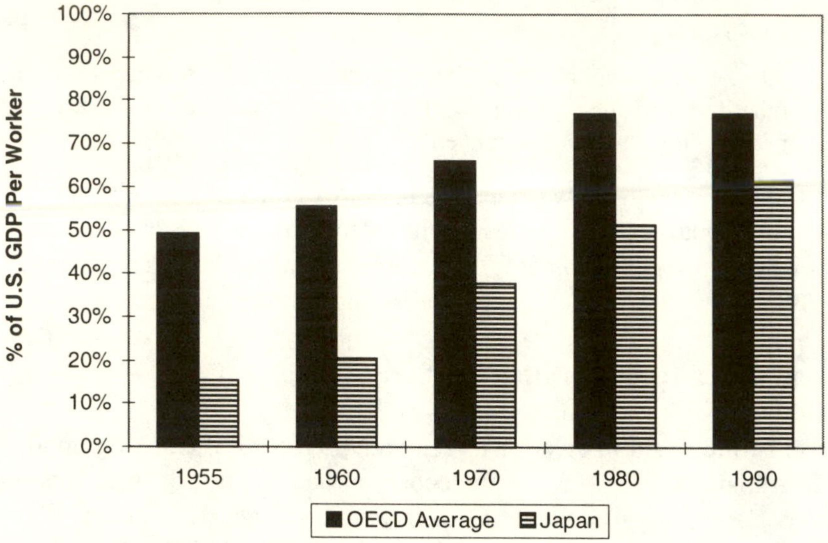

Source: Summers and Heston (1995)

So the mere fact that Japan grew faster than the U.S. or European countries over the past four decades is neither a surprise nor, in and of itself, a great achievement.

What really distinguishes Japan during the high-growth era is the *speed* of its catch-up. Japan skillfully used industrial and trade policies to *accelerate* the normal catch-up process.

While not all countries hop aboard the catch-up train, those that do follow a regular pattern. Growth starts off slowly, often only 1–2 percent per year. Then, as they approach the middle-income range, growth accelerates, hitting a peak of 4 percent or more. Finally, as countries mature, growth slows to 2–3 percent and the variation in growth rates shrinks (top panel of Figure 6.6).

The reason that growth rates arc in this manner is the relationship between investment and development. Investment rates—i.e., the investment:GDP ratio—follow the same arcing pattern as growth. Moreover, returns to investment—how much growth a country gains as a result of a certain amount of investment—likewise show the same arcing pattern. Both investment rates and growth returns to investment start off at low rates in very poor countries, then rise in middle income countries, and fall again in rich countries. (The arcing pattern of investment rates was shown

Figure 6.5 **To Catch Up, the Poorer Countries Have to Grow Faster**

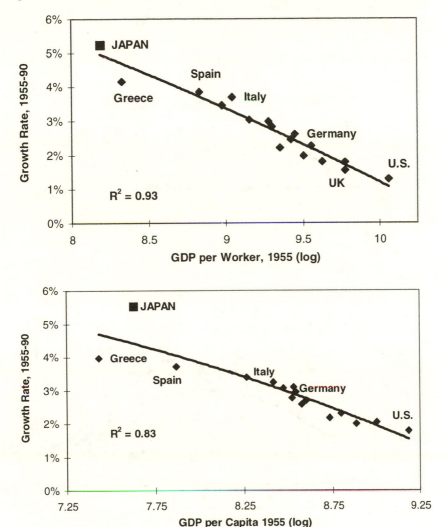

Source: Summers and Heston (1995)

Note: These two charts include 19 populous countries in the OECD. Japan does better on the per capita chart than the per worker chart. The reason is that, during this era, its labor force was growing faster than its total population. Taking the entire 1955-90 era amalgamates the above-par 1955-73 and below-par 1973-90 performance. This gives Japan an average performance on the GDP per worker chart. $R^2 = 0.93$ in the top panel means that 93 percent of the variation in the growth rates can be explained just by differences in the intitial GDP.

Figure 6.6 **The "Arc of Catch-Up" Growth**

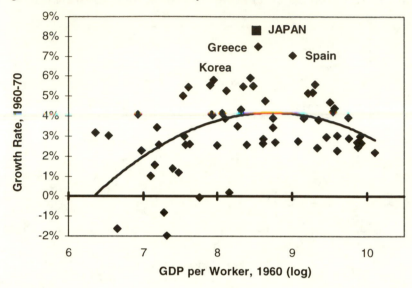

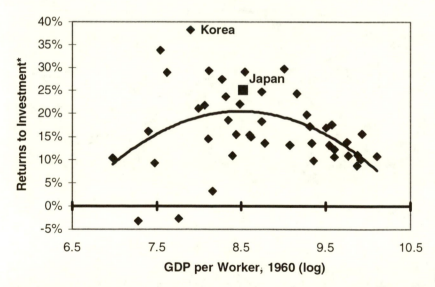

Source: Summers and Heston (1995)

Note: The top panel plots growth rates among 63 advanced and developing countries with populations of at least 4 million. The bottom panel plots the "growth return" to capital among a subset of 45 of these countries. A rough estimate of the growth return to capital was calculated by dividing the growth rate by the investment:GDP ratio (see endnote 39 for an explanation). Japan grew quickly because its investment was high (Figure 4.8) and its returns to investment were high.

in Figure 4.8; the arcing pattern of returns to investment is shown in the bottom panel of Figure 6.6.)[41]

In very poor countries, most people are too close to subsistence to save, i.e., to postpone consumption; these countries invest no more than a small share of their national income. So, the economy grows slowly. Moreover, returns to investment tend to be low as well, due to lack of education, poor financial institutions, undeveloped management skills, and so forth.

As countries get a bit richer, they can invest a larger share of their national income. Moreover, once investment hits a critical mass, countries can temporarily enjoy *increasing* returns from that investment. Give a farmer a tractor and his output will rise. Combine the tractor with irrigation, chemicals, modern storage, and so forth, and his output will really zoom. The combination of these different elements has a synergistic effect—the whole is greater than the sum of the parts. Moreover, because educational levels are higher than in poorer countries, these middle income countries import more advanced technology. As management skills improve, the capital is used more efficiently. As financial institutions improve, capital is allocated to better uses.

Soon, a virtuous cycle ensues. As growth accelerates, these countries can invest at still higher rates, which yields an ever faster increase in GDP per worker, leading to still higher investment rates. It is this virtuous cycle between growth and investment that produces the explosive growth "takeoff" among Newly Industrializing Countries. So, NICs grow fast for two reasons: higher investment rates and high returns from that investment.

Finally, as countries mature, they inevitably face diminishing returns to their investment (the tenth tractor doesn't boost output as much as the first one). In response, investment rates slow down. So, growth in rich countries is slower than in NICs due to both lower investment rates and lower returns from that investment. Japan, as we saw in Chapter 4, tried to make up for its low returns by keeping investment rates high.

This whole process is intimately bound up with the process of industrialization, for reasons we will explain below. The fastest growing countries are neither the poor, not-yet-industrialized countries, nor the rich, already-industrialized countries. The fastest growers are the countries in transition. Indeed, the faster growth is produced *by* the transition. It is the process of industrialization that produces the higher returns to investment. Typically, as manufacturing moves from about 10 percent of GDP to 25 percent, growth accelerates (Figure 6.7).

Figure 6.7 **Industrializing Countries Have the Fastest Growth**

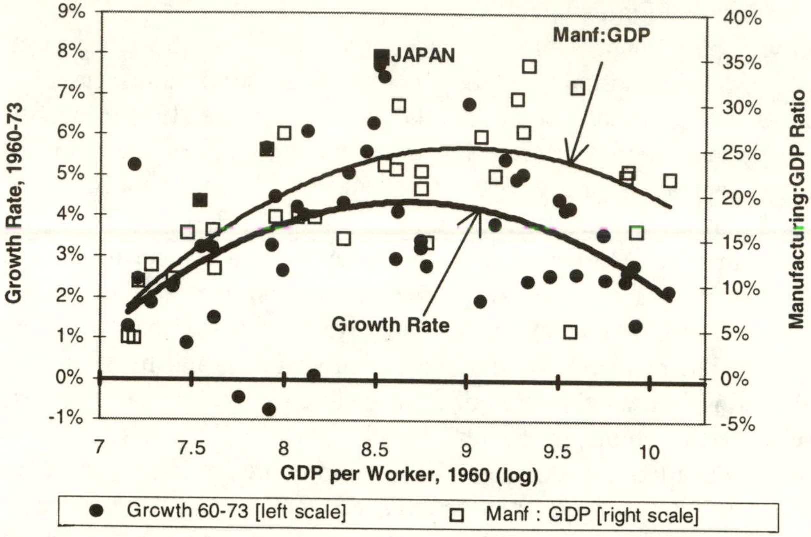

Source: Summers and Heston (1995); World Bank (1995)
Note: The chart plots a country's growth rate and its manufacturing:GDP ratio against its level of GDP per worker in 1960. The block labeled Japan shows Japan's growth rate during 1960-73.

Japan traversed the same "arc of catch-up" as other countries. Japan's highest growth—8–10 percent a year—came during its era of industrial takeoff. During that era, manufacturing more than doubled its role in the economy, going from 11 percent of GDP to a peak of 27 percent (Figure 6.8). Conversely, agriculture fell from 17 percent of GDP to 5 percent.[42] Farm labor plummeted from 45 percent of the labor force in 1950 to 13 percent by 1975. Meanwhile, workers in the secondary sector (manufacturing, construction, utilities) went from 29 percent of the labor force to 42 percent.[43]

Equally dramatic was the "reversal of fortune" within manufacturing. The land once famed for its "dollar blouses" and easily broken toys metamorphosed into the country that supplied the world with high-quality steel, ships, autos, and TVs. In 1950, textiles comprised almost a quarter of Japan's entire manufacturing output and about half of its exports. By 1975, the role of textiles was tiny. Machinery, a minor player in 1950, zoomed to the top. By 1975, machinery comprised a third of Japan's manufacturing output and well over half of its exports (refer to Figure 6.3).[44]

Figure 6.8 **Japan's High Growth Came During Industrial Takeoff**

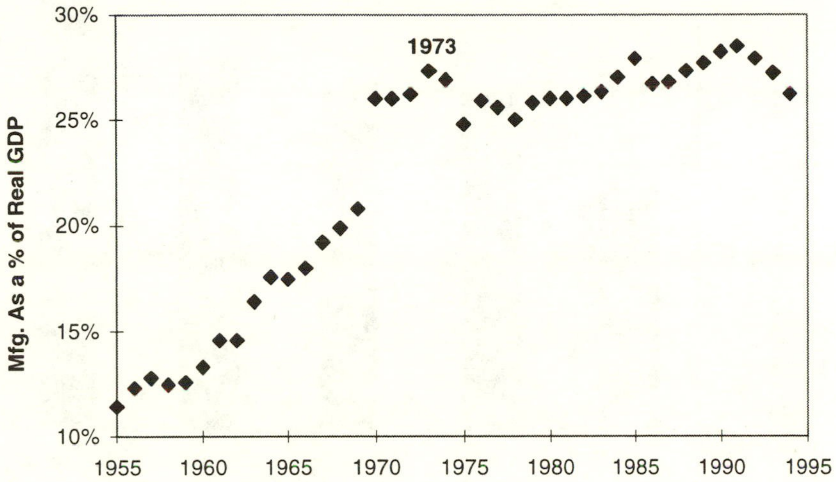

Source: Summers and Heston (1995), EPA (1996)

Many other countries have trod a similar path, but none as explosively as Japan. In only 15 years, from 1955 to 1970, Japan nearly tripled its GDP per worker from $3,600 to $11,500. In a blink of an eye, it went from a rural country at the income level of 1990 India to a burgeoning industrial powerhouse nearly at the level of 1990 Korea. No other country has accomplished this all-important task in such a short time, including the Asian NICs (Figure 6.9).

In the final analysis, Japan had its temporary burst of super-growth because its "developmentalist" industrial policy accelerated the "arc of catch-up." Japan temporarily grew faster than others because it industrialized faster.

Japan's super-growth could not last. Of the 9.5 percent annual GDP growth that Japan achieved during the 1960s, a full two-thirds (6.3 percent) was due solely to the extra growth provided by the catch-up transition.[45] Just as growth slowed in every other country as it matured, so it slowed in Japan as well.

But Japan's growth did not have to slow as much as it did. That was due to poor policy, not maturation. The man who races the mile in less time than anyone else may not go on to win the marathon—and he certainly won't do so by using the tactics of a miler.

Figure 6.9 **Japan Takes Fewer Years to Industrialize Than Others**

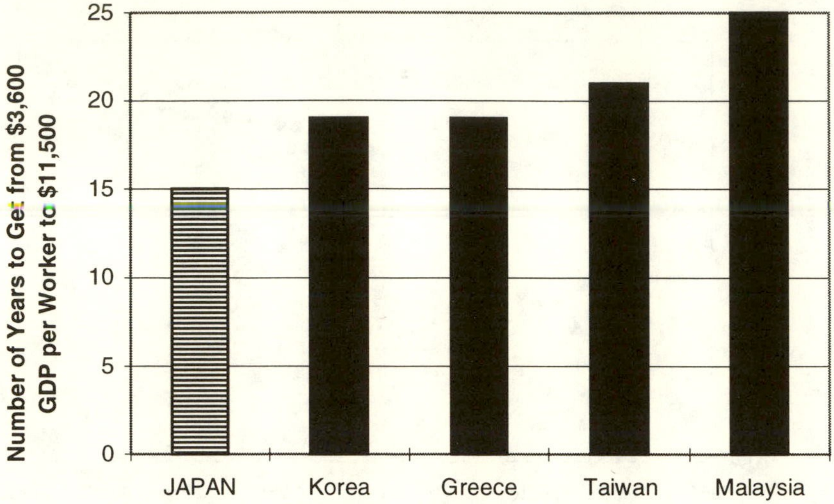

Source: Summers and Heston (1995)

Why Japan Grew So Fast during Industrial Takeoff

Saying that Japan accelerated the industrial takeoff just begs the question. How did it do so? The answer is policies that accelerated productivity growth.

When it comes to growth in living standards, productivity is the name of the game. The only way each person can consume more is if each worker produces more. In all countries, the catch-up process itself entails an inherent leap in productivity, as economies shift from low-productivity farming and textiles to higher-productivity manufacturing, and as they make farming and textiles more productive. In Japan this natural benefit was amplified by conscious policy measures.

To see how, we need to look in more detail at the sources of Japanese growth. In Japan, as in every country, there are three sources of GDP growth: more labor, more capital and finally more productivity—not just labor productivity, but what is known as Total Factor Productivity, i.e., more output for each unit of labor plus capital. In Japan, GDP grew 8 percent in the 1950s and 9 percent in the 1960s (Table 6.3); less than half of the growth came from adding more inputs of capital and labor. The majority—57 percent in the 1950s and 53 percent in the 1960s—came from growth in Total Factor Productivity.

Most people are more familiar with the concept of labor productivity,

135

Table 6.3

The Sources of Japan's High Growth

	Growth Rate		Share of Total Growth	
	1953–61	1961–71	1953–61	1961–71
Growth rate per year	8.1%	9.3%	100%	100%
Caused by additional inputs	3.5%	4.4%	43%	47%
Growth of labor inputs*	(1.9%)	(1.8%)	(23%)	(19%)
Growth of capital inputs	(1.6%)	(2.6%)	(20%)	(28%)
Caused by greater output per unit of input (Total factor productivity)	4.6%	4.9%	57%	53%
Growth in labor productivity (GDP per manhour)	6.2%	7.5%	100%	100%
Due to increased capital-labor ratio	1.6%	2.6%	26%	34%
Due to increased total factor productivity	4.6%	4.9%	74%	66%
Increased Total Factor Productivity	4.6%	4.9%	100%	100%
Economies of scale	1.9%	2.0%	41%	40%
Within sectors	(1.0%)	(1.1%)	(21%)	(23%)
Structural shift	(0.9%)	(0.8%)	(20%)	(17%)
Moving labor from farm to factory**	1.1%	0.8%	23%	16%
Advances in technology	1.4%	2.4%	31%	49%
Increased education*	0.3%	0.4%	7%	7%

Source: Denison and Chung (1976), p. 94

Notes: *Increased education is considered part of Labor Inputs. **This includes moving labor from farming and traditional self-employment into the modern business sector.

i.e., growth in output per worker (or per manhour). And that is very important. By achieving astronomical increases in labor productivity of 6.2 percent in the 1950s and 7.5 percent in the 1960s, Japan was able to *quadruple* living standards in less than two decades.

There are only two ways to gain such extraordinary leaps in labor productivity.

One is to give each worker more tools, i.e., increase the capital–labor ratio. This, however, has two drawbacks. The first is that the more a country has to invest to boost output, the less it has left over for consumption. The second is that the benefits don't last forever. Due to diminishing returns, it gets harder and harder to sustain growth through investment alone.

The second method is getting more bang for the buck from both labor and capital, i.e., Total Factor Productivity (TFP).

Now, its certainly true that Japan invested a lot. But high savings did not define Japan as a miracle; high productivity growth did. During the high-growth era, only a quarter to a third of Japan's improved living standards came from giving each worker more tools. The lion's share—74 percent in the 1950s and 66 percent in the 1960s—came from growth in TFP.

To a certain degree, relatively high TFP is part of the catch-up process. But Japan's TFP record in its high-growth era is unmatched by any other country at a similar stage of development, including the Asian NICs. By contrast, after 1973, TFP growth shrunk precipitously—much more so than occurs in most countries with the end of catch-up. And that is the ultimate reason why the miracle ended (Figure 6.10).[46]

If increases in TFP gave Japan's high-growth era its high growth, what caused the high TFP growth? The key elements were: economies of scale, a structural shift to higher-productivity industries, importing technology, increasing farm productivity, and high rates of investment. Let's look at each of these.

Economies of Scale

Economies of scale was the single largest contributor to TFP growth. It's the closest thing economics provides to a free lunch. Double your inputs and you more than double your output. Economies of scale were particularly prevalent in the newer manufacturing industries. At the plant level, in big capital-intensive industries like steel and autos, factories need to reach a certain size to be efficient. At the firm level, the "learning

Figure 6.10 **Productivity: Superb in Catch-Up Era, Then Poor**

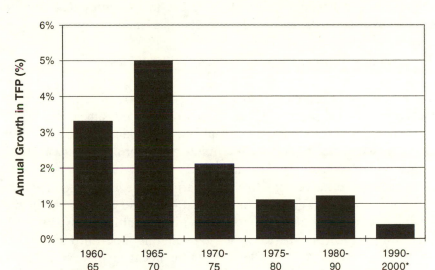

Source: For 1960-80, Dale Jorgenson and Masahiro Kuroda. For 1980-2000, Japan Center for Economic Research. Both are cited in Okubo (1996), pg. 36.
Note: TFP = Total Factor Productivity (output per unit of labor plus capital). *1990-2000 is a projection.

curve" means that companies become better as they gain more experience. At the industry level, a market that is big enough to support several competing firms creates the competitive pressure cooker that forces firms to keep on improving their efficiency. Larger industry size also allows greater specialization and it attracts high-grade suppliers and inventors. The founder of modern neoclassical economics, Alfred Marshall (Keynes' teacher at Cambridge University), was famous for pointing out the importance of industry-level economies of scale, using the term "external economies."

Economies of scale supplied 40 percent of the entire increase in TFP in the 1950s and 35 percent in the 1960s. Indeed during 1953–61, economies of scale were even more important than capital investment for Japan's total GDP growth (1.9 percent for economies of scale versus 1.6 percent for investment).

Even without industrial policy, Japan would have enjoyed some economies of scale as did other countries in their catch-up era. In Germany, France and Italy, economies of scale added 1 to 1.5 percent per year in GDP growth. As the economy matures, economies of scale diminish and so in the U.S. economies of scale added only 0.4 percent a year to growth during the 1960s. However, as we saw in the case of autos, steel and shipbuilding, deliberately shifting resources to industries that enjoyed economies of scale was a major facet of Japanese industrial policy.

The Structural Shift to Higher-Productivity Industries

The essence of industrial development is the shift of labor from farm to factory and, within manufacturing, from textiles to machinery. Since, for most countries at the point of industrial takeoff, productivity in manufacturing is about twice as high as in farming, every farmer who switches to the factory immediately doubles his output per hour.

In Japan, the movement from the farm to the factory alone supplied a quarter of TFP growth in the 1950s and 15 percent in the 1960s, not counting any of the shifts within manufacturing. Overall, according to growth expert Dale Jorgenson, only one-third of Japan's productivity hikes during 1960–79 came because makers of toys, textiles, steel and cars became more efficient at what they were doing. Two-thirds came from shifting capital, labor and output from the farm to the factory, and within manufacturing, from sectors like textiles to industries like machinery.[47]

Moreover, half of the growth from economies of scale arose due to shifts from industries with smaller scale economies to industries with greater scale economies (Table 6.3).

While such shifts in industrial structure are inherent in the catch-up process, consciously accelerating these normal shifts was the whole point of Japan's industrial structure policy, as we saw in the case of the effort to change Japan's export mix. Indeed, there is even an Industrial Structure Division within MITI whose sole purpose is to focus on this kind of issue (Figure 6.11).

These kinds of results, and MITI's role in them, have unfortunately led to misinterpretations about "good industries" vs. "bad industries" and to suggestions that America could improve its competitiveness by promoting the high value-added, high-tech industries. The fact is, most of the huge discrepancies in productivity among sectors are an artifact of the early stages of industrialization. As economies develop, these productivity gaps lessen and the pace of structural shift slows. Once countries industrialize, even the productivity gap between farming and manufacturing eventually disappears as farming goes high-tech. Indeed, one of the clues to Japan's problems is that, as late as 1987, the productivity gap

Figure 6.11 **Rapid Structural Change Is the Hallmark of Catch-up**

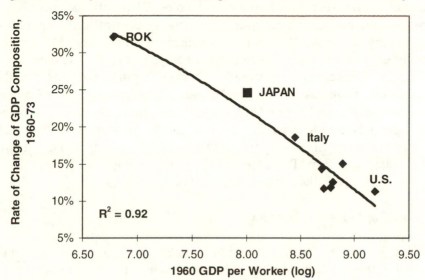

Source: Summers and Heston (1995); Saxonhouse (1988), pg. 227-229

Note: This chart shows that the speed with which the composition of a country's GDP changes, e.g. the shift from farm to factory or from textiles to machinery, is fastest in middle-income countries. $R^2 = 0.92$ means 92 percent of the variation of the pace of structural change can be explained by a country's position in the catch-up process.

between manufacturing and the protected farming sector had actually widened instead of shrinking.[48]

Importing Technology

Advances in technology are one of the most important "advantages of backwardness" for a country in the catch-up era. In building a steel plant, a late industrializer can import technology and build the most modern kind of plant. It doesn't have to settle for the technology that the leaders had when they were at the same stage of development. And so it is not surprising that, whereas advances in technology added 2 percent a year to Japan's growth during the 1950s and 1960s, they only helped U.S. growth half as much.[49] Advances in technology contributed a third of all TFP growth in the 1950s and half in the 1960s.

Once again, industrial policies aimed at insuring that Japan would gain as much as possible from imported technology. Up until the late 1960s, and in some industries even later, MITI strictly controlled the import of technology under the 1949 Foreign Exchange Control Law. MITI commonly used this power to force foreign companies to license their technology to Japanese companies rather than selling their products directly themselves. Given Japan's import barriers at the time, as well as its severe restrictions on Foreign Direct Investment, for many foreign companies, the only way to reach the Japanese market was by either licensing the technology outright to a Japanese firm, or else forming a joint venture with a Japanese firm. Thus, the transfer of technology to Japanese firms was far greater than would have occurred in a free market.[50]

Increasing Farm Productivity

Although promoting farm productivity is not singled out in Table 6.3, it is probably the single most powerful step a country can take to accelerate industrialization. Indeed, it may be indispensable. Higher farm productivity frees up farm labor to move to the factory. At the same time, lower food prices free up consumer spending for purchases of industrial output. The World Bank's *East Asia Miracle* report rightly points out:

> Across developing regions, agriculture's share of output and employment has declined the most and fastest where agricultural output and productivity have grown the most.[51]

After leaping 10 percent in 1954 and an astounding 20 percent in 1955, Japanese labor productivity in farming rose 4 percent a year throughout the late 1960s. TFP grew 3.2 percent a year in 1956–60 and 2.5 percent in 1960–70. This growth was due in part to the postwar land reform and in part to government programs that subsidized the use of fertilizer and mechanization.[52]

But by 1970, government farm policy had been reduced to a pure boondoggle, aimed at supporting high farm prices in order to garner farm votes for the LDP, particularly the Tanaka faction. Whereas farm prices had been falling relative to the industrial prices in the 1950s and 1960s, from that time onward, they increased rapidly. And, not surprisingly, TFP in agriculture fell to virtually zero in the 1970s. This was one of the worst aspects of the post-1973 dual economy.[53]

What About Japan's High Savings and Investment?

By focusing on TFP growth, we don't mean to diminish in any way the critical role of investment. Indeed, most of the TFP growth could not have occurred without heavy investment. About 80 percent of technology is "embodied" in capital goods. And surely neither economies of scale nor shifts in industrial structure could have occurred without investment in the new industries.

But to say that Japan succeeded because it saved and invested a great deal begs the question. Why were Japan's savings and investment so high? The Japanese people are no more "natural savers" than anyone else. Prior to World War II and up through the early 1950s, Japan's household savings rates, at about 7–9 percent of income, were not especially high by international standards. The rates did rise in the late 1950s and 1960s, going from 12 percent in 1955 to 20 percent by 1973. This was the product of a number of practices that induced greater savings, from tax-free savings accounts to the twice-yearly corporate bonus. As the share of income paid in twice-yearly big bonuses rose from 12 percent of income in 1958 to 20 percent in 1974, savings rates rose in tandem. As the share of income paid in bonuses peaked and retreated, so did savings rates.[54]

However, because household income actually declined *as a share of GDP* during industrialization, household savings did *not* rise relative to GDP. Virtually all of the increase in Japan's gross savings rate came from business savings rather households. As Japan developed, corporate cash flow took a greater and greater share of national income while increasingly smaller portions went to labor and farmers. And so, much of the nation's legendary savings sprang from the profits of companies, not the frugality of families (Figure 6.12).

Accelerating the Industrial Takeoff: Exports Lead the Way

If Japan's rapid industrialization was responsible for its high growth during the "arc of catch-up," then its export drive was in turn indispensable to the rapid industrialization. This occurred not only because exports paid for indispensable imports. Beyond that, exports were crucial to the shift from farm to factory. At the most basic level, exports provided an unbelievably large share of the growth in virtually all the key industries that

Figure 6.12 **Profits Take Greater Share of Income, Supply Savings**

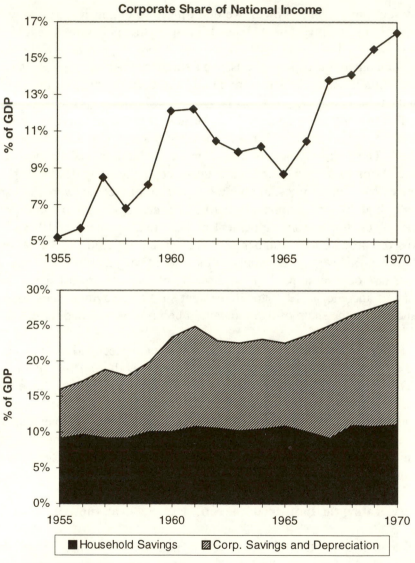

Source: EPA (1995a) NIPA Tables, in current yen

Figure 6.13 **Almost All Ships Are Exported**

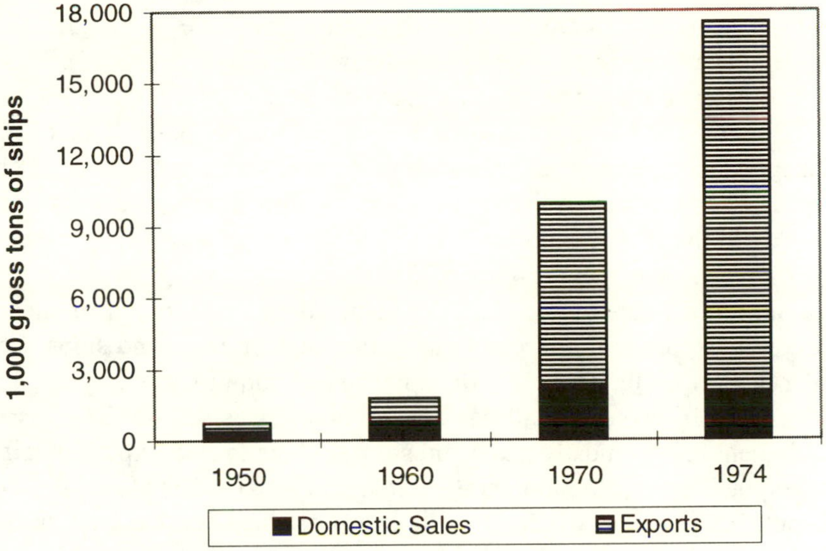

Source: Tsuru (1993), pg. 84

propelled Japan's industrial takeoff. If not for exports, industrialization would have proceeded much more slowly.

Exports: The Demand Driver for Manufacturing

Let's start off by considering three of the classic export industries of Japan's heavy industry: ships, steel and autos. In 1975, these three items alone accounted for a third of Japan's industrial output and 40 percent of Japan's exports, up from 11 percent in 1950.[55]

With all the talk of VCRs and computer chips, it's easy to forget how recently it was that shipbuilding was a major stimulus to Japan's economy, including its role as a big market for steel and machine tools. As late as 1975, Japan exported as much in ships as in cars, with each accounting for about 11 percent of total exports. As early as 1955, shipbuilding depended on exports for a bit more than half of sales. By the 1970s, almost every ship built was exported (Figure 6.13).

Then there's cars. In 1960, as the industry was being nurtured in the protected domestic market, only 4 percent of its output was exported. By 1965, exports were up to 15 percent and by 1980 the majority (56 percent) of total output was exported. Without exports, the industry would have grown to only half its actual size. From 1965 to 1970, exports provided 42 percent of all growth in Japanese car output; from 1970 to 1980, almost all (83 percent) of the growth. If not for exports, the industry would have virtually stopped growing after 1970 (Figure 6.14).[56]

The case of steel, the final member of the early Big Three, is even more interesting because it shows the importance of "positive feedback" linkages among industries. As with autos and ships, with each passing decade, the industry relied upon exports more and more to achieve growth. In the 1960s, exports provided 24 percent of growth; by the early 1970s, it was 60 percent (Figure 6.15).

But these figures understate the reality because so much of Japan's steel was exported, not directly but in the form of autos and ships. Consider this: in 1970, 20 percent of Japan's steel output was exported. That same year, 16 percent of all basic metal output was sent to the transport equipment sector (mostly autos and ships), which in turn exported half of its output. That means, another 8 percent (.50 × .16 = .08) of Japan's steel output that year was exported in the form of ships and cars, an amount equal to half as much as direct exports.[57]

As Japan moved from the age of heavy industry into the electronics age, the same pattern persisted: export-led growth.

As of 1980, the heavily promoted machine tool industry exported 30 percent of its output, much of which was numerically controlled tools.

In a marvel of synergy, television and semiconductors—both promoted by a combination of protection, subsidies and government-authorized export cartels—helped each other grow. TVs provided the crucial initial demand and testing ground for Japan's semiconductor output while solid-state circuitry, in turn, helped Japanese TV makers beat out the U.S. competition, which was slow to move to the new technology.

In both industries, export growth was crucial to growth, with 75 percent of Japanese TV output being exported by 1980 (Figure 6.16). As for semiconductors, by the mid-1990s, Japan was exporting almost as many computer chips as cars.[58]

The indispensability of exports to Japan's industrial takeoff can be easily seen by dividing Japanese manufacturing into two groups: growth and non-growth sectors. Machinery, chemicals, and metals are the growth sectors, while all the rest are in the non-growth category. As we consider, it becomes evident that only a few sectors accounted for the lion's share of Japan's manufacturing growth and that these were the sectors whose own growth was driven by exports.

Figure 6.14 **Exports Provide Brunt of Car Growth after 1965**

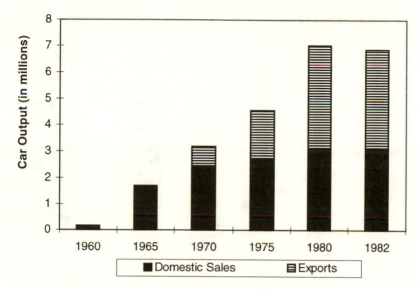

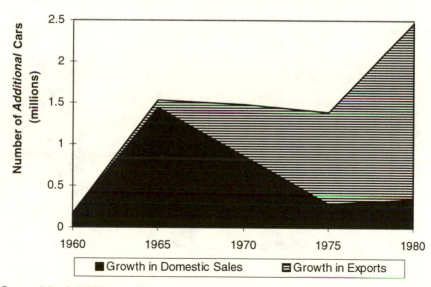

Source: Mutoh (1988), pg. 319

Figure 6.15 **Exports Drive Steel Growth**

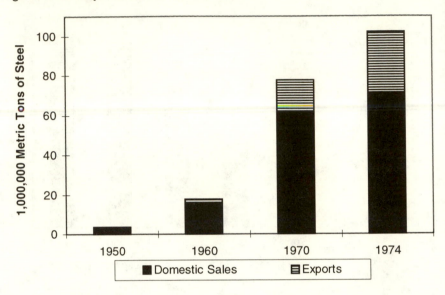

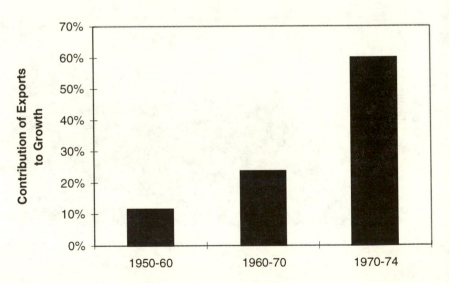

Source: Tsuru (1993), pg. 83

Figure 6.16 **Exports Lead TV Output**

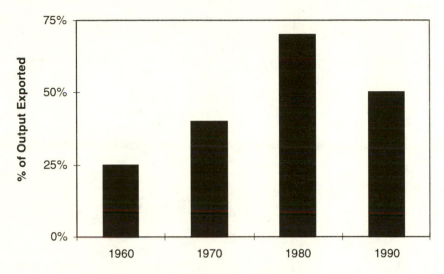

Source: Yamamura and Vandenberg (1986); Katz (1994a)

In Table 6.4a, we can see a rapid "reversal of fortune" between the growth and non-growth sectors. The three growth sectors steadily rose from 39 percent of manufacturing output in 1955 to 60 percent in 1970 to 75 percent by 1987. Machinery alone rose from 11 percent in 1955 to 41 percent in 1987.

During the 1956–70 industrial takeoff, the three growth sectors provided 66 percent of all manufacturing growth. This figure rose to an astonishing 92 percent in 1970–87 (Table 6.4b).

What is equally striking is that the growth sectors are the ones that increasingly depend on exports for their own growth. Exports rose from 8 percent of output in 1955 to 11 percent by 1970 and 18 percent by 1987. By contrast, in the non-growth grouping, exports virtually disappeared.

All of this is illustrated in Figure 6.17, where the sectors making the strongest contribution to overall industrial growth are sectors like machinery and chemicals whose own growth is being accelerated by exports. (An increase in the export–output ratio means exports grew faster than domestic demand and hence caused overall sales to rise faster than they would have done without exports.)

For example, in 1956–70, machinery and chemicals both showed a 4 percent increase in export-dependence and, together, they accounted for just about half of Japan's entire manufacturing growth during that period.

Table 6.4a

Exporting Industries Are the Growth Industries

	1955 Share of Mfg.	1955 Export: Output Ratio	1970 Share of Mfg.	1970 Export: Output ratio	1987 Share of Mfg.	1987 Export: Output Ratio
Machinery	11%	9%	24%	13%	41%	24%
Chemicals	16%	5%	19%	9%	21%	10%
Metals and metal prod.	12%	9%	18%	8%	14%	7%
Foods	22%	1%	15%	2%	10%	1%
Textiles	13%	18%	8%	13%	4%	11%
Others	26%	8%	17%	5%	11%	3%
All manufacturing		8%		9%		12%
Growth industries	39%	8%	60%	11%	75%	18%
Non-growth industries	61%	7%	40%	5%	25%	3%

Table 6.4b

Exporting Industries Propel Overall Industrial Growth

	1956–70 Change in Export Ratio	1956–70 Contribution to Growth	1956–70 Growth Rate	1970–87 Change in Export Ratio	1970–87 Contribution to Growth	1970–87 Growth Rate
Machinery	4%	27%	19%	10%	60%	7%
Chemicals	4%	20%	13%	0%	23%	4%
Metals and products	–1%	20%	15%	–1%	9%	2%
Foods	0%	12%	8%	–1%	5%	2%
Textiles	–5%	6%	8%	–2%	0%	–1%
Others	–3%	15%		–2%	3%	
All manufacturing	1%		12%	3%		4%
Growth industries	3%	66%	16%	7%	92%	5%
Non-growth Industries	–2%	34%	8%	–2%	8%	1%

Source: Minami (1994), pp. 99–100; EPA (1995a)

Note: Growth sectors are: Machinery, Chemicals, Metals. Manufacturing shares are based on constant value. Non-growth are all the rest. Machinery includes non-electrical and electrical machinery, transport equipment, and precision instruments. The Export-Output Ratio is based on gross output, not value-added, in current value.

Figure 6.17 **Manufacturing Growth Is Led by Exporting Industries**

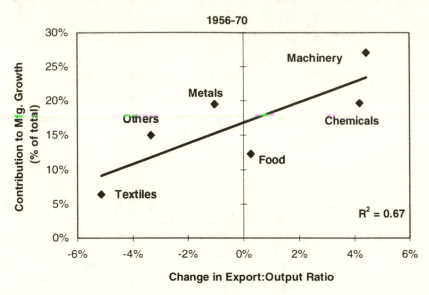

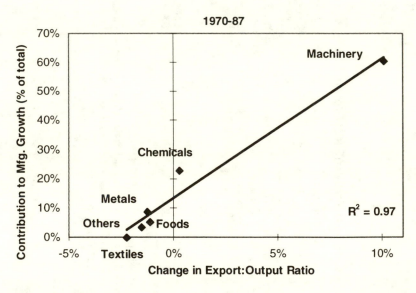

Source: See Table 6.4

Note: The sectors with the greatest increase in export:output ratios make the biggest contribution to overall industrial growth. R^2 = 0.67 in the top panel means that 67 percent of the variation in a sector's contribution to manufacturing growth can be explained by its export performance.

Metals might seem to be an exception since that industry made a big contribution to growth even though its export-dependence declined. However, as we explained above, as the auto and ship industries grew, much of steel's output was diverted to indirect, rather than direct, exports in the form of cars, ships, and other machinery.

In the low-growth period, the skewing of growth toward the exporting sectors was even more pronounced. Machinery, the one sector to increase its export-dependence, provided 60 percent of all manufacturing growth. By this time, however, as we will detail in the next chapter, this dependence on exports had become excessive and unhealthy. Exports were no longer accelerating domestic growth, but substituting for it.[59]

Exports, the Structural Shift and Growth in TFP

If the secret of Japan's high growth in the catch-up era was growth in Total Factor Productivity (TFP), then exporting industries were key to high TFP growth.

For one thing, the rapidly growing export industries were usually the most modern industries, with better productivity performance and greater economies of scale. According to economist Tuvia Blumenthal, "the rate of technological increase of exports [in Japan] is above that of domestic production by 25 percent in 1960 and 30 percent in 1965." And so every worker who shifted into modern export industries automatically raised his productivity.[60]

Beyond that, the force of economies of scale gave exports incredible leverage in turbo-charging Japan's structural shift.

As we noted on page 138, two-thirds of Japan's TFP growth came, not from improvements within each sector, but from the shift from low-productivity sectors to higher-productivity sectors. In Japan, this shift was incredibly explosive. In 1971, some 33 percent of Japan's exports consisted of products that had not been exported ten years earlier; 40 percent of all industrial output consisted of products—from color TVs to petrochemicals to air conditioners—that didn't even *exist* in the Japanese market in 1951. In 1969, 10 percent of output consisted of products that hadn't even been *invented* five years earlier.[61]

Economies of scale created enormous leverage. Due to economies of scale, anything that raised sectoral output—be it exports or domestic output—raised productivity, and thereby lowered costs. Lower prices, in turn, stimulated even more demand and thus even greater economies of scale. The forces of supply (economies of scale) and demand (price and income

Table 6.5

Exports and Domestic Growth Reinforce Each Other

1955–64 Rate of Increase in:

Industry Groups Ranked According to Export Growth	Exports	Domestic Demand	Investment	Capital Share	Labor Productivity
Group 1	1%	10%	15%	–0.7%	8.0%
Group 2	9%	14%	18%	–0.7%	8.6%
Group 3	16%	13%	25%	0.5%	9.8%
Group 4	23%	18%	26%	3.3%	10.8%
Group 5	44%	24%	31%	1.0%	10.4%

Correlation of Growth in:	Exports	Domestic Demand	Investment	Capital Share	Labor Productivity
Exports	1.00				
Domestic demand	0.97	1.00			
Investment	0.95	0.88	1.00		
Capital share	0.54	0.55	0.66	1.00	
Labor productivity	0.81	0.77	0.92	0.89	1.00

Source: Kanamori (1968), p. 318, 322
Note: The bottom panel shows an almost perfect (97%) correlation between the industries growing quickly on the basis of exports and those growing due to domestic sales. Capital share is the portion of the industry's value-added that goes to profits instead of wages.

elasticities) reinforced each other in an explosive virtuous spiral upward.

Under these conditions, growth from exports stimulated domestic growth and vice versa. Not surprisingly, then, the industries growing fastest through exports were also the ones enjoying the fastest growth in domestic sales, investment, labor productivity and profits (Table 6.5).

The role of exports in accelerating the upgrading of the domestic industrial structure is by no means unique to Japan. It is the norm. Countries with the most rapid shifts in their export mix usually have the most rapid structural change at home (Figure 6.18). The distinctive thing about Japan is the extent to which accelerating this natural transformation process was consciously integrated into industrial policy.

A lot of ink has been wasted in a debate over whether Japan's high growth was export-led or led by domestic demand. This is a false dichotomy. Under conditions of economies of scale, exports and domestic demand are partners, not alternatives. Anything that speeds up the change in the export mix will speed up changes in the domestic industrial structure, and vice versa. Economist Hisao Kanamori put it this way:

The causes of [Japan's] export increase—increased competitive strength and a change in commodity composition—were made possible by domestic factors, such as increased domestic investment and an enlarged home market . . . and increased labor productivity. Productivity increase, in turn, is closely related to an increase in the scale of output, presumably because a manufacturing industry whose production scale is rapidly expanding adopts new techniques and methods with higher productivity. . . .

Once the expansion of domestic demand and investment begins to promote exports, a kind of circular action begins. *An industry whose market was enlarged through growing exports attracts more investment and thus strengthens its competitive position.* . . . [T]here is a general tendency that, in industries with growing exports, both capital shares and productivity increased rapidly. This indicates that these industries enjoyed a favorable circle; they attracted new capital, which raised productivity and led to further growth in exports [emphasis added].[62]

Profitable exports helped make Japan's overall investment rates very high. For high investment rates, not only high savings, but attractive

Figure 6.18 **Shift in Exports Leads to Shift in Domestic GDP**

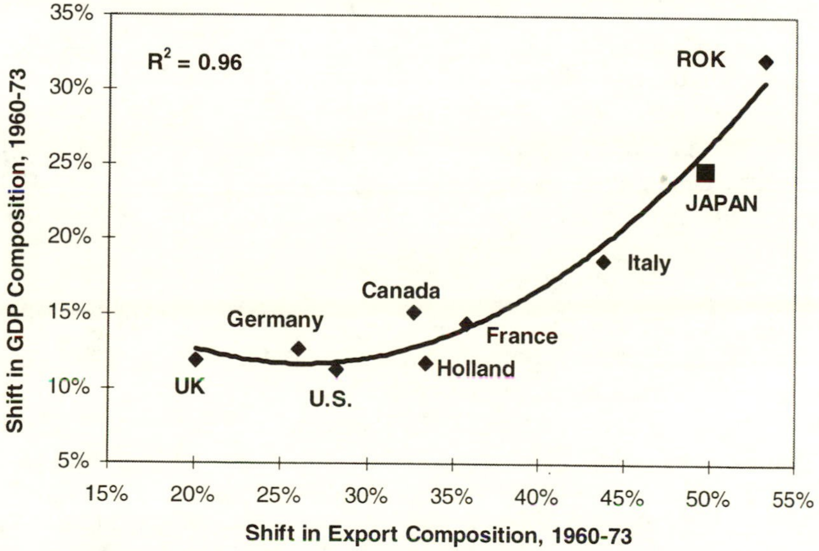

Source: Raw data from Saxonhouse (1988), pg. 227-229

Note: R^2 = 0.96 means that 96 percent of the difference in how fast countries change their domestic structure can be explained by how fast they change their export mix. Even if one adjusts for "catch-up," an econometric regression shows that a shift in exports still hastens the domestic transformation.

investment outlets are required. The high rates of return in the exporting sectors (Table 6.5) helped on both sides: it made investment very attractive and it gave the corporations the cash flow to plow back into new plants and equipment. Dollar and Wolff note:

> There is no cultural basis for the high savings rate of Japan or Korea. . . . It is more likely the pull of expected gains in technology and productivity rather than a large push of available savings that is at the heart of their rapid capital accumulation.[63]

Subsidies and Protection: The Foundation for Export Promotion

And now we can see what a crucial role industrial policy played in Japan's export-led catch-up. When Japan's future export stars were infants, the gap between Japanese production costs and world prices was so high that a *temporary* dose of subsidies and import protection was needed to help close the gap. Industrial policy gave these future exporters the indispensable breathing space they needed for takeoff.

For some industries, subsidies were huge. For example, to encourage purchases of domestic machine tools in the early 1950s, buyers were subsidized to the tune of *half* of the entire purchase price.[64]

Target industries were also awarded huge tax breaks, particularly for exports. These included deductions on export earnings from 1953 to 1963, and accelerated depreciation allowances for exports during 1964–71. For some key exporting industries, like steel, the subsidy was huge, in some years in the 1950s amounting to as much as 25 percent of profits.[65]

Financing was critical. As we have seen, many of these industries received government loans in their takeoff period. Gradually, private lending became much more important than government loans, but the government often subsidized private borrowing, particularly for exports. For example, the Bank of Japan (BOJ) "discounted" export-related paper for banks at rates 1–2 percent below normal market rates; these below-market loans provided *half* of all export-related bank lending from 1946 all the way to 1972. On the whole, on private borrowing, large-scale modern industries usually paid interest rates of 8–10 percent, far below the normal market level, which was 12–15 percent in those capital-scarce early days.[66]

While these subsidies were helpful, the initial gap between Japanese and world prices was so huge that subsidies alone could not do the trick.

These future exporters had to be protected from world competition until they could grow bigger on the basis of domestic demand.

It is hard to remember now, since it was so long ago. But, for nearly 20 years from the end of World War II until the mid-1960s, there simply was no free market in imports. Rather, under the Occupation and then under the 1949 Foreign Exchange Law promoted by the U.S. Occupation authorities, anyone wanting to import anything had to receive an allocation of then-scarce foreign exchange from the government. The original rationale was that Japan was chronically short of foreign exchange to buy vital food and raw materials. Eventually, the system became MITI's most powerful tool for influencing the private economy. Since Japan ran a chronic current account deficit until the mid-1960s, this was a true rationing system with teeth. Not until 1964, when Japan assumed so-called Article 8 status in the International Monetary Fund (IMF), did MITI lose this power.

It wasn't only goods that needed approval. Anything, from a technology license to a foreign direct investment, required approval. Suffice it to say that, once the Occupation ended in 1952, virtually no foreign firm was allowed to form a majority-owned subsidiary while MITI retained this power. They were pressured into forming joint ventures with Japanese companies or just licensing their technology outright.

The principles for allocating foreign exchange were simple and clear: protect future export industries from competition; make sure favored industries get the supplies they need; pressure foreign firms to license technology to Japanese companies; and don't let anyone "waste" scarce foreign exchange on unnecessary or competing consumer goods.[67]

To gain foreign exchange for vital raw materials, a firm often had to prove its worthiness due to its *export* performance.[68] If exporters were in an especially important industry, like shipbuilding, they could even get lucrative import licenses in unrelated areas, as a form of subsidy.

> Import licenses for such lucrative consumer goods as bananas, whiskey and crude sugar were given to the trading firms which had already met the export targets for ships, rolling-stock, and machine tools. The export of ships was particularly subsidized through this linking process.[69]

MITI's typical tactics are captured in the fascinating symbiosis in support for the sewing machine and machine tool industries. As was often the case, MITI aided an industry, not just because it was an important export earner on its own, but also because it was a critical customer or supplier for another priority exporter.

Sewing machines were a priority because they exported a third of their output as early as 1949, thereby bringing in valuable foreign exchange. But equally important, they were a major customer for an industry of the future: machine tools.

Tokyo not only blocked imports of sewing machines, but it would not allow Singer even to form a joint venture in Japan until 1958, and even then it limited Singer's output. Then it took a step that both lowered sewing machine prices and promoted machine tools in one fell swoop. As Shigeto Tsuru explains:

> Costs [of sewing machines] were declining very rapidly in those years; and one of the factors contributing to the productivity rise was the subsidy scheme introduced in 1951 by the government for importation of up-to-date machine tools. As much as *50 percent of their import price was paid by the government*; and, in addition, *domestic manufacturing of such machine tools in imitation* was in the initial stage subsidized again to the extent of *one half* of the cost. The purpose of this subsidy scheme was the promotion of the machine tool industry in general. However, since other industries using machine tools were not sufficiently developed at that time (such as domestic electric appliances) or were only in the burgeoning stage (such as automobiles), the main beneficiary was the sewing machine industry [emphasis added].[70]

By the mid-1960s, MITI's power to allocate foreign exchange ended. For one thing, MITI's allocation is a kind of rationing that can only take place in an environment of scarcity. By the late-1960s, when Japan turned into a chronic trade surplus country, such rationing was impossible.

Beyond that, international pressure forced MITI to end the system. After Japan joined GATT (The General Agreement on Tariffs and Trade) in 1955, it became clear it would eventually have to eliminate the outright quotas in order to adhere to GATT's free trade rules. The deadline for beginning the process was 1964, when Japan would have to adhere to so-called Article 8 status of the IMF. The quotas started to come down in the early 1960s, but Tokyo dragged out the process as long as possible. Many quotas, particularly in the electronics field, remained in existence until the mid-1970s. The removal of quotas came in successive waves: e.g., buses and trucks in 1961, color televisions in 1964, passenger cars in 1965, color film in 1971, calculators and cash registers in 1973, integrated circuits in 1974 and computers in 1975.[71]

In the place of quotas, Japan applied stiff tariffs. In fact, Japan's tariffs, which under the quota system had been unnecessary and therefore low, were systematically raised as quotas came off. They hit their peak in 1965.

Tariff rates escalated as one went from raw materials to consumer goods, with effective rates of protection (ERP) reaching as high as 36 percent for consumer goods as late as 1968. *As late as 1978*, the effective rate of protection for manufacturing was *as high as 22 percent.*[72]

Eventually, as export industries like autos, TVs and machine tools became more competitive and they exported ever-larger proportions of their output, overt protection became superfluous. So, it was reduced.

Had the liberalization process continued, then developmentalism would have served its purpose and been abandoned like the butterfly abandons the cocoon. Unfortunately, as we shall see, this did not happen.

Private "Structural Impediments" Replace Direct State Protection

The major reason liberalization didn't continue was that, while formal barriers went down, the power of private restraint of trade went up—with the encouragement, and sometimes at the instigation, of the government.

At first, MITI wanted to respond to the foreign challenge with heightened "state control." In 1963, it proposed a law called the Special Measures Law for the Promotion of Designated Industries. This law would have given MITI enlarged powers to guide, or sometimes direct, internal firm rationalization, mergers, intra-industry cooperation, bank lending and so forth. But industry and banking, the Finance Ministry and others all resisted MITI's grab for power. Despite approval by the Cabinet, the Diet refused to even vote on it.[73]

Industry "self-control," not state control, was going to take the lead. MITI acquiesced. Calling investment liberalization "the second coming of the Black Ships," MITI and the MOF actively strengthened *keiretsu* ties and industry collusion so they could replace quotas and tariffs as the shield of Japanese industry.[74]

To be sure, institutions like *keiretsu* and industry associations are deeply rooted in Japanese history. The Japanese corporate world has long been permeated by horizontal multi-industry conglomerates like Mitsui, Mitsubishi, Sumitomo and so forth. In addition, vertical production and distribution *keiretsu* unite companies like Toyota and Matsushita with their suppliers and distributors. In these arrangements, *keiretsu* brethren, customers, suppliers, banks, insurance companies and so forth not only buy each other's products. They also hold each other's shares to cement the relationships, and as "stable shareholders" refuse to sell.

In some cases, particularly the *vertical* production *keiretsu*, these ties have proven to be an authentic institutional innovation that, if not taken to extremes, can significantly improve productivity and quality control.[75]

However, in other cases, particularly in the *horizontal* conglomerate-type *keiretsu*, efficiency is sometimes sacrificed for security and stability. Profits of companies in the six big *keiretsu* are often smaller than in non-*keiretsu* counterparts. Why, then, do companies participate in them? One reason is that, in time of trouble, they can expect to be aided by their *keiretsu* bank or other *keiretsu* partner. Sumitomo kept Mazda afloat. Mitsui in 1997 went to the aid of a construction firm on the verge of bankruptcy. Lower profits are a kind of insurance premium.[76]

Because this "insurance" function is such a large part of *keiretsu*'s *raison d'être*, the *keiretsu* often act to keep up sales by excluding both Japanese and foreign newcomers from the market.

As investment and import liberalization loomed ever closer, the government encouraged the strengthening of both *keiretsu* and cross-shareholding as part of a deliberate effort to create a thicket too difficult for foreigners to penetrate. Indeed, these measures are known in MITI parlance as "liberalization countermeasures" as in MITI's Capital Transactions Liberalization Countermeasures Special Committee (Table 6.6).[77]

MITI encouraged Japanese companies to increase their cross-shareholding to such a high level that foreign buyouts would become unfeasible. MITI even changed Japan's Commerce Law so that corporate boards could issue new shares and place them directly with other corporations—without requiring the approval of shareholders who might object to the dilution of their ownership. Consequently, in Japan, the percentage of shares held by "stable shareholder" allies suddenly jumped from 42 percent in 1964 to 55 percent in 1968 and 62 percent by 1973. This made a foreign—or domestic—takeover virtually impossible.[78]

This effective anti-takeover device held down foreign investment to a negligible level even after all formal barriers had been removed. That's because, in most countries, up to 80 percent of foreign entry comes by buying up an existing company—and thereby immediately gaining all its staff, suppliers, customers, distributors, bankers and so forth, rather than starting from scratch. And since imports by foreign affiliates are a major route to exports by the parent, the low level of foreign direct investment (FDI) in itself constituted a powerful impediment to imports.

Table 6.6

Keiretsu Dominate Key Industries (% of industry sales)

	Mitsui	Mitsubishi	Sumitomo	Fuyo	Sanwa	Dai-Ichi	Total
Rubber	0	5	45	13	17	19	99
Shipbuilding	9	38	0	1	10	39	97
Electrical machinery	19	11	38	20	1	8	97
Nonferrous metals	43	20	16	4	0	10	93
Textiles and apparel	26	18	14	8	20	0	87
Drugs	11	2	53	1	15	4	86
Petroleum	6	13	0	40	16	8	84
Construction	11	6	21	17	13	14	82
Chemicals	18	28	13	10	11	2	82
Nonelectrical machinery	11	10	34	7	9	8	79
Wire and cable	9	9	25	0	0	26	69
Precision equipment	0	36	5	11	0	12	64
Metal Products	20	8	11	2	3	13	58
Steel	2	1	13	19	15	11	60
Motor vehicles	31	8	10	3	2	0	55

Source: Okimoto (1989), p. 146
Note: The data show the market share of each *keiretsu* in 1974.

Beyond investment, *keiretsu* ties all by themselves served as an effective barrier to imports. How eager were Toyota, Nissan, Nippon Steel, Toshiba, NEC, Matsushita, Mitsubishi Heavy Industries and others to buy imports that competed with the suppliers whose shares they held? Robert Lawrence has shown that, the more that *keiretsu* dominate a product, the smaller the imports of that product.[79]

Moreover, as *keiretsu* domination of key industries proliferated, inter-*keiretsu* collusion increased, particularly in old-line materials industries. Both Hiroya Ueno and Kozo Yamamura have shown that, where concentration increased, so did price rigidity.[80]

No wonder competing imports made little headway in penetrating the Japanese market.[81]

Export Cartels: The Symbiosis of Semiconductors and TVs

While Japan's pervasive barriers to imports are well known, less well-understood is the role these barriers have played in the export drive of many industries. All too often, what allowed Japanese firms to charge low prices abroad was the higher prices at home made possible by their impenetrable sanctuary. During the high-growth era and beyond, this "two-tier pricing" was pervasive.[82]

Take semiconductors, for example. Even after the sector was officially liberalized in 1974 (one of the last to be liberalized), imports still didn't increase their market share. The main restraint was that many of the electronics giants that made semiconductors were also the main purchasers of them. In cases where companies specialized in different types of chips, these companies preferred to buy from another Japanese company, even a competitor, rather than a foreigner. The motivation was simple: as long as such collusion kept out imports and everyone played by the rules of the game, they could all maintain high prices at home. That, in turn, financed their all-important export drive.

> [U]ntil late 1978, Japanese producers apparently used a two-tier price strategy. They kept RAM [Random Access Memory chips for computers —rk] prices high in their controlled domestic market, thereby subsidizing their ability to offer lower prices in the U.S. markets. Prices [in Japan] came down only in response to the ITC's "dumping investigation" [referring to the U.S. International Trade Commission —rk].[83]

The strategy bore fruit in the late 1970s. During the 1974–75 recession, financially strapped U.S. firms had to curtail investment. When the market turned up and U.S. makers could not gear up production fast enough, a big shortage emerged. But their Japanese competitors—backed up not only by stable shareholders and their main banks but also by high prices/profits at home due to the private import barriers—had continued to build up capacity even during the much-worse recession in Japan. They quickly moved in to fill the U.S. gap by offering high-quality products at low prices. By the end of 1979 they had taken 43 percent of the domestic U.S. market for 16K computer memory (DRAM) chips.[84]

But wait a minute: if electronics giants like NEC, Toshiba and Matsushita—and/or their affiliates—were both producing and buying the chips, weren't they just charging higher prices to themselves? How could that benefit them? It couldn't. Unless, of course, they were able to pass their costs on to someone else: the Japanese consumer. Peeling back that layer of the onion brings us to the crucial role of export cartels—in this case, the TV cartel, one of the biggest customers for the semiconductor industry.

As occurred so often in Japan, protection and promotion were used to aid both the supplier and the customer industry. Like almost every other exporting industry, televisions had been protected from imports by strict quotas. Although it was already strong enough to export 25 percent of its output in 1960, import liberalization was held off until 1964.

Since many of the same companies made both TVs and semiconductors, it was not surprising that, in the 1960s and early 1970s, Japanese TV makers rapidly moved into solid-state circuitry. Their American competitors meanwhile foolishly resisted this shift and tried to compete by sending assembly offshore. The move to solid-state TV not only boosted the quality and competitiveness of Japan's TV makers; it provided the vital initial market for Japan's semiconductor output.[85]

And so support for the TV industry helped boost demand for Japanese semiconductors, while aid to the semiconductor industry in turn improved the competitiveness of TVs and later other consumer electronics.

If TVs provided the demand for semiconductors, exports provided the demand for TVs. By 1970, 40 percent of all Japanese TVs were exported; by 1980, it was 70 percent.

And two-tier pricing—made possible by the shield of import barriers and the sword of export cartels—was critical to the export drive.

Activities that would have sent U.S. executives to prison were quite

Table 6.7

Export Cartels Proliferate

	Total Cartels	Export Cartels
1964	970	201
1965	999	208
1966	1,079	211
1967	1,040	206
1968	1,003	213
1969	948	217
1970	898	214
1971	844	192
1972	976	175
1973	985	180

Source: Caves and Uekasa (1976), p. 487
Note: Export cartels were second in number only to small business cartels.

legal—and common—in Japan. In any year, there were upwards of 200 legal export cartels under the 1953 Export and Import Trading Act, which permitted industry cartels to fix prices, limit imports, and carve up export markets (Table 6.7).[86]

During an industry downturn in 1956, six of the biggest TV firms—including Matsushita (Panasonic) but *not* Sony—established a cartel. They fixed prices and cut off supplies to any wholesaler trying to gain markets by undercutting the price guidelines. These high prices at home were then used to subsidize prices in the U.S. market that were only *half* as high—a practice known as "dumping." The cartel members even allocated U.S. customers among themselves. The export cartel set *minimum* export prices. In other words, while the cartel wanted to use low prices to gain share at the expense of American firms, they didn't want to create a ruinous price war amongst themselves.[87]

As part of an officially authorized export cartel, they enjoyed MITI's full official approval for their practices in the U.S.—even though that meant they were willfully violating U.S. anti-dumping law and were thus subject to legal penalties.[88]

When the U.S. brought these practices to light through an anti-dumping case in 1967, unsuspecting Japanese housewives, angry at having to pay prices twice those in the U.S., launched a nationwide boycott of the Japanese TV makers. And Japan's Fair Trade Commission (JFTC) even found that many of the TV makers' cartel practices within Japan violated Japan's anti-monopoly law. And yet, in typical fashion, the JFTC took no enforcement action. Not surprisingly, the price differential between domestic and foreign prices continued throughout the 1970s.[89]

None of this—the export cartel, high prices at home, the dumping—would have been possible if not for the combination of import protection and industry oligopoly that blocked all newcomers in Japan, foreign or domestic.[90] Successful cartels need tight collusion.

Despite all this, prominent economist Ryutaro Komiya lists color television manufacturing as among the industries (along with sewing machines, machine tools, and a host of others) that supposedly:

> developed without any dependence on industrial protection and promotion policies. . . . Given the chance to speak, [executives from these industries] would proclaim that they had succeeded on their own . . . and not because of government favors that seldom came their way.[91]

Komiya may be right. The same television executives who ran the MITI-authorized cartel probably would proclaim that they received no government favors. But that doesn't make it so. Incidentally, Komiya also proclaims that Japan has no import barriers.[92]

In TVs, semiconductors, steel and a host of other industries, cartels played a crucial role in industrial policy in the catch-up era. Cartels and *keiretsu* ties blocked imports, promoted exports and, by making profits more secure, created a foundation for higher investment rates. The cartels, collusion and *keiretsu* also created a phenomenon that, for a while, seemed to make Japanese exporters unbeatable in world competition: the *profit sanctuary*. By keeping the domestic market closed to imports, and therefore being able to charge high prices at home, companies earned high enough profits at home to be able to subsidize low prices on the export front, and thereby seize foreign market share. This became a common pattern among many, albeit not all, Japanese exporting industries.

An effort to document this pattern is one reason why, as part of the Structural Impediments Initiative (SII), Washington successfully obtained Tokyo's agreement to conduct joint surveys that compared prices of Japanese and U.S. goods in both markets.

Beginning in the 1980s, a number of U.S. industries, such as chipmakers and computer makers, realized they could only protect themselves against Japanese competitors by bringing the market battle to the Japanese turf. They had to destroy the profit sanctuary in Japan and they could only do this by gaining access to the Japanese market. Indeed, as we will discuss in Chapter 9, even a small increase in import penetration has often created tremendous "price destruction" in many of Japan's closed markets. Going after the "profit sanctuary" is one reason why George Fisher, a veteran of Motorola's battles for market access in Japan, launched the famous (and failed) Section 301 case against Fuji Photo Film after he became CEO of Kodak.[93]

In the colorful words of former USTR Carla Hills, those who sought to open Japan's market were the "crowbar faction" in American trade politics. They were very different from the protectionists who sought to close America's market to Japanese goods.

The success of the profit sanctuary in promoting exports as well as higher investment within Japan itself misled many Japanese as well as Americans into seeing cartels and collusion as a long-term boon to Japan. But this view ignored the prominent downside: cartelization may have benefited individual firms or industries. But it cemented a pattern of corporate and government behavior that became absolutely dysfunctional for Japan as a whole once the economy matured.

"Developmental State" or State of Development?

Japan's industrial policy did succeed brilliantly during the high-growth era. But not because Japan had developed a superior variant of capitalism, as American "revisionists" and some Japanese analysts came to believe. It worked because, when industrial policy was applied to genuine infant industries with economies of scale, inter-industry spillovers, and so forth, it greatly accelerated the natural process of catch-up. The problem, as we shall see in the next chapter, was continuing the same patterns after the catch-up era was over. Then, many of the same facets of the economy that had previously been fountainheads of vigor—import barriers, cartels, extensive cross-shareholding, banker-dominated finance, and so forth—turned into vessels of infirmity. "Developmental state" policies only make sense for an economy still in the state of development.

Chapter 7

1973–90: The System Sours

At first . . . by free trade with nations of higher culture, [countries] emerge from barbarism, and improve their agriculture; then, by means of restrictions, they give an impulse to manufactures, fisheries, navigation, and foreign commerce; then, finally, having reached the highest degree of skill, wealth, and power, by a gradual return to the principle of free trade *and free competition in their own and foreign markets, they keep agriculturists from inaction, their manufacturers and their merchants from indolence, and stimulate them to wholesome activity, that they may* maintain the supremacy *which they have acquired [emphasis added].*

—Friedrich List, 1841[1]

Devolution: From "Accelerationism" to "Preservationism"

The 1970s and 1980s should have been Japan's big payoff from all the hard work of the 1950s and 1960s. Instead, growth fell off a cliff.

Even in the best of circumstances, growth would have slowed somewhat as Japan matured. There are signs this was already beginning to occur during 1971–73.[2]

Then came the 1973 oil shock. Once the initial recession was over, Japan was expected to recover to growth rates of 6–7 percent. Instead, growth *halved* from rates of 8–10 percent to rates of only 4 percent. It was a far worse slowdown than that of European countries at similar levels of GDP per worker, far worse than can be explained by the oil shock, and far, far worse than economists of the time expected.[3]

The oil shock only triggered the slowdown; it did not cause it. According to renowned growth expert Angus Maddison, higher oil prices only lowered Japan's growth by 0.2 percent a year during 1973–84. Had the oil shock been the only problem, growth would have recovered far more than it did.[4]

Just prior to the first oil shock, the Japanese government planned on growth rates up to 10 percent at least through the 1980s. As late as 1978, MITI still assumed 6 percent growth rates through the year 2000.[5]

While MITI's forecast may seem wildly optimistic in hindsight, actually, it was quite in line with estimates by many of the most respected private economists. Writing in 1975, Denison and Chung also projected 6 percent growth rates through 1990, on the way to a gradual descent of the potential growth rate down to 3.25 percent by the year 2002 as the "transitional elements" of the catch-up process gradually receded. Hugh Patrick writing in 1977 thought Japan could achieve 6–7 percent in the 1980s.[6]

Growth has never gotten back to more than a subpar level and, without reform, it never will.

The problem was not the oil shock per se, nor any of the other big external changes occurring at the same time: the end of the fixed-rate monetary system in 1971 and the subsequent appreciation of the yen; or the rise of the NICs. Rather, the problem was Japan's poor reaction to these changes.

The miracle ended because the overall thrust of Japan's industrial policy switched from "*accelerationism*" to "*preservationism*." Instead of accelerating economic transformation, Japan was now resisting it. Increasingly, the thrust of policy was to *preserve* already existing industries, in order to protect sunk costs in capital-intensive sectors, to prevent unemployment, and to maintain wage equality. Market-conforming industrial policy was replaced by market-defying industrial policy.[7]

Poor Demand: The Shock of the 1970s

There is some truth to the argument made by Kent Calder that much of Japan's policymaking can be explained by pure bureaucratic inertia and long-standing political ties between Ministries and their industry clients. Japan supported shipbuilding, agriculture, coal mining, steel, textiles, petroleum refining and so forth in the 1950s and continued to support them later on. Calder notes that the 1986 loan portfolio of certain Japanese government agencies shows a remarkable similarity to that of 1953.[8]

No doubt there was a lot of inertia. However, there were also some tendencies toward liberalization at the end of the 1960s. Without the oil shock, it is hard to say whether protection or liberalization would have won out.

More importantly, inertia hardly explains the energetic and activist steps that Japan's state agencies took to protect the country's lagging sectors in the post-1973 era. As Robert Uriu demonstrates in *Troubled Industries*, MITI undertook active efforts in response to high-pressure lobbying by Japan's declining sectors.[9] Some sectors received more protection than others—all depending on their political connections, size of their labor force and other factors. Not inertia alone, but clientelism—in the context of a severe economic shock and a political system dominated by Tanaka's money politics—is the culprit.

The shock effect of the 1973 oil crisis was the initial impetus for the new wave of retrograde protectionism that gripped Japan. Once the oil shock occurred, everything seemed to change.

Back in the glory days of the high-growth era, Japan enjoyed a "Field of Dreams" economy: "If you build it, they will buy." Not so after 1973. Growth halved. Once-prosperous industries were suddenly plagued by chronic excess capacity, some never to recover. Even a minimal list showed that the industries in trouble accounted for *half* of Japan's manufacturing assets, almost *half* of its manufacturing output, and a *third* of its factory workers (see Table 7.1).

The problems were not limited to the labor-intensive and resource-intensive industries that employed about 20 percent of Japan's manufacturing workers. These were industries like textiles and wood products where Japan had long since lost comparative advantage. Low demand also plagued the capital-intensive and energy-intensive materials-producing industries (steel, chemicals, cement, paper, glass, nonferrous metals, and so forth). While these industries employed only 15 percent of all manufacturing workers, they accounted for 40 percent of both output and assets.

The latter were the industries that had led growth during the investment-driven stage of Japan's comparative advantage, but they were not going to be leaders in the innovation-driven stage. *From 1973 through 1982, these industries suffered virtually zero growth in output.*[10]

For some industries, such as aluminum or petrochemicals, the problem was that the double whammy of high oil prices and the rising yen permanently priced them out of the market. For others, such as steel or shipbuilding or cement, the problem was that the whole structure of the economy had changed in ways that permanently reduced demand for their output. The growth sectors of the economy, mainly machinery, simply used a lot less material than bulkier products. At the same time, slowing investment meant fewer new plants, hence less need for cement and steel (Table 7.2).

Table 7.1

Japan's Heavy Industries Hit the Wall

Role in Manufacturing in 1980	% of Assets	% of Output	# of Workers	% of Workers	Demand Problem
Steel	17.0	8.4	428,000	4.2	Output falls 20% from 1974 to 1978. Japan prices 50% above import prices 1981–91.
Cement, glass, ceramics	5.6	3.9	505,000	4.9	20% drop in demand. 1973–75. Domestic prices 57% above import prices.
Cement	1.2	0.5	13,000	0.1	
Chemicals	10.5	8.5	409,000	4.0	Capacity usage drops to 55% by 1975. Domestic prices 60% above import prices, 1982–92.
Petrochemicals	5.1	3.8	111,000	1.1	
Paper, pulp and products	4.8	3.2	279,000	2.7	Resource- and energy-intensive. Can't compete.
Nonferrous metals	3.7	3.8	187,000	1.8	Oil shock causes costs to rise 50% above world levels. By 1987, 97% shut down.
Aluminum	0.9	0.3	8,000	0.1	
Petroleum and coal prod.	4.4	7.1	44,000	0.4	
Shipbuilding	1.3	0.8	93,000	0.9	Index of ship orders falls from 100 in 1973 to 20 in 1975 and 10 in 1978.
Textiles (not inc. apparel)	3.2	3.7	691,000	6.7	Too labor-intensive. Can't compete.
Apparel	0.9	1.4	498,000	4.8	Too labor-intensive. Can't compete.
Lumber and wood products	2.0	2.5	362,000	3.5	Resource-intensive. Can't compete.
Total	53.3	43.3	3.6 mil.	33.9	

Sources: Tilton (1996), pp. 9, 15, 39, 40, 89, 62, 130, 204; Yonezawa (1988), p. 437

Table 7.2

Declining Demand for Materials-Producing Industries

	Input Item as % of Total Cost of Product Output	
	Basic Materials (1985)	Labor (1980)
General machinery	15	18
Electrical machinery	12	15
Transport equipment	10	11
Precision instruments	10	19
Construction	29	

Source: Tilton (1996), p. 15

Unfortunately, the materials-producing industries had built capacity like crazy in anticipation of never-ending high growth. As late as 1969, Mitsui Bussan, in pursuit of the full-set strategy and *against* the advice of MITI, added a whole new aluminum company to an already crowded market. MITI's own investment subsidies in petrochemicals had led to a flood of now-useless capacity in that sector.[11]

Faced with this crisis of sales, it is not entirely surprising that Japan's governmental and industrial leaders did what came naturally: protectionism. Exports boosted sales, while imports hurt them.

When Japan's macroeconomic dilemmas are thrown into the equation, the lunge for neomercantilism (i.e., policies that boost exports and restrict imports) seems even more comprehensible. As growth slowed, so did investment. Since growth had always been driven by investment, Japan now developed a chronic problem of insufficient overall demand. The response was an unprecedented export drive. Indeed, during the 1975–85 decade, a growing trade surplus supplied the stimulus for almost half of all economic growth. Never before had Japan been so dependent on trade surpluses to drive growth. No wonder imports were seen as the enemy.[12]

Recession Cartels: A Cure That Worsened the Disease

There are cures, sometimes, that make the initial malady even worse. That is what happened in Japan.

The "accelerationist" response to Japan's economic shocks would have been to apply macroeconomic stimulus to keep a floor underneath growth; to use subsidies and other devices to accelerate the transfer of capital and labor from the declining sectors into rising sectors; and to provide a temporary social safety net for afflicted individual workers.

In fact, this is exactly what MITI and other agencies *claimed* they were doing. There are some prominent observers of Japanese policy who believe them—Chalmers Johnson, for one:

> Thanks to MITI, Japan came to possess more knowledge and more practical experience of how to *phase out old industries* and phase in new ones than any other nation in the world [emphasis added].[13]

This is about half right. Japan had a brilliant policy for phasing in sunrise industries—at least during what Michael Porter calls the investment-driven stage of development. But, even in the high-growth era, it never had an effective policy for phasing out sunset industries. On the contrary, from coal to agriculture to cotton textiles, Japan's declining industries mightily resisted downsizing.

Under the pressures of the low-growth era, the syndrome only worsened. Year after year, Japan poured resources down the drain in sectors with no real hope for the future. Even when, as in aluminum or textiles, inevitability was recognized, everything was done to slow and forestall the decline. Capacity-reduction cartels seemed to create a never-ending cycle of cuts and buildups and cuts again. Wage subsidies advertised as helping workers move to new companies in new sectors were often used simply to move workers to a different company in the same troubled industry. Industry association gatekeepers kept imports out of declining industries, even when domestic prices were far higher than world prices and even when no formal import barriers existed.[14]

If preserving weak industries was a tolerable defect in the catch-up era, then prolonging the decline of troubled sectors was the fatal norm in the post-1973 period.

Despite the pretense that Japan is a kind of "non-capitalist market economy" with "companies by, for, and of the employees," capital received a lot more protection than labor. The number of steelworkers declined by 34 percent in the 1970s while the number of aluminum workers fell by 76 percent. Some capital was lost, 11 percent in cement, for example, but the effort was made to preserve as much as possible.[15]

In industry after industry, MITI formed so-called recession cartels under a series of laws in the 1970s and 1980s. These cartels allowed MITI (or another Ministry depending upon the industry) and the relevant Industry Association to coordinate prices, production levels, capacity reduction, investment and modernization plans and, covertly, to limit imports. Thousands of these cartels in dozens of industries have come and gone—often several times within the same industry. In many cases, the industry association was a lineal descendant of the "imperial control associations" that administered similar cartels before and during World War II.[16]

It was, of course, often recognized that the concerned industry would ultimately shrink somewhat. But these cartels tried to resist and delay the decline, slow it down, or even shift the burden to foreign producers (i.e., by exporting at "dumping" prices, which forced companies in other countries to take a greater share of global cutbacks).

Under MITI guidance, the cartel came up with a plan whose goal was to establish minimum prices to which everyone had to adhere—so as to maintain profits. Since overcapacity exerted downward pressure on prices, the cartel was obliged to come up with a plan to reduce output and capacity. Sometimes, the minimum price was not explicit. What was explicit was a planned reduction in production or capacity aimed at putting an unspecified floor under prices.

When overcapacity decimates prices in a market situation, there is a shakeout and the high-cost firms fall by the wayside. With the most efficient firms remaining, the average efficiency of the industry as a whole is raised, albeit in a smaller industry.

In Japan, by contrast, the cartel system ended up reinforcing inefficiency. In the name of egalitarianism, all firms were obliged to make *pro rata* cuts according to their share of the market or their share of capacity. To help out the weakest, the bigger or stronger firms were sometimes pressured to take an extra-large cut. The Japanese call this a "convoy" system in which the whole convoy can move no faster than the slowest ship.[17]

Indeed, *efficient producers were often coerced to make cuts* under penalty of government fines and industry association boycotts. They couldn't be allowed to stay out of the cartel if it was to work. As in OPEC, once one or two significant players underprice the cartel, the whole monopolistic structure collapses.

One of the more famous cases is that of Tokyo Steel, a mini-mill producing steel rods. In the electric-furnace-based steel industry, legal cartels were organized eight times during the 1970s and 1980s. Still, there were many small producers of steel rods who resisted the cartel. In 1977, the National Small Steel Rod Industry Association asked MITI to rein in the mavericks. MITI did so, ordering them to cut output by 35 percent or face fines. Masanari Ikeya, president of Tokyo Steel, complained to the *Asahi Shinbun*, "Though the industry was supposedly suffering from a recession, our firm was healthy. Can a healthy person be forcibly hospitalized?" He considered appealing to the courts, but decided he couldn't win against the government, and reluctantly surrendered.[18]

In the shipbuilding industry, supervised by the Ministry of Transportation rather than MITI, firms not reducing their capacity by the allotted amount had to pay fines up to ¥100,000 ($900) per gross ton on the excess.[19]

Often the main enforcer was not the government but industry associations. In a typical example, the Cement Association and construction associations got together and agreed that the construction firms would not buy from any cement maker who sold below the cartel price; nor would the cement makers sell to any construction company that bought from "cheaters." This "refusal to deal," illegal under the seldom-enforced Japanese Anti-Monopoly Law, is the main power behind the cartels. However, as Mark Tilton stresses:

> It is crucial to recognize that this unofficial trade association policy . . . was facilitated by restrictions on competition aggressively pushed by MITI. . . . Only by restricting competition *among* the members of the trade associations could refusal-to-deal agreements *between* trade associations [of buyer and supplier industries —rk] become possible [emphasis added].[20]

The end result of cartelization was to make an industry even less efficient. Companies expecting a government bailout down the road didn't feel a lot of pressure to improve. In the food and drink industry, a classic sheltered industry, fixed costs almost doubled from ¥1.8 trillion to ¥3.0 trillion during 1984–94, even as fixed expenses were slashed in export-oriented industries in the same period.[21] As Japanese economist Sueo Sekiguchi put it:

> A recession cartel has never played the role of letting the costly producers exit while the more efficient stay. The arrangement instead protected the weaker at a cost to the stronger at the expense of consumers.[22]

While the cartel system is advertised as implementing smooth *exit* from declining industries, in fact it promotes *entry*. Since cuts are distributed according to market share, and since firms expect the government to put a floor under prices and profits, firms rush to increase capacity and market share once there is a slightest upturn. This is done in anticipation of the next depression cartel. As one business executive cited by Kozo Yamamura put it:

We know there is too much output and capacity in our industry. . . . So why do we increase our own output and capacity? Primarily, because we expect the government to protect our profits before very many of us fail. . . . In such a control scheme, the larger our share of our industry's capacity or output, [then] the larger our share of the market will be under controls, and the better off we are likely to be in the long run.[23]

In other words, "cartels beget cartels." Some industries have gone through this cycle of overcapacity, bailout, more overcapacity, more bailouts over and over again. The polyvinyl chloride resin industry formed legal cartels eight times between 1958 and 1978. The stainless steel producers implemented five legal cartels between 1965 and 1973.[24]

Even a dying industry like aluminum—or "canned electricity" as it was called—attracted investment even after the oil shock put the hand-writing on the wall. Everyone knew that Japan would have to exit this industry entirely, as it eventually did by the end of the 1980s. Yet, Japan's recession cartels prolonged the death agony for more than a decade at immense cost. In 1975–77, Japanese refiners added 20 percent additional capacity to what was already the world's largest aluminum refining industry. And yet MITI points to aluminum as a successful exit policy.[25]

True, cartels were used in the high-growth era as well. However, over time their purpose changed: from smoothing the up and down cycles of a growing industry into propping up "senile industries." James Vestal comments:

[A]s time passed, there was a decreasing emphasis on promoting the development of infant industries and an increased emphasis on using these laws to maintain the *status quo* or to assist in adjustment. Since these laws were used to form cartels in industries such as textile machinery, bearings, and woodworking machinery whose further survival was questionable . . . [they fit] under anti-growth rather than pro-growth policy.[26]

The same verdict fits the wage subsidies that were applied in textiles and other labor-intensive industries. Tokyo offered generous wage subsidies to companies that hired workers who had been laid off in depressed industries. Supposedly, this would help shift workers to rising sectors, and so it met the OECD's (Organization of Economic Cooperation and Development) criterion for "positive adjustment subsidies." In reality, it *cheapened the cost of labor within textiles*, thus enabling textile companies and workers to *stay* in that sector. According to a 1983 study by Japan's Ministry of Labor:

> [M]ost textile workers who changed jobs *moved to other enterprises in the same industry* . . . thus protecting the declining sector. . . . But with such assistance *lasting for over a decade*, the overall result is "counter-positive adjustment" as far as moving resources out of a declining sector is concerned [emphasis added].[27]

Meanwhile, MITI was surreptitiously protecting textiles from imports, thereby further propping up prices and profits:

> MITI warned major textile importers to refrain from importation to avoid excess supply. . . . In general however, there was no *acknowledged* use of import restrictions as part of adjustment assistance at this point [emphasis added].[28]

The Japan Textile Importers' Association collected import data in order to prevent "unguided imports." Meanwhile, MITI officials, from time to time, contacted firms whose imports rose above the amount projected by the Textile Industry Council.

> The Division [of MITI] cannot ask the importers to cancel their contracts, but it does request them to delay the deliveries and refrain from entering into new contracts.[29]

Under criticism by the U.S. that the cartels blocked imports, Japan changed its law in 1987 to stop using overt cartels. Instead, under the Structural Conversion Facilitation Law (SCFL), MITI talks with individual producers. But there is little doubt that the combination of MITI "administrative guidance" and the power of industry associations produces the same result in a less transparent manner.[30]

Cartels and Import Impediments

For the cartels to work, imports must be blocked. Since the whole purpose is to raise prices, how could this be accomplished if cheaper imports were allowed to come in and seize market share?[31]

Even economists from Japan's own Finance Ministry have acknowledged that the very existence of the cartels was proof positive that Japan had no free market in imports in the cartelized sectors:

> In domestic markets that are perfectly competitive, when the prices of imported products supplied by foreign competitors decline due to appreciation of the value of the yen, it [should] become impossible for the Japanese firms to maintain high prices for their own products which they sell in Japan. However, observed facts show that this [maintenance of high prices] is possible.[32]

This is the reason "price destruction" has been so dramatic even in cases where the penetration of imports has increased by only a few percent. Tuna prices, for example, dropped 63 percent during 1995, beer fell 32 percent, whiskey 17 percent, gasoline 25–30 percent.[33]

Wherever industries have been successfully cartelized, imports remain very low even though Japanese prices are far above world levels. In steel, for example, imports were held to less than 7 percent of consumption even though Japanese prices were 60 percent above world levels.[34]

The amazing thing, as Sekiguchi and others have noted, is that there were no *formal* import barriers in the cartelized industries. That would have been politically untenable in light of the U.S.–Japan trade friction.

And yet, often-illegal boycotts and refusals to deal organized by various industry associations, along with MITI administrative guidance, managed to restrict imports even in the most uncompetitive industries. Among seven sectors that Sekiguchi studied:

> In some sectors, penetration was nil—generally areas where costs are easily passed onto the consumer. . . . Industry associations may have created barriers to foreign products trying to penetrate the domestic market. . . .
>
> Factors such as the closeness of producer-distributor networks undoubtedly had more to do with how well imports did than the presence or absence of a [formal] cartel. . . .
>
> Fertilizer, cement, electric furnace steel, and electrical wire are such examples. Nil or slow import penetration may have alleviated adjustment difficulties for producers, but it was at the expense of users. . . .
>
> MITI has argued that this is not a result of government policy, but rather, the private sector is responsible for this behavior. This argument is not persuasive however, because MITI's strategy that domestic producers and distributors promote mergers and business cooperation is likely to strengthen closer ties among domestic units. While the system of desig-

> nated cartels was abolished, recession cartels and other joint actions may
> contribute to reducing imports in a climate where the members easily
> collude with each other. Import monitoring and early warning by each
> industry division within MITI may also restrain aggressive importing
> under the rubric of orderly importation.
>
> It is abnormal that Japan has no imports in such declining sectors as electric
> furnace steel, chemical fertilizers, electrical wire and other products.[35]

In certain industries, like aluminum, where Japan was so uncompetitive
that industry survival was hopeless, Sekiguchi reports that "users were
able to *lobby* policymakers for more imports [emphasis added]." This is
absolutely remarkable. If the market were really open, why was it necessary for users to "lobby?" Why couldn't they just buy what they wanted?

Cartels, whether official or not, and import barriers protect each other.
The more effective industry collusion is, the more effective the barriers to
imports. And the more effective the barriers to imports, then the more
powerful the cartel.

Where Was the JFTC?

Where was Japan's antitrust enforcer, the Japan Fair Trade Commission
(JFTC), while all this was going on? Various laws required JFTC approval before the MITI-led cartels could go into force. However, rather
than resisting cartels, the JFTC—which is dominated by MOF officials—
mostly embraced them. At most, the JFTC tried to regulate them rather
than stop them.

What about the illegal cartels, the price-fixing, boycotts, refusals to
deal, and other illegal activities by the industrial associations?

Consider the case of glass. Long supported by MITI and closely allied
with the construction industry, flat glass is completely dominated by a
three-company cartel. For almost three decades now, they have each had
the same market share, hardly deviating by as much as 1 percent. Asahi
Glass always has 50 percent, Nippon Sheet Glass has 30 percent and
Central Glass Co. has 20 percent.

The foreign share is still no more than 3 percent despite the fact that
prices are higher in Japan and the industry has had to be rescued by a
MITI-organized depression cartel. The glass issue has long been the subject of a bitter U.S.–Japan trade dispute. The two governments have even
signed an agreement to resolve the problem, but little has changed.

In 1993, the JFTC conducted a study of the industry. It found:

There were incidents of [dealers] being pressured by manufacturers or contract agencies in one form or another as a result of handling imported products, such as . . . *suggestions that the supply of domestically produced goods would be terminated* and others. Furthermore, among retail outlets, there were evidently some that felt that there were probable disadvantages in terms of receiving supplies of timely deliveries of domestic products or when requiring the assistance of contract agencies, if they expanded purchases of imported products or initiated new purchases [emphasis added].[36]

And yet, the JFTC said it was "*unable to find evidence of Anti-Monopoly Law violation.*" Instead, it noted that:

All three companies have written manuals on the Anti-Monopoly law, including regulations banning action to exclude imports. There is great expectation that effective implementation of the rules *will continue* [sic!] [emphasis added].[37]

This has happened time and time again in many industries, often to the consternation of some career JFTC officials at the working level who feel hog-tied in trying to enforce the law.[38]

Hardening of the Arteries

The end result of all this cartelization was to take what had been perhaps the world's most dynamic economy and slowly to clog its arteries. The rapid flow of capital, labor and output from one sector to another—the very hallmark of Japan's accelerationism—became increasingly sticky. Workers and capital that should have been forced by overcapacity to move to new sectors were instead kept in their old moribund industries (Figure 7.1).

As this happened, what had once been a "virtuous cycle" between structural change and growth metamorphosed into a "vicious cycle." When the economy was growing rapidly, workers didn't mind losing jobs in sunset sectors because they knew there were new, higher-paying jobs in the sunrise sectors. But now, as the economy slowed, they put pressure on the politicians and bureaucrats to maintain their jobs in the sunset sectors. And so, slowing growth led to a slowdown in structural change. But the slowdown in structural change created an even larger decline of productivity growth and thus slower overall economic growth. That in turn meant fewer new jobs in the sunrise industries, starting the cycle all

Figure 7.1 **Rigidity and Slow Growth Reinforce Each Other**

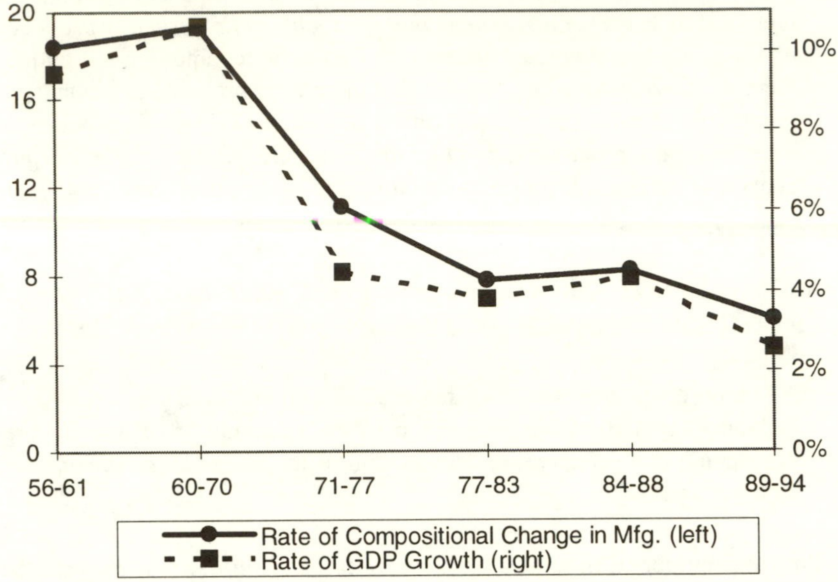

Rate of Compositional Change in Mfg. (left)
Rate of GDP Growth (right)

Source: EPA (1995a); Imai (1982), pg. 51; UNIDO (1995), Statistical Annex. The figures for the 1950s through the 1970s come from Imai; the later ones from UNIDO. Since
UNIDO is the ultimate source for Imai, the extrapolation gives an accurate picture of the
trend.
Note: The Rate of Compositional change is an index that shows how rapidly output is
changing from sector to sector, such as textiles to electronics.

over again. The slowdown in growth and the slowdown in structural
change reinforced each other—downward.

Some immobility is unavoidable in any country. Steel mills do not turn
themselves into VCR assembly lines. Autoworkers don't suddenly become software programmers. But accelerationism eases the transformation; preservationism resists it.

Even the most basic price mechanisms failed to work properly as the
economy became increasingly cartelized:

> Economists had no difficulty in showing that the price of products of
> highly oligopolistic markets had grown more rigid and less responsive to
> the supply and demand in many markets.[39]

There had always been some barriers to entry and exit in Japan's
institutional setup. But these institutions were geared to a growth econ-

omy. When the growth slowed down, many of them became dysfunctional.

One of the most important is Japan's lifetime employment system. This is mostly used at big companies and covers less than half of the labor force. Under this system, workers are recruited upon graduation and then stay until they retire. Salary is based on seniority. Under conditions of high growth, this system had benefits for both worker and company. Because workers were assured of job security and rising income as they aged and the company prospered, they didn't resist labor-saving technologies. Because the company knew the workers would stay, they invested a great deal in training them.

The downside appeared when growth slowed. Suddenly, younger employees and even middle management found fewer slots for promotion. The salary bill rose because the average age of workers rose and, due to seniority-based pay, the average wage rose with it. Even in declining sectors, workers were reluctant to leave their job because other companies are reluctant to hire someone above the normal recruitment age, especially a "job hopper." Nor could companies easily let redundant workers go; they had a commitment to uphold. And so the lifetime employment system became a barrier to *exit*, creating even greater pressure on the government to provide the protection necessary to preserve jobs in sunset industries. The lifetime system is under strain and some say it is eroding, but it still exerts great social pressure in Japan.

Capital is just as tied up as labor, due to Japan's financial setup. If American capital has the problem of being too short-term-oriented and flighty, Japanese capital goes to the opposite extreme. It is too tied up in specific companies. Japan's corporate financing is bank-centered with the stock and bond markets playing a minor role. Under the main bank system (in which banks often own shares of their corporate borrowers and vice versa), banks are very closely tied to their customers.

The huge sunk costs in capital-intensive industry have made both managers and bankers reluctant to let companies fail. And because companies need to keep sales going to support their labor forces, banks are also reluctant to let them shrink. In Japan, as demand for steel declined, steel companies, with the help of their bankers, tried to move into everything from semiconductors to amusement parks. Stock and bond investors, by contrast, would have simply sold their stock and move on, shifting capital from sunset sectors to sunrise sectors.

Since, under the convoy system, the government would not let any banks fail, it had to help make sure that not too many bank debtors failed either. Once again, the barriers to exit meant the political pressures to bail out troubled sectors were enormous.

Who Pays for the Cartels? Cartels Beget Cartels

Cartels can work only if somehow the cartel can pass its high costs on to its customers. But how do those customers then pass their costs along? They too must be cartelized and protected from cheaper imports. And then so must their customers. Each time Japan protects an industry, that sets up a chain reaction from industry to industry to industry until finally the taxpayer and/or consumer is hit with the final bill. Cartels beget cartels and protection begets protection. U.S. political scientists Mark Tilton and Robert Uriu, and a few Japanese economists, have documented this pattern via industry case studies. A look at these cases shows why the burden of the system has become insupportable.

Passing Along Costs to the Taxpayer: Cement and Construction

The cement industry, a subject of repeated recession cartels, is a micro-cosm of all the problems that plague cartelized Japan.[40]

It would seem that Japan should be a major importer of cement and that the domestic industry should be shrinking. Domestic prices are far above world prices (68 percent over import prices during 1986–93). And, in Korea and Taiwan it has major low-cost producers right nearby able to supply much of Japan by using cheap water transport.

And yet, this has not happened. Except in 1973, Japan imported no cement at all from the end of the World War II until 1984. Furthermore, despite the absence of any formal barriers in recent years, imports were a scant 1.2 percent of consumption in 1992.

Far from exiting this uncompetitive industry, Japan has been a net ex-porter, often shipping as much as 10 percent of output overseas. It achieved this through massive dumping, with export prices 32 percent below domestic prices in 1980–85 and 60 percent below domestic prices in 1986–93.[41]

The key to the whole situation is a cozy deal between the concentrated cement industry, where only five firms control 60 percent of sales, and the construction cartels. As Tilton reports:

> [T]he core policy that restricts the flow of imports into the Japanese market is a refusal-to-deal agreement. . . . Construction trade associations agreed to buy only from members of the domestic cement trade association, while

members of the cement association agreed to sell only to construction association members that abide by the agreement. If a construction company buys imported cement, domestic companies will no longer sell to that company.[42]

Every once in a while, some company tries to make money by "cheating." It's not easy, as some companies found out when, during a time of shortage, they tried to bypass the cartel and import some cement from Asia:

> At the port of Kobe, the dock workers union formally refused to unload the cement. At other ports, longshoremen showed up the first day to unload but failed to report to work the following day. . . .[In one case] the longshoring company said it could not do the work because Japanese cement companies had told it they would no longer give the company work if it handled foreign cement.[43]

Similar arrangements were set up with the Trucking Association. The Cement Association members would use only members of the Trucking Association and the latter would ensure that their members would not transport Korean cement. When Korean firms nonetheless found some truckers, the *Nihon Keizai Sangyo Shimbun* reported that Japanese cement firms followed the trucks to identify the "criminals who are buying imported cement," vowing to cut off all future sales to these "criminals."[44]

The cement industry gets away with its outrageously cartelized prices because it sells all of its output to the cartelized construction industry.

The notoriously corrupt construction industry in turn passes its grossly inflated prices (15–45 percent above international levels)[45] on to its own favorite customer: the Japanese government. Half of all construction jobs are public works projects. Prices are inflated by the notorious *dango* system, whereby major construction companies decide beforehand who will submit the "low" bid and for how much. A government audit found that *dango* was used in 90 percent of all national and local government projects in 1992 and 1993. A Construction Ministry official defended the practice as a kind of disguised unemployment.

> If the practice is changed, smaller construction firms will go bankrupt one after another and things will be plunged into confusion.[46]

The Construction Ministry even helps enforce industry association retaliation. Only cement companies approved by the Ministry are allowed to sell to the government. The same applies to steel. Tokyo Steel Manufacturing, a mini-mill making steel from scrap, offered prices 50 percent cheaper than those of the big blast furnace operators. Yet it could not sell to construction companies, partly because the Japanese government was unwilling to authorize steel purchases from outsiders for public works, and partly because the construction firms feared retaliation from the steel cartel.[47]

Substantial contributions to Liberal-Democratic Party (LDP) politicians and cozy post-retirement sinecures for Construction Ministry bureaucrats help keep the system going—all at a huge cost to the taxpayer.

Cement is hardly the only industry for which construction provides this service. As one of Japan's largest industries—accounting for 10 percent of its GDP and 10 percent of its workforce—construction is one of the biggest customers for many of Japan's materials-producing sectors, from glass to steel. Half of all Japanese steel is bought by the construction industry. In fact, 30 percent of total construction industry costs are made up of material costs, largely from some of Japan's most important, depressed, and overpriced materials industries. Without the ability to pass their costs onto the construction companies, the materials industries would be hard pressed to maintain their own cartelized prices.

It is not only the taxpayer who pays higher prices. Padded construction costs raise the costs of everything from housing, to the electric bills paid by Nippon Steel, to the factories that build Toyotas.[48]

When the 1973 oil shock and the subsequent recession cut cement demand by 20 percent, MITI sprang to the cement industry's rescue—even though high costs were hurting MITI's heavy industry clients. Over the next several years, the industry formed legal (and sometimes illegal)[49] cartels again and again.

In the 1980s, even these measures no longer worked and MITI had to organize a cartel to reduce capacity from 130 million tons to about 100 million tons. This was resisted by the construction companies, who feared even higher prices, and the plan became a subject of negotiations between the Construction Ministry and MITI. Eventually, capacity was reduced, with the larger companies making proportionally greater cuts.

The end result is that Japanese prices remain way above world levels, imports remain tiny, and the industry remains far larger than it would in a free market. MITI may claim it smoothed the downsizing because it organized a 25 percent capacity cut. But the reality is: had MITI and the Construction Ministry not created a cartel that could block imports, the industry size might have dropped by 50 percent, maybe more, and cheaper imports would have come in, thereby lowering costs throughout the Japanese supply chain.

Steel and Its Customers in Autos and Shipbuilding

While cement had always had its troubles, steel proudly paraded itself as one of Japan's stars, the "rice of industry," a national treasure. In the 1960s it had been Japan's top exporter, accounting for 18 percent of all exports, and it remained the top exporter until as late as 1977.[50]

The 1970s put the industry into crisis. From its 1974 peak at 119 million tons, output fell to a low of 102 million tons by 1978. It has never recovered the 1974 high.

By the beginning of the 1990s, Japan's steelmakers, once the world's low-cost producers, were now the world's high-cost producers. The soaring yen, global overcapacity, and a shrinking demand for materials all combined to make Japan's steel industry uncompetitive.

And yet, somehow, the steel industry achieved record profits in 1981. Even in the early 1990s profits averaged around four times the 1970 level. How was this possible? The answer is: the steel cartel.

Protected by MITI and dominated by five big firms who produce 70 percent of Japan's steel, the industry has long been able to collude and insist upon industry-wide oligopolistic prices. Beginning in 1950, the Big Three—Yawata Steel, Fuji Steel and Nippon Kokkan—met together and decided upon a "designated price," which the other steelmakers followed.

Later, when "excess competition" in the high-growth boom made this system unstable, MITI and Japan's top business leaders helped organize the merger of Yawata and Fuji to form Nippon Steel in 1970. One purpose was to restore the system of price leadership. According to one Japanese analyst, without the merger, domestic steel prices in 1971–75 would have been 14 percent lower, and export prices would have been higher.[51]

Today, 80 percent of all steel sold to Japanese manufacturers is sold at the so-called big buyer price—despite the fact that this is far above both the import and export price, and above even domestic "spot" or "dealer" prices.

The big buyer price is not decided by negotiations between individual company buyers and sellers. In the high-growth era, the "big buyer price" was negotiated between the steel companies and the shipbuilding industry, with Mitsubishi Heavy Industries (MHI) serving as the shipbuilders' representative. Today, the automakers, which account for 23 percent of domestic steel demand (second after construction), fill this role. Every year, the basic price is negotiated between Nippon Steel and Toyota Motors. Once this is decided, the rest of Japan falls in line.

One can understand the power of the steel cartel during the high-growth period, when Japanese steel was competitive and Japanese buyers wanted to be sure of adequate supply. What is fascinating is the iron grip that the steel cartel continues to exert despite its big price disadvantage.

Japanese domestic prices are much higher than import prices. During 1981–84, even before the rise of the yen, the "big buyer" price averaged 31 percent above import prices. By 1991, after the yen had risen, the price differential had risen to 57 percent. Despite this, imports were not able to make much headway in the Japanese market. From less than 1 percent in 1980, penetration slowly rose, but as of 1992, it was still only 6–7 percent. The fact that headlines were made a couple of years back when Mitsubishi Motors merely *considered* buying Korean steel shows the lock of the cartel.

The reluctance of Japanese automakers and others to buy imports is legendary. Back in 1986, when the rising yen was hurting the automakers' ability to export, they begged the steelmakers to cut prices. They pointed out how the rising yen and falling oil prices had cut the steelmakers' own costs for coal, iron ore and energy. The steelmakers were intransigent. When some automakers hinted they might want to look at cheaper Korean steel, the steel cartel—led by Yoshiro Inayama, a former head of Keidanren and of Nippon Steel—called the automakers' bluff. Inayama bluntly told them they had to stick with Japanese steel "built with the blood of the Japanese people." In the end, the automakers didn't buy the imports and the steel industry relented somewhat on price.

Not all such restraint was voluntary. In a scene reminiscent of the cement story, trucks carrying Korean steel at the port of Kobe were reportedly trailed by agents of the Japanese steelmakers to see who was buying foreign steel. The latter were threatened with a cutoff of supply.[52]

Even the powerful Mitsubishi Heavy Industries was faced with threats when it wanted to buy a bit of steel from Korea's Pohang Steel at a time when Japanese prices were 60 percent higher. The *Nikkei Sangyo Shinbun* reported that MHI:

> has been unable to [buy South Korean steel] because it has been concerned with the fact that [Japanese] steel manufacturers are both its suppliers and among its principal customers.[53]

MHI was concerned that the steel cartel would tell the shipping companies used by the steelmakers not to buy from MHI, and might even cut off MHI's supply of steel. At the end of the bargaining process between two powerful industries, MHI received a kind of tacit permission to buy minimal amounts of Pohang's steel. Its imports never went above 10 percent of usage. MHI was also considered an "exception" since it had supplied equipment to Pohang Steel.

In the end, MHI decided it could better afford to acquiesce to the cartel than to wreck the web of mutual protection.

As a shipbuilder, MHI was an ongoing participant in government protection, subsidies, and cartels. It was not in a position to complain when steelmakers used similar devices. Besides, MHI in turn passed along the high steel costs to both the taxpayer and its *keiretsu* brother, the NYK shipping line. The shipping companies in turn enjoy their own subsidies and collusion.

Moreover, along with Toshiba and Hitachi, MHI is one of the biggest providers of heavy machinery to the nine big electric utilities. These utilities in turn pass their costs (for machinery, steel, construction work, and heavy petroleum) onto their customers. Japan has the industrial world's highest utility rates.[54]

The utilities, who have always been one of the LDP's biggest campaign contributors, have long been both wards and supporters of the state. Most have always had a former senior MITI official on their boards, and continue to enjoy below-market financing by the Japan Development Bank (JDB) that, as late as 1991, provided 27 percent of the utilities' outstanding credit. In turn, when the economy needs boosting, MITI asks the utilities to step up investment by buying equipment they don't really need from MHI, Toshiba and Hitachi.[55]

As the yen rose and cost pressures on exporters increased, it became clear that not all imported steel could be kept out. And so a "gatekeeper" scheme was set up. The Japanese importers were organized into the Japan Iron and Steel Institute to regulate the volume and pricing of imports under the rubric of "orderly marketing." Foreign producers like Korea's Pohang agreed with the Japanese steelmakers to abide by informal restraints on price and volume in return for not being totally locked out.[56]

The high price of Japanese steel did, of course, hurt the Japanese steelmakers on the export front. Exports fell from a third of all output in 1982 to only about 15 percent by 1992. Moreover, even to get these sales, Japanese steelmakers had to "dump," with export prices nearly 30 percent below the domestic "big buyer" price during 1985–91. As with cement, steelmakers facing huge fixed costs seemed satisfied if they could merely meet variable costs on the export front.

The shrinking of export markets made it even more imperative to keep control of the price structure on the domestic front. And so, in 1986–87, with MITI's blessing, the steelmakers formed an informal cartel (as opposed to an official MITI-authorized cartel) to cut capacity by about a third to 100 million tons. There was cheating, as always, but basically the cartel held. Steel prices and profits were maintained. Through attrition, the labor force was gradually cut from 430,000 to 340,000 during the 1980s.

Without the cartel to keep prices and profits artificially high, the cutback in steel would have been even more severe. The capacity-reduction cartel was not a device to smooth exit, but to resist it.

Protecting the Japanese Victims of Japanese Protection: Petrochemicals

The classic case of the "chain reaction of protection" is from petroleum refining to petrochemicals, and then from petrochemicals to synthetic textiles, detergent and consumer electronics.[57]

MITI began promoting petrochemicals in 1951. Lacking the U.S. access to cheap natural gas, Japan's petrochemical industry was compelled by MITI to buy naphtha from Japanese refiners. To help ease the cost-pressure, MITI instructed the petroleum refiners to charge higher prices for consumer products like gasoline in order to subsidize lower prices for naphtha. Nonetheless, prices for Japanese naphtha remained far above world prices. Despite this, petrochemical firms were initially compelled by MITI to sell their products at world prices. Petrochemicals was forced to take the loss to help the refiners.

To help the petrochemical industry export, MITI repeatedly organized export cartels from 1957 through 1972. This allowed the industry to gain markets by selling abroad at prices far below domestic prices, but not so low as to be ruinous. Even had the oil shock not occurred, the industry would never have been able to compete on its own. Yet, encouraged by MITI, it was building capacity *en masse*.

Then came the two oil shocks and the rise of new low-cost producers. MITI responded with the usual tools. A legal "recession cartel" orchestrated cuts in capacity of about 25 percent and allowed competing firms to organize "joint sales" efforts in order to maintain prices.

However, what the industry really needed and wanted was access to cheap petroleum. It had to go to MITI since petroleum product imports were still controlled under the 1962 Petroleum Industry Law. MITI was split. Its Basic Industries Bureau, petrochemicals' protector, wanted naphtha prices brought down. Its Energy Agency wanted to keep prices high to support the refiners.

Finally, in 1982—nine years after the first oil shock—MITI reached a compromise. It allowed petrochemical firms to import when their requirements went above the capacity of the local petroleum refiners. At the same time, MITI directed the respective industry associations to negotiate price and quantity on a quarterly basis. Under this system, imports of naphtha gradually increased, even overcoming domestic output, but the domestic prices still remained far above import prices.

During 1980–92, domestic prices were 64 percent over import prices and 60 percent over export prices.

Despite this incredible price disadvantage, Japan managed to use "dumping" to be a *net exporter* of ethylene-based goods as late as 1992. In that year, exports amounted to 15 percent of output, down somewhat from 22 percent in 1975.

Just as remarkably, while import penetration had risen a bit from virtually zero in 1975, it was still no higher than 8 percent as late as 1992. As in steel, most Japanese industrial customers did not abandon ship.

How was this possible? Once again, the answer is the chain reaction of protection.

One of the biggest customer industries for petrochemicals is synthetic textiles, a longtime target of MITI help. In the 1970s and 1980s, this industry was also organized into cartels by MITI. That protection allowed it to pay high prices to the petrochemical firms and pass them along to the Japanese consumer.

However, the textile industry also relies heavily on exports. How does it pass costs along in that market? The compromise worked out by MITI was the following: to lower costs, the textile industry was allowed to import about 40 percent of its petrochemical supplies, but no more. Meanwhile, the textile firms still had to pay a huge premium on the remainder that they did buy domestically.

Another big share of the petrochemical output goes to makers of detergent and home cleaning products. Since there is little competition in Japan from imports, these costs easily are passed along to consumers.

Still, some costs can't be passed along at home. A full 30 percent of petrochemical output is sold to export-dependent auto and electronics firms. Nonetheless, the auto firms have agreed to abide by an industry-wide "cost-plus" pricing formula set by the chemical cartel.

Once again, the efficient sectors have agreed to bail out the inefficient, intensifying the former's own need for protection and high prices at home.

Why Do Exporters Submit to Cartel Prices?

The really interesting question is *why* and *how* did efficient exporters continue to submit to the cartel? Does Toyota really need Nippon Steel more than vice versa? How does Toyota pass along high prices when domestic sales are humdrum and a high yen is already putting pressure on export prices? How does shipbuilding pass along high prices when it suffers an $8 million cost disadvantage per oil tanker vis-à-vis Korean competitors simply due to the fact that Japanese steel costs more than Korean steel?[58]

Part of the answer is, as we noted, fear of retaliation. It doesn't exist in all industries. It's weak where there is fierce competition within Japan; Japanese firms had no fear of switching from NEC PCs to Compaq. But the fear is remarkably pervasive whenever Japanese buyers face a concentrated industry with a history of MITI cartels. The editor of one of Japan's biggest newspapers recalled asking his purchasing manager why they couldn't import foreign newsprint since it was so much cheaper. The buyer replied that, in times of shortage, the newspaper had to know it could always get its supply. The inference was that, if it used imported paper, its supplier might not be as willing to make such assurances. Besides, the Japanese supplier was going to build a plant in Canada, and then the newspaper would get its cheaper paper.[59]

And yet, neither fear of retaliation nor the ability to pass along costs is sufficient to explain why industry users continue to tolerate the intolerable. The fact is that this newspaper is so big that many paper companies would like to sell to it. It could call the paper industry's bluff, particularly if it lined up support from other publishers in the same situation.

The ultimate answer is that Japan is still in the iron grip of an insular mentality. There is the web of mutual back-scratching in which each sector desires its own collusion and protection from imports. There is the gut sense that only other Japanese firms with whom one has long worked can really be relied upon to play by the rules of the mutual support game in a time of crisis. There is the fear-based "full-set psychology" that says control over supply and pricing will only be secure if Japan makes everything it needs. Each industry must support protection of the other, even at the cost of "short-term" economic losses. Otherwise, the entire system might crumble. As one electronics executive told Tilton:

> If we and other big companies buy our steel overseas, then these steel companies would go out of business and we would lose our customers. Our company would have to leave Japan too. *And then we wouldn't be able to use Japanese trading practices anymore* [emphasis added].[60]

Hence, in the auto industry, despite intense pressure from a rising yen in the early 1990s, Tatsuro Toyoda (of Toyota) and his former high school classmate Kei Imai (of Nippon Steel) personally worked out a deal for the automakers that avoided importing cheaper foreign steel in return for slightly reduced prices. With steel only 5 percent of the total cost of building a car, the automakers apparently felt they could afford it.[61]

If these outmoded practices explain *why* efficient exporters go along with costly protection of their suppliers, it doesn't explain *how* they are able to do it. Pass-along is part of the answer of how. But, increasingly, Japan's industrial users *cannot* continue to absorb these costs. Using the efficient sectors to bail out the inefficient is rapidly becoming untenable. That's why Japan's dual economy is facing an unavoidable crisis. That's why the efficient exporters are going offshore. The irony is that it is easier for Toyota and Matsushita to leave Japan than to change it. The system designed to keep the inefficient supplier industries in Japan is forcing the efficient consumer industries to leave.

When Imports Are Inescapable, Buy the Foreign Producers: The Aluminum Model

Japan's policy in aluminum is a crucial test case, for it may be the model of what Japan will do when imports are inescapable: don't buy the foreign product; buy the foreign producers. Already, according to Jesper Koll, chief economist of J.P. Morgan's Tokyo office, two-thirds of the growth in manufactured imports over the past 15 years is from Japanese overseas subsidiaries.[62]

The aluminum case is commonly cited by those who argue that Japan has a good model for organizing exit in declining industries. In reality, when the oil shocks made domestic production of aluminum unviable, MITI delayed the shutdown of domestic capacity as long as possible.

Then, as it obstructed imports from foreign firms, it promoted Japanese investment overseas.

The results speak for themselves. In 1977, Japan produced almost all the aluminum it consumed. Sixteen years later in 1993, it was producing virtually none. However, *80 percent* of the lost output was replaced by imports from *Japanese-owned* plants overseas.[63]

Aluminum is often nicknamed "canned electricity." Even before the oil shock, energy accounted for 30 percent of the cost of refining aluminum. With the rise in oil prices, energy costs jumped to 60–70 percent of total costs. Since Japan's electricity rates in the early 1980s were ¥15–17 per kilowatt hour, versus ¥1–2 in Canada and ¥3–5 in the U.S., continuing to produce in Japan was ludicrous. Even after declining oil prices and the rising yen lowered energy costs, aluminum prices in Japan still averaged 25–60 percent above world prices. This was one industry that Japan's consuming industries refused to subsidize.

MITI wanted it both ways. On the one hand, it said it was switching goals from maintaining full domestic self-sufficiency to developing *Japanese-owned* production facilities overseas and importing from them. On the other hand, as late as 1981, a MITI report insisted that at least 700,000 tons of domestic capacity, about half of Japan's usage, was "indispensable."

In any case, MITI encouraged aluminum refiners in Japan to scrap some of their facilities and invest overseas. To this end, it organized the usual capacity-reduction cartel. In addition, it provided ¥82 billion ($713 million at ¥115 per dollar) in subsidies between 1978 and 1985, along with ¥276 billion ($2.4 billion) in low-interest loans for investment overseas. Tariffs were crafted to favor imports from these Japanese-owned plants.

At the same time, MITI *delayed* the shutdown both of domestic capacity and of competing imports until Japanese-owned imports were ready to come on line. In 1978 and again in 1981, MITI asked aluminum users to restrain their imports. Meanwhile, Washington protested that MITI was using tariff rebates to keep out competing imports. The MITI system granted tariff rebates to domestic aluminum firms based on how much domestic capacity they had replaced with overseas capacity. As late as 1981, MITI protested a Finance Ministry effort to cut aluminum tariffs, arguing that Japanese capacity overseas was not yet sufficient to replace domestic output, while importing from foreign-owned firms was not an acceptable alternative.[64]

As in other cases, the artificially high prices created by MITI-organized cartels induced *more* investment in the declining industry. During 1975–77, at the same time that MITI was organizing a 40 percent *production* cut, Japanese refiners expanded *capacity* 20 percent.

Too Many "Barbers"

Unless the dual economy is corrected, Japanese growth is doomed to become slower and slower. As the efficient sectors go offshore and as the inefficient sectors employ ever-larger portions of the labor force, the productivity growth and the GDP growth of the entire economy will gradually decline to the low growth rates of the stagnant sectors. Unless Japan ends its "convoy system" of protecting the inefficient, then the speed of the "convoy" known as Japan will gradually slow to the pace of its slowest ships. This is due to the "forces of unbalanced growth" that were explained more than a decade ago by economists Baumol, Blackman and Wolff.[65]

To see why, ask yourself: why does a barber earn so much more today than fifty years ago? Has his productivity really improved that much—or at all? Or, is it that the productivity of his *customers* has improved so that they are able and willing to pay more? In Japan's dual economy, there are far too many "barbers" living off the productivity gains of others.

Japan has tried to use a hefty trade surplus to provide more demand for the efficient manufacturers, thus enabling them to support the "barbers." But, as we shall see, ultimately this is futile. The only long-term answer is to improve the productivity of Japan's stagnant domestic sectors.

Consider a dual economy divided between a "progressive" sector with good productivity growth and a "stagnant" one with poor productivity growth. For the sake of simplicity, let's call them manufacturing and services. So, in flashlight batteries, output per man-hour grows at a hefty pace; by contrast, it takes a barber the same amount of time to cut someone's hair as 100 years ago.

In this situation, what happens over time is that labor shifts from manufacturing to services, and the growth of the whole economy slows down the stagnant productivity growth in services. The reason is the following. Suppose that productivity in manufacturing grows about 14 percent so that 86 workers can do the work that it previously took 100. Now, suppose that demand for manufactured goods goes up 10 percent. In that case, there is only need for 95 factory workers and five will have to be laid off ($86 \times 1.10 = 95$). Now, suppose that in services, productivity goes up much more slowly, say 5 percent, so that it now takes 95 workers to produce what it previously took 100. Suppose demand for services goes up by the same 10 percent as in manufacturing. In that case, the number of workers in services must *rise* by five (95 × 1.1 = 105). The slower growth of productivity in services causes five workers to switch from manufacturing to services.

As more and more workers shift, the rate of growth in the economy slows to the growth rate of the stagnant sector. To see why, suppose that, regardless of price changes, people need to buy the same number of flashlight batteries and haircuts every year. This is not unrealistic. In a cross section of 34 poor countries, as GDP per capita increased, the share of GDP devoted to services did *not* increase in price-adjusted terms. The same is true of the U.S. and Japan. Yes, in *nominal* terms, there was a huge switch in demand in Japan from goods to services amounting to almost 15 percent of total final consumption (Figure 7.2). But, once we adjust for price changes, the change is less than a third of that, less than 5 percent.[66]

To see why growth slows, let's take an extreme example. Suppose the manufacturing and service sectors each comprise half of GDP and half of the labor force.*

Now, suppose productivity rises by 10 percent in manufacturing and by zero in services. In that case, the entire growth in Japan's overall national income would come solely from productivity growth in manufacturing.

Since the population wants, in *real* (i.e., price-adjusted) terms, to spend half of its income on goods and half on services, the following *has* to occur:

1. GDP will grow by 5 percent (10 percent growth in manufacturing × 50 percent of GDP = 5 percent total growth).
2. The real wages of *all* workers will rise by 5 percent. In other words, manufacturing workers receive only half of their productivity improvement; the rest goes to pay for wage increases of the service workers.
3. The share in *real* GDP of the progressive and stagnant sectors stays at a 50:50 ratio.
4. The *price* of services (like haircuts) has to rise relative to that of goods to pay for the higher wages of the service workers. This is

---

*To make the arithmetic simple, let's assume that the two sectors start at the same level of output per worker, that labor is the sole input, that all workers get the same pay, and that the labor force doesn't grow so that all economic growth comes from increases in productivity.

Figure 7.2 **Real vs. Nominal Demand for Goods and Services**

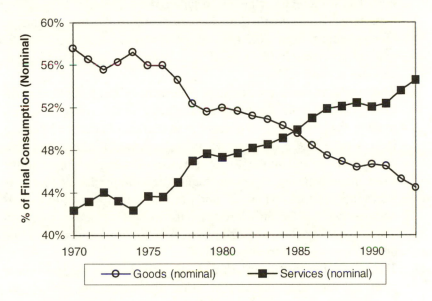

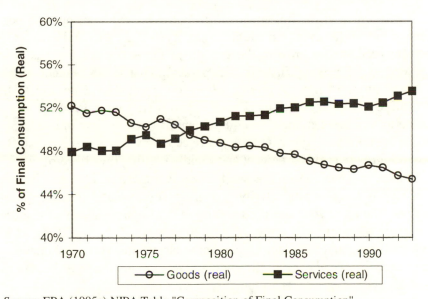

Source: EPA (1995a) NIPA Table "Composition of Final Consumption"

why inflation in the service sectors is always higher than in the manufacturing sector, whether in Japan or the U.S.

5. Consequently, in *nominal* terms, the share of the two sectors in GDP changes from 50:50 to 45 percent manufacturing and 55 percent services. It *looks* as if it is becoming a "post-industrial services economy."

6. The next part is the crucial step: 5 percent of the labor force will *have* to move from the progressive sector to the stagnant sector, making the labor ratio 45 percent in manufacturing and 55 percent in services. That's because 45 manufacturing workers can now produce as much output as 55 service workers. Workers move from manufacturing to services and the country looks like it is "deindustrializing." This is *not* because manufacturing is uncompetitive, but because productivity in services is so stagnant. This is exactly what we see for Japan in Figure 7.3 and the same phenomenon is also true for the U.S.

7. That's why the shift from goods to services is very big in *nominal* terms but very small in *real* (i.e., price-adjusted) terms.

It gets worse in the following years. In the second year, only 45 percent of the workers are in manufacturing. Even if they have the same 10 percent productivity growth, the growth of the entire economy is now reduced to 4.5 percent, instead of 5 percent. That is, 45 percent of the workers times 10 percent productivity growth equals 4.5 percent GDP growth. Consequently, 4.5 percent of the workers switch from manufacturing to services, leaving about 40 percent of workers in manufacturing. So, in the third year, growth of the entire economy drops to 4 percent. By year 15, growth is only 1 percent and rapidly hurtling toward zero!

Is there any way to stop this syndrome? Sure there is. The most important step is to raise productivity growth in services and other *stagnant* sectors. The more you raise productivity in the *stagnant* sectors, the more the entire economy will grow. If only 20 percent of the workforce is in manufacturing and the other 80 percent is elsewhere, you would have to raise each factory worker's efficiency 4 percent to get the same benefit as raising every other worker's productivity by 1 percent.

Japan's preservationist policy has done precisely the opposite. It has lowered the productivity of the stagnant sectors.

What Japan's leaders—as well as certain U.S. advocates of the "manufacturing matters" school—didn't recognize is this: under these condi-

Figure 7.3 **Poor Productivity in Services Draws in Labor**

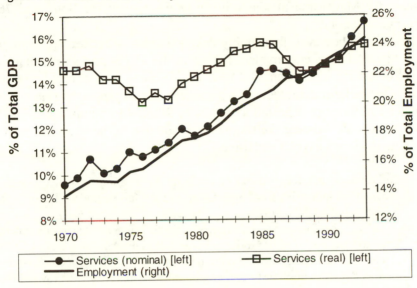

Services (nominal) [left]   Services (real) [left]
Employment (right)

Source: EPA (1995a) NIPA Table "GDP By Industry"
Note: This figure, unlike Figure 7.2, uses the narrow definition of "services" from the GDP tables. Because productivity is so poor in services, a much larger portion of the labor force has had to shift to the service sector to provide the same share of real GDP as in 1970. See text for explanation.

tions, it is not only counterproductive but *futile* to try to shove more workers into the progressive sector. Given the demand conditions, this simply cannot be done. There is not enough demand for the output of such additional workers.

The Futility of Japanese Neomercantilism

There is, of course, an illusory and temporary solution to the "unbalanced growth" dilemma for a trading economy. A country can expand demand for its progressive sector at the expense of its trading partners by exporting more and more of the output of the progressive sectors and limiting imports in those sectors.

This is the path that Japan took. In all of its key industries, such as autos, exports began to supply more and more of the growth. As late as 1990, exports provided 17 percent of the market for steel, 34 percent for machine tools, 45 percent for cars, 60 percent for electrical machinery, and 95 percent for videocassette recorders. Among the big electronics companies, reliance on exports ranged from 18 percent for NEC and 35 percent for Matsushita all the way up to 64 percent for Sony and 76 percent for Canon.[67]

Ultimately, however, this simply delays the day of reckoning. Sure, it kept manufacturing employment higher in the 1970s and 1980s than it might otherwise have been. But now the chickens are coming home to roost. One million manufacturing jobs were lost in the early 1990s and another 1 million are expected to be lost by 2002. More importantly, this approach simply worsens the stagnation in the rest of the sheltered economy. As Dollar and Wolff underline:

> Countries do not forge ahead or catch up by stealing jobs in the high-value-added industries from others, nor do they fall behind by losing jobs in high-value-added industries.
>
> Indeed, the forces of "unbalanced growth" suggest that employment tends to shift out of high-productivity-growth industries or sectors almost in step with its rate of labor productivity growth. . . . In an open economy there is a greater possibility that employment shares may shift toward the high-productivity-growth sectors, provided the exports of those industries can be continually expanded. *But, even in the export-oriented economies of Japan and Korea, this was not the case*; employment shifts were dominated by relative productivity growth movements. Thus the "high-value-added strategy" is generally a losing battle: it is almost impossible to maintain labor force share in high-productivity-growth sectors let alone expand them . . . [emphasis added][68]

Hollowing Out: Push Comes to Shove

If the costs of "preservationism" were simply slower growth, the existing system might still be salvageable, albeit with sub-optimum results. But, as we detailed in Chapter 3, the preservationist system is steadily driving away the geese that lay the golden eggs. It is raising costs in the strong sector so prohibitively that Japan's strong exporters are fleeing Japan. Moreover, as we shall see in the next chapter, the dual economy has created a witch's brew of macroeconomic distortions that lie behind Japan's current financial turmoil. The system cannot go on as it is.

Chapter 8

Economic Anorexia: From Bubble to Bust

The End of the Road

Just like buildings, economies with an underlying rot do not sink slowly into the pavement. For quite a long time, they go about their business apparently in fine shape, while out of view the support beams silently corrode. Then, one day, the walls cave in. So it was with the Soviet Union when Mikhail Gorbachev started pulling on the threads. So it was with Japan when the bottom fell out of the stock market in 1990.

What brought on the breakdown was that Japan's slow structural decline turned into a macroeconomic crisis. Just as a light bulb flashes brightest just before it burns out, so the economic gloom of the 1990s was heralded by the financial euphoria of the 1980s. Due to this sequence, many observers mistakenly regard the late-1980s "bubble" as the primary cause of today's stagnation. The bubble, in turn, is commonly viewed as the product of a bad mistake, i.e., an excessively expansionary monetary policy by the Bank of Japan. However, it's hard to believe that Japan's monetary authorities suddenly suffered an outbreak of mass stupidity. Nor is there any substance to the after-the-fact claim by the Ministry of Finance that the BOJ's monetary looseness was forced upon it by an agreement to support the dollar or the U.S. stock market.[1]

The reality is that the bubble was a perniciously false solution to a very real problem: Japan's cartelized economy is so distorted that it suffers a kind of "economic anorexia." In other words, private domestic demand is chronically too deficient to consume all that Japan produces. The bubble, a futile attempt to make up for that deficiency, was more a sysmptom of Japan's systemic problems than a cause. But it was a symptom that worsened the disease.

This "anorexia" did not exist in the high-growth era when rapid investment drove growth. However, as Japan matured, investment slowed down. In most countries when this happens, personal consumption rises to take up the slack—but not in Japan.

Figure 8.1 **1973-85: Trade Surpluses Provide Half of All Growth**

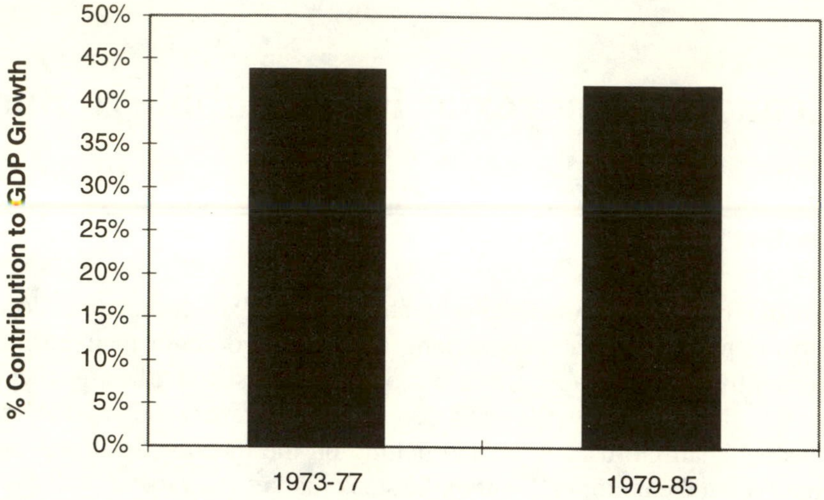

Source: EPA (1995a) NIPA Table "Contribution to GDE Growth," in constant yen, with deflators normalized to 1980=100. GDE = GDP.

To keep the economy afloat, Japan had to resort to a series of artificial stimuli, from enormous budget deficits to massive trade surpluses. True, exports had been critical to industrialization because they created demand for the new industries. But, from a macroeconomic standpoint, they supplemented, rather than substituted for, domestic demand. Not so after 1973. Japan's rising trade surpluses after 1973 were not a sign of health, but a way of stimulating an economy unable to grow on its own. A few Japanese economists pointed this out at the time:

> The structural change that occurred around 1970 made exports the main engine of growth of the Japanese economy, in place of domestic demand.[2]

Indeed, during 1973–85 (with the brief exception of 1978–79), nearly *half* of all GDP growth came from a growing trade surplus (Figure 8.1).

But it takes two to tango. Japan could only keep generating ever-larger trade surpluses as long the rest of the world—particularly the U.S.—was willing and able to absorb ever-larger deficits. The trade frictions of the 1980s and the "*endaka* (high yen) shock" that followed the Plaza Accords of 1985 signaled that this willingness was coming to an end. From that moment on, Japan would suffer the worst of both worlds. Its trade surpluses were high enough to antagonize its trading partners, but these surpluses would never again grow fast enough to propel GDP growth for more than a year or two.

As the yen began soaring in 1986 and Japanese exports were increasingly priced out of the market, the economy gulped. Industrial production started falling. At that key fork in the road, reformers, exemplified by the famous Maekawa Commission Report of 1986, warned that Japan must become a consumer-led economy, one more open to the world. A more open economy would force greater efficiencies, while greater consumption at home would enhance overall demand. Derisively brushing off that warning, Japan's leaders instead injected the economy with monetary steroids, unleashing the late 1980s bubble.[3]

For a while, the bubble provided a temporary boost to growth. It stimulated something that looked like investment. Factories and buildings went up. But, in the end, they had little real economic value, as can be seen in empty offices and in the red ink flowing from bank balance sheets.

When the bubble met its inevitable demise, the economy collapsed. Anorexia returned with a vengeance. Once again, Japan faced the same dilemmas addressed in the 1986 Maekawa Report, but by then it was in far worse shape.

Why Is Japan Anorexic?

At the heart of Japan's post-1973 anorexia is its low personal consumption. In this as in so many other areas, Japan is an international outlier.

Normally, during the era of industrial takeoff, a country's personal consumption declines as a percentage of GDP (Figure 8.2). In fact, consumption must decline relative to GDP in order for investment rates to rise.

But this is still a good deal for consumers. Because they are willing to take a smaller share of the pie today, the pie is much bigger ten years later. In Japan, even as consumption fell from 62 percent of GDP to only 54 percent, real consumption per person *tripled* in only 18 years (1955 to 1973)![4] Consumption fell relative to GDP only because it was growing slightly more slowly, "only" 8.3 percent a year compared to 9 percent for total GDP. Over time, compounding magnifies even tiny differences into huge differentials. It was the slower pace of consumption growth that made room for the share of GDP devoted to investment to soar from 7 percent in 1955 to 25 percent in 1970 (Figure 8.3).

In most countries, as the industrial takeoff eases, the pattern reverses.

Figure 8.2 **Japan Stands Alone with No Revival of Consumption**

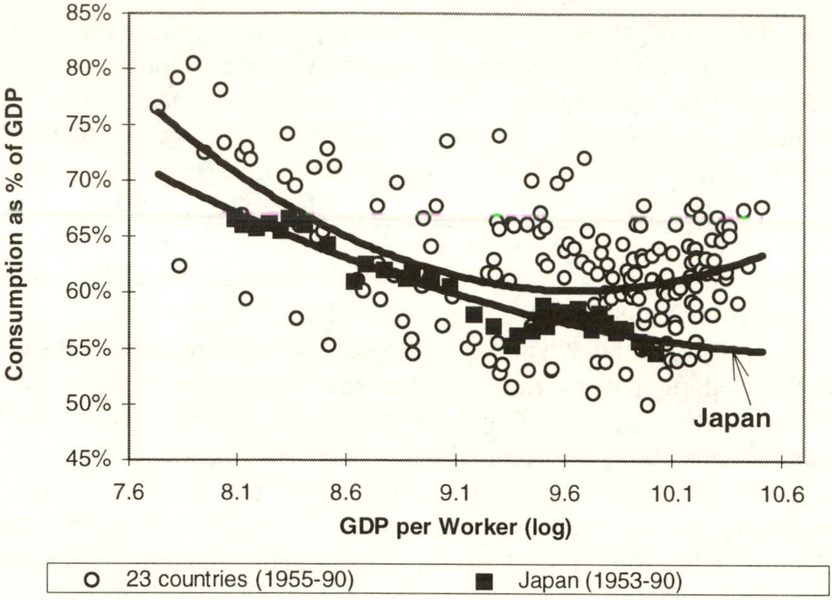

Source: Summers and Heston (1995)

Investment needs slow down and the return on investment declines. As companies invest less, the share of GDP devoted to investment declines, and the share devoted to consumption rebounds. Among the 23 countries in Figure 8.2, the consumption share of GDP typically turned up again once GDP per worker reached about $15,500. This is the level Japan reached in 1979 and Korea reached in 1990.

For a few years in the early 1970s, Japan appeared to be following the normal pattern. The consumption share of GDP did rise a bit. Then came the oil shock, Japan's preservationist response and the creation of the high price structure. Suddenly, despite Japan's maturation, the consumption:GDP ratio resumed its decline.

As the 1970s turned into the 1980s, Japan fell more and more out of step with international norms. By 1990, when Japan's GDP per worker was $22,600, consumption was just 55 percent of GDP. It was almost at its lowest rate in the entire postwar period. In the typical country at that level of GDP, consumption was 60 percent of GDP. That's the rate Germany reached when its GDP level hit $22,000 in 1970.

Of course, even though the consumption *share* of GDP declined, living standards still rose. This point needs to be underlined because there is

Figure 8.3 **Consumption vs. Investment during the High-Growth Era**

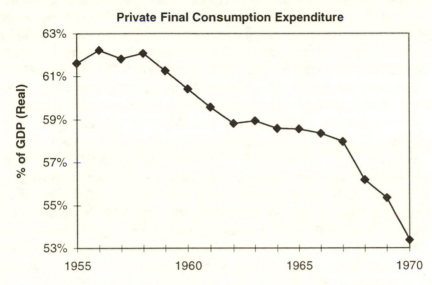

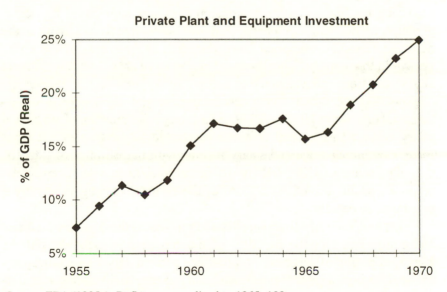

Source: EPA (1995a). Deflators normalized to 1965=100.

such a misconception about this. For example, James Fallows, in his zeal to show that Japan's economy is rigged to benefit producers at the expense of consumers, has insisted that "in Japan, individuals remained poor so that industries could grow strong." Fallows reported that, as he looked out of his window upon his Tokyo neighborhood, "modern plumbing was rare" and "most of our neighbors had no cars."[5]

Fallows must have lived in the most unusual neighborhood in all of Tokyo. Today, virtually every Japanese household has a car, piped-in water, a washing machine, a refrigerator, and a color TV (Table 8.1). Only a few decades ago, few enjoyed these accouterments of the middle-class life.[6]

Nonetheless, *relative to GDP*, consumption was declining at the same time that investment was slowing. What then was the source of demand in the economy? Increasingly, the answer was budget deficits and trade surpluses. And this is the source of so much of the U.S.–Japan economic friction as well as of Japan's internal financial mess.

As with so many of Japan's troubles, former strengths were the source of current weakness. Having learned how to limit consumption and promote savings during the high-growth era, Japan found it hard to shift gears when the times changed.

During the high-growth era, consumption was suppressed by demographics. Some 14 million people fled the countryside to seek work in the new factories. They supplied more than half (55 percent) of the entire growth in the nonfarm labor force.[7] This "reserve army" of new workers kept wages from rising as much as output.

Consequently, urban wages and salaries stayed at 50 percent of national income from 1955 to 1970 even though the number of wage and salary earners had jumped from 62 percent to 82 percent of the labor force. Combining wage and salary income with the earnings of farmers, the labor share of GDP fell by 18 percent! (Figure 8.4). Conversely, corporate profits tripled their share of the national income from only 5 percent to 16 percent.

Firms took their newfound profits and reinvested them in new factories and equipment. Not the frugality of the Japanese households, but the increased profits of Japanese corporations created Japan's extraordinary national savings. Japanese households did increase their savings rate during the high-growth era. But, since the labor share of national income was going down, this canceled out the higher personal savings rates. As a share of GDP, household savings did not budge throughout the high-growth era (Figure 8.5).

Table 8.1

From Poverty to Middle-Class Life in Two Generations

Number per 100 Households:	1957	1960	1965	1970	1975	1980	1990	1996
Car		1		22	41	57	77	80
Electric clothes washer	20	45	69	88	98	99	108	108
Electric refrigerator	3	16	51	85	97	99	116	119
Black-and-white TV	8	55	90	90				
Color TV				26	90	98	197	215
VCR							82	104
Microwave oven							71	90
% of Dwellings with:		1963	1968		1973	1978	1990	1993
Piped water		68%	80%		87%	93%	94%	95%
Flush toilets		9%	17%		31%	46%		77%
Flush toilets in dwellings built after 1991								90%

Source: Bronfenbrenner and Yasuba (1987), pp. 106–107, with updates from Statistics Bureau, Office of the Prime Minister

Figure 8.4 **1955-70: Labor Share Plummets, Capital Share Soars**

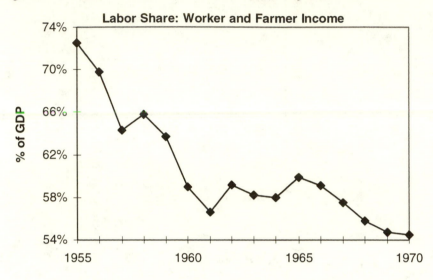

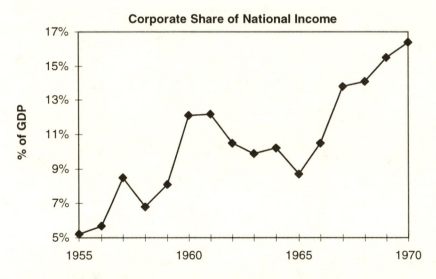

Source: EPA (1995a) NIPA Table "Distribution of National Income" in current yen

Figure 8.5 **Business, Not Households, Provides Added Savings**

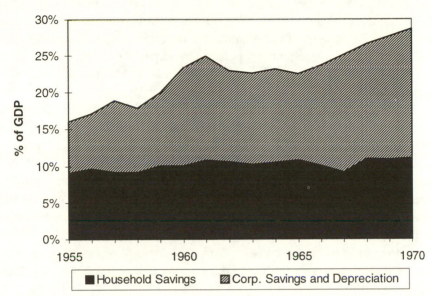

Source: EPA (1995a) NIPA Tables: "Income and Outlay by Institutional Sectors"

High savings and investment are the supply-side ingredients of rapid growth. But growth needs demand too. Companies are not going to invest unless they can sell their output profitably. So, with consumption going down relative to GDP, what provided the demand?

Amazingly, during the high-growth era, the answer is: investment itself. As Japanese economists put it at the time, "investment breeds investment." When Toyota builds and operates an auto plant, that creates more demand throughout the economy for the materials and machinery that Toyota needs, the materials and machinery for Toyota's suppliers, and all the purchases by the construction workers and then the Toyota workers. Through the so-called multiplier effect, the initial investment in an auto plant will create demand throughout the economy several times higher than the initial investment.

In fact, to some degree during the takeoff stage, investment can sometimes stimulate demand even more than it expands supply. This was the case for Japan in the 1960s. When this happens, then an increase in investment paradoxically appears to create a *shortage* of capacity, requiring still more investment. Under these conditions, growth explodes.[8]

During 1966–73, a decomposition of gross domestic demand showed that the majority, 52 percent, of the growth in gross domestic demand was propelled by investment, 20 percent by exports and 27 percent by gross domestic demand itself. When investment in turn was examined, it was found that 73 percent of the demand for investment was ultimately propelled by other investment, 15 percent by exports and 13 percent from growth in overall domestic demand. Japan was an investment-driven economy.[9]

However, machines building machines to build machines cannot go on forever. At some point, there must be a final outlet for all this investment.

In part, exports supplied this need. By rising as a share of GDP, exports enabled Japan to simultaneously limit the rise of consumption, thereby increasing savings, and yet still have a final outlet for all the investment. Nonetheless, as a source of overall demand in the economy, exports played second fiddle to investment (Figure 8.6).

Anticipation of *future* consumption was critical. Although consumption was declining as a share of GDP, it was still rising quite rapidly in absolute terms. Economist Hiroshi Yoshikawa has argued quite cogently that the movement of households to the city provided a powerful source of demand for the new goods being produced by industry, from cars to refrigerators to washing machines to TVs, and thus for the goods embodied in them, from steel to electricity.[10] Much of Japan's investment was made in anticipation of current, but especially *future*, demand for consumption as well as exports.

Then, in the early 1970s, Japan experienced the turning point that comes to all industrializing countries: the surplus labor from the farm ran out. The flow of farmers to the cities fell to half the rate of the 1960s.[11] Whereas the supply of new labor had previously exceeded the demand for labor, now the new supply couldn't keep up with the still rapidly growing demand. In response, wages soared. And so did the labor share of national income (Figure 8.7). As a result of the income shift, consumption rose as a share of GDP (Figure 8.8).

This rise in wages and consumption was exactly what Japan needed. Japan had by now built up its capital stock. Investment no longer bred new investment. After 1970, investment started slowing (Figure 8.9).

Had this pattern of slowing investment and accelerating consumption continued, Japan would have followed the normal path of development.[12]

But then something mysterious happened. Following the oil shock, the labor share of international income fell back again. Hence, the capital

Figure 8.6 **Exports Double Share of GDP, but Still Second to Investment as Growth Driver**

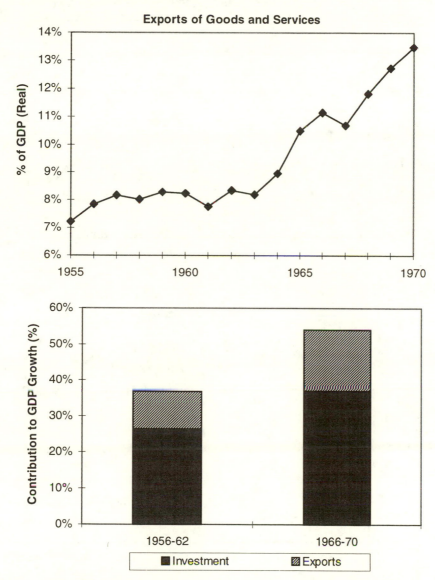

Source: EPA (1995a), constant 1965 yen (1990 deflators normalized to 1965)
Note: Private corporate investment accounted for only 20% of GDP in 1966-70, but it supplied nearly 40% of the growth. Exports were 12% of GDP, but supplied 17% of the growth.

Figure 8.7 **In 1970s: At First Labor Share Leaps, Then Falls Back**

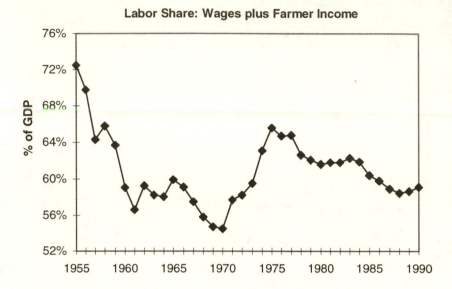

Labor Share: Wages plus Farmer Income

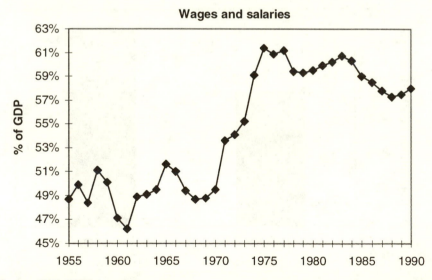

Wages and salaries

Source: EPA (1995a), current yen

Note: As in other countries, once the surplus of farmers coming to the factories slowed down, wages soared. But, in Japan, unlike elsewhere, the labor share fell back after the first oil shock, and stayed down. Compare with Figure 8.2

Figure 8.8 **1970s-80s: Consumption Share Rises, Then Falls Back**

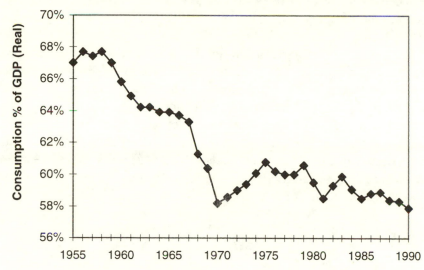

Figure 8.9 **After 1970, Investment Rate Falls--Until Bubble Era**

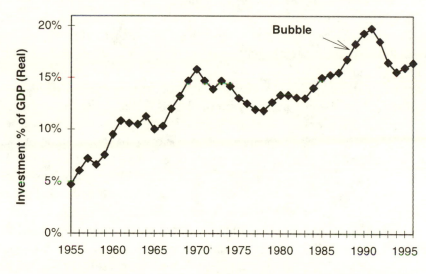

Source: EPA (1997) NIPA Table "Gross Domestic Expenditures" in constant 1990 yen
Note: Because these figures are in constant 1990 yen, the exact numbers, but not the
trend, differ from Figure 8.3, where the figures are in constant 1965 yen.

share, which had begun to recede as in all countries at this stage, re-bounded again. With workers earning too small a portion of the national income, the consumption share also fell back (Figure 8.7, Figure 8.8, Figure 8.10).

The culprit in this retreat from normal development was Japan's protectionism. Protection of farming required protection of food processing. Protection of steel required protection of autos and machinery. Protection of cement required protection of construction. All these layers of protection padded profits up and down the line. They also made consumer prices so high that consumers simply could not afford to pay them all; they consumed less. What individuals gained in security as wage earners they lost in income and living standards as consumers. The dual economy is what created the anorexic economy.

Japan's Chronic "Excess Savings"

In the jargon of economics, the other side of the coin of under-consumption is "excess savings." This term undoubtedly sounds strange to people in both Japan and the U.S. But, as we will show, while the U.S. saves far too little, Japan saves far too much.

This is not because Japanese individuals are obsessive penny-pinchers. On the contrary, as Japan reached maturity and growth slowed, households lowered their savings rates just as they do in most every other country (Figure 8.11).

Japan's national savings stayed too high because too much of Japan's income was still being gathered into the hands of its corporations. In the high-growth era, corporate cash flow was high but investment needs were even higher. Hence, companies needed to borrow what households saved. At the level of the economy as a whole, there was a good balance between savings and investment. But, following 1973, corporations were still raking in cash as they had done in the old days and yet their investment needs had declined. Japanese corporations had more cash than they knew what to do with. Given all that excess cash, companies had less need to borrow additional funds from household savings. In fact, corporate borrowing fell even faster than household savings fell. The result, at the national level, was excess savings, i.e., gross savings much higher than gross investment. In a typical post-1973 year, the gap between what households saved and what companies could profitably use ranged as high as 4–5 percent of GDP (Figure 8.12).

Figure 8.10 **After initial drop in early 1970s, Capital Share Rebounds**

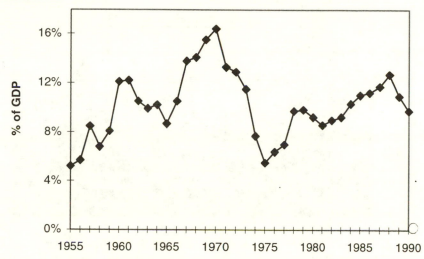

Source: EPA (1995a) NIPA Table "Distribution of National Income" in current yen

Figure 8.11 **After Mid-1970s, Households Reduce Savings Rate**

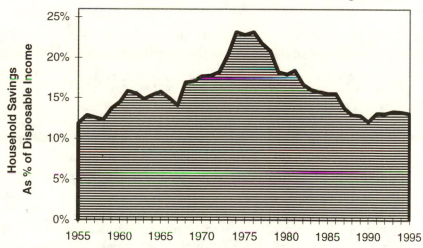

As a mature economy, Japan should generate and export some surplus savings, perhaps 1–2 percent of GDP. But Japan's excess savings have been so excessive that they created enormous distortions for both itself and its trading partners.

Here's why. Excess savings is the same thing as insufficient demand.

Figure 8.12 **Japan's Excess Savings Dilemma**

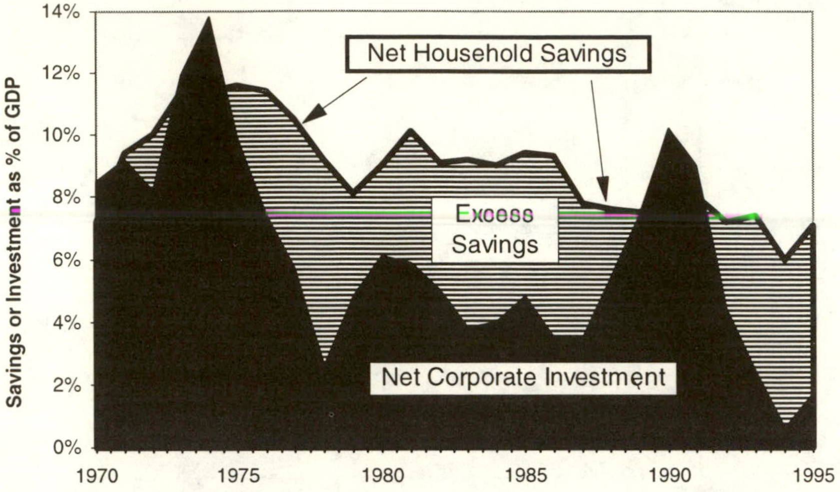

Source: (EPA 1997) NIPA Tables "Household Savings Rate" and "Capital Finance Accounts by Institutional Sectors"

Note: Figure 8.12 shows the gap between net household savings and net corporate investment. The latter is the amount of corporate investment that cannot be financed from internal cash flow, and for which the companies must borrow. In the 1980s, and again in the mid-1990s, the gap was several percent of GDP.

Ultimately, savings and investment have to equal each other. If savings is larger than investment, the result is a leakage of purchasing power for the overall economy. The reason is that savings comes out of income and represents a decision by certain people not to spend. It is a decrease of demand in the economy. When other people borrow those savings and invest, they are plowing the purchasing power back into the economy. So, when savings and investment equal each other, the total purchasing power in the economy remains the same; it is just spent by different people. But if those savings are not spent, then the purchasing power is not plowed back in. There is a drain.

What then happens? Consider this: one person's income is the result of another person's spending, and that income, in turn, allows for new spending. Just as savings and investment must equal each other at the economy-wide level, so must income and spending. If investment is less than savings, that means that spending in a given year is less than the income earned that year. That shortfall in spending, in turn, will reduce income in the next cycle, which, in turn, reduces spending still further. GDP will keep on shrinking until finally savings are as low as investment, or, what amounts to the same thing, income is as low as spending. In fact, this is how recessions or prolonged stagnation occurs.

When, as in Japan, a country chronically saves far more than it can invest, the economy faces the ever-present danger of recession unless some new way is found to absorb those savings. This is the classic Keynesian dilemma.

Unless private investment can be stimulated and/or consumption unleashed, the only alternative for a *closed* society (i.e., one that does not trade with the rest of the world) is a big budget deficit. Let the government borrow and spend more than its own "income," i.e., taxes.

In a trading economy, the alternative is a growing trade surplus. Lend the foreigners the excess savings, so that they can buy Japanese exports. This shows up as a big trade surplus and an equally big surge in overseas investments.

During the past two decades, Japan has alternated between these two "solutions."

With the post-1973 slowdown, the budget deficit exploded, hitting 5.5 percent by 1978. During 1974–79, deficit spending accounted for 17 percent of all growth (Figure 8.13).

As important as deficit spending seemed, the real action was on the trade front. During 1973–85 (except for 1978 and 1979), *nearly half of all GDP growth came from a growing trade surplus* (Figure 8.14). As the trade surplus took over, Japan was able to start reducing its budget deficit. Even in the 1979–85 period when investment rebounded, Japan's growth was far more dependent on the trade surplus than on investment.

Then the Japanese export boom hit a brick wall: the 1985 Plaza Accord, which sent the yen soaring. Suddenly, Japanese exports were priced out of the market and the trade surplus began to shrink. A trade surplus that had amounted to as much as 4.3 percent of GDP at the peak in 1985 rapidly plunged to less than 1 percent by 1989 (Figure 8.15).

To be sure, the trade surplus remained high enough to fuel trade friction. But a high surplus in and of itself does not add to GDP growth. Only a *growing* trade surplus does. A high surplus that is shrinking does Japan no good at all. As the trade surplus shrank, it detracted from growth. The accumulated decline of the surplus by 3 percent of GDP from 1985 to 1989 is equivalent to a good-sized recession. Indeed, in 1986, growth did pause. Industrial production did not just slow; it actually started falling.

It was at the onset of this process that the commission led by former Bank of Japan Governor Haruo Maekawa issued its famous report. For

Figure 8.13 **Deficit Spending Explodes to Keep Economy Afloat**

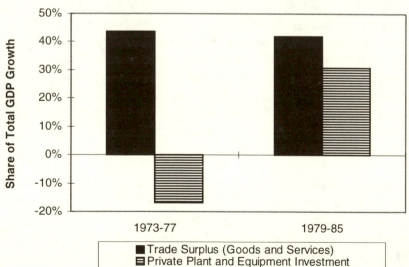

Source: EPA (1997) "Capital Finance Accounts by Institutional Sectors." Calendar year, in current yen; *1996 is from the Bank of Japan "Flow of Funds" figures.
Note: The budget balance figures refer to all government activities at the national and local level, social security and government-owned enterprises.

Figure 8-14 **Trade Surplus Replaces Investment as Growth Driver**

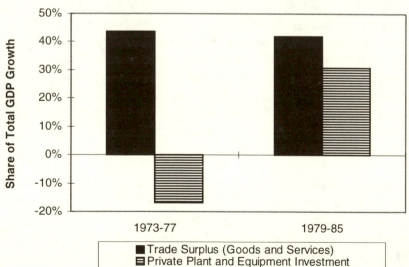

Source: EPA (1995a) NIPA Table "Contribution to GDE Growth," in constant yen, with deflators normalized to 1980=100. GDE = GDP.

Figure 8.15 **As Yen Soars, Trade Surplus Route to Growth Falters**

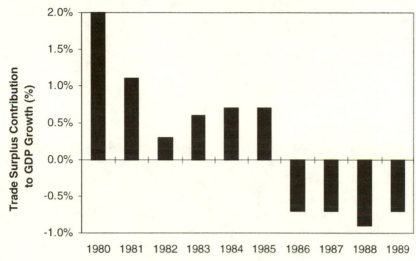

Source: EPA (1997) NIPA Table "Sources of GDE Growth"
Note: This chart shows the amount that GDP is raised or lowered by a rsing or falling trade surplus, e.g., in 1986, a falling trade surplus lowered GDP by 0.7%. GDE = GDP.

the first time, an official Japanese body pointed the finger for Japan's internal problems and its chronic trade surplus straight at the homegrown syndrome of excess savings. What the report lacked in specific solutions and political will, it made up in its clear philosophy: a proposal for a radical change to a consumer-led economy open to imports.

Implementing the Maekawa approach was a political hornet's nest because Japan was caught in a particularly nasty vicious cycle. Excess savings led Japan to rely on expanding trade surpluses to fuel growth; in other words: more exports, fewer imports. Yet, protection led to high prices in inefficient sectors at home. Those high prices, in turn, stifled consumer demand, which ended up exacerbating the problem of excess savings. That required still greater trade surpluses. This dead end is what the Maekawa Report was trying to correct.

To create an economy led by consumer demand, Japan needed more import-led "price destruction" in the protected and cartelized domestic sectors. Import liberalization and consumer-led growth walked hand in hand. However, while the urban middle class and exporters would benefit, it would mean a direct attack on all the cartels and construction *dango* and retailer/farmer *koenkai* that kept the LDP in power.

Since so much of Japan's political elite refused to accept the radical political-economic prescription, they had to discredit the diagnosis. Aside from exceptional reform economists like Iwao Nakatani, the diagnosis of excess savings was derided by many of Japan's most prominent economists, including Ryutaro Komiya of Tokyo University, Masaru Yoshitomi, formerly chief economist for the EPA, and Osamu Shimomura, a giant of the high-growth era. Surprisingly, even such prominent Americans as economist Martin Feldstein and former Federal Reserve Chairman Paul Volcker joined in the criticism. These Americans joined the MOF in arguing that Japan's excess savings and consequent trade surplus were a benefit to a capital-starved world.[13]

Rather than reform the economy, Japan's leaders chose to gun the money supply and drive down interest rates, thereby inadvertently launching the infamous "bubble" of the late 1980s. The monetary steroids artificially—and temporarily—revived investment and made the economy boom, thereby appearing to solve the problem of excess savings.

Investment rose to replace the falling trade surplus as the prime stimulant (Figure 8.16). During 1985–91, investment provided 42 percent of all growth.[14] In fact, while the bubble lasted, investment rates even topped those of the high-growth era (refer to Figure 8.9).

At first, the monetary stimulus did little more than simply stimulate investment and raise prices of stocks and real estate. But soon asset prices began to feed on themselves way beyond any economic justification. People who bought stocks or real estate stopped caring whether the companies earned good profits or the buildings exacted high rents. Rather, in accordance with the "greater fool theory," they bought these assets only because they expected someone else to pay an even higher price later on. To make matters worse, investors not only *bought* real estate for this reason; they also *built* it. The same thing happened with factories. As the stock market soared, it valued companies—and by implication, their factories—far in excess of what it actually cost to build those factories. Companies took this as a signal to build many more factories than the economy really needed.

Naturally, this investment boom could not be sustained—because the real return to these investments was often negligible. Some of the "bubble buildings" are the loveliest in all of Tokyo. Yet, in far too many cases, they were the economic equivalent of digging ditches and filling them up again. In creating new factories to make exports, Japanese companies were all too often navigating through a rear-view mirror, building for markets that would never exist because the high yen would price them out of existence.

While the party lasted, everything seemed fine. The economy boomed.

Figure 8.16 Bubble-Fed Investment Replaces Trade Surplus as Demand Driver

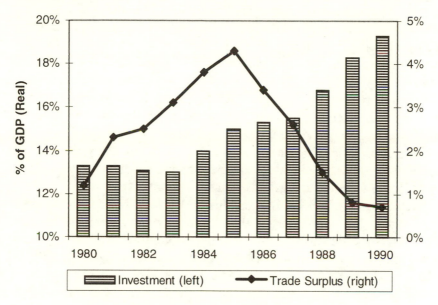

Source: EPA (1997) NIPA Tables, in constant 1990 yen, calendar year
Note: This charts shows the size of investment and of the trade surplus (in goods and services) as a percent of GDP.

Corporate borrowing soared to nearly 10 percent of GDP—levels not seen since the catch-up era—and sopped up all the excess savings (refer to Figure 8.12).

Inevitably, the day came to pay the piper. Without genuine economic profits, there was no way for the borrowers to repay the banks, bondholders and other investors. The sky-high level of nonperforming bank loans is simply the financial manifestation of this deeper problem.

Once the bubble burst, the process reversed itself. Just as rising asset prices artificially stimulated investment, so falling asset prices depressed investment. That, in turn, depressed the whole economy. The downturn was exacerbated and prolonged by the refusal of the MOF to apply fiscal stimulus early on. Despite interest rates almost at zero and a budget deficit that eventually ballooned out of control, the economy has yet to recover.

Excess Savings and the Banking Crisis

Japan's notorious banking mess is the financial mirror of the excess savings syndrome. Every year trillions of yen of unneeded deposits flooded into the banks, along with enormous unwanted premiums into the insurance companies, and mounting investment funds into the securities houses. The banks and other financiers frantically searched for a way to invest that money so that they could meet the interest and dividend payments. The supply of savings grew so much faster than the need for them that banks' commercial loans soared from 73 percent of GDP in 1987 to 97 percent by 1992.

When there is so much superfluous money to invest, it is not likely to be allocated wisely. International bankers found this out in the 1970s when they suddenly had to recycle tens of billions of "petrodollars." They lent much of it to Latin American dictators and paid the price with the 1980s debt crisis. While this "petrodollar recycling" was a one-time event, Japan faces the equivalent dilemma year after year.

Despite loose talk about the benefits of Japanese savings in a capital-short world, it's hard to argue that Japanese money went to the most economically efficient uses. Some went to build factories in Southeast Asia. However, 80 percent was sent to the rich countries, where $600 billion went down the drain in foreign exchange losses alone.

The outrageous prices paid for Rockefeller Center or California's Pebble Beach are only the tip of the iceberg. Tessa De Carlo, a writer in Napa Valley, California's famed wine country, recalls seeing Japanese investors driving by vineyards, stopping at one or another, and saying, "I'll buy that," without knowing anything more. An American lawyer who worked on mergers & acquisitions (M&A) in the 1980s reports that one Japanese firm looking to take over a U.S. construction company declared, "Unless we find a way to invest this money, we'll have to pay taxes on it. So find me a company to buy."

When smart people do foolish things over a long period of time, we have to look for deeper causes. The deeper cause is excess savings.

"The Japan That Has Not Yet Attained Capitalism"

A few years back, the MOF's Eisuke Sakakibara wrote an essay on the Japanese economy entitled "Beyond Capitalism."[15] A more accurate title would have been "The Japan That Has Not Yet Attained Capitalism."

Capital markets are at the heart of capitalism. The job of the financial sector is not only to raise money for companies to invest, but also to allocate it to its most efficient use. But the structural flaws in Japan's "pre-capitalist" financial system have rendered it incapable of fulfilling that role. Indeed, Japan's excess savings syndrome was tremendously compounded by the structural flaws in Japanese finance, flaws that in 1997 prompted Prime Minister Hashimoto to announce a program of "Big Bang" financial reforms. (Whether the "Big Bang" reforms will solve the problem remains to be seen.)

During the high-growth era, Japan's bank-centered financial system vacuumed up huge amounts of household savings (on which savers usually received interest rates lower than consumer inflation). The banks then shoveled that money into rapidly growing, sometimes government-targeted, capital-intensive industries.

The stock market, instead of serving its normal function as a device to raise and allocate capital, has performed mostly as an anti-takeover buffer (through cross-shareholding) and a casino. Stock issues produced less than 4 percent of new company funds as late as 1968 while bonds played a similarly negligible role. Hence stock and bond prices never served as a guide to capital allocation, the true function of the capital markets in a normal capitalist economy. Although the portion of financing supplied through the bond and stock markets has gone up somewhat, the basic picture has not changed (Table 8.2).[16]

No one denies that Japan's "main bank" system has many virtues, including patient and dedicated capital. Studies have shown that this system often restored to good health troubled firms that might have been abandoned by an impersonal capital market. There have even been calls in the U.S. for more "relationship investing."

Unfortunately, in Japan, capital was just a little too dedicated, a little too patient. One reason is that the biggest borrowers own the banks and vice versa. According to Ken Courtis, 85 percent of the stock of the big commercial banks is owned by large Japanese companies and other financial institutions. The banks in turn often hold shares of their borrowers.[17]

Capital was also a little too protected. Risk was taken out of the system. Japan's banking operates under a "convoy" system in which faster ships must restrain themselves to the speed of the slowest. Until 1997, not a single sizable bank has been allowed to fail since World War II. If it got into trouble, stronger banks had to absorb it. Since banks were not allowed to fail, not too many bank customers could be allowed to fail either. The same kind of moral hazard that afflicted American S&Ls in the 1980s existed at the core of Japan's banking system. Few companies and executives ever paid for their mistakes.

Consider this: In the aftermath of America's S&L crisis, approximately

Table 8.2

Equities, Bonds Rank Low in Japan's "Bankers' Kingdom" (Portion of corporate financing from various sources)

	External Funds		Equity Issues		Bond Issues		Bank Loans	
	Japan	U.S	Japan	U.S.	Japan	U.S.	Japan	U.S.
Portion of total financing								
1970–74	47%	62%	3%	20%	9%	9%	41%	9%
1975–79	55%	79%	7%	7%	11%	9%	27%	6%
1970–79	51%	71%	5%	13%	10%	9%	34%	8%

	Equity Issues		Bond Issues		Bank Loans	
	Japan	U.S.	Japan	U.S.	Japan	U.S.
Portion of external financing						
1970–74	5%	52%	17%	25%	78%	24%
1975–79	16%	31%	24%	41%	60%	28%
1970–79	10%	44%	20%	31%	69%	25%

Source: Okimoto (1989), p. 137

1,600 banker crooks were sent to jail. In Japan, by contrast, under a scheme unveiled in January 1998 for the government to buy preferred shares in failing banks, the MOF and LDP decided that the government dare not even ask the executives of these banks to resign. Where there is no accountability, incompetence and corruption are given free rein.

Protected by regulations and a lenient Finance Ministry Banking Bureau, the banks had no system for screening customer creditworthiness resembling anything like the screening departments of American banks. Bank loans were not based on projections of future company cash flow. Nor did banks charge different rates according to the riskiness of the loan. A former MITI official complained:

> With their government protection, banks firmly believe that all they need to do to make a profit is to increase the scale of their deposits and loans. This conviction is especially pronounced regarding the financing of land since its supply is limited ... the Japanese financial community is so reliant on government protection and supply restrictions [barriers to entry into banking —rk], it even lacks the ability to evaluate collateral or check personal credit records.[18]

Instead of using cash flow projections, banks lent to established customers (some of whose stock they may have owned) based on collateral. If a company had property, whether real estate or even stocks of other firms, it could borrow based on that collateral.

Once the bubble was launched, such a system was virtually calculated to pour oil on the flames. The monetary ease raised the value of assets like real estate and stocks. Companies could then go to their banks, point out that the value of their collateral had risen, and borrow even more—not to make their normal products—but to buy even more real estate and stocks. That raised the values of those assets even more, allowing still more borrowing to buy still more assets, ad infinitum.

In 1987, 40 percent of Toyota's profits came, not from its auto production, but from non-operating revenues, much of which was financial speculation. At Matsushita, the ratio was 60 percent. It was 65 percent at Nissan, 63 percent at Sony, and 134 percent at Sanyo.[19]

Via this process, stock prices were geared up to 100 times corporate earnings. The land underneath the Imperial Palace in Tokyo was supposedly worth more than the entire state of California. From the standpoint of the financial system as a whole, this was a house of cards destined to collapse, or, as the Japanese put it in 20/20 hindsight, a "bubble" foredoomed to pop. Yet, as far as each individual bank loan officer was concerned, there was no problem. After all, the borrower had the collateral (Figure 8.17).[20]

In 1990, the house of cards collapsed. The Finance Ministry put the bad loan total at ¥40 trillion (or $300 billion at the early 1998 yen/dollar rate), or about 5 percent of all bank loans and about 10 percent of Japanese GDP. Because MOF accounting standards allow many bad loans to be hidden, the true size of the bad loan problem was at least twice the MOF estimate, according to respected private economists like Deutsche Bank's Kenneth Courtis: in other words, 10 percent of all bank loans and a staggering 20 percent of GDP.[21]

As the years have passed, the MOF estimates also keep going up. In early 1998, the MOF put the estimate of problematic loans as high as ¥77 trillion (or almost $600 billion). Some private economists say the true number is probably closer to $800 billion.

The scary fact is that no one really knows. This is not only due to poor accounting standards and devious practices, but due to the fact that there are only several hundred bank examiners in Japan, compared to thousands in the U.S.

Japan's banking crisis makes America's S&L fiasco look like nothing. For one thing, the actual losses in America's banking crisis of the early 1990s were only 2 percent of all bank loans and about 1 percent of GDP.

Half of these non-performing loans in Japan are on the books of the 21 *largest* banks. By contrast, with the exception of a couple of big banks like Citicorp, America's crisis affected mostly Savings & Loan companies (S&Ls) in a few energy states hit hard by the 1986 crash of oil prices.

The banking crisis in Japan started off far worse than in the U.S., precisely because the underlying macroeconomic imbalances and the flaws in the financial system were far more serious. Then, resolution of the crisis was dragged out when the MOF, to avoid bankruptcies under the "convoy" ideology, used so-called Price-Keeping Operations (PKO) to prevent stock and real estate prices from hitting bottom.[22]

These figures don't even count the huge potential for defaults on government loans made through the Fiscal Loan and Investment Program (FLIP). For example, in the early 1980s, the governmental Housing Loan Corporation was lending up to $10 billion a year. In early 1998, as a credit crunch by fragile banks led to increased bankruptcies at small and medium firms and a new election loomed, the government announced a

Figure 8.17 **Real Estate: What Goes Up Too High Must Come Down**

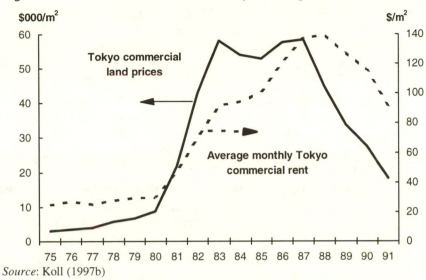

Source: Koll (1997b)

plan for the FLIP to lend up to ¥12 trillion (almost $100 billion and 2.5 percent of GDP) to small and medium companies. These companies can use these funds not only for normal operations but to pay back their bank loans. It's a scheme straight out of Kakuei Tanaka's electoral handbook. One seriously wonders how many of these loans will be paid back. There is no reason government loans should be considered any safer than housing loans by private banks. By some estimates, the unsafe assets on the government books could amount to another several percent of GDP.

Why Japan Can't Export Its Way Out of Its Problems

There are some in Japan and in the U.S. who believe Japan can export its way out of recession and the excess savings syndrome, as it did in the past. In reality, never again will Japan be able to export its way out of trouble for years on end as it did in the 1970s and 1980s. Japan is just too big for the rest of the world to bear the burden of the kind of surplus Japan would need.

Consider this: from the second quarter of 1996 to the fourth quarter of 1997, Japan's price-adjusted trade surplus in goods and services grew from a negligible level to 2.3 percent of GDP. That's a huge jump and one not easily repeated. Some of the increase came from a 17 percent boost in exports, as the effects of two years of a 40 percent yen depreciation finally kicked in. But it also reflected the weak Japanese economy: price-adjusted imports actually fell 2 percent during this period. And yet, what did this big increase in the trade surplus accomplish? Since domestic demand fell almost as much as the trade surplus rose, all that the massive growth in the trade surplus achieved was to keep the overall economy at near-zero growth rather than in deep recession.

For trade expansion to rescue Japan, its surplus would have to rise to a level even higher than the 4.5 percent of GDP it achieved in the mid-1980s just before the Plaza Accords sent the yen soaring. Given all that is going on in the rest of the world, as we shall detail below, that is simply not going to happen.

The effort at an export-led recovery began in the summer of 1995. At that time, it looked as if Japan might undergo an unmanageable banking crisis with ripple effects throughout the world. The yen was soaring to 80, exports were tanking and the economy was dead in the water. At that moment, U.S. Treasury Deputy Secretary Larry Summers and Eisuke Sakakibara, Director-General of the MOF's International Finance Bureau, arranged a deal. They would help push the yen down to stimulate Japanese exports. That would revive production, avoid a bank collapse, and give Japan a breather and avoid a banking mess. Since a stronger dollar attracted Japanese money to the U.S. and therefore temporarily lowered U.S. interest rates, the deal also helped Bill Clinton in the 1996 Presidential election.

As a result of the deal, the yen fell to 115–120 per dollar by early 1997. Japan's current account surplus, which had bottomed out at 1.5 percent of GDP toward the end of 1996, bounced back to 2.6 percent by the third quarter of 1997. Exporting companies started showing record profits—at least for a while.

This is not the first time in the 1990s that Japan has tried this route. The first time occurred in the early 1990s. Soon, however, Japan ran into the brick wall of a rising yen. The trade surplus turned south (Figure 8.18). Japan had no choice but to resort to skyrocketing budget deficits to keep the economy out of negative territory (Figure 8.19). The same trade scenario seemed to be repeating itself in the late 1990s.

The fact is: Japan cannot run a trade surplus of, say, $100 billion, unless the rest of the world is willing and able to run a trade deficit of $100 billion.

In the 1980s, Japan's dancing partner was the U.S. Rising budget deficits and falling private savings rates meant the U.S. was consuming far more than it produced. That's what keeps the U.S. addicted to trade deficits.

Figure 8.18 **Investment Falls, But Trade Surplus Can't Stay Up**

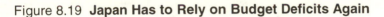

Figure 8.19 **Japan Has to Rely on Budget Deficits Again**

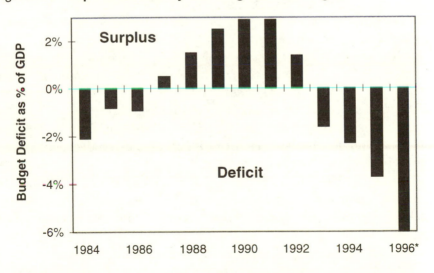

Source: EPA (1997) NIPA Tables. Calendar year, in current yen for budget, constant 1990 yen for trade and investment. *The 1996 budget figure is from the Bank of Japan "Flow of Funds" figures because the EPA number was not yet available.
Note: The budget balance figures refer to all government activities at the national and local level, social security and government-owned enterprises.

Japan and the U.S. could each maintain its own addiction only because of the other. Without Japan's rising surplus, Reaganomics would have crashed on the shoals of double digit interest rates. Without Reaganomics, Japan's rising trade surplus in the 1980s would have been stillborn. It's like a married couple where the husband is obese and the wife is anorexic. It works only because the anorexic wife surrenders her food to her husband's enormous appetite.

By the late 1990s, however, the U.S. was beginning to get its budget deficit in order. The U.S. still runs a trade deficit because private savings is still too small to finance the big rise in America's private investment. So the link between America's budget deficit and its trade deficit is not as tight as it was in the past. The bottom line, however, is that the size of the U.S. trade deficit relative to GDP in the late 1990s was far smaller than in the mid-1980s. America's ability to absorb Japanese surpluses is dwindling.

When one also considers that the troubled Asian countries, with their plummeting currencies, will also be increasing their trade surpluses vis-à-vis the U.S. and decreasing their deficits with Japan, the ability of Japan to generate a surplus big enough to solve its problems is highly dubious.

To see the U.S.–Japan symbiosis, just look at Figure 8.20. For 20 years, the ups and downs of the American budget deficit have been faithfully echoed a year or two later by proportional ups and down in the bilateral U.S.–Japan trade balance.

But, what is absolutely remarkable is that, for the same 20 years, the gyrations of the U.S. budget deficit have sent the *entire Japanese trade deficit* up and down just as faithfully (Figure 8.21). That's because the U.S. provides such a large part of Japan's total surplus.

Indeed, according to the U.S. Federal Reserve, every time the U.S. cuts its fiscal stimulus by 1 percent of GDP, Japan's current account surplus drops by 0.3 percent of Japanese GDP.[23]

That's the ultimate irony. An economic structure initially aimed at creating autonomy ended up in the post-1973 era making Japan inordinately dependent on budget machinations of U.S. politicians. A 1987 BOJ report describing the post-1973 change commented, "Japan [now] suffers extremely from the impact of business cycles in the U.S."[24]

Certainly, the causality works in both directions. Changes in Japan's trade balance are faithfully mirrored in the U.S. just as much as vice versa. Even after the trends diverged in the early 1990s, they came back together again quickly (Figure 8.22).

What about the cheap yen? Doesn't the huge gap between American

Figure 8.20 **U.S. *Budget* Deficit Drives U.S.-Japan *Trade* Balance**

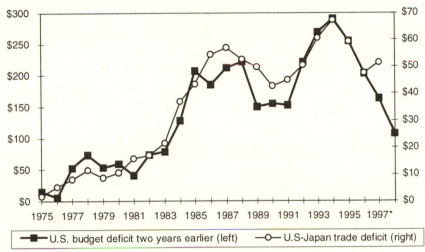

Figure 8.21 ***U.S.* Budget Gyrations Whipsaw *Japanese* Trade**

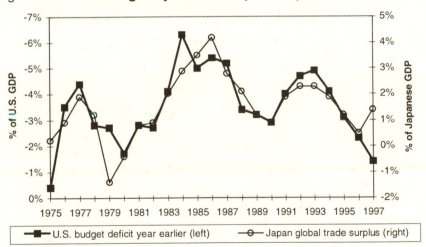

Source: EPA (1997); U.S. Commerce Department, Congressional Budget Office

Note: All in current dollars and current yen. Since it takes time for changes in the budget deficit to affect trade, in Figure 8.20, the year labeled 1995 shows the trade imbalance for 1995 and the U.S. budget deficit two years earlier, i.e., in 1993. In Figure 8.21, the year labeled 1997 shows the Japanese current account surplus for fiscal 1995 and the U.S. budget deficit for 1996. In Figure 8.21, the U.S. scale is inverted in order to compare an increase in the U.S. *deficit* and an increase in the Japanese *surplus*. The Commerce Department provides bilateral trade imbalances in goods only.

Figure 8.22 **U.S. and Japanese Trade Deficits Mirror Each Other**

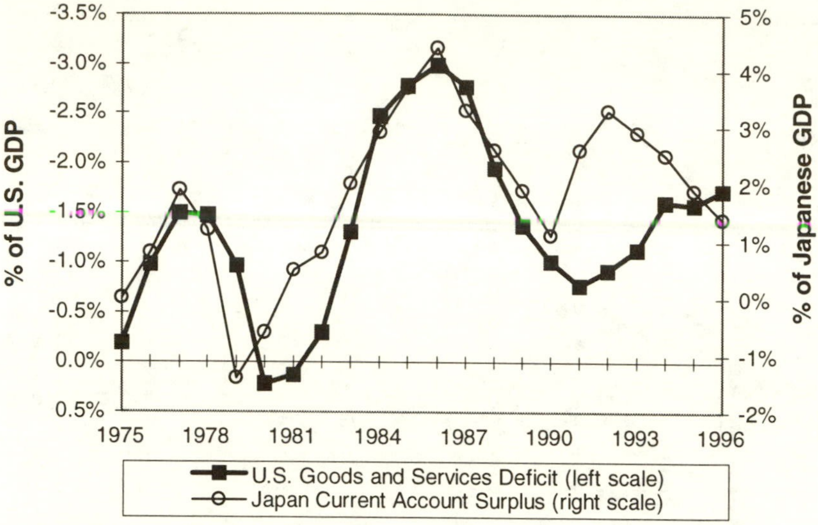

Source: EPA (1997) "Net Lending and Borrowing by Sectors", except 1996, which is from the NIPA tables,. U.S. Department of Commerce

Note: The U.S. scale is inverted so that an increase in the U.S. *deficit* and an increase in the Japanese *surplus* can be compared. The U.S. current account figures for 1991 and 1992 were adjusted to overcome distortions caused by payments to the U.S. due to the Gulf War. All figures are calendar year, constant yen and dollars.

and Japanese interest rates keep the yen lower? Won't that keep raising Japan's trade surplus? Yes, it does—but only temporarily as we saw for a few years in the early 1990s. American interest rates in 1997 were 4–5 percent higher than those in Japan. With Japan's stock market and banks so shaky, investors shifted assets from Japan to the U.S., thereby strengthening the dollar and weakening the yen (Figure 8.23).

But no matter how low the yen goes, unless some other country, or countries, run corresponding deficits, Japan cannot run a trade surplus. Who would be Japan's partners? Southeast Asian countries have been a big absorber of Japanese surpluses since the late 1980s. However, the currency crises of 1997 will result in smaller trade deficits on their part.

To a certain extent, the cheap yen forces other countries to absorb somewhat larger deficits than they otherwise might. But that, too, has its limits. Given the trends in other countries, a yen at 130 or even 140 will not produce as large a surplus as it would have even a few years ago. In the end, if Japan cannot find partners, what will happen is what has always happened in the past. When Japan's trade surplus gets too big for

Figure 8.23 **Japan–U.S. Interest Rate Gap Pushes Yen Downward**

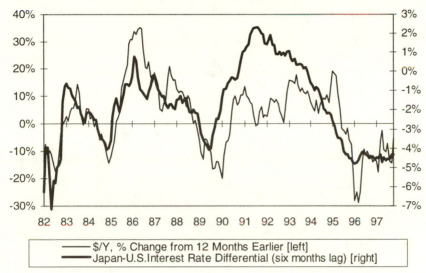

——— $/Y, % Change from 12 Months Earlier [left]
——— Japan-U.S.Interest Rate Differential (six months lag) [right]

But Rebound in Japan's Trade Surplus Pushes It Back Up

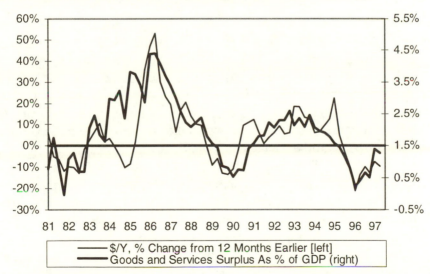

——— $/Y, % Change from 12 Months Earlier [left]
——— Goods and Services Surplus As % of GDP (right)

Source: Deutsche Morgan Grenfell; EPA (1997)
Note: Over the past two decades, whenever Japanese interest rates were at least 3% below those in the U.S., money left Japan, causing the yen to fall vis-à-vis the dollar. On
the other hand, whenever Japan's surplus on trade in goods and services reached about
1.5% of GDP (nominal), the yen rose.

Figure 8.24 **The Yen's "Roller Coaster Path"**

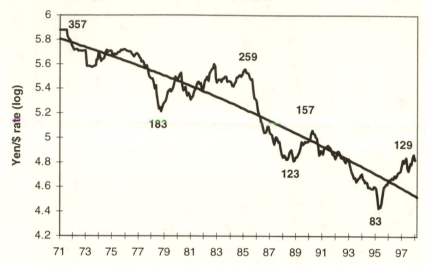

Source: Deutsche Morgan Grenfell
Note: Every few years, the yen cycles between overshooting and undershooting its long-term trend toward greater strength. The chart is rendered in a logarithm scale so that a 10% change from 300 and a 10% change from 100 are proportional.

other countries to absorb, the yen rises again (Figure 8.23, bottom panel).

That is why the yen has gone in roller coaster cycles over the past 25 years. A falling yen produces a Japanese trade surplus too big for its partners to absorb, and so the yen has to rise to rein in Japan's exports. That lowers the trade surplus. Then, Japan's excess savings sends money flowing out of the country, which lowers the yen, raises the trade surplus and starts the cycle all over again (Figure 8.24).

In February of 1997, as the yen fell to 124 and the trade surplus was rebounding rapidly, Treasury Secretary Robert Rubin finally called for a halt to further yen depreciation at the Group of Seven meeting. Larry Summers let it be known that a Japanese surplus at 2.5 percent of GDP is close to the line in the sand requiring a U.S. response.

If Japan's global current account surplus stays at around 2.5 percent of GDP but does not grow further, that will just antagonize Japan's neighbors without adding further to Japanese growth.

Currencies can remain out of line with fundamentals for quite some time, as we saw in the early 1980s. And, as they do, they also distort economic fundamentals. History has shown that the farther currencies and macroeconomic fundamentals get out of line and the longer they remain so, the sharper the ultimate correction. As of early 1998, capital flows (Figure 8.23a) were still telling the yen to fall while trade flows (Figure 8.24b) were telling it to rise.

As of January 1998, the shaky state of Japanese banks and the stock market, as well as the desire of Japanese savers to seek higher rates abroad, had sent the yen to 125–130. So, capital forces were stronger than trade forces at that point. But that cannot go on forever.

Indeed, at the beginning of 1998, when the yen hit 130, the Japanese Finance Ministry started worrying that, if the yen kept falling, it would hurt Japan more on the financial side than it would help on the trade side. A falling yen makes Japanese assets less attractive. Thus, it contributes to the weakness of the Japanese stock market. Since the fragile balance sheets of the banks depend on high stock prices, an excessively weak yen could indirectly exacerbate Japan's banking problems. Thus, in early January, Sakakibara went to Washington, pleading for Rubin's help in bolstering the yen—exactly the opposite of his request two years earlier. Rubin reportedly responded that, unless Japan changed its fundamentals, including more fiscal stimulus, there was little he could do that would be effective.

The bottom line of the all the gyrations of the yen, interest rates, U.S. budget politics and so forth is this: Japan may be able to use exports to avoid the need for reform for a while—but not for long. It certainly cannot be a permanent strategy.

The Japan That Can't Say Grow?

In 1995–96 it looked for a while as if Japan was finally recovering from the doldrums of the early 1990s. By the spring of 1997, leaders in both Tokyo and Washington said that the cyclical recovery that had been promised for three years in a row had finally arrived. Then, no sooner had the economy raised its head from the mat than it plopped down again. Problems seemed more intractable than ever. In the second quarter of 1997, GDP plummeted at an enormous 12 percent annual rate. Forecasts as of early 1998 said the economy would grow below 1 percent for three more years through at least fiscal 1999. Even when Japan does recover, recovery is defined as 2 percent growth. The 4 percent growth rates that Japan enjoyed in the 1970s and 1980s are gone forever (Figure 8.25).

What produced the new downturn in 1997 was the return of economic anorexia. For a while, that anorexia was disguised by massive government stimulus, but in early 1997, it began to manifest itself again.

Figure 8.25 **Still Waiting for Recovery: GDP Growth in the 1990s**

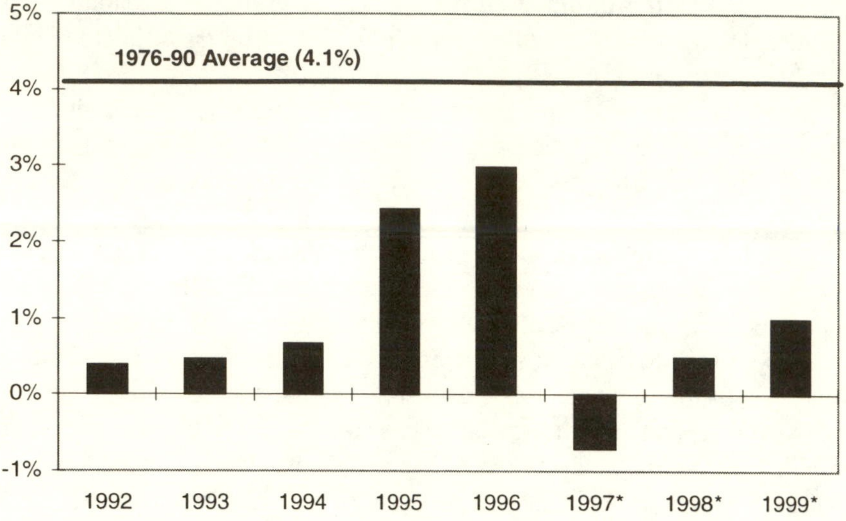

Source: EPA (1997) for 1991-96. All are fiscal years. *1997 through 1999 are consensus forecasts as of March 1998.

From the first quarter of 1992 until the second quarter of 1996, Japan's entire GDP grew only 5 percent—less than it had grown in the single year of 1990. Almost two-thirds of this growth was accounted for by government spending on "investment." In fiscal 1995–96, the economy even gave the illusion of recovery as GDP grew 2.8 percent and 3.2 percent respectively. Then, in mid-1996, as budget deficits hit 6–7 percent of GDP and pressure for "fiscal reform" appeared, spending on public works was pared back. Then in the spring of 1997, taxes were hiked. Once fiscal stimulus retreated, the air went out of the entire economy and the sub-1 percent doldrums of 1992–94 returned.

At the beginning of 1998, it looked as though the Hashimoto Administration was going to reverse itself once again and apply a new round of fiscal steroids. If it does, that could once again give demand a boost and produce somewhat higher rates of growth than are now expected. But there is a big difference between a temporary use of fiscal stimulus that jump-starts a flagging economy into a self-sustaining recovery, and budget deficits that are needed as a permanent crutch. The latter is the situation in Japan.

There are those in Japan who argue that fiscal stimulus is a means of making the patient strong enough to withstand the surgery of tough economic reform. If indeed Tokyo were actually following that policy, that would be sound. The economy truly needs a macroeconomic safety net to tide it over the initially depressive effects of the bankruptcies and layoffs that would inevitably (and temporarily) accompany serious reform. However, in all likelihood, if the politicians and bureaucrats running Japan in early 1998 remain in power, they will not use fiscal stimulus as a means to help reform, but as a device to avoid it.

Clearly, Japan's long-term structural flaws are far from cured. In 1983, the International Monetary Fund (IMF) figured that Japan's medium-term potential growth rate was about 4 percent a year. Four years later, the IMF downgraded Japan's growth potential to half that level. And then, early in the next century, growth potential is expected to slow even more. Without reform, MITI predicted Japan would grow at most about 2 percent in the late 1990s, then 1.8 percent in 2000–2010, and then plunge to 0.9 percent thereafter.

Actually, Japan has two obstacles to growth: a supply-side problem and a demand-side problem. The supply-side problem is the low productivity growth caused by its dual economy. As a result of this, even if Japan ran at full capacity, its growth would be limited to 2 percent or so for the next several years. The demand-side problem is economic anorexia. That makes it difficult for Japan to run at full capacity. In fact, according to some estimates, the gap between Japan's full-capacity GDP and its actual GDP is now the largest in the postwar era. Because of that gap, if Japan could get demand going again, it could grow for a few years at more than its 2 percent long-term potential— until it reached full capacity.

Where do these long-term growth forecasts of 2 percent or even less come from? In any economy, the growth rate is a combination of how fast the labor force is growing and how fast output per worker is growing. If labor is growing 1 percent and productivity is growing 1.5 percent, then the economy can only grow 2.5 percent in the long term. That's what the Federal Reserve figures is the situation for the U.S.

In Japan, the labor force peaked in 1995 and is now declining. People aged 15–65 years old were 70 percent of the population in 1995. They will decline to only 60 percent by 2024. Hence, for the next couple of decades, the only source of growth of Japan will have to be productivity growth. In fact, even if Japan's output per man hour grew at 2 percent a year, its per capita GDP would actually grow much less—because of the labor force shrinkage. There will be more and more retired people for every working person to support.

Even with 2 percent productivity growth, per capita income growth would sink to only 1 percent for much of the next two decades, less than one-third the rate of the 1970s and 1980s (Figure 8.26). This compares to America's record of 1.6 percent per capita growth during 1973–96.

If Japan wants better results, it has to become more efficient. If it wants to be more efficient, it has to end the dual economy. But it won't achieve even the meager growth rates now projected unless it ends its economic anorexia.

Without reform, stop-go growth is Japan's future.

Figure 8.26 **If Labor Productivity Growth Stays below 2% . . .**

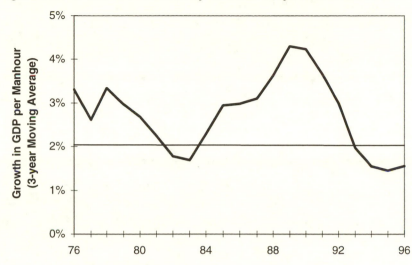

. . . Japan's Per Capita Income Growth Will Drop to 1%

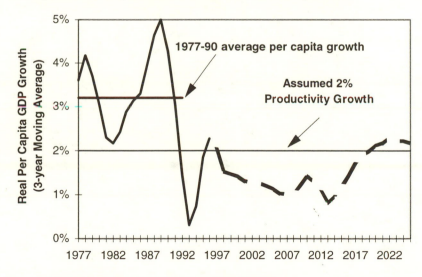

Source: Adapted by author from data from Koll (1997b)

Note: In the top panel, 1996 is an estimate. Japan's labor force is now declining. For the next couple of decades, even if Japan's output per manhour grows at 2% a year, its per capita growth will not be any higher than 1% a year. The reason is this: if output per manhour grows 2% and manhours decline, say 0.5%, then GDP will only grow 1.5%. If the population grows 0.5%, then per capita GDP growth will be only 1%.

Part Three

Open Trade: The Heavy Artillery of Economic Reform

Chapter 9

If Poland Can Reform, Why Not Japan?

> *The cheap prices of its commodities are the heavy artillery with which [capitalism] batters down all Chinese walls.*
> —Karl Marx, 1848[1]

Trade and Reform

Poland outshining Japan? It's unbelievable, but it's true. Ever since 1994, the once-moribund Poland has been one of Europe's fastest-growing economies, expanding at an almost Asia-like pace of 6 percent. Moreover, if reforms continue, this pace is expected to continue for at least a couple of decades to come.[2] Why is economic reform flowering in Poland and still floundering in Japan?

A big part of the answer lies in international trade. At the core of Poland's post-Communist "shock therapy" was the decision to hitch its star to expanded integration with Western Europe. Cheap commodities from Western Europe are the heavy artillery battering down the vestiges of Poland's enforced experiment with Stalinism. Poland is getting rid of its dinosaurs and forging vibrant new private enterprises in their place. Trade in Poland is not an economic force, but a political one. The old institutions cannot survive under the pressure of international competition. If the European Union follows through on its intention to let Poland eventually join, progress should be even faster.

True, the initial costs in social dislocation were enormous and this in turn sparked serious political resentment. Nor can anyone deny that there have been serious setbacks along the way. Undoubtedly there will be more to come. The high budget and trade deficits that emerged in 1997 were a serious warning. Still, the long-term rewards in growth and efficiency are already being felt.

While Poland was brave enough to risk this social turmoil, Japan has so far been unwilling to risk the much milder disruption entailed in exposing its own weak sectors to world competition. Quite the contrary, ever since the early 1970s, Japan has been going in the wrong direction. In the high-growth era, Japan was as trade dependent as any other country. But while the rest of the world continued to raise its interdependence, Japan reversed course. Alone of all major countries, Japan actually trades *less* today relative to GDP than it did four decades ago—19 percent of GDP in 1996 versus 24 percent in 1956.

This is a tragedy. For, while Poland is a particularly dramatic case, it is hardly unique. All over the world, wherever economic reform has succeeded, trade opening was at the heart of the effort. And whenever reform has failed, failure to expose the market to international competition was usually present.

In Japan, as well, trade opening will probably prove to be indispensable to economic reform. Without trade opening the forces of cartelization could prove too powerful, and too well connected politically, to tear down.

Trade and Growth: The Global Dual Economy

To see why the force of trade opening is so powerful, let's take a step back and look at a broad spectrum of countries. We find that Japan's dual economy is, in a sense, replicated on a world scale. Countries that are open to high levels of trade grow quickly. Closed countries with too little trade grow slowly or even shrink. Figure 9.1, adapted from the work of Jeffrey Sachs, a Harvard economist who helped design Poland's reform, tells the story.[3] (See also Table 9.1.)

The open economies—where trade dependence was twice as high as in the closed countries—achieved an average growth rate of 2.8 percent per worker each year. Among the developing economies in the open group, the average growth rate per worker was 4.3 percent. Indeed, the *average* open developing country grew faster than the *fastest* closed economy (Guinea at 3.8 percent).

While virtually *none* of the open developing countries showed growth below 3 percent, almost *all* of the closed economies did. Even 1 percent was too difficult for most of the closed economies to attain. In fact, a full third of the closed economies actually shrank instead of growing!

The most striking difference between the open and closed economies is that, among open economies, the poorer countries are growing so fast that they are rapidly catching up to the living standards of their richer fore-

Figure 9.1 Open Economies Grow Faster Than Closed Ones

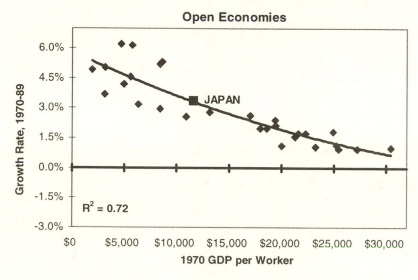

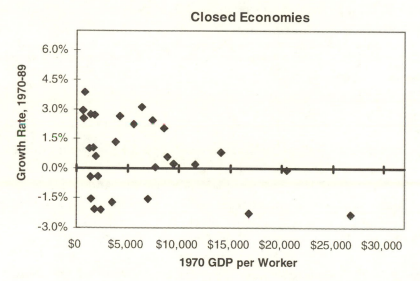

Source: Summers and Heston (1995) for data. See Sachs and Warner (1995) for classification of "open" and "closed."
Note: This charts plots growth in GDP per worker during 1970-89 against initial GDP
per worker in 1970. Among open economies, the poorer countries regularly grow faster
than the richer ones, thereby catching up to the leaders. $R^2 = 0.72$ in the top panel
means that 72 percent of the difference in growth rates among open economies can be
explained by their level of development. Among closed economies, there is no pattern of
"catch-up."

bears. Occasionally, you can find a few closed economies that are catching up as well, but most are falling further behind.

Contrary to popular impression, we do not live in a world where the rich get richer and the poor get poorer. Rather, the rich get richer; those poor who choose to trade get richer even faster; and those poor who choose not to trade remain in misery.

Among the open economies, there is a clear "catch-up" process. Trade and foreign investment are the transmission belt for transferring technology, capital, management techniques, and modern institutions. In open economies, this catch-up process is so regular that a full 72 percent of the difference in growth rates among open economies can be explained just by looking at their initial GDP per worker (top panel of Figure 9.1).

As a result, among advanced countries, GDP per worker grew from 67 percent of U.S. levels in 1970 to 77 percent by 1989. Japan grew from 38 percent of U.S. levels to 60 percent. Among open developing countries, relative GDP per worker almost doubled from 20 percent of U.S. levels to 37 percent. While 11 of the open countries were poor in 1970—with GDP below $10,000 per worker and about $4,000 per person—all but three had lifted themselves out of poverty by 1989.

Among the closed economies, there is no consistent "catch-up." Most started off poor and stayed that way. Out of the 24 closed countries that were poor in 1970, 21 were still poor as of 1989.

Trade Catalyzes Productivity-Enhancing Institutional Change

This record just begs the question: *why* do open or "outward-oriented" economies grow faster?

The main reason is higher growth in productivity. And this is not just better labor productivity, which a nation can temporarily achieve by pouring on more and more capital per worker. This is more output from each unit of labor *plus* capital, called Total Factor Productivity (TFP).

Among the strongly outward-oriented countries in Table 9.2, the growth in TFP alone was more than the *total* growth of the strongly inward-oriented countries. Indeed, productivity actually *fell* in the inward-oriented countries. They had to run faster just to stay in place.

We can also see that the strongly outward-oriented countries in Table 9.2 showed higher investment rates. This suggests that the returns to capital were so much better that companies were willing to invest more.

Hence, the outward-orientation produced a double benefit: it induced

Table 9.1

The Global Dual Economy: Trading Countries Grow Faster

	Open	Closed
	29 Total 12 Developing	30 Total 29 Developing
Average trade:GDP ratio (population-weighted)*	66%	37%
Number poor in 1970 (below $10,000 GDP per worker)	11	24
Number still poor in 1989 (below $10,000 GDP per worker)	3	21
Number extremely poor in 1970 (below $5,000 per worker)	5	16
Number still extremely poor in 1989 (below $5,000)	1	15
Advanced countries GDP per worker as % of U.S. in 1970	67%	NA**
Advanced countries GDP per worker as % of U.S. in 1989	77%	NA**
Developing countries GDP per worker as % of U.S. in 1970	20%	20%
Developing countries GDP per worker as % of U.S. in 1989	37%	18%
Average growth all countries	2.9%	0.6%
Average growth, developed	1.8%	NA**
Average growth, developing	4.5%	0.6%
Avg. growth of developing countries with positive growth	4.5%	1.7%
Number above 4% growth	8	0
Number above 3% growth	12	2
Number above 2% growth	20	8
Number above 1% growth	27	11
Number below 3% growth, developing	1	27
Number below 2% growth, developing	0	21
Number below 1% growth, developing	0	18
Number below 0% growth	0	10

Source: See Figure 9.1

*On population-adjusted trade: GDP ratios, see footnote 3. **New Zealand was the one developed economy among the closed group.

Note: All figures are measured in constant 1990 dollars.

Table 9.2

Open Countries Grow Faster Due to Better Productivity

	GDP Growth Rate	% of GDP Growth Contributed by:		
		Labor	Capital	Total Factor Productivity
Strongly outward-oriented countries				
1975–82	8.4	1.1	4.6	2.7
1983–89	7.7	0.7	3.3	3.7
Moderately outward-oriented countries				
1975–82	4.6	1.3	2.8	0.5
1983–89	4.1	1.2	1.7	1.2
Moderately inward-oriented countries				
1975–82	4.0	1.5	2.6	–0.2
1983–89	2.7	1.5	1.4	–0.2
Strongly inward-oriented countries				
1975–82	2.3	1.6	1.6	–0.9
1983–89	2.2	1.6	0.7	–0.9

Source: Krueger (1996), p. 198

Note: In all countries, GDP growth equals the sum of three factors: more labor, more capital and greater output for each unit of labor plus capital (known as Total Factor Productivity). This table is based on World Bank classifications of developing countries according to its "outward-oriented" index. See Appendix E for more on trade and growth.

more investment and yielded more bang for the buck. These two factors reinforced each other.

But why, exactly, does increased trade produce higher productivity growth?

There is no way to explain this in narrow economic terms. Sure, trade helps countries switch their production base. They shift to making the products where they are most efficient and import those that they cannot make as efficiently. Undoubtedly, that improvement in "resource allocation" helps. But careful studies show this can only explain a tiny part of the increased productivity.[4]

No, the major reason is that increased trade both reflects, and helps trigger, wholesale institutional changes. In most cases, the extremely poor closed countries did not start off poor because they were closed. Usually, the causality worked the other way around: they were closed because they were poor. A combination of circumstances—the legacies of colonialism, poor education and health facilities, lack of modern political and economic experience—left these countries not only poor, but encumbered by a host of institutions that are hostile to entrepreneurship and growth. These range from kleptocratic governments to local monopolies and "crony capitalism" to dysfunctional financial systems. Being closed to international trade is just part and parcel of this whole institutional setup.

But being closed to international trade is what *keeps* them poor. These countries need wholesale reform of their institutions. And the fact is: were they to open their economies to international competition, few of their uncompetitive growth-suppressing domestic practices could survive.

Financial institutions are a classic case. How fast a country grows depends critically upon how much it saves. But suppose people live in a country where the president of a bank can abscond with the deposits and get away with it by paying off crooked cops. How much of that country's savings will go into mattresses and how much go into banks or the stock market? Now, suppose the government lets Citibank, Merrill Lynch and others set up branches throughout that country. How long will it take before depositors shift their money? How long before local banks know that, to survive, they'd better be able to ensure that they are as reliable as Citibank or Merrill?

If that country wants to attract foreign funds to finance growth, is it more likely to attract them with a healthy policing of its banks and securities markets, or without it?

Not surprisingly then, in virtually every country where reform has succeeded, making trade and foreign direct investment more open has been a key catalyst. Sachs and Warner comment:

> The international opening of the economy is the *sine qua non* of the overall reform process. Trade liberalization not only establishes powerful direct linkages between the economy and the world system, but also effectively forces the government to take actions on other parts of the reform program under the pressure of international competition. For these reasons, it is convenient and fairly accurate to judge a country's *overall* reform program according to the progress of its trade liberalization.[5]

"Price Destruction in Japan"

While the poor countries post a particularly stark case for the benefits of trade, even advanced nations show extraordinary productivity and growth gains from trade.

That's because advanced nations can also be plagued by dysfunctional practices. All over Japan, there is money to be made by colluding with competitors to jack up prices to monopolistic levels.

Imports are heavy artillery that batters down the walls of oligopolies, collusion and cartels—and the political arrangements that protect them.[6]

Just look at the "price destruction" that Japan experienced in the early 1990s when a soaring yen forced greater imports in previously closed sectors. Even tiny gains in imports brought down prices in a way that years of complaining to the Japan Fair Trade Commission (JFTC) never did.

- When Compaq sent PCs to Japan in 1992 at cut-rate prices, it not only gained a 4 percent share; it also revolutionized the market. Prices dropped by a third and NEC's share plummeted from 53 percent to 40 percent, as Japanese firms like Fujitsu joined the price war. Now, Japanese PC buyers get to use the international standard, Windows, rather than NEC's proprietary system.
- When giant discount retailer Daiei brought in private-label beer from Holland, prices dropped *32 percent.* Entrenched liquor stores and struggling new discount shops are now battling it out. Although this has not yet compelled Japanese beer makers to import foreign bottles or cans to boost their competitiveness vis-à-vis the imported beer, the pressure on them has increased.
- Just the announcement that gasoline imports would finally be liberalized—up until 1996 gasoline imports by anyone other than refiners were illegal—initially sent prices crashing 25 percent. While tight control over distribution by the refiners has kept imports low, in 1997 Daiei and the Marubeni trading company cooperated to open gasoline "superstores." They charged ¥90–95 per liter, way down from the typical price of ¥107–108 per liter. Prices started heading toward ¥90 per liter across Japan. The entry of British Petroleum into the gas station market along with an end to the prohibition on self-service gas stations is expected to send prices even lower.[7]
- General Electric, Whirlpool and other appliance makers were told for years that they had to sell at high prices to preserve their cachet. Then, GE and Whirlpool allied with Japanese retailers to bring in large models at prices as much as 20–30 percent below domestic makes. Sales exploded and GE announced ambitions to sell a million a year.

- By 1997, it seemed that everyone in Japan was walking around with a "handyphone." It wasn't that way a few years back, when high prices suppressed demand for cellular phones. Motorola's pressure to open the market and change regulations and practices created a revolution. Companies sold phones cheaply instead of leasing them at high rates. Phone call rates tumbled. And, in response, demand soared. From January 1994 to June 1997 the number of cell phone subscribers increased from 500,000 to 24 million. In fact, according to Takashi Kiuchi, chief economist at the Long-Term Credit Bank (LTCB), the purchase of cell phones and use of them increased GDP by about ¥1 trillion, or 0.2 percent of GDP, during that period.

Even among advanced countries, trade promotes growth because competition forces managers to live up to their potential. Only half of the overall gap in manufacturing productivity between Japan and the U.S. can be explained by tangible factors like the capital–labor ratio or the age of equipment. The other half is caused by management practices. Those in turn depend on the degree of competition that managers face. And that, in turn, depends upon the level of international trade.[8]

Not surprisingly then, even among advanced nations and NICs who are successfully on the catch-up path, those who trade more increase their productivity faster and therefore grow faster. In Japan's case, suppose that, during 1973–90, instead of its actual 23 percent trade:GDP ratio, the ratio had been 33 percent. (This is the level our economic model in Chapter 11 projects Japan would have if its trade patterns conformed to international patterns.) In that case, Japan's growth would have been 3.25 percent a year instead of 3.0 percent.[9] That may not sound like a lot. But that's the kind of difference that, when experienced year after year for as little as 10 years, makes the whole economy 5 percent bigger. It spells the difference between being able to pay Social Security costs or not. That's the kind of differential that has allowed the U.S. to pare down its once-intractable budget deficit.

The Critical Factor: Trade in Competing Products

Because it is the "creative destruction" engendered by trade that creates the gains, the greatest benefits come from trade in products that *compete* with local producers, rather than mere *inputs* like oil and raw materials.[10]

Table 9.3

Most Countries Except Japan Import *Competing* Products

Passenger cars (1,000 units) 1995	Production	Exports	Imports	Exports: Output Ratio	Imports: Consumption Ratio
Japan	**7,611**	**2,896**	**362**	**38**	**7**
U.S.	6,601	522	4,114	8	40
Germany	**4,360**	**2,465**	**1,756**	**57**	**48**
France	3,051	1,852	1,259	61	51
Spain	1,959	1,537	414	78	50
UK	1,532	746	1,160	49	60
Canada	1,339	935	739	70	65
Korea	1,986	856	9	43	1
Italy	1,422	642	NA	45	NA

Machine tools ($ mil), 1994	Production	Exports	Imports	Exports: Output Ratio	Imports: Consumption Ratio
Japan	**6,811**	**4,214**	**353**	**62**	**12**
Germany	**5,188**	**3,786**	**1,174**	**73**	**46**
U.S.	4,080	1,267	2,808	31	50
Italy	2,240	1,431	576	64	42
Switzerland	1,730	1,518	252	88	54
Taiwan	1,167	756	496	65	55
UK	1,003	561	572	56	56
Korea	834	150	1,000	18	59
France	627	314	663	50	68

Source: Keizai Koho Center (1997), p. 27
Note: Even countries with "comparative advantage" in cars and machine tools still import a lot, unless they have explicit barriers (such as Italian and Korean restrictions on auto imports). Japan is the exception. The U.S. exports so few cars because its European affiliates make the cars sold there.

Not surprisingly, then, in most modern countries *except Japan*, the lion's share of trade is in competing products, also known as intra-industry trade. Germany, for example, is not only one of the world's biggest exporters of steel and cars and machine tools, but one of the biggest importers of those items as well (Table 9.3). This is what keeps its companies on their toes. In Japan, by contrast, not only is overall trade low, but very little of what Japan does import are products that compete with domestic producers. In Japan's dual economy, only its exporters face competition.

Japanese officials often claim that Japan imports so little in competing manufactured goods because, as a resourceless country, it must spend its money on oil, food and raw materials. But Germany, too, has no resources except coal. Nonetheless, manufactured goods comprise 84 percent of its imports.

It is Japan's cartelized economy, not its lack of resources, that explains its trade patterns. And those trade patterns, in turn, help keep the economy cartelized.

If Japan wants to improve its productivity, it must break the Gordian knot somewhere. As in other countries that had to reform, Japan needs to bring in the big guns of imports and foreign direct investment to break up the cartels.

Chapter 10

Asia Versus Japan in the Race
to Reform

Over the last few years, there has been a lot of talk about an "Asian model" of development. Thus, when many of the Asian countries were thrown into crisis at the same time as Japan entered a new downturn, this was widely seen as a setback for the entire "Japan–Asia" model of development. In our view, we need a more differentiated picture. It is true that there are some things Japan and the Asian NICs have in common, including a prominent role for the government in the economy. But when it comes to the role of trade in growth strategy, Asia and Japan are poles apart.

The Asian countries practice *trade-led growth* whereas Japan emphasizes *investment-led growth*. This has enormous consequences for their long-term growth potential as well as the welfare of their populations. Moreover, as we shall discuss below, the Asian countries' greater exposure to international trade and investment means that most of them are likely to reform far more quickly than Japan.

Any country's growth is the combination of three factors: how fast labor is growing; how fast capital is growing; and, how much growth there is in total factor productivity (TFP), i.e., the ability to get more output out of each unit of labor and capital input. Let's say we have two countries growing at 4 percent a year with labor growing at 1 percent a year in each, so that growth per worker is 3 percent in each country. In that case, how much a country has to invest in order to achieve that growth depends entirely on its productivity. If TFP is growing only 1 percent a year, then the remaining 2 percent of growth has to come from an awful lot of investment. But if TFP is growing at 2 percent a year, then the investment required to create the remaining 1 percent of growth is much, much less.

Since trade helps growth by raising TFP, a country that trades more can invest less without sacrificing any growth at all. And the less it needs to invest to get its growth, the more its people can consume. Of course, countries need both to invest and to trade; it's a question of balance.

Let's take the case of Japan. We said in Chapter 9 that if Japan traded as much as our model predicted, its growth in 1973–90 would have been 3.25 percent a year instead of 3.0 percent. To get that same extra growth through investment, Japan would have to raise its already sky-high investment rate another 3.5 percent from 35 percent of GDP to 38.5 percent. That, in turn would cut living standards by 6 percent without yielding an iota of better growth (3.5 percent of GDP diverted from consumption to investment multiplied by consumption at 55 percent of GDP = 6.3 percent lower consumption).

Since the whole purpose of investment is to be able to create larger consumption down the road, if that greater growth can be achieved through trade, then why not choose the trade route to growth? It was not chosen because opening the country to greater trade would expose Japan's inefficient sectors to competition. Instead, as we detailed in Chapter 4, Japan poured on more and more investment while getting less and less growth for its investment every year.

The Asian NICs, by contrast, chose the trade route to expansion. All of the East Asian NICs trade far more and invest far less than Japan to get their growth. While Japan invested 35 percent of its GDP in 1973–90, the five East Asian countries in Figure 10.1 (Malaysia, Thailand, Indonesia, Korea, and Taiwan) invested on average only two-thirds as much, about 24 percent. The highest investor was Korea at 29 percent. Conversely, while Japan's trade was a meager 24 percent of GDP, the five Asian NICs were premier traders at an average 74 percent of GDP. The lowest trade dependence in the Asia group, Indonesia at 47 percent, was still twice as high as Japan at 23 percent.[1]

Japan stands as the great outlier, with far too much investment and far too little trade. The East Asian countries, by contrast, fit within the international norms of the trade versus investment trade-off.

Since competition is the source of the benefits from trade, it is crucial that Asia lets in imports in the same industries where it produces and exports. In the jargon of economics, it practices "intra-industry" trade. Japan, by contrast, does not (Table 10.1).

Normally, poor countries practice little intra-industry trade. They import capital goods and other advanced manufactures while exporting primary goods or simple manufactures. Then, as the catch-up process unfolds, intra-industry trade grows. This is what we see in the Asian

Figure 10.1 **Asia's Trade-Led Growth Differs from Japan Model**

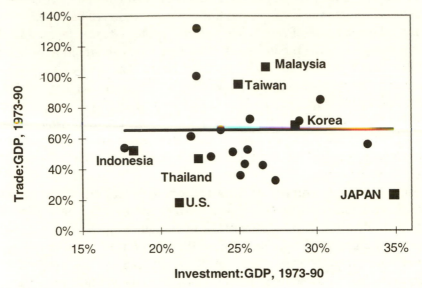

Source: Summers and Heston (1995)
Note: The trend line divides high-trade countries from low-trade countries.

NICs. Korea, for example, went from an intra-industry trade index of 0.19 in 1970 to 0.48 in 1990. Once again, Japan stands out as the exception. Back in 1970, when Japan was richer than the rest of Asia, its 0.33 index number ranked it sixth out of 15 Pacific countries. As other countries improved and Japan did not—even though Japan had gotten much richer—its ranking fell to twelfth. All of the Asian NICs, save Indonesia, the poorest of the lot, now engage in more intra-industry trade than Japan. They accept competing products.

Moreover, aside from Korea, the Asian countries are far more open to foreign direct investment (FDI) than is Japan. FDI into Japan is negligible. In 1993, foreign-affiliated companies had a negligible 0.9 percent share of sales. By contrast, the Asian boom is built on foreign direct investment. One company alone, Matsushita, accounts for 4 percent of Malaysia's GDP.

As a result, Asian NICs like Taiwan, Hong Kong, and Korea have among the very highest rates of TFP growth in the world. Moreover, while most low- and middle-income countries derived only 10–20 percent of their growth from TFP, Taiwan, Korea, Hong Kong and Thailand obtained over a third of their growth from TFP. This led the World Bank

Table 10.1

Asian NICs Import Competing Products; Japan Does Not (Index of intra-industry trade in manufacturing in 15 Pacific nations)

	1970		1980		1990	
	Index	Rank	Index	Rank	Index	Rank
Singapore	0.44	3	0.65	1	0.71	1
U.S.	**0.57**	**2**	**0.62**	**3**	**0.69**	**2**
Canada	0.63	1	0.62	2	0.68	3
Malaysia	0.13	13	0.37	6	0.58	4
Hong Kong	0.33	5	0.46	4	0.50	5
Taiwan	0.36	4	0.35	8	0.49	6
KOREA	**0.19**	**9**	**0.39**	**5**	**0.48**	**7**
Mexico	0.29	7	0.36	7	0.48	8
Philippines	0.07	14	0.17	14	0.42	9
China	0.19	10	0.28	10	0.40	10
Thailand	0.05	15	0.24	13	0.39	11
JAPAN	**0.33**	**6**	**0.27**	**11**	**0.36**	**12**
New Zealand	0.16	11	0.27	12	0.32	13
Australia	0.28	8	0.29	9	0.26	14
Indonesia	0.14	12	0.08	15	0.19	15
France	0.78		0.82		0.84	
Germany	0.60		0.66			

Sources: Bergsten and Noland (1993), pp. 32 and 209; Lincoln (1990), p. 47 for Germany.
   Note: This table shows an index of "intraindustry trade," i.e., how much a country imports the same products that it exports. Japan' s ranking steadily dropped as other countries increased their interdependence and Japan did not. This index is not affected by Japan's lack of natural resources because it measures intra-industry trade *within* manufacturing alone. Korea, despite its protectionism and lack of natural resources, used to rank lower than Japan but now ranks higher.

to call them "productivity-driven economies." Even Indonesia, Malaysia and Singapore, which the World Bank labels "investment-driven," still obtained about 20 percent of their growth from TFP, far more than the vast majority of non-Asian developing countries.[2]

Ironically, Paul Krugman's thesis of the "Myth of the Asian Miracle" has more application to post-1973 Japan than to most of the Asian NICs.[3]

International Exposure Will Hasten Asia's Reform

If a frog is thrown into a boiling pot of water, it will jump out. But, if a frog is put into a pot of water and then the heat is gradually turned up, it is said that it will sit there until it dies.

That, in a nutshell, is the difference between the malaise afflicting Japan and the tumultuous financial storms that began battering so many other East Asian countries in late 1997. The boiling water in this case is international trade, investment, and money flows.

Japan is suffering from a deep-seated, long-term structural malaise that produces low productivity and long-term economic stagnation. The economy neither plummets nor booms. It just limps along. The danger for Japan is not cataclysm, but drift. Unlike the rest of Asia, which depends on foreign funds, Japan can finance its own needs. If its banks are in trouble, the Bank of Japan can just print more money. This does, of course, have long-term deleterious effects. Still, Japan can, if it so chooses, try to muddle through. The cost of muddling through is a lot worse than most leaders in Tokyo recognize, but it has been done for eight years so far and can be done for several more, albeit not indefinitely.

For Korea, Indonesia, Thailand, Malaysia and so forth, muddling through is simply not an option. They are dependent, not only on international trade, but on international money flows. If they do not enact the reforms necessary to instill confidence, both domestic and foreign investors will flee the country. Facing a stark choice between reform or chaos, they are more likely to choose the former.

There is no guarantee, of course. The peculiarities of each country, from corruption to succession crises, make a big difference. Still, history has shown that countries which are more open to international trade and investment are far more likely to reform than those which are not.

The prospect of reform also depends, of course, on the international support given these countries. History has shown that, to prevent crises from turning into Depressions, it is necessary for a country, or group of countries, to act as both "lenders of last resort" and "importers of last resort." The U.S., the IMF and Japan have all played a role in the first function, the lending function. But for the countries to be able to pay back loans, as well as restore confidence of private investors, they have to show their ability to earn export income.

One of the most disheartening aspects of the crisis is Japan's inability and unwillingness to play the "importer of last resort" role—at least as of early 1998. Japan has been so paralyzed by its own crisis that it has been unable to rescue even itself, never mind its neighbors. When Prime Minister Hashimoto was asked by President Clinton to play this importer of last resort role along with the U.S., Hashimoto promptly told the press that, "Japan is not so arrogant as to think it can play the role of locomotive for other countries." Indeed, to some extent, Japan is trying to export its way out of its own problems at the expense of its Asian neighbors. Its efforts won't be enough to rescue Japan, but they could be enough to slow Asian recovery.

Ten years ago, some people claimed Japan was a threat because it was too strong; today, Japan is a problem because it is too weak.

It should also be stressed that, aside from the case of Korea, the crises facing East Asian countries are far different from the structural malaise afflicting Japan.

In most of Asia, the current crisis is basically a sharp macroeconomic crunch. It is akin to the tumultuous boom-bust cycles that America and Europe suffered in the 19th and early 20th centuries when they too were in their industrializing heyday.

The boom part of the cycle over the past decade was based on an international trade/investment triangle comprising Japan, Asia and the U.S. Following the rise of the yen in the mid-1980s, Japan invested massively in manufacturing facilities in Asia, thereby running a trade surplus with the region. Indeed, a full third of Japan's entire global exports of capital goods consist of shipments to Japan's own overseas affiliates, many of them in Asia. Asia, in turn, exported shiploads of goods to the U.S., thereby piling up a big surplus with the U.S. It was the surplus with the U.S. that initially allowed these countries to finance their deficit with Japan. Aside from imports from its own affiliates in Asia, Japan imported few manufacturing goods from the Asian countries.

Once the Asia boom began, then additional money flocked to Asia in the form of bank loans, stock purchases and so forth. In fact, in typical boomtown fashion, more money came in than these countries could use wisely. In particular, as the bust in Japan lowered interest rates toward 1 percent, Japanese investors sought higher returns elsewhere. Japan flooded Asia with money, in effect exporting its late 1980s bubble. Cash went into buildings for which there were no renters, factories in industries already suffering global overcapacity, unscreened bank loans, overvalued stocks, and so forth. Soon, European and American funds joined the party.

The end of the boom was triggered when the U.S. dropped out of the trade triangle. Partly this was because America's trade deficit was shifting from the offshore Asian countries to China. America's trade deficit with the four big Asian NICs (Korea, Hong Kong, Singapore and Taiwan), virtually disappeared during 1997. The deficit with ASEAN, which had risen from a negligible level in 1988 to hit a peak of $23 billion in 1996, dropped by 25 percent to an annualized rate of $17.6 billion during the first six months of 1997.[4]

Had it only been the trade *balance* in the Asian countries that was falling, these countries might have adjusted over time. After all, many developing countries grow while running a big trade deficit. However, the absolute level of exports to the rest of the world hit a brick wall. Some of this was due to the incredible drop of electronics prices that sent computer memory chips down from $50 in 1995 to $5 in 1997. In country after country, exports plummeted from double-digit growth in 1995–96 to negligible or even negative growth by the summer of 1997, when the crisis broke out.[5]

Since exports provided the income not only to pay for current imports but to pay back past loans and investments, this resulted in a sudden bulge in these countries' trade and current account deficits.

Eventually, as it became clear that these countries would not be able to sustain these rising trade imbalances, a few investors broke ranks. Soon, everyone headed for the exits. The hot money which had flowed in so quickly left just as quickly. This set off the crisis.

We do not mean to imply that this crisis is merely a short-term financial phenomenon and that no changes are needed. On the contrary, long-term structural reforms are needed, as many leaders in the region acknowledge. These countries have developed too much to continue with obsolete ways. Over time, primitive financial systems must be modernized. Corruption and "crony capitalism" must be uprooted. These countries need economic and political institutions as modern as their factories. The good news is that, under the current financial pressure, they are likely to adopt many of those needed reforms. The other good news is that, because of these countries' international openness and productivity-based growth, once they do get through the storm and enact the needed reforms, they are likely to return to impressive growth—even if not as high as what they previously enjoyed.

While the spark for the crisis in Korea has many features in common with Southeast Asia, the overall dilemma in that country is better described as a more tumultuous version of the maturation crisis that Japan faced in the aftermath of the 1973 oil shock. To a larger extent than in other Asian countries, Korea modeled its political economy on that of high-growth era Japan, including large *chaebol* that mirror the *keiretsu*, as well as government-directed bank credit to favored industries and firms. While this produced a tremendous jump-start in Korea's industrial takeoff, it also meant that pampered and politically connected conglomerates built too much capacity in glutted industries. As in Japan, it was time to move to a more market-oriented setup. To some degree, Korea tried, but failed, to make this transition in time. Now, it faces a crisis and must accelerate the transition. Because of Korea's greater dependence on international trade and funds, it, unlike Japan, will find it very hard to maintain the old system.

It is certainly possible to think of disaster scenarios that could derail Asia's revival. Except for a possible political meltdown in one or two countries, most of the pessimistic scenarios involve circumstances beyond developing Asia's control: from a massive currency devaluation by China, to Japan's failure to absorb enough Asian exports, to a protectionist reaction in the U.S. While these scenarios cannot be ruled out, the odds are, when the new millennium dawns, most of Asia will probably be well on its way to full recovery. But when it comes to Japan—a nation whose fate is almost entirely in its own hands—we will still be waiting for the sun to rise.

Chapter 11

Japan's Peculiar Trade:
Too Few Imports, Too Few Exports

Japan's Outlier Status

One of the crowning glories of the post–World War II international economy is the steady increase in global interdependence. The lowering of trade barriers, cheapening of transport costs, new technologies, and the spread of foreign direct investment all fueled a steady globalization trend. Globalization in turn helped fuel faster rates of growth than for any comparable period in the history of the world. Nations now grow as much in a single year as they used to grow in a decade. A greater portion of the world's population has entered the industrial age and left abject poverty behind than ever before.

Among the advanced nations, virtually every major nation *except Japan* drastically increased its trade volumes relative to GDP. In Germany—a country, like Japan, with no natural resources (other than coal)—the trade: GDP ratio soared from less than 30 percent to more than 60 percent. Even America, a country with twice Japan's population, has more than doubled its trade:GDP ratio from a low 9 percent to 22 percent.

As we detailed in Chapter 10, this trend includes the Asian NICs as well. Korea's trade:GDP ratio exploded from 11 percent in 1955 to 63 percent in 1990, Taiwan's went from 21 percent to 90 percent, Thailand's from 45 percent to 75 percent and Indonesia's from 25 percent to 53 percent.

Japan alone stood aside from this global process. Except for the period of high oil prices, its trade openness ratio shows a clear *declining* trend throughout the postwar era. It was virtually the only nation that traded less in 1996 than it had four decades earlier in 1956. Today, relative to GDP, Japan trades even less than the U.S. (Figure 11.1).

Japan is the only major country whose imports grow more slowly than GDP (Table 11.1). Among Japan's trading partners, imports grow faster than GDP. In the U.S., every time GDP rises 1 percent, imports go up 1.3 percent; in Germany they go up 2.8 percent. On the whole, when-

Figure 11.1 **Japan's Trade Slips; America's and Germany's Soars**

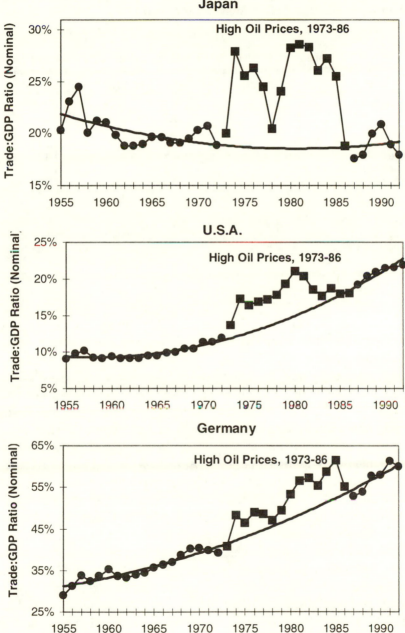

Source: Summers and Heston (1995)

Table 11.1

Only in Japan Do Imports Rise More Slowly Than GDP

	Column A	Column B	Ratio B/A
	% that *imports* rise for every 1% rise in *own* GDP	% that *exports* rise for every 1% rise in GDP of trading partners	Why Japan's trade surplus keeps expanding
JAPAN	0.8	1.7	2.06
U.S.	1.3	1.7	1.30
Canada	1.7	2.9	1.73
Belgium	2.0	1.2	0.62
Austria	2.6	3.1	1.18
Netherlands	2.7	3.9	1.45
Germany	2.8	2.2	0.76
Italy	3.7	2.4	0.66

Source: Krugman (1995), p. 55

Note: This table covers 1970–86. Japan is the *only* major nation whose imports rise less than 1% for every 1% rise in GDP. On the other hand, when the GDP of its customer nations rises 1%, Japan's exports to them rise 1.7%. Even considering differences in growth rates, these trends mean that Japan's imports do not keep up with exports, creating a tendency toward ever-higher trade surpluses. See Appendix F.

ever GDP grows 1 percent in Japan's customer countries, their purchases of Japanese exports go up 1.7 percent. No wonder Japan's trade surplus keeps expanding.

Japan was not always an "under-trader." During the high-growth era, its trade dependence was as high, or even higher, than similarly situated countries. However, from 1975 onward, as the rest of the world raced ahead toward greater interdependence and a resistant Japan remained stuck behind the starting line, it fell further and further behind global trends. Whereas Japan's trade:GDP ratio had been almost half of the 25-country average in 1995, it fell to less than a third by 1990 (top panel of Figure 11.2).

Had Japan simply kept up with world trends, its trade in 1990 would have amounted to 30 percent of GDP, nearly 1.5 times the 21 percent ratio it actually attained (bottom panel of Figure 11.2).

If we use a more sophisticated analysis—based on standard economic models that show how a country's trade is typically affected by its population, distance from other countries, income levels and membership (or lack of) in trade blocs—then the gap becomes even larger. Had Japan acted like a typical country, then in 1990 its combined exports and imports would have amounted to 37 percent of GDP, almost *twice* the 21 percent it actually attained (Figure 11.3).[1]

Figure 11.2 **Japan Falls Behind World Trends, U.S. Is Catching Up**

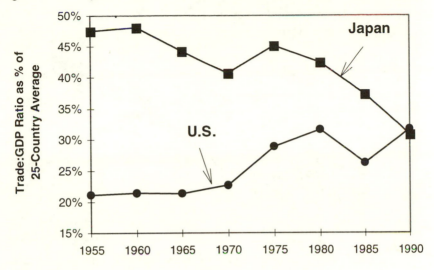

If Japan Had Kept Up, Its Trade Would Be 1.5 Times As High

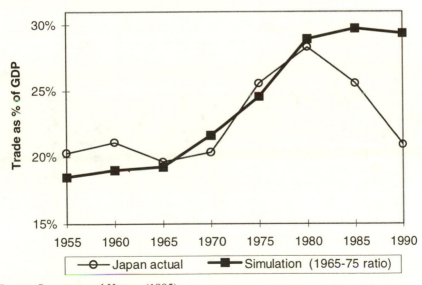

Source: Summers and Heston (1995)

Note: The simulation in the bottom panel assumed that Japan's trade:GDP ratio was sustained at 44% of the 25-country average, the relationship to world trends it had maintained during 1965-75.

Figure 11.3 **Japan Moves from "Excess" Trade to Too Little Trade**

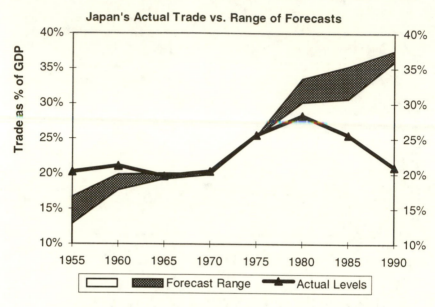

Japan's Actual Trade vs. Range of Forecasts

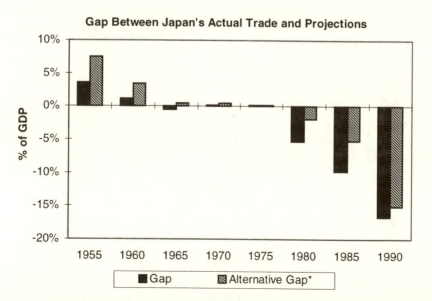

Gap Between Japan's Actual Trade and Projections

Source: For actual trade levels, Summers and Heston (1995). For projections and the methods used to produce them, see Appendix F. *Alternative Gap is based on use of a special adjustment for East Asia.

The irony is that, relative to world trends, Japan was more closed in 1990, when it was ostensibly "open," than in 1960, when it was avowedly restrictive. In terms of the volume of its trade—the objective measure of openness—Japan in the 1960s was in line with what one would expect. Its restrictions on imports only changed their *composition* but not their overall *volume*. Meanwhile, its boosts to exports more than counterbalanced its restrictions on imports. However, from the mid-1970s onward, its cartelized economy not only distorted the composition of trade, but also increasingly suppressed its volume.[2]

In terms of the global dual economy that we discussed in Chapter 9, it was almost as if Japan had moved from the community of the open economies to the world of the closed ones. As it did so, it began to suffer all the productivity problems and institutional paralysis that typically afflict closed economies.

Why Japan's Trade Is So Low: A Dearth of Competing Imports

Since it is trade in *competing* products that produces the biggest gains in productivity, Japan's trade patterns are particularly self-defeating. Not only is Japan's overall level of trade too low, but, among Japan's imports, very few are in goods that put competitive pressure on domestic firms.

In fact, the reason that Japan's overall trade is so low is precisely because it imports so few competing manufactured goods. Low imports of competing products leads to low total imports and, as we shall see, low *im*ports lead to low *ex*ports.[3]

Most countries import two kinds of products: (1) those that *complement* domestic output, such as inputs like oil and raw materials, or specialized products (like an Intel microprocessor); and (2) those that *substitute* for and compete with domestic output, e.g., Japanese cars in America, or British steel in Germany. The growing trade in substitutes, i.e., competing products, is reflected in the high intra-industry trade indexes that we saw for most advanced countries other than Japan (refer to Table 9.3).

Japan, however, until very recently limited itself almost entirely to the first type of import, the complements. The lion's share of its imports have been food, oil, raw materials, or indispensable specialty items that Japan does not produce itself. Substitutes have a hard time getting into Japan's cartelized economy no matter how cheap the price. As recently as 1992, despite domestic prices in that were 60–70 percent (!) above world levels, Japan imported only 7 percent of the steel, 1.2 percent of the cement and

8 percent of the petrochemicals that it consumed.[4] Imagine how powerful cartels have to be to keep imports down with even that great a price discrepancy.

Imports are not low because individual Japanese consumers are hostile to foreign goods. On the contrary, studies have shown that Japanese consumers have little problem in buying imported goods—but they cannot find them on the shelves. It is primarily the government and firms in vertical supplier–buyer cartels that refuse to buy competitive imports. Peter Petri has documented that business and government purchase practices reduce import penetration 15–16 percent below what households tend to purchase. As for consumers, Prof. Petri shows that where producer concentration is high and distributors have a lot of control, import penetration is small; where controls are looser, imports are higher. Cartels, not consumer choice, dictate Japan's low imports.[5]

It is often claimed by Japanese economists that Japan imports so few manufactured items because it has no natural resources. Therefore, it has to import raw materials instead of manufactured goods. The implication seems to be that imports are like a child's seesaw: the more raw materials Japan imports, the fewer manufactured goods it can import. Typical is the following passage by two of Japan's most prestigious economists, Ryutaro Komiya and Motoshige Itoh (Komiya, besides being a Tokyo University professor, formerly headed the MITI-affiliated Research Institute on International Trade and Industry):

> The low levels of manufactured goods in Japan's total imports, as well as relative to GDP, can be explained as follows. The share of minerals, fuel, raw materials, and food in the total imports of Japan is quite large because of its poor endowments of natural resources and land. Japan has a strong comparative disadvantage in natural resources and agriculture and an equally strong comparative advantage over a wide range of manufactures.[6]

At first blush, this sounds reasonable. However, on closer inspection, this explanation does not hold water.

First of all, it's simply not the case that Japan has to import raw materials just because it has none of its own. As economist Ed Lincoln has pointed out,[7] Japan has no need to import a single drop of oil. It could import finished petroleum products instead—just like scores of other countries do. Indeed, comparative advantage suggests that Japan should import petroleum products rather than crude oil since its own refiners are so inefficient. Why does Japan need to import a single ton of copper ore when others are so much more efficient at making copper products? And yet, 65 percent of Japan's copper imports come in the form of iron ores and concentrates and 31 percent in the form of unwrought metal.

Japan does not import a lot of raw materials because it lacks them. It imports them because it chooses to do so rather than import finished products that might compete with local producers. Aside from coal, Germany is just as deprived of natural resources as Japan. Yet Germany imports these resources in the form of finished products.

Secondly, despite the assertion of Komiya and Itoh, Japan does *not* have strong comparative advantage over a "wide range" of manufacturers. On the contrary, due to the dual economy, Japan's comparative advantage is limited to an unusually *narrow* range of goods. In stark contrast to other advanced countries, most of Japan's exports are concentrated in only a few products, primarily autos, electronics and producers' machinery. For example, in 1985, Japan's top 10 exports amounted to a full 36 percent of all its exports, and all but one of these top 10 products were part of the automotive or electronics industries. By contrast Germany's top 10 exports added up to only 22 percent of total exports and they came from a broader array of sectors.[8] Japan's excessive concentration of exports means that, in those few industries where it does export, its share of world trade is unusually high. That is one of the reasons its exports cause such disruption in the few sectors where they are focused. This phenomenon is yet another facet of Japan's trade patterns where it is an international outlier.

Thirdly, compared to other countries, Japan's import bill for raw materials is not that large. In 1990, its raw material and oil imports amounted to about 4.5 percent of GDP. This places it 16th among the 21 advanced and developing countries shown in Figure 11.4.

Most important of all, even if Japan did need to import a lot of raw materials, that in itself does not mean it has to import fewer manufactured goods. It could import a lot of both—as does most every other country.

If the "seesaw theory of imports" were correct, countries all over the world with a high dependence on raw material imports would import few manufactured goods. But, as we can see in Figure 11.4, that is not the case. Most countries that import a lot of raw materials also import a lot of manufactured goods as well. Their total imports are high. (In the top panel of Figure 11.4, the trend line is pointing upward; if the seesaw theory were correct, it would be pointing downward). Hence, there is absolutely no trade-off whatsoever between a country's raw material imports and its manufactured goods imports. Nor is there any correlation at

Figure 11.4 **Other Low-Resource Nations Import Manufactures**

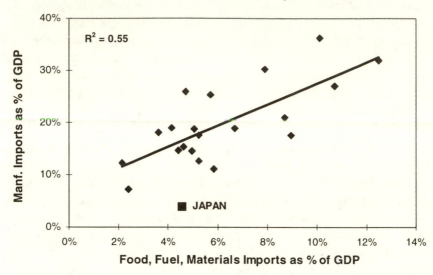

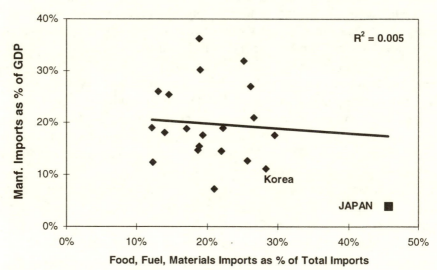

Source: World Bank (1997); Summers and Heston (1995)
Note: 21 countries in the year 1990. The top panel shows that countries which import a lot raw materials also import a lot of manufactures. The bottom panel shows there is no trade-off (i.e., R^2 is close to zero) between the proportion of a country's imports used for raw materials and its imports of manufactured goods. Japan is simply an outlier. The trend line is drawn without including Japan.

all between how much of a country's import bill goes to buy raw materials and that country's total trade volume (bottom panel). Japan is simply an extreme outlier that imports a lot of raw materials and low-grade manufactures and far too little of everything else. The seesaw theory is wrong.

To see why Japan's overall trade is so low, consider the following arithmetic. Suppose Country A imports raw materials equal to 5 percent of GDP, but excludes everything else. In that case, raw materials would amount to 100 percent of imports, manufactured goods 0 percent, and imports would be 5 percent of GDP. Now, suppose Country B likewise imports raw materials equal to 5 percent of GDP but also imports manufactured goods equal to 5 percent of GDP. In that case, its raw materials would amount to 50 percent of imports, manufactured goods 50 percent of imports, and total imports would be 10 percent of GDP. Japan is like Country A and the rest of the world acts like Country B.

In sum, the Japanese argument stands logic and arithmetic on its head. It is not the case that Japan imports few manufactures because it has a high ratio of raw materials to total imports. Rather, it has a high ratio of raw materials to imports because it imports so few manufactures.

True, Japan's ratio of manufactured goods to total imports has increased in recent years, but not all that much. Moreover, it seems that progress occurs only in the wake of repeated hikes in the yen/dollar rate. In 1987, after oil prices collapsed, the ratio rebounded to 44 percent. A year later, with the yen soaring, the ratio rose to 50 percent. There it stayed for another few years until another ratcheting of the yen brought it up to 55 percent in 1994—still far below the OECD average, which is over 80 percent.[9]

It is a staple of economics that barriers to imports turn out to be barriers to exports as well. (We discussed this in Chapter 3 and will explore it further in Appendix F. Essentially, the reason is that, when imports are too low, the yen rises. This in turn prices Japanese exports out of the market.) So, in the end, it is Japan's refusal to import competing imports that explains why its exports, and not just its imports, are too low. The victims of Japanese protection include not just Chrysler and Motorola but Toyota and Toshiba as well.

Could the World Absorb More Japanese Exports?

If Japan did reform and double its trade to 37 percent of GDP, could the world absorb all those exports? One economist, upon hearing this, protested, "Needless to say, such an expansion would give rise to intensified trade frictions. This venue is definitely unrealistic.[11]

But, in fact, the world can absorb all the exports Japan is able to put out—*as long as Japan is willing to match its rising exports with rising imports.* Global trade is growing faster than global GDP. Every major country except Japan is increasing both exports and imports at a rapid pace. What the world cannot tolerate is a continually rising trade *surplus.* It is not excessive trade, but insufficient trade (caused by Japan's low imports) which leads to friction.

Why is it that Japan's surpluses provoke a backlash but Germany's do not? The reason, as economist Robert Lawrence has pointed out, is that Germany is not only one of the largest exporters of autos and steel, but also one of the largest importers of such items. No car or steel company is going to complain about Germany being closed—despite its large surplus. In 1986, when Lawrence made his analysis, both Japan and Germany ran similar surpluses in merchandise trade (4.3 percent and 5.8 percent of GDP respectively). Germany's exports amounted to 27 percent of GDP while imports added up to 21 percent of GDP. By contrast, Japan exported 10 percent of GDP, but imported only 6 percent. The trade balances were similar, but, at 48 percent of GDP, Germany's total trade was three times as high as Japan's 16 percent.[11]

Japan's Distance from Trading Partners Is No Explanation

Those who wish to deny that Japan's market is closed often claim that Japan's trade is low because it is so far away from other industrial countries.[12] Sure, Germany trades a lot, they say. So would Japan if it had more than a dozen industrial countries within a couple hundred miles of its major cities. Again, the following passage by Komiya and Itoh is typical:

> Moreover, Japan has no neighboring countries that are similar in language, culture and income level. The last condition seems to be an important aspect of the low levels of imports of manufacturers.[13]

Distance does, of course, matter somewhat. Michigan does a lot more trade with Ontario than it does with Texas. Germany is always going to trade more than Japan. On the other hand, Japan seems to have little problem getting oil from the Mideast or shipping cars to the U.S.

But all of this misses the main point. It is true that, at any given moment in time, Japan's distance might explain why it trades less than

Figure 11.5 **Distance Does Not Explain Japan's Low Trade**

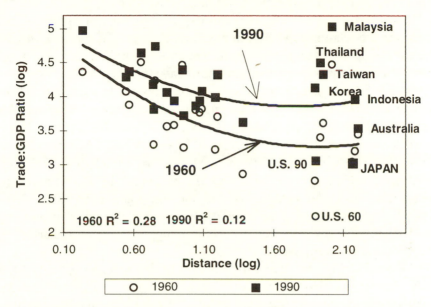

Source: Barro and Lee (1994); Summers and Heston (1995)

Note: The chart, using a logarithmic scale, shows that the farther away a country is from its 20 largest trading partners, the less it trades. The box next to Japan shows Japan's trade in both 1960 and 1990 since its trade:GDP ratio has hardly changed. The higher trend line for 1990 compared to 1960 means that all countries are trading more, regardless of distance. The R^2 numbers mean that, in 1960, 28% of the variation in the trade:GDP ratio among countries could be explained by their distance from trading partners. By 1990, distance could only explain 12% of the variation. See text for further explanation.

Germany. However, that does not explain why Japan is the only country that did not become more trade dependent *over time*. Japan's Asian neighbors are far more industrialized than 30 years ago. They all trade far more than they used to, much of it on industrial imports from Japan. This suggests that Japan's trade dependence should have increased rather than decreased.

Moreover, distance is simply nowhere near as big an obstacle as it used to be—especially now that Japan ships more computer chips and fewer cars. On a global scale, transportation costs have dropped from 20 percent of the cost of the goods traded in 1948, to 10 percent by 1960, and only 6 percent in 1990. That's less than currencies can fluctuate in a year.[14]

In 1960, distance accounted for about 28 percent of the reason why Germany trades more than Japan or the U.S. (i.e., $R^2 = 0.28$ in Figure 11.5).

Today, distance can account for only about 12 percent of the trade differences among countries (i.e., $R^2 = 0.12$).

Moreover, in 1960, Japan was more or less in line with international trends in the relationship between trade and distance. By 1990, it was far below trends. It is notable that other countries in Asia, just as far away from major partners, engage in a lot more trade than Japan.

In any case, distance has always been a less important factor than population size in determining how much a country trades. Four decades ago, nations with big populations did not do all that much trade. But a small country had no choice. How could a country of 4 million or even 10 million produce by itself all the cars it needs, including all the steel, glass, and rubber that go into it, all the parts and all the machines to make those parts and materials, and all the consumer needs of the workers who make all these things? Small countries had to trade. By contrast, aside from vital raw materials and so forth, bigger nations could afford to be *relatively* self-sufficient.

So, traditionally, the larger a country was, the smaller its trade:GDP ratio. In fact, population size used to be more important in determining a country's trade dependence than all other factors *combined*—including distance. All by itself, population size could provide *half* of the explanation of why some countries trade more than others (i.e., $R^2 = 0.50$ in Figure 11.6).

But, over the past four decades, population differences have become less important in explaining trade patterns. (R^2 fell to 0.35, which means only 35 percent of the difference in countries' trade volumes can be explained by population size.) It's not just cheaper transport and communication costs along with eased tariff barriers: specialization yields more benefits than ever before. America is better at making airplanes and microprocessors than Japan; the latter is better at making cars and memory chips. Software engineers in Bombay can write Microsoft programs while programmers in Seattle sleep and then they can send the results over the phone line. This produces the kind of trade that no one even imagined a few years ago. Overall, the cost:benefit equation has so changed that even large nations find it pays to specialize.

Against this background, Japan stands out. In 1960, Japan's trade dependence was almost exactly in line with its population (Figure 11.6). But, as the rest of the world traded more but Japan did not, it fell far behind world trends. By contrast, the U.S. has moved up and now trades more than Japan even though it has twice Japan's population.

Figure 11.6 **These Days, Big Countries Trade a Lot--Except Japan**

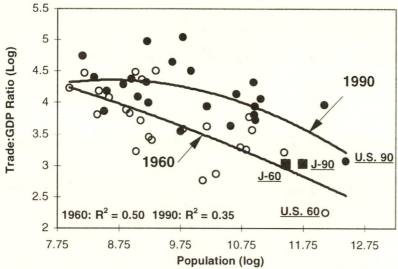

Source: Summers and Heston (1995)

Note: This chart, in logarithm form, shows how much a country's trade:GDP ratio decreases as its population increases. In 1960, Japan--indicated by J-60--was right on the international trend line. By 1990, it was far below it. The higher trend line for 1990 compared to 1960 means that both big and small countries are more trade-dependent. R^2 numbers means that, in 1960, 50% of the variation in trade among countries could be explained by their population; in 1990, only 35% of the trade variation could be explained by population. See text.

The bottom line is that external, uncontrollable factors like population and distance simply matter less than they used to. It is to Japan's policies and economic structures, not to any external circumstances, that we must look for the cause of its low trade.[15]

Chapter 12

Is Japan Opening Up?

Progress of Early 1990s Stalls Out

Some will argue that everything we have said about Japan's limited trade is ancient history. Japan, it is said, is now increasing its import penetration and has been doing so steadily over the past few years.

To some extent, this is true. Under the pressure of the rising yen, import volumes (actual number of sweaters, TVs, square feet of lumber, and so forth) swelled substantially in the early 1990s. Among manufactured goods, the progress was particularly impressive—a 21 percent hike in 1994 and another 31 percent in 1995.

By 1996, imports of TVs began to outpace domestically made units. Imports supplied over 30 percent of textile consumption, up from a meager 10 percent in 1985.

While all of this is good news, it's a little premature to celebrate. For one thing, there are reasons to wonder whether this a genuine sea change, or just one more of the temporary blips Japan has experienced whenever the yen soars. After the yen reversed itself in 1995 and started weakening again, the progress on imports stalled out. From 1995 through the end of 1997 there has been virtual zero growth in import volumes (number of sweaters, TVs, square feet of lumber, etc.).

Japan's imports have repeatedly bounced up and down—depending on the price of oil, the yen and Japan's growth rate. However, relative to GDP, there is certainly no increasing trend in the data. Indeed, as a percentage of GDP, imports in 1996 were still below the level of 1990, not to mention 1960 (top panel of Figure 12.1).

In fact, Japan is so import-resistant that it spent barely a yen more on imports in 1994 than it had spent in 1980. Since barriers to imports turn out to be barriers to exports as well, revenue from exports in 1996 was no higher than in 1984 (bottom panel of Figure 12.1).

The failure of imports to increase for so long is astonishing since,

Figure 12.1 **Relative to GDP, Japan's Imports *and Exports* Decline**

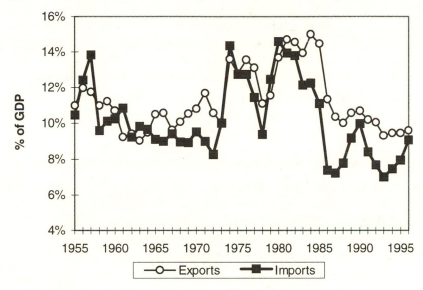

Spending on Imports Barely Higher in 1994 Than 1980

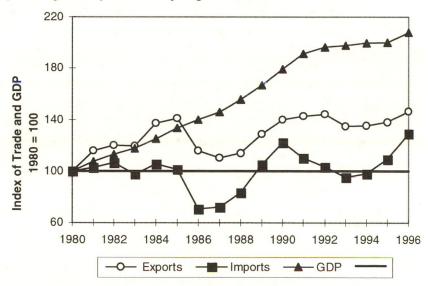

Source: EPA (1997), all in current yen.

Note: Even though the volume of imports increased, this increase was less than the price drop, so the money spent on imports fell. See text for explanation.

during that time, Japan's nominal GDP had doubled and the combination of falling oil prices and a soaring yen had reduced the price of imports by half.

In most countries, such price drops would have produced an enormous surge of imports as consumers and companies switched from domestic products to imports. But in Japan, both the government and companies are reluctant to buy imports and consumers still find it hard to locate imports on their shelves. Hence, while imports did increase substantially in price-adjusted terms, there was nowhere near the kind of import surge that such price cuts normally produce and certainly not enough to increase overall spending on imports such as occurs in most countries. (If cutting the price of a $100 item by 10 percent leads customers to buy 20 percent more imports, then spending on imports will *rise* 8 percent, i.e., $90 × 1.20 = $108. This is what happens in most countries. But, if the price falls from $100 to $90 and customers buy only 5 percent more of the item, then their spending on imports will actually go *down* 5 percent, i.e., $90 × 1.05 = $95. This is what happened in Japan.)

Beyond the simple level of imports, there is another nagging issue. Not all imports are created equal. In recent years, the lion's share of the growth in manufactured imports has come not from *competing* firms, but from the overseas affiliates of *Japanese* firms. Most of those imported TVs, for example, are made by Japanese companies in Southeast Asia. Clearly, such "captive imports" (called "reverse imports" by MITI) are not positioned or priced to challenge the cartelized price and industry structure at home (Figure 12.2).

Japan has an unfortunate pattern. When imports are unavoidable, the approach is: buy the foreign producers, not the foreign product.

When the oil shocks made domestic production of aluminum completely nonviable, MITI delayed the shutdown of domestic output until Japanese firms could build up overseas capacity. By 1993, 80 percent of Japan's lost output at home was replaced by imports from *Japanese-owned* plants overseas.[1] When beef imports were finally liberalized, Japanese investors decided to buy cattle ranches in Montana. Now that Japanese consumers are demanding cheaper food and clothing, and imports have begun to come in, Japanese food and textile companies are moving offshore.

Consumer products imported from Japanese affiliates have doubled from 13 percent of all consumer goods imported in 1991 to 27 percent in 1995. Overall such "captive imports" accounted for 13.6 percent of Japan's total imports in 1995, double the 6 percent ratio in 1990.[2] Indeed,

Figure 12.2 **Captive Consumer Imports Outpace Competitive Imports**

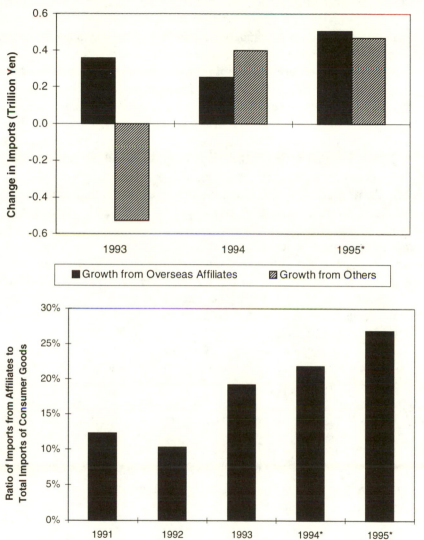

Source: MITI (1994a, 1994b), *1995 is an estimate by MITI.

according to Jesper Koll, chief economist of J.P. Morgan's Tokyo office, two-thirds of the entire growth in manufactured imports from the early 1980s to the mid-1990s was from Japanese subsidiaries overseas.[3]

The rise of the yen has changed the location of the factory but not the nationality of the producer.

Captive imports do not provide the productivity kick that comes from competing imports. What Japan really needs is a tidal wave of imports from *non-Japanese* companies. Where even a small amount of imports can get their foot in the door, the effect on bringing down monopolistic prices—"price destruction" the Japanese call it—has been phenomenal. Tuna prices dropped 63 percent during 1995, beer fell 32 percent, whiskey 17 percent, PCs 30 percent and gasoline 20–25 percent.[4]

Overall, if imports were no longer blocked by structural impediments, *keiretsu* and so forth, then, says economist Marc Noland, "Japanese [retail] prices would fall by 41 percent."[5]

Individual Japanese consumers have always been quite willing to buy imports—if only they could get their hands on them. Those who snickered at Washington's focus on the Large-Scale Retail Store Law have good reason to reconsider. Strengthening the power of big retailers, and therefore consumers, vis-à-vis manufacturers may be one of the most powerful weapons of reform.

If the positive trends of the early 1990s had continued for several more years, we might have truly seen some far-reaching and irreversible structural changes in Japan.

Unfortunately, with the U-turn of the yen after 1995, progress on imports seems to have stalled, perhaps even reversed. While overall import volumes—numbers of PCs, yards of cloth, tons of oil, and so forth—rose 13 percent in 1994 and 13 percent again in 1995, they rose only 2.3 percent in 1996. In the first half of 1997, import volumes were no higher than they had been in the last half of 1996. Manufactured imports, which had increased 31 percent in 1995, have shown a similar slowdown. Due to the yen hike, manufactured imports rose from 50 percent of all imports in 1990 to 60 percent by 1990. But, as of July 1997, this ratio had not improved any further.

As Salomon Brothers economist Tomoko Fujii stresses, without the pressure of constantly rising yen, it is hard to maintain progress:

> As the yen's past appreciation has begun to reverse, the rise in the import share ratio for producer goods appears to be stalling. Moreover the relative stability of this ratio during periods without yen appreciation in the past

suggests that producers are not willing to boost sourcing from abroad at the expense of their traditional domestic suppliers, once they have weathered their profitability crisis. . . . [Regarding final goods like consumer durables and capital goods], a further acceleration of growth for these imports probably will require additional downward pressure on prices—whether from further yen appreciation, deregulation, or technological innovation.[6]

Nor has there been any progress in foreign direct investment (FDI) into Japan. In 1993, according to MITI, foreign-affiliated companies had a negligible 1.6 percent share of the market for manufactured goods in Japan (not counting petroleum refiners). This is no higher than the share they had back in 1984. In all industries, the share of foreign affiliates was only 0.9 percent—*down* from the 1.5 percent share that they had back in 1984. By contrast, foreign affiliates have more than 10 percent of the U.S. market and more than 20 percent of the European market.[7]

This investment issue is particularly important for two reasons. Firstly, studies have shown that competition from foreign affiliates on the ground can sometimes provide an even bigger productivity kick than imports. It was not until the Japanese automakers put transplants on American soil that the U.S. "Big Three" started emulating their best practices.

Secondly, the dearth of foreign investment in Japan is itself one of the biggest structural impediments to more imports. U.S. multinationals sell twice as much overseas through their foreign affiliates as through direct exports. Moreover, much of their exports are to their own affiliates. In the case of Japan, *half* of all purchases by foreign affiliates are imports, either from their parents or from others. Even though foreign affiliates account for only 1 percent of all sales in Japan, they account for 9 percent of Japan's total imports. If FDI in Japan were greater, Japan's imports would also be greater.

The Market Test of Opening: Do Imports Respond to Prices?

We'll know that there has been a fundamental and irreversible sea change in Japan when the market starts working normally, i.e., when Japan's imports begin to respond to price changes in the same way that imports in other countries do. There has been some improvement on this front since the yen started rising in the late 1980s, but so far not enough to break the power of the cartels.

Historically, most of Japan's imports have been restricted primarily to items that *complement* domestic output rather than *substitute* for (or compete with) it. In other words, items like oil, raw materials, feedgrains, low-level manufactures, or specialized items that Japan doesn't make, like airplanes. Imports of these complements tend to grow proportionately with the growth of manufacturing or GDP, but they don't respond very readily to price changes. If a company is producing 1 million tons of steel, then it needs a certain amount of iron ore and coking coal, regardless of whether the price goes up 10 percent or down 20 percent. If steel output doubles, then so will its imports.

Substitutes, i.e., competing products, on the other hand, are very sensitive to price changes. If the price of imported cars or steel or wine goes up or down, companies and consumers in most countries readily switch from the domestic producer to the import and back again. A 10 percent drop in price might lead, for example, to a 15 percent or 25 percent rise in imports.

And so, in most countries, the growth of imports is a result of two factors: the growth of output (which affects complements) and the change in import prices relative to domestic prices (which affects substitutes). But in Japan, up until very recently, only the first of these factors had much impact. The market, i.e., responsiveness to price changes, was not being allowed to function.

Up until very recently, Japan's imports rose strictly in proportion to manufacturing or overall GDP (Figure 12.3), but, unlike in almost every other country, they were almost entirely insensitive to price changes. This was widely recognized and understood during the high-growth era when restrictions on competing imports were explicit. Indeed, when Krause and Sekiguchi modeled Japan's trade during the high-growth, they explicitly presumed absolutely zero responsiveness to price ("price elasticity" in the economics jargon).[8]

The amazing thing is that this insensitivity to prices continued in the 1970s and 1980s—even though overt trade restrictions had been lifted and the market was ostensibly open. The reality was: despite formal opening, the cartelized economy did not allow market forces to operate.

In 1974–94, import prices gyrated as oil prices exploded and imploded and the yen soared in a "three steps forward, one step backward" fashion. And still, up through the late 1980s, prices had little effect on Japan's imports (Figure 12.4).

Then, finally in the late 1980s, following the post-1985 explosion in the yen rate, the picture changed dramatically. As we see in Figure 12.4, the path of imports and import prices began to overlap. Price now seemed to matter a great deal.

Figure 12.3 **Imports March in Lockstep with Manufacturing Growth**

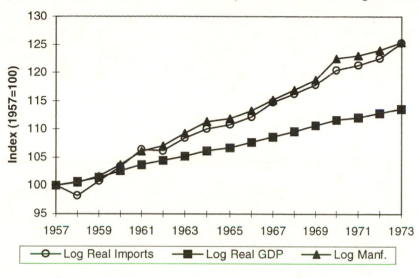

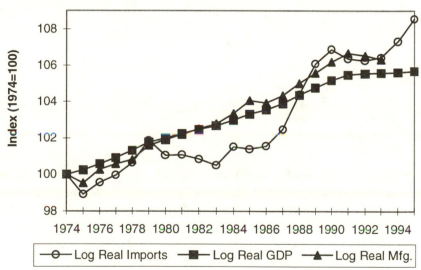

Source: EPA (1995a)

Note: In 1957-73, imports marched in almost complete lockstep with manufacturing and price had almost zero influence. Since manufacturing grew faster than GDP, so did price-adjusted imports. Since the prices of imports fell, the amount of yen spent on imports fell as a percent of GDP, as we saw in Figure 12.1. During 1974-95, except for a few years after the second oil shock in 1979, imports more or less grew in lockstep with manufacturing as well As the yen rose in the late 1980s and again in early 1990s, imports rose a bit faster. All numbers are in logarithm scale.

Figure 12.4 **Until the High Yen, Price Had Little Impact on Imports**

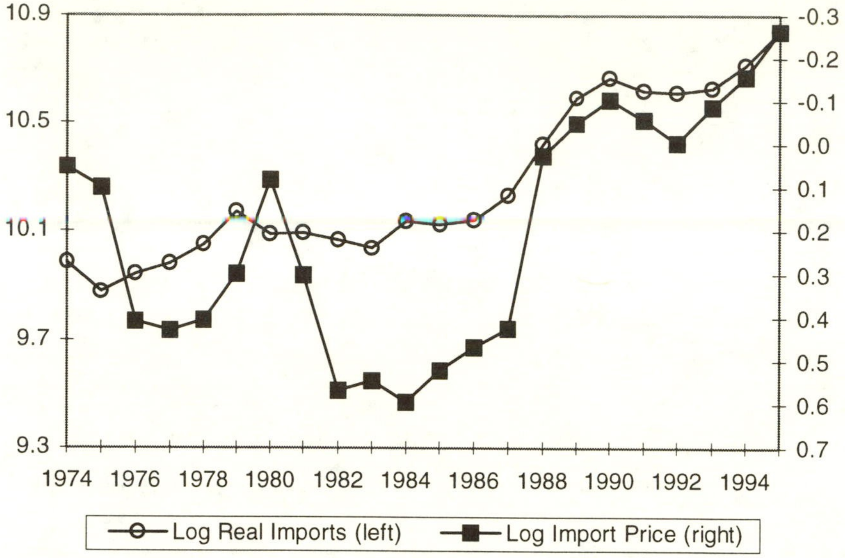

Source: EPA (1995a)

Note: This charts compares the growth of real imports to the change in the price of imports relative to domestic prices. From 1974 to 1987, the two lines move independently, showing that changes in price have a negligible impact on real imports. After 1987, they overlap showing that imports have become price-sensitive. This result is confirmed by econometric regressions. There is a 2-year lag on imports since it takes a while for price effects to show up. The figure for 1994 means the imports in 1994 and the price in 1992. Price is: Ln (Import deflator/GDP deflator). The price scale is inverted so that falling prices are indicated a rising line.

At first blush, it might seem that the high yen has finally broken the back of Japanese protectionism and that Japan is now importing competing products that substitute for domestic output. Prior to the rise of the yen, for every 1 percent drop in import prices, Japan's imports would rise only about 0.3 percent. After the yen rose, the situation changed. For every 1 percent drop in import prices, Japan's imports started increasing about 0.9 percent. This is certainly a welcome and dramatic change.

Yet, we cannot leap to the conclusion that market forces are now working properly. As we noted earlier, the lion's share of the increase in imports came from Japanese affiliates overseas. *Thus, price has come to matter a great deal as to where the goods are produced, but not the nationality of the producers.*

Moreover, while the increased price responsiveness (elasticity) is a lot better than before, it is still not enough for a yen rise to produce more spending on imports. In order for that to happen, Japan's imports must rise a bit more than 1 percent every time prices fall 1 percent.

Moreover, there are indications that, now that the yen has reversed course and started falling, Japanese firms are going back to old patterns and imports are once again becoming relatively insensitive to price.

A Rising Yen: "The Single Greatest Force for Reform"

Fuji-Xerox chieftain Yotaro Kobayashi has repeatedly stressed that "the rising yen is the greatest single force for reform."[9] He's right. When the yen rose sharply in the early 1990s, progress on both imports and domestic reform was seen; when the yen depreciated again after 1995 progress stalled or even reversed.

A rising yen promotes reform because it heightens the penalty that Japan's exporters pay for Japanese protectionism. Whenever the yen rises, Toyota gets fewer yen for each car that it sells. Suppose, because of the high input costs at home, it costs Toyota ¥2 million to make a Camry. Then at ¥100 per dollar, it can sell the car for $20,000. But if the yen rises in value to ¥80 per dollar, then Toyota faces a dilemma. If it keeps the price at $20,000, it will get only ¥1.6 million instead of ¥2 million and lose a bundle. If it wants to recoup its ¥2 million cost, it must charge $25,000—sending a lot of Americans scurrying to the Taurus showroom. Or else, Toyota must stop exporting from Japan and start building in Kentucky.

But exporters like Toyota and Matsushita cannot totally avoid the costs of protection by going to Kentucky and Malaysia. They still depend on domestic customers for the brunt of their sales and still have to support a domestic workforce that, under Japan's "lifetime employment" social contract, they cannot lay off.

Consequently, a rising yen increases the pressure on Japan's exporters to push for more imports in Japan's less-competitive sectors in order to bring down the monopolistic price structure.

The reason why the yen is so powerful is *not* because, as in other countries, a given rise in the yen produces X increase in imports. The reason why a drastic, abrupt appreciation of the yen works is that it's like Poland's "shock therapy." It breaks the old relationships; it changes the rules of the game.

Up to a limit, Japan's cartels will accept higher prices at home. But at some point, when the differential between domestic and foreign prices gets so high, and the pressure on export sales becomes so tough, the cartel cannot be maintained. It breaks down. And then, suddenly, imports begin to respond to price—not in a gradual fashion as in other countries, but in an abrupt shifting upward. Cartels break up. And then comes the "price destruction" as collusion cannot sustain monopolistic prices anymore.[10]

The soaring yen is not so much an economic constraint as a political bombshell.

For this reason, we have to question the 1995 decision by Deputy Treasury Secretary Lawrence Summers to ally with the Ministry of Finance's Eisuke Sakakibara—currently Vice Finance Minister for International Affairs and one of Japan's most unabashed opponents of reform[11]—and, in a reversal of years of U.S. policy, to push down the value of the yen.

For more than a year, it was massive Bank of Japan intervention supported by Washington, not market forces alone, that stood behind much of the yen's current weakness. The BOJ spent $54 billion in 1995 and another $14 billion through August of 1996 to send the yen south. The repeated mantra of Treasury Secretary Robert Rubin that "a strong dollar is in U.S. interests" finally convinced traders that the U.S. was no longer pushing for a stronger yen/weaker dollar. That, combined with U.S. interest rates 4–5 percent higher than those in Japan, and then, in late 1997, dwindling confidence in the Japanese banking system lured money out of Japan and into the U.S. This weakened the yen without further intervention.

But, as a consequence, Japan's current account surplus (the broadest measure of the trade surplus), which had receded to a bit more than 1 percent of GDP in early 1996, rebounded to 2.5 percent by the first half of 1997. Even Summers and Rubin have expressed their concern, with Summers reportedly saying that a Japanese trade surplus at 2.5 percent represents a "line in the sand."

Neither Summers nor his boss, Secretary Rubin, has really explained their actions. It is often presumed that they moved to prevent Japan's terrible banking crisis from turning into an economic calamity. If so, quick action to calm the currency and financial markets was the most responsible thing to do. But why was a short-term emergency tactic turned into a long-term policy?

Moreover, it is true that a higher dollar/yen rate *temporarily* keeps U.S. inflation and interest rates a little lower. It could even be argued that the benefit from lower interest rates outweighs any gains from exports to Japan or even long-term interest in Japanese reform.

But ultimately, as Japan's trade surplus rises, the yen will ratchet upward again. Yet another cycle of the roller coaster yen (refer to Figure 8.24) to correct Japan's exploding trade surplus will unfold. When the inevitable happens, U.S. interest rates will go up as they did in 1994.

As we saw in the early 1980s, currency rates can remain out of whack for quite a long time before they eventually correct. But the longer they remain out of whack, and the farther away they are from a sustainable rate, the worse will be the stomach-turning reverse course on the roller coaster of currency rates and interest rates. Meanwhile, Japanese exporters feel less pressure either to import more or to push for economic reform.

Could an Excessively Weak Yen Be a Force for Reform?

While a high and sharply rising yen is a force for reform because of its trade impact on exporters, some analysts argue that an excessively weak and sharply falling yen is also a force for reform because of its impact on bankers.

Beginning in 1997, there began a startlingly close correlation between the Banking Index on the Tokyo Stock Exchange and the yen rate. Whenever confidence in Japan's banks waned, both Japanese and foreign investors fled Japan for dollar assets and so the yen plummeted. When confidence in the banks rebounded, so did the yen (Figure 12.5).

But the fall of the yen not only reflected the decline in bank stocks and other stocks, it also exacerbated it. If investors expected the yen to keep falling, then they would tend to move out of Japanese assets and into dollar assets. Thus, at the end of 1997, the expectation of a further fall in the yen and in Japanese stocks became a self-fulfilling prophecy. As the Nikkei 225 index headed toward 15,000, the yen sank to 130/$.

If Japanese officials earlier welcomed the weakening of the yen because it helped promote exports and thus boosted economic growth, by the end of 1997 they began to fear an excessive fall. Indeed, in December of 1997, the BOJ spent up to $6–7 billion buying yen in a futile effort to boost its value. In January, the MOF's Sakakibara visited Washington to seek Robert Rubin's help in raising the value of the yen—the exact opposite of his request two years earlier. Rubin reportedly replied that there was little he could do that would be effective in the markets until Japan undertook more fundamental correction of its problems.

Figure 12.5: **The Yen: A Referendum on Confidence in Japan's Banks**

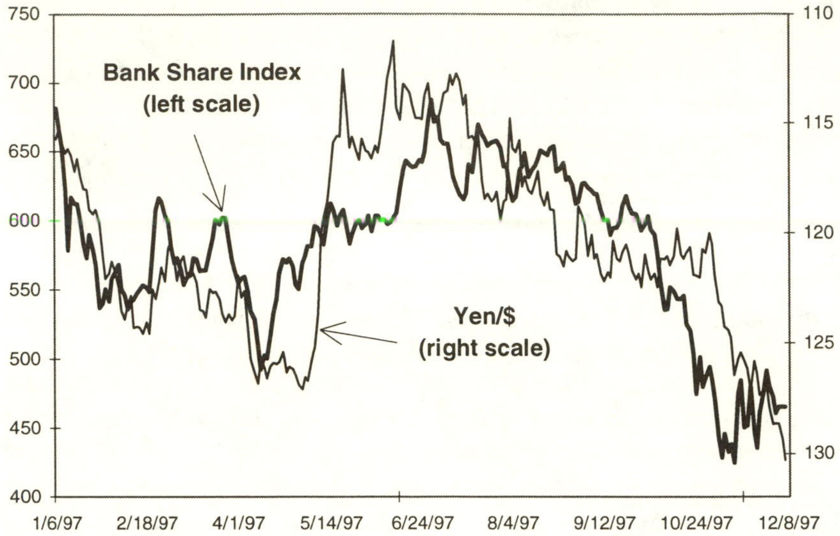

Source: Deutsche Morgan Grenfell Japan
Note: See text for explanation.

As long as a weak yen merely boosts exports and doesn't harm the price of stocks (or even helps them because investors expect stronger growth and higher profits), then a weak yen seems to be a boon for Japan. But, if an excessively falling yen brings down stock prices, that is a big danger sign.

The fragile balance sheets of Japanese banks depend on high stock prices. That's because their holdings of stocks are a vital part of their capital base. If stocks fall too low, they can no longer meet the 8 percent capital:asset ratio mandated by the Bank for International Settlements (BIS) and must unload poor assets. This pressure has already caused banks to lower their overall loan portfolio, creating a serious credit crunch among their borrowers.

Those who see a declining yen as a force for reform took the premise that investors would not be appeased until Tokyo made it clear that it would finally clean up the banking mess. In that scenario, currency pressures on Japan would act as a milder version of the currency crisis forcing reform in Asia's developing countries.

It remains unclear whether it will turn out that way. In response to the crisis, in January of 1988, Tokyo went on an all-out effort to shore up the banks. Rather than force the banks finally to bite the bullet and rid themselves of bad assets, the LDP came up with a scheme to spend more than $200 billion to shore up the banks, partly by having the government buy preferred shares in banks, partly by having the BOJ stand ready to make loans. Meanwhile, to ease the growing credit crunch on small and medium companies, the MOF postponed for a year the Prompt Corrective Action (PCA) measures previously scheduled for April of 1998 as part of the "Big Bang." The PCA would have put greater pressure on the banks to rid themselves of bad loans.

At least for a while, the markets were appeased by these moves and both the yen and stocks revived sharply. How long they will revive remains unclear as of January 1998.

The bottom line politically is that the currency and stock markets have yet to make it clear that they demand fundamental reform as the price for investing in Japan. On the issue of whether they demand this or not rests the issue of whether a sinking yen can be a force for reform.

Part Four

The Road Ahead

Chapter 13

Beyond Revisionism
and Traditionalism:
A New Paradigm to Guide Policy

A Quiet Revolution in American Thinking

The travails of the 1990s have sparked a revolution in thinking not only in Japan. They have also prompted some welcome rethinking in America as well. In the effort to discover why Japan's miracle soured, analysts are finding that they have to go beyond the "revisionist" versus "traditionalist" debate that has polarized, and paralyzed, U.S. analysis for the past two decades. Neither of these two dominant paradigms either predicted, or can explain in hindsight, why the Japanese miracle soured. Neither has proven an effective guide to policymaking.

The traditionalist versus revisionist debate was an unfortunate sidetrack in the evolution of U.S. understanding of Japan, an artifact of the fierce trade wars that engulfed Japan and the U.S. beginning in the early 1970s. Over time, both sides increasingly ceased to deal with Japan as the complex multifaceted country that it was. Instead, analysis was shoehorned into one narrow and artificial confine: was or was not Japan "different" from the U.S.? At one pole, the "revisionists" argued that Japan's economic system was so "different" and so "superior" in its trade and economic performance that special measures were needed to deal with this mounting threat. At the other pole, "traditionalists" seeking to maintain free trade and economic harmony with a vital ally insisted that Japan followed the same free market, free trade patterns as America. Hence, no special measures were necessary.

As the years passed, the debate became increasingly acrimonious and personal. Some traditionalists called their opponents "Japanbashers" and "crypto-racists" while some revisionists used terms like "Japanapologists" and "intellectual geishas." Revisionists like Pat Choate accused traditionalists of being on the Japanese payroll and traditionalists countered with accusations of McCarthyism.[1]

This bitter schism among U.S. analysts of Japan did not always exist. Nor did the absence of "shades of grey" always prevail. Even in the worst moments of the 1980s, academic investigators were producing illuminating new understandings of Japan, many of which we have cited in this book. Unfortunately, that work was consigned to the ivory towers while the two poles captured the op-ed pages.

If we are to regain a valid guide to thinking about Japan, it is probably necessary to begin by understanding how and why Japan analysis went off the track.

The Original "Traditionalist" View: Japan Is Different Because It Is a NIC

Back in the 1950s and early 1960s, before the trade wars erupted, descriptions of Japan were both more nuanced and more straightforward. All that we have described in this book—government subsidies and controls; the control over foreign exchange, barriers to entry, and promotion of exports; the cartelized economy, with *keiretsu*, collusion, and industry associations; and the pervasive role of negotiation and lobbying to reach compromise between winners and losers—was the standard description. Evaluations differed, of course. But few analysts objected to the classic portrayal made by renowned economist William Lockwood in his influential 1965 essay, "Japan's 'New Capitalism'":

> The metaphor that comes to mind is a typical Japanese web of influences and pressures interweaving through government and business, rather than a streamlined pyramid of authoritarian control.... A web it may be, but a web with no spider ...
>
> The industrial bureaus of MITI proliferate sectoral targets and plans; they confer, they tinker, they exhort. This is "economics by admonition" to a degree inconceivable in Washington or London. Business makes few major decisions without consulting the appropriate governmental authority; the same is true in reverse.[2]

Lockwood's essay was published in a volume which he edited, entitled *The State and Economic Enterprise in Japan*. It was one volume in an authoritative series put out by Princeton University Press, edited by the nation's top Japanologists, and used by scholars, journalists, and in university courses all over the country throughout the middle and late 1960s.

In that same volume, economist Martin Bronfenbrenner explained how Japan's *Yudo Keizai* (Guided Economy) promoted high investment rates by using government-authorized cartels to enable Japanese firms to ride out periodic bouts of excess capacity, and even avoid more than minimal reduction of investment during these slumps. Through the mechanisms of the Guided Economy, "by carrot rather than stick, the Japanese firm is kept under constant expansionary pressure—but by Ministry bureaucrats," as he explains:

> What are those "peculiar institutions of the Guided Economy"? They vary from one industry to another, but in general and in resistance to Occupation nudges toward free competition, they consist of alliances between trade associations (cartels) and the appropriate sections of a Ministry, normally MITI. These alliances divide responsibility for maintaining profitable prices and allocating output limitations in case excess plagues the industry.[3]

Bronfenbrenner then discusses how this created "investment races" and "excess competition" and in terms very similar to our discussion in Chapter 5 (pp. 88–97).

If anyone stood for orthodoxy in that period it was certainly Edwin Reischauer. His book, *East Asia: Tradition and Transformation* (co-written with John K. Fairbank and Albert Craig) has been the standard text in hundreds of classrooms for three decades. It was recently named by *Foreign Affairs* as one of the most important books of the past 75 years. In 1973, the chapter on "The New Japan" reported matter-of-factly:

> A final factor of great importance for economic growth was the particular Japanese combination of free enterprise and government guidance.... A number of points may be noted: 1) Banking credit, backed ultimately by the government, made heavy capital investment possible.... Commercial banks lent out a high percentage of their funds for purchases of fixed capital with the tacit backing and guidance of the Bank of Japan.... 2) The government was more deeply involved in planning than the government of any other nonsocialist state.... The Finance Ministry and the Ministry of International Trade and Industry ... cooperated in charting Japan's future growth. Growth industries were targeted, production goals were set, and foreign markets were estimated. Growth was rewarded with high depreciation, cheap loans, subsidies and light taxes.... 3) The government successfully carried out a policy of protection.... Infant indus-

tries, particularly in new technologies, were protected by successive walls
of tariffs, quotas, currency controls, foreign investment controls, and bureaucratic red tape. . . . 4) Japanese businessmen often chafed at bureaucratic regulations and government interference and argued that it was their
own efficiency and hard work that was responsible for their success. This
was not untrue. . . . Yet the attitude of businessmen toward the government
took for granted a favorable supportive business climate such as did not
exist in most countries.[4]

In those days, Tokyo proudly trumpeted the role of government in
Japan's post–World War II revival—sometimes prompting accusations of
"puffery." The famous 1970 report of the OECD (Organization of Economic Cooperation and Development), *The Industrial Policy of Japan*,
was based on accounts provided by MITI itself. As MITI Vice Minister
Yoshihisa Ojimi told the OECD:

> MITI decided to establish in Japan industries . . . such as steel, oil refining,
> petrochemicals, automobiles, aircraft, industrial machinery of all sorts, and
> electronics, including electronic computers. From a short-run static view-
> point, encouragement of such industries would seem to conflict with eco-
> nomic rationalism. But, from a long-range viewpoint, these are precisely
> the industries where income elasticity of demand is high, technological
> progress is rapid, and labor productivity rises fast. . . . Japan has been able
> to concentrate its scant capital in strategic industries . . .
>   MITI policies have succeeded . . . mainly through encouragement of
> industry and promotion of exports . . . in building on a cramped land area a
> giant economy that ranks second in the free world.[5]

The point is: none of these distinct characteristics of Japan's political
economy were surprising or exotic or even particularly Japanese. Nor
were they expected to last.

That's because, while Japan operated very differently from the U.S., it
had a lot of similarity with other developing countries. And that's exactly
what Japan was at the time—a Newly Industrializing Country (NIC) in
today's terminology. In 1960, its per capita GDP was no higher than
Chile's. Everyone knew that, in NICs all over the world, from Brazil to
India to Korea, government played a strong role in the economy. Because
these countries were plagued by scarcity and lacked modern institutions,
the government, for better or worse, tended to fill the gap.

This understanding was even incorporated into the rules of the OECD,
the IMF (International Monetary Fund), the World Bank, the GATT

(General Agreement on Tariffs and Trade), and other global institutions. All these institutions applied special rules to developing countries, *including Japan*, that removed them from the tougher strictures applied to advanced countries. Infant industry protection and promotion by these countries were accepted. Naturally, these institutions envisioned a "graduation" process. As a country's economy and institutions matured, it would "graduate" and have to adhere to international norms of free trade, currency convertibility, "national treatment" of foreign investment, rules on government subsidy, and so forth. Such graduation was a requirement for joining the OECD, the so-called rich countries' club.

This developmental process, ran the consensus among scholars of the 1950s and early 1960s, was precisely the case with Japan. Japan was so poor that it had not yet been required to abandon its industrial policy practices by the global institutions. But, once Japan did graduate and adhere to advanced country rules—as it began doing in the mid-1960s— then it was expected to become a "normal" modern, capitalist nation.

In short, Japan's differences from the U.S. were an artifact, not of some eternal peculiarly Japanese corporate culture, but of clear and identifiable rules and policies. When the rules changed, so would the practice.

Typical of mainstream thinking in this era is this 1972 passage by economist Gary Saxonhouse:

> While these [trade and investment] *restrictions may well have once played a central role in calling forth a more socially optimal amount of modernizing activity* on the part of Japanese management, why do they remain important today? It has been noted that elements of the Japanese trading pattern appear highly unusual by international standards. The very low ratio of manufacturing production, the lack of intra-industry specialization, the high ratio of raw materials to total imports, *cannot be explained simply by Japan's resource endowment, its physical distance from other countries*, its cultural distinctiveness or special characteristics of its wage structure. Other developed countries with comparable resource bases do not exhibit this Japanese phenomenon. Similarly, as distance and cultural distinctiveness present no problem for Japanese manufactured exports and raw material imports, why should manufactured imports present a special case? *Japanese trade restrictions probably play an important role in explaining this unusual pattern* [emphasis added].[6]

At the time, noted Saxonhouse, both American and Japanese officials readily acknowledged that "Japanese commercial policy was a major cause" of its unusual trade pattern. Japanese officials gave assurances that, once Japan adhered to international rules, there would be "a radical change in [its] import structure."[7]

Trade Wars Popularize the "Japan, Inc." Thesis

Then, in the late 1960s and early 1970s, something very surprising happened. Japan's rules did change and, by the mid-1970s, it had pretty much graduated in formal terms. Yet, the real operation of both the internal economy and international trade patterns did not change anywhere near as much as had been expected. Despite all the formal liberalization of Japan's trade, it still imported very few manufactured products that competed with domestic producers. Foreign investment remained negligible (and still does).

This unanticipated gap between formal graduation and substantive lack of change produced three consequences in U.S.–Japan relations. In the trade arena, chronic frictions developed of a character quite unlike U.S. frictions with any other country. In the political arena, calls for harsh protectionism against Japan began undermining the free trade political consensus that had reigned in the U.S. since World War II. And finally, in the intellectual arena, explanations had to be developed to explain the gap between extensive formal change and substantive stasis. And this is when Japan analysis went off the track. Amidst this new type of trade friction, discussion of Japan's economic setup was no longer a matter of academic investigation. It became an ideological weapon on both sides of the trade debates.

Trade frictions between Japan and other countries had existed for some time, of course. Even in the 1950s, Washington had asked Japan to restrain shipments of its famous "dollar blouses." This, however, was little different from the minor frictions the U.S. had with a myriad of developing countries.

In the late 1960s, however, the character of Japan's trade patterns began to diverge from the norm. On the one hand, Japan imported fewer manufactured goods than any other industrialized country. On the other hand, Japanese exports of manufactures flooded the American market. Moreover, Japan did not follow the pattern of other countries, where small amounts of a wide variety of goods were shipped, thereby causing little disruption. Japan's exports seemed be focused on just a few items at any point in time. As Japan moved up the industrial ladder, its exports created inordinate dislocation in one industry after another. They almost wiped out the American TV industry, decimated steel, made huge head-way in cars, and virtually eliminated the computer memory chip industry.

Countries like Germany also shipped a lot of goods to the U.S., of course, and ran huge trade surpluses to boot. But, they imported manufac-tured goods as well. Germany not only exported cars and steel, it im-ported cars and steel. It allowed—even encouraged—GM and Ford to set up factories within Germany. No one was about to launch a broad protec-tionist drive against Germany. Japan, on the other hand, did not import goods in the categories where it exported, nor in many other manufac-tured areas either. Japan, unlike Germany, had won itself few allies among American exporters.

The political impact of Japan's exports was particularly great since it affected many large-scale, unionized industries like autos and steel. Begin-ning in the late 1960s, the call for protection against Japanese exports grew louder and louder. These calls were made even harder to ignore by the fact that the previously unchallenged free trade ideal was now under attack. As former U.S. trade surpluses turned into deficits and U.S. factories increas-ingly invested offshore, the AFL-CIO dropped out of the free trade coali-tion. Congress called for tough action on a host of trade fronts and, in 1969, created the Office of Special Trade Representative (now the USTR) to heighten the priority of trade issues in the Executive branch.

Eventually, Administrations of both parties decided that, if they were to maintain the free trade regime, they had to take action against a now-industrialized country that seemed to be violating its norms. In 1970, as Japan racked up trade surpluses that seemed to know no limit, Assistant Secretary of State for Economic Affairs Philip Trezise declared, "I seri-ously question whether the international system can stand a Japanese global trade surplus of $12 billion in 1975."[8]

As Japan moved up the industrial ladder, so did the U.S. response. First came the 1967 anti-dumping case in TVs and an eventual Voluntary Restraint Agreement (VRA) on Japanese TV exports. This was followed in succession by export restraints in steel in 1966 and the trigger price system for steel in 1977, the 1981 VRA in autos, the 1985 VRA in machine tools, and the 1986 anti-dumping and market access agreement in semiconductors.

(It should be stressed that not all of these responses to Japan were politically or economically equivalent. The initial response was a call for thinly veiled protectionism by old-line American industries like textiles, steel and autos, who sought to restrict the imports of Japanese goods into the U.S. Beginning in the 1980s, however, Washington policy was increasingly shaped by newer high-tech industries from computer chips and computers to banking and securities. These sectors sought, not closing the U.S., but opening Japan; not fewer Japanese goods in the U.S., but more foreign goods and services in Japan. The first goal would hurt both countries; the latter would help both.)

Inevitably, the rise of trade friction produced a change in the intellectual scene. Policymakers needed a conceptual framework to explain all that had happened and to guide policy. Why was there so little change in Japan even though it seemed formally open? Why did Japan's trade patterns continue to differ so much from those of other countries? Why was Japan able to grow so fast even though it seemed to be violating the norms of free-market economics? Would Japan ever become a "normal" nation?

In 1970, business consultant James Abegglen came up with answers to these questions that immediately caught fire: the "Japan, Inc." theory. Most Americans presumed that in every modern country, as long as government does not interfere, atomistic corporations and consumers will each act independently to maximize their profits and welfare. This, argued Abegglen, was not the case in Japan. Instead, corporations and employees all played assigned roles in a unified national effort:

> Perhaps "Japan, Inc.," the label a Japanese businessman recently applied to his country's economy, best indicates how the system functions. In this analogy, the Japanese government corresponds to corporate headquarters, responsible for planning and coordination, long-term policy formation, and major investment decisions. The country's large corporations are thus analogous to corporate divisions: they have a good deal of autonomy within an overall policy framework, are free to compete with one another, and are charged with operating responsibility. . . .
>
> Moreover, "Japan, Inc." is a special kind of corporation: a conglomerate in U.S. terms. A conglomerate can channel cash flows from low-growth to high-growth areas and apply the debt capacity of safe, mature businesses to capitalize rapidly growing but unstable ventures. It can move into a dynamic new industry and bring to it financial power that no existing competitors can match. . . . The result is that the conglomerate is in a position to dominate a new industry by setting prices so low that existing competitors cannot finance adequate growth. . . . In all these senses, "Japan, Inc." is indeed a conglomerate, a *zaibatsu* of *zaibatsu*. The Bank of Japan is the financial center, and with the bank's help each rapidly growing industry can incur more debt than it could on its own; the borrowing power of the

entire portfolio—Japan itself—is available to each industry. Hence the economy as a whole funds new enterprises, holds prices down, competes successfully in the world market, and earns large profits.[9]

Suddenly, the Japanese web had a very big spider. In the U.S. the "Japan, Inc." concept was quickly adopted by both industry lobbyists and government officials. Steel lobbyists now had a ready answer for those who said they were suffering only because they had failed to adopt continuous casting and other modern technologies as fast as their Japanese counterparts. On the contrary, said the lobbyists, Japanese steelmakers— as well as their counterparts in machine tools, TVs and autos—were able to succeed only because of government aid to industry, and even government control of industry.

Government officials also adopted the new concept. In 1971, the year America devalued the dollar and applied a 10 percent import surcharge, Nixon's Assistant to the President for International Economic Affairs, Peter Peterson, described Japan in language straight out of Abegglen's text. Japan, said Peterson, is:

> a type of informal conglomerate . . . a form of business organization which, through strong financial management, can channel cash flows rapidly from low-growth to high-growth sectors. The Bank of Japan is the financial center and, following guidelines of the Planning Agency, determines the nature and direction of growth.[10]

A year later, the Commerce Department—where Peterson had become Secretary—put out a politically explosive report based on the "Japan, Inc." concept, entitled *Japan: The Government:Business Relationship (A Guide for the American Businessman)*. (Ironically, Peterson later became chair of the New York Japan Society, and James Abegglen now insists that Japan is pretty much wide open to imports and foreign investment.)[11]

Once the "Japan, Inc." concept caught on, the whole nature of discussion of Japan changed. Almost overnight, simply to acknowledge what had previously been standard—that Japan's government had been effective in promoting industry—seemed equivalent to acquiescing to the cries for special measures to deal with Japan.

Even *domestic* U.S. economic policy and analysis of Japan became hopelessly intertwined as calls arose to "fight fire with fire." Chalmers Johnson argued that industrial policy had worked so well in Japan that America should emulate it. Economist Charles Schultze of the Brookings

Institution, determined that the U.S. not adopt industrial policy, apparently felt compelled to fortify his stance by contending it had not worked in Japan either.

It was in this heated atmosphere that the polarization emerged between what came to be known as "traditionalist" and "revisionist" views of Japan.

The First "Revisionists": Japan Is Just Like Us

What is now known as "traditionalism" got its start in 1976 when the Brookings Institution published a huge volume entitled *Asia's New Giant* that even today remains a "bible" among Japan analysts. Edited by two prominent scholars, Hugh Patrick and Henry Rosovsky, it was the product of years of study by some two dozen researchers. As neoclassical economists, Patrick, Rosovsky and many of the other contributors had an innate skepticism that industrial policy could improve on the market. Hence, they were inclined to give greater credence to evidence that suggested industrial policy was deleterious, ineffective or just plain irrelevant, and they often discounted evidence that suggested it had played a critical role in Japan's development. Beyond that, however, the analysis showed a clear intent to discredit the "Japan, Inc." caricature and consequently the justification for special treatment of Japan.

> Anti-Japanese articles have been easy to find in newspapers and magazines, especially amid the tension of 1971–72; often these featured sinister descriptions of "Japan, Inc.," that mythical, all-powerful instrument of the national will. If it really existed, presumably no one could compete with it according to gentlemanly rules of the game and therefore special rules might be permissible and desirable.[12]

In this effort, Patrick and Rosovsky, joined by former Assistant Secretary of State Philip Trezise and some of the other contributors, supplied the necessary correction—and then went far beyond it.

And that is the great irony of the whole "traditionalist" versus "revisionist" fracas. The economists now known as "traditionalists" were in fact the original *revisionists*. They made no bones about the fact that they were iconoclasts out to revise what Trezise called "a more or less standard political model." "Destroying graven images" and "reformulating stereotypes" is how they put it.[13] In their determination to knock down the "Japan Inc." caricature, these economists also overturned much of what had been traditional analysis of the Reischauer, Lockwood and

Bronfenbrenner variety. To an unfortunate degree, they threw the baby out with the bath water.

The Brookings authors insisted that "what happened to the Japanese economy after World War II cannot be described as miraculous. . . . We need not live in awe or fear of Japan." Traditional descriptions of industrial policy were "subject to so substantial a discount as to make them largely valueless"; Japan had been pretty much a free market economy all along. The government provided a "supportive environment" rather than a guiding role; the government–business relationship in Japan was typical of capitalist countries in Europe; and it was America that was "the atypical case." Industry was hardly more concentrated in Japan than in the U.S.; there is "very little cooperation among companies"; and, in any case, "where collusive practices were permitted . . . no particular benefits to growth ensued." As for Japan's low levels of trade, that was "due mainly to Japan's distance from major world markets."[14]

Patrick, Rosovsky and Trezise were not content to argue that Japan now operated on the same principles as other capitalist countries because its overt control mechanisms had been dismantled. Rather, they contended that it always had adhered to the free market paradigm. As Patrick put it:

> I am of the school which interprets Japanese economic performance as due primarily to the actions and efforts of private individuals and enterprises responding to the opportunities provided in quite free markets for commodities and labor. While the government has been supportive and indeed has done much to create the environment for growth, its role has often been exaggerated.[15]

In a recent interview, Patrick explained, "I was not trying to say that government was unimportant. Certainly there was a cooperative spirit between government and business in Japan that differed from the antagonism often seen in the U.S. But government's role was to provide a supportive environment for private business decisions. For example, governmental '5-year plans' gave business information about the direction of the economy and government spending plans, thereby reducing the risk in their investment decisions."

Patrick also cautioned against projecting the heat of the ideological battles of the late 1980s and early 1990s onto the mid-1970s when *Asia's New Giant* was published. "I and others thought the Japan Inc. view was wrong. But our sense was that we were doing a simple workmanlike job of criticizing an inaccurate account. The atmosphere was not as emotional as it later became."

Patrick and Rosovsky did acknowledge that, in Japan, "protection was certainly important, as has been typical of the economic history of industrializing countries (other than England)." But they simultaneously discounted its significance in Japan's success and insisted that it was a thing of the past:

> Between 1971 and 1973, Japan carried out a major trade liberalization, moving from being one of the most restrictive to being *one of the more liberal of the advanced industrial nations*. By mid-1974, the tension of 1971–72 between the U.S. and Japan on economic issues had evaporated; there appeared to most policymakers to be *no serious bilateral economic problems* [emphasis added].[16]

Soon, the insistence that Japan was fully open to imports became a shibboleth among this school. In support of this view economist Gary Saxonhouse came up with a sophisticated statistics-based model in 1982. It appeared to show—against all evidence to the contrary—that Japan did not limit imports of competing manufactured goods. The very arguments about distance and resource endowment that Saxonhouse had so sharply dismissed back in 1972 were now resurrected. He was candid enough to acknowledge the change.[17]

Later it was pointed out that, if the equations in Saxonhouse's model really were correct, then Japan would look like a liberal trader even in rice. In reality, Japanese law banned the import of even a single grain. Moreover, after economist Robert Lawrence proved in 1987 that Japan did under-import manufactured goods, the Lawrence view was confirmed, and amplified, by the majority of economists who conducted original empirical research on Japanese trade.[18]

Disregarding the empirical studies of Lawrence, Ed Lincoln, Marc Noland and others, most orthodox economists who were *not* experts in Japanese trade quickly gave credence to the Saxonhouse analysis. After all, their training had told them that a country that violated free trade norms could hardly have grown so fast. By 1993, economist Jagdish Bhagwati was able to line up dozens of America's most prominent economists to condemn the allegedly "crude and simplistic view that Japan is importing too few manufactures owing to structural barriers."[19]

The Patrick–Saxonhouse analysis was also embraced by political-military experts looking for a reason to downplay trade issues. To security-minded analysts, trade frictions were seen as a sideshow, an irritant that, if not suppressed, could corrode the alliance between the U.S. and Japan. As U.S.-Soviet tensions mounted in the late 1970s and early 1980s, security officials asked, in effect, "Is it worth jeopardizing our air and naval bases in Japan just to sell a few more oranges or just to win a few more votes in Michigan." A theory that seemed to justify that political stance was welcome. When some adherents to the opposing theory, revisionism, began to call into question the alliance itself and suggest that Japan was not an ally, but a security threat, that drove these security officials into an even tighter embrace of the Patrick–Saxonhouse view. But what these security officials ignored was that Japan's insularity on trade and its insularity on security affairs were two sides of the same coin. In any case, having been adopted by both Washington and the academic elite, the Brookings–Saxonhouse view slowly took on the aura that it had been the mainstream "traditionalist" view all along.

Revisionism Round Two: Japan Has a Superior, and Threatening, Model

Just like "traditionalism," "revisionism" originally began as a corrective. It officially began in 1982 when political science professor Chalmers Johnson published his long-awaited book, *MITI and the Japanese Miracle: The Growth of Industrial Policy, 1925–1975*.[20]

While Johnson was later labeled the "godfather of revisionism," by *Business Week*'s Robert Neff, Johnson always saw himself instead as a "restorationist." In his eyes, he was simply reviving the past standard appreciation for the role of state-led industrial policy in promoting Japan's economic takeoff. He even dedicated the book to Lockwood. But since the Patrick–Trezise–Saxonhouse view had been embraced by traditional policymakers, it was perhaps inevitable that Johnson was perceived as a revisionist.[21]

Johnson's most important theoretical contribution was his distinction between what he called the "capitalist regulatory state" that he said was common among the early industrializers and the "capitalist development state" needed by late industrializers like Japan in order to catch up:

> In states that were late to industrialize, the state itself led the industrialization drive, that is, it took on *developmental* functions. . . .The U.S. government has many regulations concerning the antitrust implications of the size of firms, but it does not concern itself with what industries ought to exist

and what industries are no longer needed. The developmental, or plan-rational, state, by contrast, has as its dominant feature precisely the setting of such substantive social and economic goals [emphasis in original]. . . .

In the plan-rational state, the government will give greatest precedence to industrial policy, that is, to a concern with the structure of domestic industry and with promoting the structure that enhances the nation's competitiveness.[22]

Just as Patrick and Trezise went too far in their attempt to correct the "Japan Inc." image, so Johnson went too far in trying to remedy the Patrick–Trezise swing of the pendulum.

For one thing, in his political schema, he painted a sort of "bureaucratic authoritarian" state in which "the bureaucrats rule and politicians reign."[23] The "puppet Diet" served only as a "safety valve" for public discontent but played no genuine policymaking role. In this depoliticized state, business humbly submits with "responsive dependence" to a super-rational bureaucracy single-mindedly pursuing Japan's national economic interests. Policy and influence flows in one direction: from the state to society. Because of this supposed immunity from political pressure, Japan, according to Johnson, had the world's most effective policy for both entry and exit. Despite Johnson's protests to the contrary, it looked very much like the "Japan, Inc." thesis in new clothes.[24]

Moreover, Johnson portrayed Japan's industrial policy not as a temporary strategy enabling late industrializers to catch up, but as a permanently superior form of capitalism. He even suggested that America emulate Japan, create its own MITI-like pilot agency, and reduce America's elected representatives to a mere "safety valve."[25]

While Johnson initially suggested America should emulate Japan, in 1988 former trade negotiator Clyde Prestowitz portrayed Japan's economic and trade practices as a threat. Japanese exporters, he contended, were backed up by a national economic system that enabled them to defeat their U.S. competitors in virtually any head-to-head contest. His book *Trading Places: How We Allowed Japan to Take the Lead* argued that America's loss to Japan was certified in 1987, when the stock market crash "signaled as clearly as any bugle call the most serious defeat the U.S. has ever suffered."[26] Prestowitz insisted that it served no purpose for the U.S. to call Japan's system "unfair" and demand that they change. Rather, he said, Washington should recognize that this system served Japanese interests well, that therefore Japan had no intention of changing. Consequently, the U.S. needed to find new ways to counter the Japanese challenge.

It was not long before Japan came to be commonly portrayed as a "national security hazard." James Fallows wrote of "containing Japan." The head of the CIA's Japan Desk, Nathan White, spoke at a closed-door conference in 1992 of a "collision course" between Japan and the U.S. The following year, a CIA contractor wrote a report, *Japan 2000*, charging that the alleged Japanese attempt to "exercise dominion" over the world "represents significant national security threats to the U.S." As late as 1996, Johnson labeled Japan, along with China, as "the only countries on earth that could threaten the national security of the U.S." Pat Choate painted a picture of Washington dominated by Japanese "agents of influence."[27]

By the mid-1990s, with Japan's economy in so much trouble, the revisionist theory of the Japanese economic juggernaut was becoming harder to maintain. Its theoretical nadir came in 1995 with the attempt to deny that those troubles really existed, as exemplified by the publication of Eammon Fingleton's *Blindside: Why Japan Is Still on Track to Overtake the U.S. by the Year 2000*. The thesis of this book was that Japan's eminent troubles—the "collapse that never was"—were all part of a timeworn Japanese strategy of "acting out pantomimes of exaggerated anxiety" in order to "foster complacency among the foreign rivals." In other words, to lull America into dropping its guard until Japan was ready to "blindside" it. This book—praised in *Business Week* and excerpted at length in *Fortune* and *Foreign Affairs* at a time when revisionists complained about being muzzled—proved too much even for others sympathetic to the revisionist camp, like Taggart Murphy and Patrick Smith.[28]

A Revisionist Revises Friedrich List

In the course of revisionism's evolution, James Fallows and some other revisionists developed the theory that Japan operated via a species of capitalism entirely different from the so-called Anglo-American or Anglo-Saxon variety prevalent in the U.S. In *Looking at the Sun*, Fallows claimed that the Japanese version of capitalism was inspired by the nationalist school of economic thought led by the nineteenth-century German economist Friedrich List. This school arose out of fear that the free market ideas of Adam Smith and David Ricardo were being used by Great Britain to block emerging industries in Europe and the U.S. This, feared List, might lock these countries into a permanent less-developed and dependent status. In response, List helped mobilize the fractious German states into a unified customs union (the Zollverein)—who practiced free trade among themselves in order to be able to compete with Britain.[29]

Now, it is certainly true that List was influential in Japan, after being translated in 1889. This, however, was long after the Meiji era pattern of state-promoted industrialization had already gotten underway. His ideas were popular among those who were trying to revise the unequal tariff treaties first imposed by the Western powers in the 1850s (Japan finally regained tariff autonomy in 1911). But the ideas of Adam Smith and his disciples were also popular. Meiji intellectual leader Yukichi Fukuzawa, who is often regarded as both a liberal and a nationalist, was among the first to translate and comment on Smith's disciples. Indeed, in the very earliest stage of the Meiji era, because of the problems facing Japan at that early point, many of Smith's free market notions were seen as a particularly effective intellectual battering ram against some of the customary practices of the pre-Meiji era. One of these was the granting of state monopolies to certain merchants, a practice, not coincidentally, also denounced in Smith's *Wealth of Nations*.[30]

In any case, Fallows' treatment is marred by a glaring omission. He fails to mention that both List and his Japanese followers in the Meiji era saw trade protection as a *temporary* phase of development. Agricultural countries should practice free trade. As follower countries begin to industrialize, they should practice protectionism—until they have succeeded in industrializing. Then they should practice free trade.

In fact, List himself seems to have predicted Japan's post-1973 problems when he suggested that the "indolence" created by protection maintained for too long would lose manufacturers the very supremacy they had earlier attained by that protection (see the quotation from List at the opening of Chapter 7). List advocated that the world's most advanced nation of his time, England, tolerate protectionism by that era's NICs (the U.S., Germany, and so forth) while practicing free trade itself. This, he predicted, would allow those emerging nations to industrialize, and lead to a world of advanced manufacturing nations operating on an equal status, practicing free trade amongst themselves, and living in harmony. In what sounds like a warning to present-day Japan and the U.S., List said England should:

> . . . recognize the legitimacy of protective systems in those [emerging] nations, although she will herself more and more favor free trade; the theory [List's evolutionary theory] having taught her that a nation which has already attained manufacturing supremacy, can only protect its own manufacturers and merchants against retrogression and indolence, by the

free importation of means of subsistence and raw materials, and by the competition of foreign manufactured goods. . .

[T]he nations which aspire, after the example of England, to attain to a large manufacturing power can very well attain their object without the humiliation of England; that England need not become poorer than she is because others become richer.[31]

List's first Japanese translator, Sadamasu Oshima, adopted the same evolutionary standpoint in his own writings, as did many others in Meiji era Japan:

When a country which is still in a savage state starts to communicate with other countries, its people, not knowing the benefits of modern industry, should be ready to import the manufactured commodities of foreign countries and to export its raw products, thus learning about mutual interests. At such a stage, a free trade policy should be adopted. By the time that the people have come to appreciate the benefit of trade and to wish to become acquainted with the modern way of manufacturing things, protectionism should be adopted. Once the country has developed modern manufacturing with a solid enough foundation to compete with others, then a free trade policy should again be adopted.[32]

Indeed, the "infant industry" analysis that we have used throughout this book is often considered to be the adoption by classical economics via John Stuart Mill and later Alfred Marshall of some of the ideas advocated by List and his predecessors.

Nor does Fallows mention List's American roots. Doing so would undermine his thesis that List's ideas are somehow more congenial to the "Asian mindset" than the "Anglo-American" one. The irony is that this supposed "German" system of thought was, at least in part, "Made in America." List lived for years in the U.S. as a political exile, and one of his first works was the 1827 book *Outline of American Political Economy*. List was influenced by American nationalists such as Alexander Hamilton and Henry Clay and was an associate of the American protectionist Henry Carey. List eventually became very influential in nineteenth-century America. Although Carey is generally regarded as an inferior economist, he was first translated into Japanese in 1874, fifteen years before List. Henry Carey's disciple, E. Peshine Smith, spent nine years in Japan as a State Department legal adviser beginning in 1871. His job was to help Japan's Foreign Office in its efforts to regain tariff autonomy for Japan.[33]

The point of all this is that there is nothing particularly German, or Japanese or American, about these protectionist or developmentalist ideas. These ideas are commonly popular among "late industrializers" all over the world as they first make efforts to modernize.

As John K. Galbraith commented in his usual wry manner, the current resurrection of List turns List's actual ideas upside down:

> As seen by List . . . protection . . . was not useful for a country in the early or primitive stage and was not necessary for one in the final stage [a mature industrial state]. . . . [Regarding] the present demand in the U.S., Britain and variously in Europe for the protection of steel, textile, automobile, electronic and other industries from the superior competence of Japan, Korea, Taiwan . . . the former infant-industries exception [to free trade] has become the aged- and senile-industries exception. In tactful modern terminology, it is called not protection but industrial policy.[34]

The Lost Middle Ground: An Evolutionary View of Industrial Policy

Throughout the 1980s and early 1990s, there were many efforts to find a middle ground between "revisionism" and "traditionalism."

Only one strand among these efforts was influential in policy circles. That was the analytical work of Robert Lawrence, Ed Lincoln, Marcus Noland and others on trade. Lawrence demonstrated that it was entirely possible to show that Japan was exclusionist and still remain well within the camp of free trade policy. An economist with unchallenged neoclassical credentials, Lawrence proved in 1987 that Japan was indeed an underimporter of manufactured goods. But he insisted on using free trade tools, e.g., trust-busting, to solve the problem. As we will discuss below, Lawrence's work would become influential in Washington policymaking during the Bush years and Clinton years—though not always in ways that he approved.[35]

However, when it came to broader analysis of Japan, the middle ground was influential only within academia. One of the most farsighted works was an essay called "Success That Soured" published back in 1982 by University of Washington Prof. Kozo Yamamura. In that essay, Yamamura pointed out that Japan was still dominated by legal and illegal cartels, import restrictions, and other vestiges of the high-growth era. However, any positive role for these practices had run out of steam:

MITI policy was successful in accomplishing its goals for nearly two decades. Taking full advantage of expanding world trade and availability of advanced technology, MITI effectively guided the investment race to increase industrial capacity, productivity and exports. Cartels, legal and de facto, minimized price competition, thus reducing one of the major risks of adopting large-scale new technology rapidly. Understandably, the industries cooperated with MITI policy most willingly and pursued their profitable market share-maximizing strategy. . . .

However, the honeymoon ended. The conditions that were necessary for the continued success of the MITI policy began to disappear in the mid-sixties. . . .

As the growth rate decelerated the problems and consequences of this policy that had long been ignored or tolerated grew in magnitude. It was no longer possible to deny that cartels beget more cartels, and that an increasing number of them were having a negative effect on the economy. But MITI could not and did not reverse its policy.[36]

A few years later, in *The Competition*, Thomas Pepper, Merit Janow and Jimmy Wheeler likewise put Japan's industrial policy in an evolutionary context. They characterized both the Johnson view and the Brookings view as one-sided. For example, while the Brookings authors showed how Japan's high savings and investment led to high growth, they did not investigate the role of government policy in promoting high investment rates in the first place:

The question remains: Should the increase in capital stock be in turn attributed to governmental policies? In other words did the selective application of a then-detailed system of trade and foreign exchange controls enable the Japanese government to use international competition to hold down the price of capital goods while providing a protected, high-priced domestic market for consumer goods produced primarily at home? . . .

To the degree that they [the scholars who contributed to the Brookings volume] discuss how this process [of industrial policy] worked, they do so as part of a discussion of the role of government policy *versus* the role of the market [emphasis in original].[37]

At the same time, these analysts faulted Johnson for "contradict[ing] himself" in suggesting that the U.S. adopt Japanese-style industrial policy. This, they say, seems to violate his own analysis that "a plan-rational economy is characteristic of later developing countries and a market-rational economy is characteristic of already developed countries." In

Japan, where "the economy is no longer in as much of a 'catch up' phase," industrial policy faces:

> declining importance, compared with other factors, as the economy itself has matured. . . . Barring an outbreak of global protectionism, the vestiges of Japan's once-detailed trade, investment, capital, and foreign exchange controls will become increasingly costly to the domestic economy.[38]

Eleanor Hadley, famed as the trust-buster who guided the dissolution of the prewar *zaibatsu* during the Occupation era, likewise tried to emphasize that neither of the polar views had captured the complexities either of government–private interaction or of inter-corporate behavior. In a review of the essay by Richard Caves and Masu Uekasa on Japanese corporate behavior in the Brookings volume, Hadley disagreed with their assessment that industrial market competition works the same way in Japan as in the U.S. and Western Europe.[39] In a 1983 essay, "The Secret of Japan's Success," Hadley wrote that both the Brookings volume and the Johnson book told only half the story:

> [Philip] Trezise staunchly believes there is no significant difference in the role of government in Japan's economy and in the U.S. economy. . . .
> [A]fter complaining that economists told only half the story, that of the private sector, [Chalmers Johnson] turned around and proceeded to tell only the other half of the story himself—the government side. The private sector is scarcely mentioned in Johnson's study.[40]

In the political science arena, there were myriad efforts to develop a political analysis of Japan that avoided extremes of both the free-market Brookings model and the bureaucratic authoritarian revisionist model. The authors we have cited throughout this book—Kent Calder, John Haley, Ellis Krauss, Daniel Okimoto, T.J. Pempel, and Richard Samuels—were only a few of those working at this. Their work paralleled similar approaches being made by Japanese counterparts.

Unfortunately, in the heat of the 1980s ideological wars between "revisionists" and "traditionalists," most of this "shades of grey" middle ground was consigned to the ivory tower. The op-ed pages were dominated by the two poles. The year 1982 saw the publication of Johnson's book, Saxonhouse's analysis, and Yamamura's essay. Of these three, only the two extremes—Johnson and Saxonhouse—resonated in the corridors of power.

From Analysis to Policy: False Answers to Real Questions

If both "traditionalism" and "revisionism" were as misguided as we claim, then how do we explain their strong intellectual hold? The answer, in our view, was that both served a need.

Whatever other mistakes the traditionalists may have made, at least they did not confuse an ally with an adversary. In the view of security experts in the early 1970s, when it looked as if the LDP could fall to Socialists and Communists, sacrificing some sales of steel and oranges seemed a small price to pay. A school of thought that justified that policy held great attraction.

However, the ineffective trade policies resulting from the tradition-alists' view created a vacuum. The real pain of millions of workers in heavy industry, as well as the challenge to America's stake in high-tech industries like semiconductors, could not be wished away by homilies on free trade. Revisionism filled this vacuum. Had the traditionalist policies been more effective, revisionism could never have become influential in the first place.

During the Bush years, it looked for a time as if a middle ground on policy might have some sway. In 1989, the Lawrence analysis that Japan was an under-importer was adopted by corporate advisers to the Bush Administration. However, to Lawrence's consternation, they advocated "numerical targets" as the solution.[41] The Bush Administration, however, came up with another solution that reconciled free trade methods with the undeniable fact that Japan was an under-importer.

To a large extent the Administration acted only because of heavy pressure from Congress to do something. Congress had almost passed the Gephardt Amendment calling for widespread protection against imports from Japan and did pass the "Super-301" provision in 1988 calling for retaliation against Japan's barriers to imports. As an alternative, the Bush Administration came up with the Structural Impediments Initiative (SII). The premise of the SII was that Japan did differ structurally from other capitalist countries in ways that hindered imports and foreign direct investment. The solution, however, was not protectionism, but getting Japan to remove its structural impediments. One may fault the Administration on how aggressively or skillfully it pursued the SII, but the premise of the policy was correct. In fact, as we will discuss below, on some of the SII items, the U.S. position had behind-the-scenes support of some constituencies in Japan. The latter were eager to use the time-honored technique of *gaiatsu* (foreign pressure) to get the reforms they wanted for their own reasons.[42]

Most revisionists dismissed the SII as the naive act of "economic missionaries" trying to impose American ways upon Japan. They insisted that the U.S. go for "measurable results" rather than changes in rules that seemed to lead nowhere. Their model was the 1986 Semiconductor Agreement, which discussed a 20 percent foreign market share in Japan. The Bush Administration did, in fact, negotiate two sectoral agreements—one on paper and one on computers—that required monitoring of objective indicators of market access such as import data, according to then-Deputy Assistant Trade Representative Merit Janow. However, in neither case were there numerical goals anything like the Semiconductor Agreement's 20 percent number.[43]

This was not what the revisionists and other critics wanted. They wanted specific targets, using the phrase "results-oriented negotiations." After all, said one former U.S. trade negotiator, the paper agreement with Japan was a "total failure" in raising American market share, while the computer agreement was only a "partial success." Without clear, measurable targets, it would be very hard to get results. When the Clinton Administration came to power, revisionism finally got its chance. And that's when it suffered the tragedy besetting all false theories. Someone tried it out.

An article of faith among revisionists was that, if only Washington were firm enough, Japan would agree to negotiate market shares for imports. It had done so in 1986 when Deputy U.S. Trade Representative Michael Smith hammered out the semiconductor agreement and would do so again, said revisionists. In a 1992 speech, and presumably in the briefings he later gave at the Clinton White House, Prestowitz said he had inside information that Japan would respond positively to such an approach:

> U.S. policy should be aimed at jointly setting targets in the manner of the semiconductor agreement. . . . [T]here is every reason to expect that such negotiations would be successful. . . . [T]hese views are not just those of an unreconstructed revisionist. The proposals presented here have been discussed with MITI and Japanese industry leaders who in private conversation . . . even go so far as to propose development of a kind of joint industrial policy. Thus, there is every reason to expect that the new policy can be successful.[44]

Even those who did not accept the full-fledged revisionist analysis were willing to go for the results-oriented negotiating strategy if that's what it took to open Japan's markets. Both in 1989 and in 1993 the USTR's corporate advisors, ACTPN—which included the CEOs of such top-ranking firms as American Express, Corning, Mobil, Motorola, Allied Signal, The Gap, AT&T, IBM, Chase Manhattan, Boeing, and a few dozen others—called for what they called "temporary quantitative indicators" (TQI) in their official reports.[45]

The concept of the TQI was that, if targets like those in the semiconductor agreement were set in other sectors and met, then imports would reach such a critical mass that Japanese collusion would break down and the market would start to function normally. For example, even though there is no longer a formal target for imported chips, the foreign share of the Japanese semiconductor market still remains well above a third. As one former chip buyer for a Japanese electronics firm acknowledged:

> Before the 1986 Agreement we didn't think U.S. chips had high quality. We wanted to stick with the suppliers we already knew and trusted. That was enough for us. But under the Agreement, we were forced to buy some U.S. chips. So, we sought out the best. Then we realized some were better than others. Now, we are used to buying good U.S. chips and we are not reluctant to buy them anymore. Even though I don't like the agreement, I have to admit that, if we had not been forced by the Agreement to try out U.S. chips, imports might still be at 10 percent.[46]

Even a growing number of political-military experts like Nathaniel Thayer, Richard Armitage, and George Packard said they were willing to accept what they called "managed trade" if that's what it took to heal the bitter rift between the two allies. "David Ricardo [the originator of free trade economic theory] never had to confront a $50 billion trade deficit," commented Thayer. "Managed trade offends me theoretically," Armitage commented, "and I can't imagine our Commerce Department running it. But for the sake of the political relationship between our two countries, we may have to consider it."[47]

All of this, however, was based on the one success of the semiconductor pact as well as on the revisionist premise that the Japanese "liked to talk numbers" and would be willing to "cut a deal" if America were only firm enough.

During various negotiations in the 1980s, the Japanese side had said, "Exactly what do you want? How much of that? How many of this?" recalled Ira Wolf, a former Assistant Trade Representative for Japan and China who had served in the Tokyo Embassy during 1983–86. Others have reported similar accounts. From these incidents, various U.S. strategists surmised that the semiconductor pattern could be replicated.[48]

Accompanied by Mickey Kantor's harsh rhetoric, Clinton tried out this theory and it blew up in his face. The Japanese government, chanting "Never Again," adamantly rebuffed the entire approach. Tokyo now refused to concede to Clinton what it had previously given Bush: objective indicators without targets. Rather than boosting the strength of the reformist Hosokawa Administration vis-à-vis the conservatives, the Clinton posture unwittingly pushed reformers into a defensive nationalistic alliance with conservatives. Hosokawa won plaudits at home for standing up to America. Tokyo seemed more intransigent than ever.

There are those like Prestowitz and some former trade negotiators who blame the failure, not on the results-oriented strategy *per se*, but on poor execution. "The Clinton Administration handled this in the clumsiest way possible," said Prestowitz, who still contends that the strategy would have worked had it been done "correctly." But he concedes that his assertion can never be proven.[49]

In any case, just as the tumbling of the Japanese economy discredited revisionist analysis, so the failure of the Clinton results-oriented negotiations derailed faith in revisionist prescriptions.

That's when revisionism died as a political force.

Yet, the clock could not be turned back to traditionalism either. Increasingly, it was widely recognized that something new was needed.

The "System That Soured" Paradigm Emerges

Today, as people try to understand why the Japanese miracle failed, new analysts are picking up the trail that disappeared in the heat of the 1980s. As they do, a "system that soured" paradigm is gradually emerging. This is by no means a completed edifice. It is an analysis being built brick by brick as various analysts individually try to figure out why the Japanese miracle failed. It is, at this stage, more a series of questions than an answer.

A good recent example is the 1993 book *Planning for Change* by investment banker James Vestal, whose distinction between anti-growth and pro-growth elements in industrial policy we cited in Chapter 5.[50] Before 1973, as Vestal shows, "pro-growth" elements predominated; after 1973, the "anti-growth" elements increasingly held sway.

An examination of the financial aspects of the situation has been offered by David Asher in his *Orbis* essay "Economic Myths Explained: What Became of the Japanese Miracle." His verdict:

> Over the last decade, the effectiveness of many of the unique Japanese institutions . . . has declined precipitously. . . . [M]any elements of the Japanese economic system that once seemed to work well no longer appear to serve the nation's needs. . . .
>
> The Japanese state . . . has largely become *anti*-developmental—retarding growth, fighting vainly against market trends, and acting selfishly to protect its vested interests.[51]

A 1997 essay in *Foreign Affairs* called "The Unraveling of Japan Inc." by Michael Hirsh and Keith Henry shows how dysfunction at home is driving Japanese companies overseas, thereby hollowing out Japan:

> Japan is losing its Inc. The interests of Japan and its giant corporations, for so long the same, are diverging. . . . The message of the multinationals is this: the low productivity and growth of this over-regulated marketplace no longer work for us.[52]

Walter Hatch, who co-authored *Asia in Japan's Embrace* with Kozo Yamamura, takes the view that Japan's multinationals are partly making up for souring of the system at home by replicating their *keiretsu* networks in Asia.

> Despite some superficial changes, Japan's domestic political economy continues to be characterized by what I call embeddedness. That is, mutually reinforcing ties between government and business, between otherwise independent entities (keiretsu), and between management and labor. This system worked well to promote economic development when Japanese industry was still adopting existing technology from the West. However, now that so many Japanese manufacturers are operating at the global technological frontier, this system produces more costs than benefits. But policies and practices that worked well in the past are not blithely abandoned. Rather than dismantling this system of embeddedness, Japanese manufacturers—with the help of the Japanese government—have tried to export it to developing Asia, where such a system creates fewer distortions. In this way, Japan has managed to "buy time," to postpone dramatic changes (toward, for example, less regulation, more competitive supply markets, and more flexible labor markets) which it otherwise would have been forced to make.[53]

Many of the conclusions of these authors differ somewhat from the ones we gave in this book, but their research is prompted by the same questions. Why did the once successful system sour? How is Japan dealing, or not dealing, with this problem? They locate Japan's "economic model" in a developmental context.

One of the more interesting books along this line is Taggart Murphy's *The Weight of the Yen*. An investment banker who worked in Tokyo, Murphy has been very much influenced by revisionists like Karel van Wolferen, and accepts the "bureaucratic authoritarian" political schema. And yet, his own investigation overturns the main revisionist thesis: that Japan benefits from its protectionism. Murphy argues that Japanese policies sowed the seeds of their own destruction. Japan required export surpluses to grow and yet Japanese policies undermined the ability of its customers to buy. The secular fall of the dollar is just one symptom of this syndrome.[54]

Other revisionists have also had some second thoughts. Clyde Prestowitz said in 1997, "I never said that Japan was superior, just that it was closed. People used to think that Japan was ten feet tall; now some people are talking as if it's two feet tall; really it's about six feet tall." Indeed, in a December 1997 op-ed in the *Washington Post* sparked by Asia's financial storms, Prestowitz ended up endorsing the main thesis of the "system that soured" paradigm. "As a catch-up machine, this [Japanese] model was unparalleled. But," he acknowledged, "once Japan caught up and several of the other [Asian countries]—South Korea, Indonesia, Malaysia, Thailand—reached advanced stages of development, problems began to arise."[55]

The "system that soured" view has even entered into official U.S. government reports. These ideas are explored in a recent U.S. Commerce Department's report, *Prospects for Growth in Japan in the 21st Century*, written by Sumiye Okubo, Director of the Office of International Macroeconomic Analysis. The view is such a reversal of past analysis that the preface by Everett Ehrlich, Undersecretary of Economic Affairs, is worth quoting at length:

> The structural opening of Japan's economy is inevitable. When it happens, not only will U.S. exports find a new and welcome home, but then and only then will Japan's economy finally find the basis for the new and sustained round of growth that has eluded it in this decade. . . .
>
> From the 1950s onward, Japan pursued an extremely successful growth strategy, one that has been emulated by other countries in Asia. This strat-

egy was based on high levels of savings and externally driven (export demand) growth, and was supported by a variety of government policies, including restrictions on imports, maintenance of an undervalued currency, incentives to save, targeted investment, and promotion of key traded sectors of the economy. . . .

[But] the Japanese created in some ways a dual economy, with less efficient industries that supply domestic customers—private and public—along with a competitive export sector. . . .

In the current world environment, Japan's past growth strategy appears less appropriate. . . .

Japan's economy has ground to a halt, plagued by . . . a form of economic organization rooted in a bygone technological age. . . . In an economy in which each competitor offers some world-class ability, the successful firm will be one that takes what the market offers and adds value to it. . . . This is exactly what Japanese firms are not good at doing. The keiretsu system is not designed to create or support the openness that allows firms to lever this higher level of specialization. Instead, it creates a walled city that shuts in its members from outside distraction. . . .

The notion of a closed economy—nations as base camps from which to leap into world market—has passed. . . .

So there are four growth policies [that Japan needs]—reform of retail and distribution, land use and construction, and financial markets, and a greater culture of openness. What is remarkable about this list is that they are all among the highest priorities of U.S. trade policy. That is the point. *We have too often thought of these policies as unilateral concessions we demand of the Japanese. It is time to think of them instead as tonics for what ails Japan* [emphasis added].[56]

"No previous U.S. government report has made this argument before," Ehrlich commented.[57]

This new analysis suggests a new approach to trade policy. In the past, both Washington and Tokyo saw U.S.–Japan trade conflicts as a zero-sum game. Whatever benefited the U.S. hurt Japan and vice versa. In the new view, domestic deregulation and trade liberalization by Japan would benefit both countries. If Japan undertook sufficient reform to end the dual economy, i.e., to raise the productivity of backward sectors to world levels, the results would be striking. According to a study cited by Sumiye Okubo, Japan would grow 1 percent a year faster and its trade surplus would vanish in a decade; meanwhile, after 10 years, America's own GDP would be 0.7 percent higher and its trade deficit cut in half.

The exact policies that flow from a "system that soured" paradigm are not yet clear. But one thing is clear. As Leonard Schoppa has documented, America has been most successful in its trade negotiations when its own demands coincided with the interests of powerful interest groups in Japan. Since Japan's own structural flaws can only be solved by greater trade opening, there are likely to be more potential allies than in the past.[58]

One precedent is the negotiations some years back to lighten Japan's limits on large discount stores. Discount stores were restricted from new openings by Japan's Large-Scale Retail Store Law, aimed at protecting small retailers. The large stores were glad to use U.S. pressure to help them get what they wanted. Payback for the U.S. came during the 1991–95 yen rise, when these stores bypassed the cartels, stocked imports and lowered prices. In addition, the change in the law finally allowed Toys R Us to get a foothold in Japan, where, after only a few years, it has become the country's largest retailer of toys. Tower Records is undercutting high prices in Japan by bringing in foreign-made CDs. Increasing the power of retailers vis-à-vis the manufacturers promotes both Japanese reform and American exports.

Similarly, in the 1996 negotiations that helped open Japan's pension fund market to U.S. securities firms, U.S. negotiators received behind-the-scenes support from Japanese corporate pension funds. The latter could no longer tolerate the low returns they were getting from Japan's life insurers. In their 1997 *Foreign Affairs* piece, Hirsh and Henry report:

> Japan's major concession last April on pension fund deregulation, for example, was more the result of the rebellion of Japan's multinational manufacturers than of pressure at the bargaining table. Although Japanese life insurers howled that they sacrificed too much . . . hard-pressed Japanese multinationals saw deregulation as essential to introducing international competition to Japan's financial sector, which had yielded abysmal returns.[59]

Japan is less of a monolith than ever before. Economic pressures are producing cracks in the former solid wall of mutual protection.

In almost all countries, the leaders in lifting domestic protection have always been the multinational and exporting companies, who benefit the most from open economies elsewhere and are willing to open their own in return. This, as Helen Milner demonstrated in *Resisting Protectionism*,[60] applied even to France, a country whose state–corporate relations and protectionism are often compared to Japan. As the conflict between the needs of Japan's domestic sectors and its efficient exporters become increasingly sharper, U.S. strategists should be geared to looking for, and amplifying, such trends in Japan as well.

U.S. negotiators report that the "seek allies" perspective is already becoming more prevalent in Washington. The same is true among some business leaders. At the July 1997 meeting of the U.S.–Japan Business Council, the leader of the U.S. side, CBS Chairman Michael Jordan, outlined with great specificity how aggressive deregulation would help both the Japanese economy and U.S. exporters.

But, no one is naive enough to think this is a "magic bullet." Past attitudes and still-current corporate hookups remain a stubborn obstacle to progress. For example, while Japanese newspapers acknowledged that much of Michael Jordan's comments were valid, they insisted it was up to Japanese, not Americans, to say such things.

The negotiators and business executives in the trenches report that seeking allies is a lot easier said than done. For one thing, Japanese businesses rarely identify domestic deregulation, which they support, with market opening to imports, which many do not. For this and other reasons—including the reluctance of Japanese firms to ally openly with foreigners against other Japanese—working out explicit cooperation is very difficult. For example, at one recent meeting of U.S. and Japanese business executives, recalled former U.S. trade negotiator Ira Wolf, the Japanese side was stressing the need for deregulation and their great frustration with Japanese political leaders. The U.S. executives then suggested an alliance. The Japanese side would draw up a list of their deregulation priorities and the U.S. side would do the same. Where the lists coincided, the two sides would work together—the Japanese from the inside and the Americans via the traditional *gaiatsu* (outside pressure). Except for one executive from a Japanese firm renowned for its unusual internationalism, all the other Japanese participants rejected the idea and said it would never work.[61]

And yet, as the examples of insurance and big stores cited above show, there is often *sotto voce* cooperation that can be very effective. Such behind-the-scenes support for the U.S. position was seen in the 1997 battle over port facilities as well.

Certainly, the seeking allies perspective will not provide a short-term fix. Nonetheless, over time, if Japan is to reform at home, it needs to open its market. Recognizing, and working with, that reality provides the best chance for success.

Chapter 14

Interregnum: Whither Japan?

The Japanese people prize stability. Maybe the prospect of 1.75 percent growth is not scary enough for the Japanese people to accept the need for reform. They may say: "1.75 percent is not so bad. We don't need reform." Japan might end up with growth too low for real vitality but not low enough to compel people to accept reform.
— Yotaro Kobayashi, CEO Fuji-Xerox, 1996[1]

Daunting Challenges

The challenges lying ahead for Japan are daunting indeed. They involve nothing less than a wholesale renovation of its major institutions. At both the governmental and corporate level, Japan is stuck with institutional vestiges of the catch-up era: a one-party state, a cartelized corporate sector, a dysfunctional financial system, and closed trade. It is high time that Japan embrace the wholesale modernization it so desperately needs.

At first blush, it may seem that simple economic reform led by deregulation is all that is required. It is certainly true that it is Japan's economic straits that make reform so urgent. Unless Japan can revive its productivity and growth, it will simply be unable to meet the burden when the aged amount to a third of the population. Unless Japan can overcome its high-cost dual economy at home, it will continue to lose its most efficient manufacturing firms to offshore investment.

And yet, the truth is, very few of the required economic reforms will take place without broader and deeper changes. If all that were needed in the economic sphere were simple deregulation, this would not be the case. But reviving the economy involves a thorough overhaul of the widespread private collusion and cartel-like activities, the cross-shareholding networks, and all the other institutional structures that limit new Japanese entrants and block imports. And these changes cannot be accomplished without breaking down the political and financial links between Japan's backward sectors and the political machines that support them. And so economic reform requires political renovation. It involves ending a system of "government by corruption."

At the minimum, Japan needs institutional renovation in four broad areas:

1. It needs a modern political system where the concerns of the broad middle class rather than narrow interest groups can dominate. This includes competitive elections where it is normal for competing parties to alternate in power, and where electoral victories are determined by policy debates rather than by "money politics" and special handouts to a small slice of the electorate. It needs a system where policy is the outcome of genuine contention in the Diet, rather than in closed-door meetings of Ministries or of politicians gathered in the back rooms of expensive restaurants. That is the best assurance that future laws and regulations will genuinely be devoted to health, safety, public welfare, and equity rather than protection of the inefficient.

The main reason for the bureaucracy's inordinate power in Japan is that Japan is still a one-party state. If parties with different programs and voter bases could genuinely alternate in power, then the bureaucracy would be a lot less powerful and the Diet more powerful. Along the same lines, it is true that there's a lot of "structural corruption" of the Diet. Yet, it's hard to think of a one-party state or one-party city where the legislature and executive are not corrupt. There's not an awful lot wrong with Japan that wouldn't be helped a great deal by nothing more esoteric than good old-fashioned political competition.

2. It needs a modern financial system. Money has to go to its most efficient use rather than to shore up outdated allies and cartelized backward industries. It needs a system where both lenders and borrowers have to pay for their mistakes. And it needs a system where savers can get a fair return on their investment. The latter will be more likely if savers are given a full spectrum of choices as to where they can put their money—whether that be inside or outside of Japan. To the extent that savers have more choice, banks are likely to scrutinize their borrowers a lot more closely.

No more convoy system that protects incompetent banks; less reliance on banks, and more on capital markets (both bond and stock); stock markets that allocate capital rather than serving as a casino and anti-takeover device; honest accounting, transparent books, and enough bank examiners—and honest ones—to do the job.

3. It needs a genuinely competitive corporate setup. Japan needs to

end the corporate collusion that undergirds its deformed dual economy and the accompanying high prices. This means seeing competition as a cleaning process, not as a source of "confusion" in the market. It requires widespread trust-busting at home. This includes an end to domination of corporate control by the incestuous system of cross-shareholding and of corporate finance by the "banker's kingdom."

It also includes a modern competitive distribution and retail system where customers actually have a choice. That will prevent cartels from passing along costs. When cartels cannot pass along costs, they cannot survive.

4. At long last, Japan needs to genuinely open its door to competing imports and to foreign direct investment. The purpose is not the static "gains from trade" of which the textbooks speak. The purpose is to shake up entrenched institutions. "Price destruction" is the heavy artillery that will knock down the walls of collusion at home. As Hugh Patrick points out, what is called "price destruction" in Japan "is really more appropriately termed 'price creation' as global market competition replaces manufacturer administrative power in price-setting."[2] As in other countries, if Japan's trade is not opened, it's questionable how far the other reforms will go.

Some in Japan say a change on this scale requires a revolution in popular attitudes as well. Throughout Japan, people interested in reform are beginning to discuss the pitfalls of its "familialist" ethic. This is Japan's counterpart to Europe's overextended social safety net. Whereas in Europe, the social safety net is woven out of overt government programs, in Japan it occurs in hidden form. Anticompetitive activities allow moribund companies and flagging industries to sustain themselves so that unemployment is disguised. Even some of the anti-unemployment schemes are organized to provide wage subsidies to preserve the redundant job, rather than help the worker move to a new job. "Japan is organized so that society's losers don't feel like losers," is how it is described by Takashi Kiuchi, chief economist at the Long-Term Credit Bank. But surely a way can be found to reconcile social compassion with efficiency. The worker should be protected, but not the job.

None of this involves asking Japan to adopt American ways, as the defenders of the status quo would have it. Every country must find its own path to striking the proper balance between the need for social cohesion and compassion on the one hand and the liberating power of countervailing institutions on the other. For too long, Japan has had too much of the former and not enough of the latter. It needs to create a better balance, lest social cohesion continue to engender stultification. Indeed, given that low growth has set one interest group against another in Japan, greater efficiency is not the enemy of social equity; it is its prerequisite.

In any case, as Yukio Noguchi points out, many of Japan's postwar institutions are hardly age-old facets of Japanese culture. They are merely relics of the pre–World War II mobilization. Saying that Japan needs to reform is not asking Japan to become more like America. It is, perhaps, asking Japan to become more like Japan.

If we gauge the Japanese reform effort by the four main tasks cited above, the verdict seems clear enough: as of early 1998, the iceberg is starting to break up, but Japan has a long way to go. It is doubtful that the task of renovation will be completed any time in the next few years. Indeed, on some fronts, change is more apparent than real.

Electoral Reform Leaves a Lot to Be Desired

In 1994, the reform-minded Hosokawa Administration overhauled the country's electoral system, hoping to usher in a new era where middle class concerns rather than corrupt "money politics" ruled. So far, this has not occurred.

To see why, we have to go back to 1990. When the financial underpinnings of Japan's dual economy crashed with the stock market in that year, its political foundations collapsed soon thereafter. The Liberal-Democratic Party (LDP), which had monopolized power as a catchall coalition of the efficient and inefficient, split apart in 1993. The split was roughly along reformer versus conservative lines. In the ensuing 1993 elections, Japanese voters rejected the LDP, forcing it to relinquish power for the first time in 38 years. A new government waving the banner of wholesale political and economic reform briefly took power.

The initial trigger for the LDP's fall was a series of corruption scandals—complete with millions of dollars worth of gold bars in the home of an LDP kingmaker, securities firms making payoffs to mobsters, and the resignation of several LDP Prime Ministers in succession, including one personally implicated in the corruption. Faith in both the system and the elites who ran it plummeted.

These scandals, however, were not the cause for the LDP's downfall, only the trigger. The underlying cause was that the political-economic foundation for LDP's catchall coalition had crumbled into sand.

"In the high-growth era, much of the economic structure involved a positive-sum game," political scientist T.J. Pempel commented at the time of the LDP's fall. "That's why the LDP could be an all-embracing coalition of the efficient and inefficient. Today, with lower growth, relations between the efficient and inefficient sectors are more of a zero-sum game. And so the LDP fell apart."[3]

The corruption issue itself was part of this split in the LDP base. The endemic corruption that so appalled Japan's urban middle class was not a matter of personal character flaws, but an artifact of the very structure of Japan's postwar political economy. Otherwise it would not have been so widespread at the very pinnacle of power. "Structural corruption," i.e., favors in exchange for enormous kickbacks, is built into the very nature of the symbiosis between the LDP and the *koenkai* (the personal support groups of Diet members discussed in Chapter 5). It is part and parcel of the dual economy. In a country where entrenched firms can keep out their rivals, payoffs have become the classic route for at least some parvenus— like Recruit Cosmos, the firm at the heart of one of the scandals—to break in. Middle-class savers suffering from falling stock and real estate prices learned that big investors were being saved from a similar fate by illegal deals with banks and securities houses. To add insult to injury, these illegal deals enjoyed the tolerance of the Finance Ministry—at least until they became public. The middle class's losses provided the safety net for the big boys.

All of this, in combination with the need to overcome the intractable economic malaise, produced widespread desire for change. Hence, when Hosokawa's anti-LDP reformist coalition took the helm in 1993, there was a revolution of expectations. Voters hoped Hosokawa would introduce a new system of competitive elections and broad social and economic reform. Finally, after nearly five decades of almost continuous rule by the LDP and its predecessor parties, Japan's urban middle-class voters, known in Japan as "the new middle mass," felt it was time for a government that represented them.

It was not long before disappointment and disillusion set in. Within months, Hosokawa himself had to resign after being personally tainted by the same series of corruption scandals that had brought down his LDP predecessors. Moreover, apart from electoral reform, the Hosokawa government had few achievements of which to boast.

A year after the LDP fell from power, it returned. It did so by allying with the very party that had been its bitterest ideological opponent for four decades: the Socialists. With the Cold War over, the two parties allied round what really counted: preserving their own power. Indeed, for a while, the LDP even allowed Socialist Tomiichi Murayama to serve as puppet Prime Minister.

The failure of this first effort by a reform coalition has led some analysts to suggest that Japan is incapable of political reform. This, however, is not so. In most countries, the first big effort at reform rarely succeeds. But it does set the stage for future efforts.

Had the reform coalition been able to maintain power for four or five years, that might have made a real difference in Japanese politics. That would have given the Opposition parties enough time to get some leverage over the budget process in Japan. Since the LDP–Ministry alliance over budgets is a key part of the spoils system that keeps LDP Diet members in power, that could have changed the rules of the game.

A reform government could have cut off budgetary funding for the rural *koenkai* and construction groups — the backbone of the anti-reformist elements in the LDP. In combination with electoral reform that increased the power of urban votes, these budget changes would have further split the LDP, while forcing it to compete as an urban-based party. Had this continued long enough, it might have created a political structure of parties alternating in power, ending Japan's skewed politics as a one-party state. That, in turn, would have elevated the role of the Diet (parliament) and the Prime Minister as the real locus of decision-making in Japan, thereby curbing the power of the permanent bureaucracy.

For a while, it looked as though this scenario stood a good chance. Although the LDP won 223 seats in the 1993 Diet elections, gradually LDP Diet members began defecting to the new government coalition. They knew that their ability to deliver to their constituents depended on being part of the ruling alliance. LDP membership in the Diet fell to 200.

But this optimistic scenario was not to be. Soon after Hosokawa's ascension, LDP tacticians began releasing information that tarred Hosokawa, a former LDP member himself, with the same corruption scandals that had brought down his LDP predecessors. Under this pressure, Hosokawa resigned.

Some analysts said Hosokawa might have saved himself if only he had leveled with the Japanese people. He might have frankly acknowledged his past, deeply apologized for it, explained that one had to be complicit in corruption to accomplish anything in that system, and declare that that's why he knew so intimately the need to dismantle the old ways. Instead, Hosokawa's reform effort ended, not with a bang, but with a whimper. This was the first of many clues that the Opposition lacked what it took to instill popular confidence.

For a while, Hosokawa was replaced as Prime Minister by another Opposition leader, Tsutomo Hata. Then, the entire Opposition cabinet fell when wire-puller Ichiro Ozawa—the Tanaka protege whose defection had brought down the LDP in the first place—became too clever for his own good. One of the parties in the reform coalition was the Socialists. Through a series of backroom maneuvers, Ozawa tried to ease them out of any cabinet post, assuming they would still support the coalition and lamely submit to whatever he dictated. After all, Ozawa reasoned, what alternative did they have? Their alternative was to join hands with their longtime adversaries: the LDP.

Nonetheless, all the king's horses and all the king's men cannot put the old political-economic system back together again. The LDP has but a shadow of its former power. In the October 1996 elections, it gained less than 40 percent of the vote and had to form a coalition government. More importantly, the traditional demographic base of the LDP—farmers, retailers, and so forth—is shrinking as a share of the population. By contrast, the demographic base of the population that the opposition would like to target—urban salaried workers and managers—is growing.

Hashimoto can read the tea leaves as well as anyone. LDP Prime Minister Ryutaro Hashimoto campaigned and ruled, not by trying to turn the clock back, but by presenting himself as the champion of change. He campaigned on the basis of a "Big Bang" reform in finance and a restructuring of the bureaucracy. By repositioning himself as a reformer, Hashimoto—a scion of the Tanaka faction and a longtime spokesman for the vested interests—was trying to repeat the trick that his old guru had pulled off in the early 1970s. He wanted to shift the LDP enough to capture a new voting base among the urban middle class while not going so far as to alienate the old base among the rural and urban *koenkai*.

Hashimoto is not a full-blooded reformer, as some observers believe. Nor is he, as others claim, merely an electioneering politician presenting the image of reform without any substance. Instead, Hashimoto is forced by his circumstances to straddle two worlds.

It is a tough straddle to manage. As economist Iwao Nakatani has pointed out, if Japan were to engage in the thorough reform it needs to revive growth, 10 million people—many of them voters for the LDP and its Socialist allies—would lose their jobs. While reform would eventually create another 11 million new jobs and raise growth, that would be little consolation to the job losers. And yet, if Japan does not reform, its manufacturing will continue to hollow out—as will the tax base. The government would be unable to meet its rising social security obligations without budget deficits in the double digits, and/or without raising taxes and social insurance to nearly 60 percent of GDP. And that is clearly impossible.

This dilemma shows why reform is so hard to achieve in Japan. There's a widespread myth in America that only the bureaucracy, jealous of its power, stands in the way of reform. In truth, as we have stressed throughout this book, many bureaucracies are often captive of the very industries they are supposedly guiding. The real obstacle to reform is that millions of voters, along with companies, would be hurt by the reform process. Indeed, as a senior MITI official commented, "Everyone says they're for reform. But when real reform happens, many people are going to be hurt. My fear is what will the politicians do when these people start screaming?"

In his maneuvering between the LDP's current and hoped-for future base, Hashimoto lacks several advantages available to Tanaka and his successors.

First and foremost, Tanaka's LDP had enough seats to rule without coalition partners. While Hashimoto's LDP finally regained a tiny majority of seats in the fall of 1997, it still felt the need for coalition partners.

Secondly, the LDP is deeply divided. One divisive issue is which parties among the Opposition would make the best allies. But the more fundamental division is over the reform process itself. While Hashimoto understands the need for some change, the dinosaurs in what journalist Peter Ennis calls Japan's "Jurassic Party" mightily resist change. Once the LDP regained its slim majority, the old arrogance returned. Why make reforms that hurt the LDP's electoral base if the party has a majority, some argued. These include former Chief Cabinet Secretary Seiroku Kajiyama, who in a private meeting with reporters lashed out at Ichiro Ozawa, the man whose defection in 1993 brought down the LDP. "He's always talking about change, change, change, we have to change. But why do we have to change? Our system has been working well for 100 years."[4]

Despite the fact that Hashimoto's personal popularity had been the LDP's biggest asset, the dinosaurs threw away this asset at the end of 1997 by pressuring Hashimoto to bring a former convicted bribe-taker into the Cabinet, and then obstructing Hashimoto's proposed reforms of the Postal Ministry in the most embarrassing way.

With all these divisions, there is no guarantee that the LDP will not split again.

Another big difference is that the Tanaka generation was able to buy votes *en masse* among both the new and old voting bases by busting the budget. Hashimoto by contrast had to bring down the budget deficit. In 1997, he pledged to reduce the national budget deficit from the 7.4 percent of GDP it hit in fiscal 1996 to less than 3 percent by 2003. Already, by 1997, cuts in public works led to a mushrooming of bankruptcies, including some very big ones, among construction companies. Considering the traditional role of construction in LDP financing and politicians' kickbacks, the need to cut the deficit was a major constraint on Hashimoto's leeway.[5]

At the beginning of 1998, there were growing signs that the weakness in the economy was forcing Hashimoto to back off from budget-cutting and return to fiscal stimulus again. Still, the already sky-high size of the deficit limits how far he can go in that direction.

Tanaka and his successors were able to cartelize the economy, thereby using high prices to support the weak sectors when aid from the budget was unavailable. But in the late 1990s, MITI and other bureaucracies insisted that Japan had to bring down high prices in order to keep Japan's efficient manufacturers from fleeing to Asia. In the spring of 1996, MITI instructed the regulated electric utilities to institute a 20 percent cut by 2001 in order to match German rates. But, if rates come down, then the utilities will find it much harder to continue absorbing the high costs of construction, refined petroleum and heavy machinery as they did in the past. So this rate cut has important ripple effects among various LDP support bases.[6]

The LDP of the Tanaka era was fortunate to have as its primary opposition the extremely ideological Socialist Party and a number of small parties. These were groups that few really wanted to see take power. The opposition of the Hashimoto era, by contrast, was composed mainly of split-offs from the LDP itself. Indeed, almost all of the opposition leaders were former members of the Tanaka faction. The opposition had ruled briefly in 1993–94. Unlike the Socialists of the 1970s, they were a realistic, if weak and divided, alternative.

Finally and perhaps most important of all, in the 1970s, most Japanese still believed in the "system." As bad as the oil shock was, it was an external event, like a hurricane, that made no reflection on Japan's own merits. The crisis of the 1990s, by contrast, is homegrown.

Consequently, in the 1990s, there has been a widespread loss of faith in the old system. This includes not only the voting public, where voter participation and party identification have been dropping. It also includes the very elites who have run the system for so long. As in the far more stark case of the former Soviet Union, it is when the very people running the system lose faith that the system topples. Once invulnerable officials started to complain of "bureaucrat bashing" by the press and the public. Journalist Tadahide Ikuta, a longtime observer of Japan's top bureaucrats, captured the mood in a passage written in 1995:

> Widespread demoralization among top-level bureaucrats is a most alarming phenomenon, as indicated by the increasing number of officials who have quit their jobs. . . . Discussion of important topics [by officials] seems far less dynamic than it used to be, and it is now pervaded with an atmosphere of anxiousness, cynicism, and intolerance. Not only is Kasumigaseki's [i.e., the headquarters of the leading Ministries —rk] structure seriously flawed, but those who are running the system are in crisis. . . .
>
> They may resist reform at their own agencies, but few seem to actually believe that the bureaucracy as a whole is wonderful the way it is, or that it does not need to change. A number of bureaucrats in their twenties or thirties are frustrated with the status quo. Many confidently declare: "When we become high officials, we will enact reform!"[7]

In the 1980s, issues of reform were reserved to arcane Commission reports that few read and even fewer believed in. By the 1990s, the fights for and against reform had become the stuff of front page headlines nearly every day.

Still, Japan seems like a country stuck between two eras. The "old Japan" has collapsed but there is not yet a "new Japan" to take its place.

Much of the reason for Japan's floundering lies in its muddled politics. Back in the heady days of 1993, Pempel predicted that the need for reform would become the focus of an electoral realignment. If the great divide in Japanese politics in the 1950s was the Cold War, said Pempel, then the great divide in the 1990s would be efficiency.

That is not how it turned out. Instead the fault lines of Japanese politics are extremely muddy. There are reformers and conservatives in all parties. Personal squabbles and factional maneuvering rather than grand ideas still determine far too much of what happens in the smoke-filled restaurants. And most of all, the Opposition parties are divided and have no compelling vision of what reform would look like.

If popular confidence in the LDP's ability to run the country is low, confidence in the Opposition is even lower. Hopefully, at some point the Opposition will find its voice, but, as of early 1998, it had not yet done so.

Part of the reason for this lies in the very nature of the electoral reform passed by the Hosokawa government. The reform abolished the old multi-seat constituency Diet. In that system, three, four or five members were elected from each district. Each voter had one vote and the top vote-getters won. That was the system that allowed Diet members to win with only 15–20 percent of the vote and that therefore boosted the power of the special interests and the *koenkai*. That was the system under which opposition parties achieved better results if they contested fewer seats, and therefore didn't divide their vote; the system that enabled the LDP to rule with less than majority support.

Under the new system, 300 members of the 500-seat Lower House of the Diet are elected in single-seat, winner-take-all elections. The other 200 are elected in a party-based proportional representation system. (The Lower House has the real power in Japan's Diet.)

At the time, it was hoped by many that the new system would break the grip of the *koenkai*. Many hoped it would reduce the influence of "money politics" and increase the electoral power of the urban middle classes and others interested in reform. Some suggested it would lead to a two-party system in which candidates needing 51 percent of the vote to win would have to appeal to broader constituencies on the basis of programs, policies and ideas. It was hoped the parties would alternate in power.

There was one big problem with such hopes. The only reform able to wend its way through the Diet was a variation on the scheme that the LDP itself had come up with in 1990 as a device for keeping itself in power! The fatal flaw was criticized by some at the time. In a January 1994 editorial, Japan's equivalent of the *Wall Street Journal*, the *Nihon Keizai Shimbun*, said of the compromise that Prime Minister Hosokawa worked out with LDP President Yohei Kono:

> The Hosokawa–Kono agreement more or less ratifies a plan put forward years ago by the LDP that was designed to preserve the existing power structure while making a gesture to a public angry about political corruption.[8]

Back in 1990, a committee considered a plan to replace the multi-seat Diet—512 Lower House members elected from 130 districts—with a system of 300 single-seat districts. The committee was headed by Tsutomo Hata. Hata knew firsthand how powerful were the pressures exerted by special interests. As Agriculture Minister, he too had to dutifully defend Japan's closed market in beef and other goods. For years, some urban reformers in the LDP had been trying to find a way simultaneously to keep the LDP in power and to reduce the influence of the rural *koenkai*.[9]

Unfortunately for the Hata committee, a computer simulation showed a big drawback to their original electoral plan of a complete move to a single-seat system. Since the winner takes all in such a system, small parties usually disappear. Voters are reluctant to throw their vote away on a small party with no chance of winning. As a result, a single-seat system would tend to cause most of the LDP's opponents to coalesce into one big anti-LDP party. Since the LDP usually failed to capture a majority of the vote, this system might eventually dethrone the LDP.

As a solution, the Hata committee came up with the idea of adding another 170 seats, which would be allotted to parties based on proportional representation. As in most other countries, such a system could be counted on to generate a plethora of small parties. That's because even parties with a few percent of the vote could get seats in the Diet. The Opposition would remain divided and the LDP would retain power even though the majority of voters preferred some other party.[10]

The electoral reform that Hosokawa passed in 1994 was basically the same scheme—except with 300 single-seat districts and 200 seats elected by proportional representation. As expected, that system encouraged small parties to keep separate identities instead of merging into a larger party. It provided few incentives to unify.

Moreover, progress against pro-rural (thus pro-LDP) gerrymandering was limited. Unlike in the U.S., where Congressional districts are changed every 10 years as people move from one place to another, the LDP allowed rural areas to keep a large number of Diet members—even though they had lost population to more urban areas. Under the pre-1994 system, in some farm districts, a single person's vote was worth as much as 2.8 urban votes. The 1994 reform made some headway on this gerrymandering but not much. After 1994, the ratio was reduced slightly to 2.3.

The plan worked brilliantly in the 1996 elections—for the LDP. In the single-seat half of the election, a mere 39 percent of the vote allowed the LDP to take 56 percent of those seats. In the proportional representation portion, the LDP got a dismal 33 percent of the vote. Together, these returns gave the LDP enough seats to rule in coalition with smaller parties.

Ironically, Hata himself became the proof of his own system. He was among those who split from the LDP in 1993. He briefly followed

Hosokawa as a reform Prime Minister in 1994. Then he was toppled by the LDP–Socialist coalition in 1994. In 1997, he led a tiny Opposition group called the Sun Party—a party that would never exist if the whole Diet were elected in a single-seat system.[11]

There was one major accomplishment of the new system. No longer could a Diet member win a seat with only 15 percent or 20 percent of the vote. In the single-seat side of the election, it took a plurality to win. The system that had enshrined narrow special interests and the *koenkai* had finally lost one of its major pillars of support.

Following the 1996 election, the Opposition became increasingly disoriented.

The man whose shove initially toppled the LDP—former LDP leader Ichiro Ozawa, sometimes called "Japan's Gorbachev"[12]—was unable to offer his party members patronage, access to the bureaucracy and money once the Hosokawa and Hata reform governments fell. In opposition, as veteran political analyst Takao Toshikawa noticed early on, Ozawa's Shinshinto party quickly seemed to lose its programmatic élan. Resentment by disgruntled party members grew. After the 1996 election, members of Ozawa's party began steadily defecting back to the LDP. By August of 1997, such defections raised the LDP Diet membership to a slim majority. By the end of 1997, Ozawa's party split and his power and influence were reduced even further.

Then, there was the other main opposition party, the Democrats (not to be confused with the Liberal-Democrats). One of its leaders, Naoto Kan, made his name when, as Health and Welfare Minister, he unearthed scandalous Ministry decisions that exposed hemophiliacs to HIV-tainted blood from Japanese companies. No one would have died had the Ministry allowed the import of heat-treated blood from U.S. firms, as some Ministry officials proposed. In a move that brought tears to the eyes of TV viewers, Kan personally offered the AIDS victims a sincere, humble and deep bow of apology for the Ministry's past actions. Unprecedented indictments against officials and company executives were handed down.

And yet, after the elections made the newly formed Democrats Japan's third largest party, Kan angled for the Democrats to join Hashimoto's coalition. Other Democratic leaders strenuously disagreed.

In any case, the Democrats lacked any clear strategy for forming a majority coalition.

And so, by default, the LDP reigned again.

If back room maneuvering, party machinations, and the mechanics of elections were all that counted, the LDP never would have fallen in the first place. All of the problems that caused the LDP to fall in 1993 still remained after the LDP returned. The basic political dilemma was as strong as ever: some powerful sections of society desperately needed for reform to work while other equally important sections would be hurt by reform. Squaring that circle would be difficult.

As long as the Opposition parties lacked a compelling vision, and as long as the electoral system made it even harder for them to unite, the job of reform rested with a party, the LDP, whose own constituents were divided. Buffeted by a storm of conflicting political and economic pressures, Tokyo responded with inconsistent policies. Some looked to promote reform. Others seemed to resist it.

Financial Reform: The Tug of War within Japan, Inc.

By definition, a capitalist economy rests on the allocation of capital. If its capital markets send money to its most efficient use, the economy is likely to prosper; if they do not, very little else will work right.

For that reason, the "Big Bang" financial reforms are at the heart of the Hashimoto Administration's initiatives. Hashimoto has heralded the "Big Bang" as turning an uncompetitive over-regulated financial system that relies on government bailouts into a more competitive system that can stand on its own. Indeed, of all the elements of reform, this is the one given the greatest chance of actually happening.[13]

And yet, the tug of war over the "Big Bang" shows that there are big conflicting interests among Japanese corporate groups—conflicts that have already caused the postponement of one major part of the "Big Bang" and that could yet cause the derailments of other parts. It is still not clear if Japan will see a "Big Bang" or a "Wee Whimper." On the one hand, many banks, securities firms and insurance companies have fiercely resisted reform because it could wipe them out of existence. If, for example, banks were allowed into the securities business as the "Big Bang" promised, half of Japan's 235 securities firms might go under, according to Moody's. With bad debts as high as 12 percent of GDP as of 1997, many weaker banks might also fail if the government ended the "convoy system" that forced stronger banks to absorb the weak. Already one major bankruptcy, that of Hokkaido Takushoku, has occurred despite the best efforts of the MOF to induce other banks to absorb it. Fear of further bankruptcies has led to a severe "credit crunch," whereby banks are reducing their loans to small and medium firms, and even some larger firms, all across Japan. Over the last few years—in order to comply with regulations that require a capital to risky asset ratio of 8 percent at a time when falling stock prices have reduced their capital, the banks have actually reduced their outstanding loans. This is not just a reduction in the volume of new loans, but a reduction in the total level of outstanding loans, in effect, negative lending. This means even creditworthy borrowers have a hard time getting funds. The mountain of bad assets is hindering the ability of the banking system to perform its most basic function.

To avoid a further credit crunch, the government has already agreed to a series of steps that cast doubt on its determination to clean up the mountain of bad assets. It has postponed for at least one year one major part of the "Big Bang." That is the "prompt corrective action" regulations that would have forced banks with bad assets to get rid of them, even at the cost of bankruptcies among borrowers. Indeed, Kajiyama and other LDP barons came up with a plan to shovel hundreds of billions of dollars of government money into the shaky banks in the form of government purchase of preferred shares as well as BOJ loans. That may temporarily alleviate the credit crunch that was developing at the beginning of 1998 but only at the cost of keeping the entire banking system mired in bad assets.

If many weaker institutions will benefit from the delay of reform, the lack of reform is a threat to other, healthier banks and securities firms. As we shall detail below, without reform, they face the prospect of being "hollowed out" like the manufacturing sector.[14]

Nowhere is the end of a monolithic "Japan, Inc." seen more sharply than in the struggle over pension reform. Securities firms and life insurance companies have benefited from outdated rules that shielded them from competition and earned them undeserved profits. On the other hand, the low returns on investments provided by these Japanese securities houses and insurance companies make it too hard for Japan's corporate pension funds to meet their obligations (Figure 14.1).

On the eve of the proposed "Big Bang," an oligopoly of 15 firms managed 95 percent of Japan's $1.7 trillion in pension funds. Moreover, regulations restricted how, where and with whom they could invest their money. For example, until the U.S.–Japan Financial Services Agreement of 1995, 95 percent of Japan's $1.7 trillion in pension funds could only be invested either in Japan's trust banks or else in the fixed-rate funds managed by Japan's insurance companies. The 1995 agreement loosened some of these restrictions, but many remained.

Figure 14.1 **Pension Funds Can't Meet Obligations**

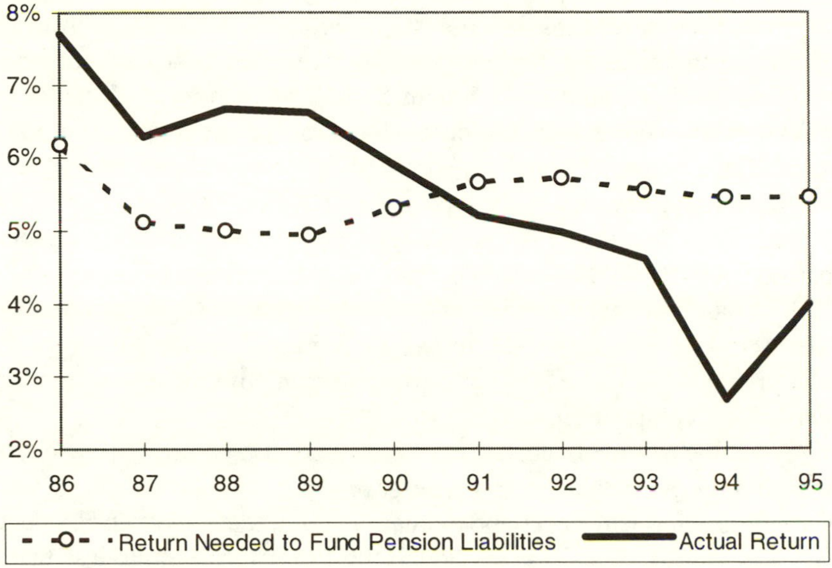

Source: Koll (1997b)

And yet the return in these funds was terrible. Over the 1985–95 decade, Japanese pension funds earned an average of 5 percent a year, only one-third of the 15 percent return averaged by U.S. pension funds. In 1996, insurance-managed funds cut their guaranteed return to only a 2.5 percent return, down from the 4.5 percent they used to provide. One reason for the low returns was that regulations required pension funds to obey the so-called 5-3-3-2 rule. This meant that, among other things, funds had to put 50 percent of their assets into low-risk (but also low-return) fixed-income assets and no more than 30 percent overseas, no more than 30 percent in domestic stocks and no more than 20 percent in real estate. For years, the Pension Fund Association, a lobbying organization of corporate pension funds, had been trying to get the MOF to loosen up, but the MOF had turned a deaf ear.

The 1995 U.S.–Japan Agreement gave Japanese corporations an alternative and they started to take it. Within only a few months of the regulatory change, Japanese pension fund managers took a reported $20 billion away from life insurance firms and put it into the hands of foreign managers. Honda entrusted $100 million to Fidelity Investments to invest in U.S. stocks. In 1996, the Pension Welfare Service Public Corp.—which manages public, not private, pensions—turned over $240 million to Goldman Sachs and the same amount to Morgan Stanley to manage. In 1996, when the insurance companies lowered their guaranteed return, Nenpuku, the national employee insurance system, withdrew $50 billion from the insurance companies and turned it over to investment management firms, including foreign ones like Goldman Sachs. As of mid-1997, Goldman Sachs was managing $1.5 billion in Japanese pension funds. In 1992, foreign firms managed only 1.7 percent of the pension funds managed by trust banks and securities advisers; by 1997, their share was up to 8.3 percent. In 1991, foreign firms managed only $360 million in Japanese pension assets; by 2005, it could be $30 billion, predicted George Curuby, a Tokyo-based financial consultant.[15]

In 1995 and 1996, as we discussed in Chapter 13, Japan's multinationals supported U.S. moves for still further opening of the pension funds to international competition.

Beyond the pension issue, the Japanese voters also earned terrible returns on their savings. Individual Japanese savers put only 10 percent of their enormous savings into stocks and mutual funds—a fraction of the U.S. level. Half was in bank deposits even though the latter were earning less than 1 percent in the late 1990s. The reason was not risk-aversion, but practices that hurt the small investor. Under Japan's system, most stocks must be bought in minimal lots of 1,000, which, given high prices, meant an outlay of $9,000.[16]

Such low returns meant that Japan's middle-class voter was not earning the money he needed to pay for his retirement—either in direct savings or in a corporate pension plan. With the population aging rapidly, this threatened to become a hot political issue.

The Japanese saver was scheduled to be given an alternative in April of 1998. New rules legislated in 1997 eased restrictions on sending money out of the country. Unless other reforms enabled institutions at home to increase returns, further "hollowing out" of finance could be expected. Fidelity and other mutual funds began moving into Japan in a big way after the 1995 agreement. In 1996, Goldman Sachs signed up Japanese investors for $4 billion in five new mutual funds. Fidelity Managing Director Roger Servison expected that Fidelity could become among Japan's top 10 fund managers within 5–7 years.[17]

Other outdated rules likewise threatened "hollowing out" for Japan's securities houses. For example, due to the high fixed commissions charged in Japan, the Tokyo Stock Exchange is losing out to London, where on any given day trading in Japanese stocks is as much as 30–40 percent of the levels in Tokyo itself. Similarly, syndicated loans and

Figure 14.2 **Banks Losing Their Best Corporate Customers**

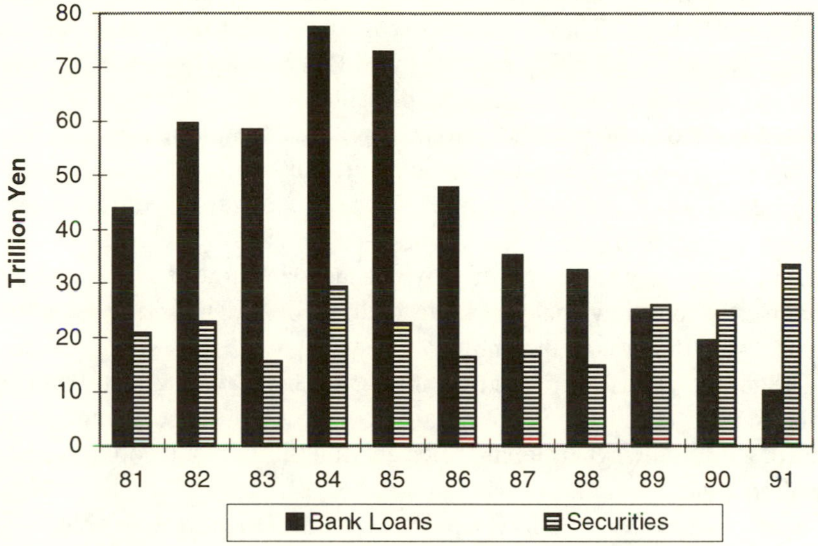

Source: Koll (1997b)

Note: The chart shows the source of funding for nonfinancial corporations from the Bank of Japan "Flow of Funds" figures.

corporate bonds are often executed in Singapore rather than Tokyo.

Banks too needed change—or at least the healthier ones did. One reason the banks had acquired so much in bad assets is that their best customers, Japan's leading corporations, had become flush with cash and no longer needed to borrow. Beyond that, the "Bankers' Kingdom" of the past was over. Previous reforms had given corporations access to other forms of financing. Hence, to the extent firms needed cash, they could find cheaper sources in the Euromarkets for commercial paper and bonds rather than bank loans. In 1996, corporations for the first time actually raised three times as much in the securities market as in bank loans (Figure 14.2). To seek business, banks have had to reach out to poorer-quality borrowers. It's like the old Groucho Marx joke: if you really need a bank loan, you're the kind of company the bank doesn't want to lend to.

For that reason, banks wanted to get into underwriting securities and business areas long denied them. This was a typical case of the pattern whereby reforms that freed up one area of finance made trouble for the still-regulated portions, leading to pressures for further reform. By 1997, due to loosened regulations, banks were underwriting a third of all corporate bonds—compared to zero in 1995. By the end of the century, banks were supposed to be let into the even more lucrative area of equity underwriting and trading. They were also scheduled to be allowed to sell mutual funds, like those being offered by Fidelity. Naturally, the securities firms, already under severe financial pressure, are fiercely resisting letting the banks encroach any further into their protected bailiwick.[18]

How Tokyo will square the circle of all these competing pressures—from banks, from securities houses, from life insurers, from corporate pension funds, from individual savers—remains to be seen. But clearly some reforms have to occur—if only because Hashimoto treated them so prominently that they took on a life of their own. They have become a litmus test in the eyes of the public.

The target year for completing the "Big Bang" was 2001. If all the changes that were promised come to pass, it would be a big change indeed. But, as always in Japan, rules are one thing; results on the ground are often quite another.

Even without deregulation, Japan's financial structure has been in the throes of drastic change. Many of the traditional financial structures behind Japan's cartelized economy have been changing rapidly and drastically. As of 1997, corporations were much more dependent on securities rather than banks than ever before. The cross-shareholding system, although still powerful, had clearly eroded somewhat. Shares held purely for relationship reasons have fallen from a peak of 72 percent in 1987 down to 60 percent (Figure 14.3). This system is expected to erode further.

Moreover, as of 1997, almost 30 percent of all shares traded on the Tokyo Stock Exchange were bought or sold through foreign brokers, up a quarter from a year earlier. Investment by foreigners accounted for a quarter of stock trades in 1997, up from one-tenth in the 1980s.[19]

What remained unclear is the degree to which the changes in the financial structure would translate into meaningful changes in the real economy. Would these changes break down the cartelization of the economy? Would the stock market really become an authentic vehicle for allocating capital? Would new firms challenging entrenched companies be able to gain financing? Would moribund, but well-connected, firms start being denied money? Would the market share held by just a few industry leaders decrease?

Some reasons for skepticism remained. For example, despite the significant erosion of cross-shareholding, the vast majority of shares were still held by stable shareholders who could be expected to support incum-

Figure 14.3 **Cross-Shareholding Erodes, but Dividends Still Low**

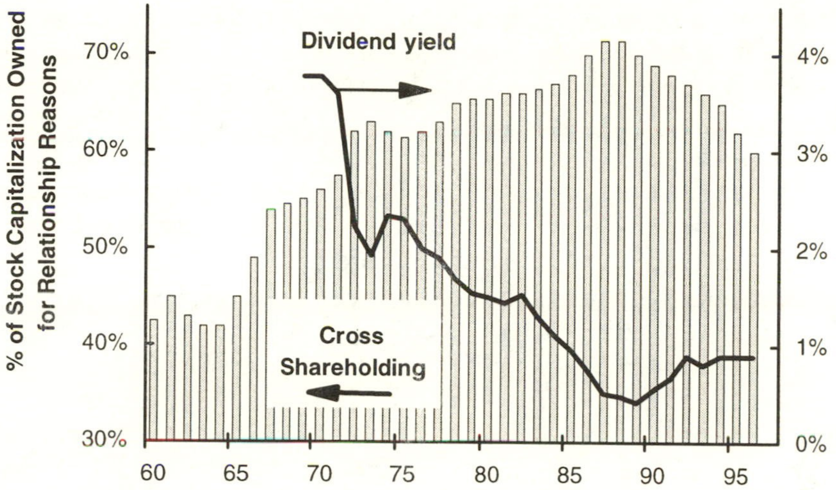

Source: Koll (1997b)

bent management. Moreover, as reflected in the still low level of dividends, shareholder power was still pretty weak (Figure 14.3).

This is not to dismiss the changes that have occurred. They are significant. The issue is whether, over time they will eventually lead to changes fundamental enough to raise Japan's dismal returns on assets and overall low productivity. On that, the jury is still out.

Will Tokyo Decartelize the Economy?

To really change things in Japan, a direct attack on the cartelization of Japan's high-cost domestic sectors is needed. Otherwise, productivity cannot be raised and hollowing out cannot be stopped.

There is no doubt that MITI, the EPA and other sections of the bureaucracy are very serious about the need to bring down the high input costs plaguing Japan's manufacturing base. If they don't, "hollowing out" of manufacturing will erode the government's tax base.[20]

The concept even made it into the "Program for Economic Reform" approved by Hashimoto's cabinet in May 1997. The object is to lower costs in several sectors, like energy, transport and distribution, telecommunications, and information to international levels. Japan's fuel prices are as much as 30–40 percent higher than in the U.S. Transport costs are 50 percent higher. Commercial rents are 75 percent higher. The sectors targeted in the cabinet order account for 30 percent of the input costs for manufacturers.

What the four sectors in the May Cabinet decision have in common is that they are highly regulated, sometimes highly concentrated, and, most importantly, they are isolated from international trade. All of this means they can pretty easily pass their costs on to their Japanese customers. For example, Japan's inefficient construction companies and petroleum refiners pass their costs on to Japan's electric utilities who pass their costs on to everyone from consumers to manufacturers.

Because the high prices in four targeted sectors depend so much on government regulation, such as "supply–demand adjustment" controls in areas like port facilities, a serious deregulation program could help deflate these prices. In the electricity field, for example, MITI has already instructed the utilities to lower their rates by 20 percent by 2001 to reach German levels. When the utilities resisted, MITI threatened to abolish regulations that prohibited non-utilities that generate electricity from selling it directly to customers in competition with the utilities.

In 1996, MITI refused to renew a decade-old law that prohibited anyone other than refiners from importing petroleum products. That change immediately lowered gasoline prices by up to 20 percent.

Still, the resistance from the protected sectors has been strong. And they still have their supporters within the bureaucracy, including within MITI itself. A MITI official whose manufacturing clients needed lower energy prices shed light on this when he said in an interview:

> We were finally able to get the restrictions on petroleum imports lifted after ten long years of fighting because the Natural Resources Agency was part of MITI and we could beat on them. But, if the Resources Agency had been a separate Ministry, we might still be fighting this battle.

In other industries, however, solving the high cost problem would be much harder. Take construction, where costs up to twice as high as in the U.S. push up the cost of so much else in the economy. That powerful industry is not covered in the deregulation order. Hashimoto's Administration has said it would seek to cut the prices paid for public works by as much as 10 percent. However, given that the prices it pays are up to 45 percent above international standards, that still leaves a lot of *dango*-based price inflation.

That makes it even more important, said one senior MITI official, that the Hashimoto Administration carry through on its pledges to reduce public works—not for fiscal reasons but for political ones. After the bubble collapsed, Tokyo poured on the public works to keep the economy afloat and one million people were added to construction payrolls. "That gave the companies a lot of money to contribute to the construction *zoku* (caucus) in the Diet," explained the MITI man. "Cutting off the public works funding of the construction firms is necessary to reduce their political clout."

Farm subsidies and protection remain a big drain on the economy, but there seems to be little progress on that front.

Beyond that, many of the high costs are created, not by explicit government regulation, but by cartelized private practices. And that underlines one of the big deficiencies of Japan's reform effort. All too often, reform has been treated as a narrow call for deregulation. But much of what plagues the Japanese economy is due, not to regulation, but to private anticompetitive activities. Those have all too often been left out of the reform discussion in Japan.

Asked about such anticompetitive activities, the senior MITI official responded, "We can't directly control that. What is needed is more antitrust enforcement by the Fair Trade Commission." Asked if he thought that would occur, the official simply shrugged his shoulders.

The Trade Front: Only Scattered Progress

Japan's most powerful weapon against the cartels, we have argued in this book, would be the "heavy artillery" of imports and foreign direct investment. And on this front, the outlook as of 1997 was not one to inspire optimism.

Many of the inefficient sectors—ports, airline practices, paper, glass and so forth—have been targets of U.S. trade negotiations with Japan. And yet, it's not just the hidebound Transport Ministry that rebuffs U.S. requests. The same MITI that is so eager to bring down the high-cost structure digs in its heels when it comes to trade opening in these sectors. That bodes ill for reform.

Nor, aside from sectoral negotiations, has there been any consistent trend toward trade opening on the ground. During the early 1990s, when the yen was rising, imports exploded and "price destruction" cracked monopolistic cartels in a host of industries. Once the yen reversed after 1995, progress stalled and even reversed. If Yotaro Kobayashi of Fuji-Xerox is right that "a rising yen is the single greatest force for reform," then the depreciation of the yen after 1995 was a setback for reform (see Chapter 12).

The biggest disappointment on the trade front is the lack of progress in the battle of ideas. When it comes to trade, a nationalist defensiveness still prevails. Even among many reform economists, there still seems to be a need to deny the obvious: that Japan is closed to imports and that this closure is hurting it immensely. The good news is that there have been some cracks on this front. At least in theory, some officials in the MITI and the EPA recognize the need for more imports to overcome the dual economy. And, in a few instances, such as the Large-Scale Retail Store Law, the law on petroleum imports, and pension fund deregulation, private constituencies in Japan have desired more foreign competition for their own reasons. Still, few understand that trade opening is critical to the overall battle for reform.

Japan Adrift?

Unlike in the rest of Asia, where the danger posed in 1997 was cataclysm, for Japan the danger is drift. Although there is widespread dissatisfaction with the current system, there is not yet any political movement either within the LDP or the Opposition with the clout and popular confidence and vision to push through fundamental change.

Nor, unlike in Asia, is the urgency so great that reform must be instituted immediately. Japan has got plenty of money to tide over fragile banks; and if tax revenues are lacking, then the BOJ can simply print the money. There may be long-term costs of this approach, but it can enable Japan to "get by" from crisis to crisis.

And so the most likely course from Japan's current leadership is a continuation of the "muddle through" approach that Tokyo has used for the past eight years. Tokyo has long believed that such "muddling through" would eventually lead to an adequate, albeit mediocre, recovery. That is not the case. Indeed, for quite a while, the economy will neither recover nor sink into the ocean. Instead, it will continue to limp along at low levels of growth, with occasional boosts from budget stimulus in a stop-go pattern. Moreover, Japan will continue to absent itself from helping to solve big problems, from the economic crisis in Asia to the integration of China into the Pacific community.

And yet, while Japan can probably get away with "muddling through" for several more years, it cannot "muddle through" indefinitely. For one thing there's the growing demographic crunch of "aging" that will wreak havoc with the national budget. More immediately, "muddling through" will only worsen the economic strains undermining Japan's political system.

The Japanese political economy—the system that gave rise to the "Japan Inc." image—is based on vast interconnecting webs of mutual support. Banks keep weak companies alive. Stronger banks keep weaker banks going. Strong companies pay higher prices to weaker ones. Companies keep redundant workers on staff. And so forth. The system was never as monolithic as some portrayals suggested. There were always conflicts within Japan Inc. But, as long as growth was good, it was possible to smooth over these conflicts. That was the job of the bureaucracy and the LDP. That's why the LDP could rule as a catchall coalition.

Now, however, with growth so low, it is becoming harder and harder to smooth over these conflicts. The options are narrowing. As we noted in the very first chapter, the low interest rates used to save the banks have caused at least one big insurance company to go bankrupt and threaten others, which in turn has led anxious policyholders to draw down their policies, straining the system even further.

And so the cracks in the webs of mutual support widen. The unemployment rate slowly rises; students who have crammed for years (and their parents who have financed cram schools) resent that they can't get jobs when they graduate; women delay marriage and have fewer children; bankruptcies of small firms increase; the government's financial straits worsen, causing it to waver between raising taxes and lowering them; banks start to cut off their less creditworthy customers; and, savers shift their funds from weaker banks to the postal savings system. From time to time, all these strains break out in a crisis, such as the spate of big bankruptcies at the end of 1997.

When such crises do erupt, the LDP and bureaucrats seem one day to call for finally biting the bullet. The next day they try to shore up the old system. They neither solidly promote reform, nor steadfastly resist it. Instead, they waver and take half-measures. They are indecisive. The mandarins no longer know how to manage—and both the common people and the elite know it.

The system cannot go on as it is because it is untenable both economically and politically. The bigger these cracks in the webs of mutual support become, the harder it is for the existing system to continue. The financial strains plaguing Japan make that more clear than ever.

And yet thoroughgoing reform cannot come until Japan has a political leadership committed to reform and until this leadership can gain the confidence of the public. What is most striking about Japan is that, at least through the beginning of 1998, the political Opposition has been completely unable to make any political hay out of the incredible mess that the LDP has created. In the U.S., in the midst of a relatively mild recession, Bill Clinton deposed an incumbent President who had just won a popular war by campaigning on the simple concept, "It's the economy, stupid." In Japan, which is in much worse straits than the U.S. was, the Opposition has so far simply been unable to get its act together. As long as the Opposition is so moribund, anti-reform barons in the LDP will be able to keep progress limited at best.

It is impossible to chart when or how the next breaking point will come. Just as no one in January of 1993 could predict that the LDP would fall scant months later, so no one in January of 1998 can predict how the new realignments will occur. What one can confidently predict is that some day, somehow, a new break will occur. A new Opposition coalition will come into being and win. Or the LDP will split again. There may have to be several rounds of such breaks and realignments before a resolution finally occurs. The resolution may occur in several steps rather than one fell swoop. The bottom line is: while one cannot chart how the change will occur, one can confidently say that reform will have to occur, because if it does not, Japan will never regain its vitality.

A Scenario for Fundamental Reform in Japan

There are five views about Japan's prospects for reform:

1. Japan won't reform because it doesn't need to reform. It's doing fine. Some revisionists like Chalmers Johnson still hold to this view.
2. Japan needs fundamental reform and this reform is already happening at a fairly rapid clip. Much of the press coverage of Hashimoto in 1997 reflected this impression.
3. Japan could use reform but it is very unlikely to reform. It will muddle through. Economist Ed Lincoln has expressed this view.
4. Japan needs reform but it's incapable of reform. Potential disaster looms. Some foreign stockbrokers in Tokyo express this fear.
5. Japan needs reform so badly that eventually fundamental changes will have to occur. But the power of the vested interests is so great that it will take years and years. And it will be a very bumpy ride. This is my view.

There are some analysts who suggest that the reform agenda proposed in this book will never happen. Some argue that a supposedly omniscient and omnipotent bureaucracy (or, in some variants, the "iron triangle" of bureaucrats, big business and the LDP) has no intention of making fundamental reforms; it will institute just enough change to restore vitality and to retain its power. There may even be some bureaucrats who believe they can do so. But in reality that is not an option. While policymakers' intentions are important, their capacities are also important. Today, the capacities of Japan's mandarins fall far short of their intentions. Hence, Japan's political crisis.

It is true that the political-economic institutions guiding Japan today most likely cannot make the necessary changes. The fact that even the relatively weak reforms proposed by Hashimoto were blocked by the LDP *apparatchiks* shows the problem. If the current system could make the necessary changes, then incremental economic reform would be sufficient. Indeed, if they could, Japan would never have gotten into as deep a mess in the first place.

What blocks the current political-economic system from making the necessary changes are the following: 1) so much of the LDP and bureaucracy rest on the support of precisely the inefficient sectors that would be hurt by genuine economic reform; and 2) more importantly, the "webs of mutual support" that distinguish Japan's political economy mean that changing one part of the system at a time threatens to bring the whole house of cards crashing down. When one starts to reform one part of the system, the threat of chaos seems to loom. Hence, the tendency to shore up the existing system.

Precisely because the current system seems incapable of making reforms, it means that even those who want only relatively minor renovation will gradually find that they have to embrace much more far-reaching political changes just to achieve their limited economic objectives. To use a Soviet analogy: did the Gorbachev of 1985 have any idea what the Gorbachev of 1990–91 would end up doing?

The current political-economic system in Japan is not Japan itself; it's just the current system. To say that the *current system* cannot reform itself is far from saying that the *nation of Japan* cannot reform itself. Japan is a great nation trapped in the straitjacket of obsolete institutions. Since those institutions seem unable to bend, they'll eventually break. But Japan will go on and thrive once it makes the necessary changes. There is no guarantee, of course. But I believe it will eventually happen.

The changes in Japan are likely to be at least as far-reaching as the reforms that Deng Xiaoping made in China in the 1970s. Political scientist T.J. Pempel uses the term "Regime Shift" to describe the degree of change that I believe Japan will have to undergo. He defines a regime shift as a change at the "middle level of politics and economics, one far deeper than the ever-recurring shifts in personalities and party strengths, but far less comprehensive than the kinds of totalistic shifts involved in, say, a transition from authoritarianism to parliamentary democracy or from a centrally planned economy to market-based capitalism."[21]

All that is necessary for that degree of change to happen is the following:

1. A growing need for change—due to continuing stagnation, rising economic strains, bankruptcies, unemployment, higher taxes, demographic stresses (aging), and all of the conflicts of interests that arise from this.
2. A growing recognition of that need for change—which we see with the ubiquitous discussion of reform even by those opposed to it).
3. A growing recognition of the inability of the present leaders and institutions to provide that change—as they waffle back and forth between tinkering and resistance and become increasingly indecisive.
4. Alternative leaders and institutions who can credibly propose a better way.

Already, within both the bureaucracy and *zaikai* (business leaders) and the general public, there are plenty of enlightened leaders who recognize that things cannot go on as they are. There are important forces in Japanese society which no longer benefit from the current system, from Japan's leading multinationals to its urban salary workers to enlightened figures in the bureaucracy, the press and academia. As of 1998, these forces are demoralized by the inability of Japan's current system to institute reform. But that demoralization itself is part of the process by which more fundamental change will eventually occur.

When does the breaking point come? Well, when George Bush, Margaret Thatcher and Mikhail Gorbachev got together in a seminar a few years back, Thatcher argued that Ronald Reagan's "Star Wars" toppled the USSR. Gorbachev, noting that he happened to be on the scene at the time, disagreed. The system fell because those, like him, charged with running it no longer believed in it. Bush agreed with Gorbachev.

Increasingly, not just the public but Japan's elites no longer have confidence in the "guardians." The elite bureaucrats no longer have confidence in themselves. The MOF is losing its credibility, not just because it is corrupt, but because it is incompetent. The importance of the MOF scandals that emerged in early 1998 is that they underscored that one reason the MOF is so incompetent is because of rampant corruption. Ordinary people in Japan—voters—are losing their jobs, unable to find careers for their college graduate sons who just spent years and years in *juku* (cram school) hell, losing their retirement nest egg just as they are about to retire—and why? Because bank examiners in the MOF were more interested in being taken by bankers to restaurants where they could be served by young girls without panties than they were in protecting the voters' savings.[22] Japan's mandarins are losing the Mandate of Heaven.

The "regime shift" in Japan will most likely take years. The current phase of this years-long process involves the unraveling of the Old System: its economic dysfunction, its increasing political dysfunction, its loss of credibility, the rising calls for reform, the inability of the present system and leadership to provide that reform, attacks on the system, defenses by the system, policy waffling and gridlock, growing dissatisfaction, head-scratching and intellectual ferment about why all this is so and about what is needed, more party realignments, more splits in the LDP, more false starts by the Opposition, various proposals for reform, trial and error, several more years of a stagnant economy, lurching from crisis to crisis, indecisiveness, more corruption scandals, and so forth.

It's easy to be cynical about Japan. Journalists and professors galore have made very nice careers for themselves on this basis. If one wants to believe that the glacial pace of change in Japan means that talk of reform is just a fraud, there is certainly plenty of grist for that mill. Certainly, some politicians who call themselves reformers are more interested in image than substance.

And perhaps Yotaro Kobayashi is right. The Japanese people may prefer stability to the risks of change.

Yet, the problems that Japan faces are so serious—and the recognition of these problems so widespread—that it's difficult to believe the nation will just let itself slide into further malaise. Economist Kenneth Courtis is right when he says, "Japan has so much to lose by the wrong policies and so much to gain by the right ones."[23] Japan is a country with immense potential trapped in the straitjacket of outmoded practices. People created those practices and people can change them.

Most important, if Keynes is right about the power of ideas, then the most hopeful sign is that Japan's once-solid wall of ideological complacency has cracked. As veteran *Yomiuri* journalist Soichi Oikawa has noted, "People no longer argue about whether or not Japan needs reform. They only debate what kind of reform." Even the opponents of reform are "for reform"—at least in public.

The major exception in the battle of ideas—and a very important one at that—is in the field of trade. As Japan experts are quick to point out, this book is hardly the first time American (and Japanese) analysts have pointed to "forks in the road" supposedly requiring "fundamental change," only to find that the Japanese power brokers have been able to patch up the cracks and muddle through. What makes today's situation different? My answer is the old saying: "If it ain't broke, don't fix it." Twenty years ago or ten years ago, the Japanese economic system wasn't broken; today, it is. Five years ago, it was broken but that wasn't manifest; today, after eight long years of malaise, it is. The preferences of Japan's power brokers may not have changed, but the objective reality confronting them has.

Long-standing institutions are not usually overturned overnight. The process will more likely take ten or twenty years rather than five, but reform will almost certainly occur.

Twice before, when confronted with fundamental challenges, Japan has shown it could virtually turn itself inside out to make the necessary changes. The first instance came in 1868 when Japanese modernizers launched the famous Meiji Restoration to avoid the semi-colonial fate of China. The second occasion came after 1945 with the Occupation-era reforms that followed the defeat of Japanese militarism. To be sure, the reform process Japan requires today will look a lot less dramatic than those previous landmark events. But, it is no less necessary and, if successful, may well prove to be just as much of a turning point. It's just not likely to come very quickly.

Appendices

This appendix section is intended to provide a more technical background to some of the issues raised in this book. It should be accessible to anyone who has taken a college-level introductory economics course. However, an effort was to make most of it approachable even to those without economics training. Most issues are explained in terms of diagrams rather than equations. Where equations are used, the mathematics is limited to algebra.

The most unfamiliar items will be the tables reporting the econometric results. However, with the background information in Appendix C, the tables can be read.

Appendix A

Why Industrial Policy Only Works in the Catch-Up Era

Economies of Scale

When the notion of using industrial policy to emulate the capital-intensive industrial structure of advanced nations was first enunciated, it was denounced as impossible. Japan had too little capital to export capital-intensive items it was said; it should instead focus on labor-intensive items like textiles and toys. Decades later, when the policy had succeeded, it was criticized as unnecessary. If industries already enjoy rapidly rising productivity and high income elasticity of demand, they will grow on their own without aid, it was argued by economists like Ryutaro Komiya. But this argument assumes that firms are able to get into the race in the first place, and this, as we shall see, was not always possible. Some of the American fans of industrial policy suggested it should go on forever—and in America too.[1]

All of these views ignore the issue of time. Industrial policy works only under certain conditions and those conditions apply only during the catch-up era when a country is in the throes of the *transition* to industrial status.

The crux of the whole issue is *economies of scale*, especially as reinforced by learning curve efficiencies, rapid technological change and inter-industry externalities.

To illustrate this, we use two diagrams, one describing successful industrial policy and one counterproductive policy.

Initially in Figure A.1—which describes an *industry-wide* cost curve—when Japanese output is less than point x1, the scale of production is too small, and the industry has too little experience, to be efficient. We are more familiar with economies of scale at the plant level, where plants must have a certain minimum output to be efficient, and this too was important in Japan's takeoff era. But economies of scale also occur at the industry level. Perhaps the industry's efficiency depends on reaching such a size that individual firms can specialize to a greater degree; hence, the pace of innovation in the industry quickens with size and innovations developed in one firm are quickly emulated by technicians in other firms. Perhaps the industry must be a certain size before it can attract

Figure A.1 **The Economics of Successful Industrial Policy**

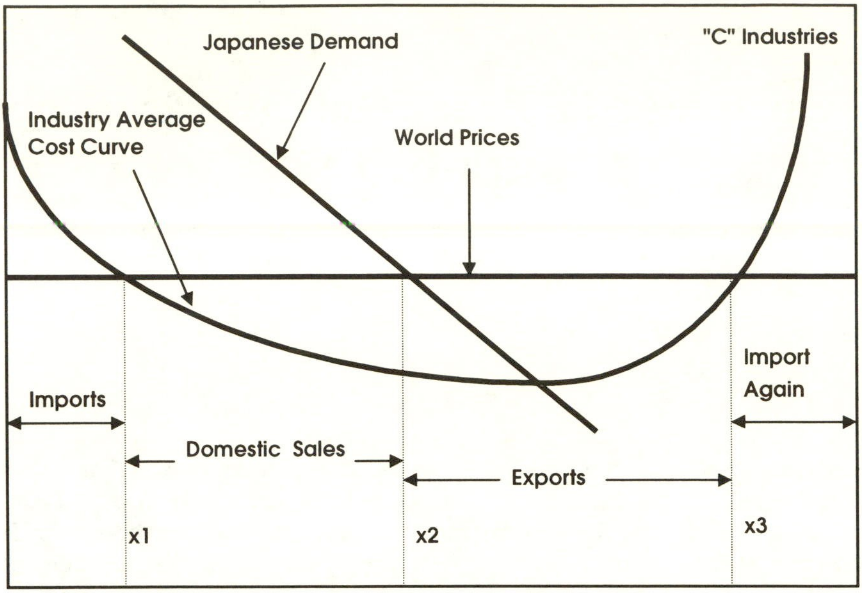

Source: Author's elaboration of chart by Itoh et. al. (1988), pg. 262
Note: The chart shows how cost per unit evolves in an industry enjoying economies of scale. Vertical axis shows cost; horizontal axis shows quantity. See text for explanation.

innovative suppliers, just as the PC industry had to reach a certain critical mass before a myriad of independent software developers sprang up. In some cases, industry efficiency may depend on the growth of other industries, e.g., perhaps steel cannot take off until rail infrastructure hits a certain size and railroads cannot take off until steel hits a certain cost level. Certainly the gathering of so many computer-related firms in Silicon Valley as well as the more general phenomenon of industry "clustering" discussed by Michael Porter[2] suggests that industry-wide economies of scale are quite widespread.

In any case, at point x1, production costs in Japan are above world prices. If the industry could somehow grow, costs would gradually decline until, after point x1, Japanese firms could compete with, and even beat, international competitors.

Because this is an *industry-wide* cost curve, not a *firm-level* cost curve, no individual producer acting on his own can either produce profitably in the sub-x1 state, or increase output above x1. Consequently, Japanese production will be *zero* and will remain there indefinitely. The product will be entirely imported.

Any modern economics textbook will tell you this is the classic condition for infant industry promotion.

(For a history of the "infant industry" and "increasing returns" arguments for protection, see Douglas Irwin's *Against the Tide* [1996], Chapters 8 and 9. Irwin notes that, in the view of many twentieth-century economists, the increasing returns argument depends on the existence of what Alfred Marshall called "external economies"—i.e., industry-wide or economy-wide returns to scale, learning-curve effects, knowledge spillovers, and so forth—rather than static firm-level returns to physical scale, known as "internal economies." Given the presence of external economies, F.Y. Edgeworth argued, each individual firm would face an upward sloping cost curve, but this cost curve would *shift* downward as industry output increased. Under these conditions, even if every *firm* supply curve sloped upward, the *industry* supply curve could still slope downward—until industry-wide increasing returns ran out. With learning-curve effects, the firm cost curve would also slope upwards, but rapidly shift downward with cumulative firm and industry experience. Prof. Motoshige Itoh and his colleagues make the same argument. Figure A.1 is based on the premise of external economies.)[3]

There are two ways to surmount the Catch-22 in Figure A.1. The first is government subsidy. Subsidies lower the cost curve in Figure A.1, thereby bringing Japanese prices closer to world prices.[4] But the gap between Japanese and world prices was so huge that subsidies were not sufficient. Temporary import protection was required.

Notice in Figure A.1 that, at small quantities, some Japanese customers are willing to pay prices far above world levels, as well as above the Japanese cost of production. Therefore, if imports were prohibited, the Japanese producers could sell profitably on the domestic market. That would give them the wherewithal to reduce their costs via economies of scale and learning-by-doing efficiencies until they were finally able to compete on their own without further aid. Itoh et al. explain:

> An alternative method [to subsidies] is to temporarily restrict the supply of the good from abroad, using domestic demand as the driving force for developing the industry. . . . Once output greater than x1 is achieved, even if import restrictions are removed, the industry will be able to develop.[5]

Indeed, if the industry develops sufficiently, its costs will actually go *below* world levels and it will no longer need protection. Indeed, beginning at point x2, it will become a major *exporter*.

Where this policy is appropriate and is applied correctly, we should see a clear evolution of industry growth in three stages:

1. Growth at first emerges under protectionism in response to domestic demand—going from zero output to x1;
2. Then, as the industry becomes able to match world prices, protection becomes superfluous and is removed. The industry grows on its own propelled mainly by domestic sales, going from x1 to x2;

3. Finally, as the industry is able to beat world prices and it has satisfied domestic demand, it becomes a major exporter. Indeed, its growth is driven primarily by exports—as it goes from x2 to x3.

This sequence is precisely what we saw in almost all of the leading industries of Japan's industrialization: autos, steel, shipbuilding, machinery, television, semiconductors, and so forth (Chapter 6).

Some economists have argued that exports played a secondary role in Japan's industrialization since most industries first became sizable and competitive by meeting domestic demand. Only then did they take on the export market. But that sequence is precisely what the model predicts.

How does the notion that import restrictions can promote growth square with the famous Bhagwati–Krueger research showing that "outward-oriented" countries grow faster than "inward-oriented" countries? The answer is this: "outward-oriented" does not mean "liberal." It simply means the country does a lot of trade, that there is an "absence of bias," meaning that any barriers to imports are balanced by boosts to exports. In Krueger's words:

> It is *bias reduction*, to a considerable *greater extent than it is liberalization* which brings about the export response [i.e., increased exports, emphasis added]. . . .
>
> [F]actors associated with better export performance explain whatever systematic differences there are in growth rates under different phases of the regime; *the fact that the regime itself is liberalized (or restricted) does not seem to have any additional independent effect* [emphasis added].[6]

In the high-growth era, Japan's trade volumes were high because its import restrictions were balanced by export promotion. It was both protectionist and outward-oriented. It was neomercantilist.

Normally, according to standard economic theory, restrictions on imports end up being restrictions on exports. A restriction on imports leads to a bigger trade surplus, thus a higher currency, and thus to lower exports. So, it may be objected: how can we argue that Japan's import restrictions have promoted exports? Paul Krugman has answered this question, using the same assumptions as the Itoh model. Under conditions of increasing return to scale, import protection can actually enhance, rather than inhibit, exports. Krugman notes:

> When businessmen try to explain the success of Japanese firms in export markets, they often mention the advantage of a protected home market. . . . They are assured of the economies of large-scale production, of selling enough over time to move down the learning curve, of earning enough to recover the costs of R&D. While charging high prices in the domestic market, they can "incrementally price" and flood foreign markets with low-cost products. . . . Yet it is an argument that economists schooled in standard trade theory tend to find incomprehensible. In a world of perfect competition and constant returns to scale, protecting a product can never

cause it to be exported. . . . [But] the businessman's view of import protection as export promotion makes sense . . . [if] markets are both oligopolistic and segmented . . . [and if there] is some kind of economies of scale.[7]

Conditions for Successful Industrial Policy

Figure A.1 makes it very clear that there are certain indispensable conditions that distinguish a successful industrial policy from crass protectionism.

Export Competitiveness Is the Test

Subsidy and protection make sense only if the industry is ultimately able to beat world prices on its own. Government protection and promotion can provide the "greenhouse" under which companies can germinate, but sooner or later they must either flower on their own, or die. The Toyota's and Sony's of Japan succeeded; aircraft and petrochemicals never did.

Hence, the issue of exports is absolutely crucial. Unless the companies expect to have to eventually meet world-class standards, protection will hinder, not help, productivity improvements.

This is what differentiates Japan's success from Latin America's failed import-substitution (ISI) strategy. Where the Japanese strategy was applied successfully, import-substitution was simply a phase on the way toward a major export presence. Eads and Yamamura comment:

> [U]nlike the industrial policies of many European states, the touchstone for these policies was competitiveness in international markets.[8]

Fierce Competition at Home

Industrial policy relieves domestic industries of foreign competition so as to give them a breathing space. However, it is competition alone that compels industries to improve. Therefore, if foreign competitors are removed from the scene, competition at home must be fierce enough to make up for the lack of foreign competition. That can only happen if the domestic market is large enough to support several competitors.

In terms of Figure A.1, that means the cost curve for individual firms must turn up well to the left of the Japanese demand curve to make it possible to have several profitable Japanese competitors.

While populous Japan was fortunate to have a large domestic market, MITI as a matter of policy simultaneously promoted several firms in key industries to ensure competition. It never promoted single "national champions," unlike the Europeans. The major exception came in telecommunications where the Ministry of Posts and Telecommunications (MPT) promoted the formerly state-owned

Nippon Telephone and Telegraph (NTT) as a national champion. On the other hand, MITI also tried—not always with success—to limit entry to the chosen few. Since economies of scale were critical, MITI wanted enough industries to maintain competition but not so many as to create what it considered "excessive competition" and price wars. As Itoh et al. put it:

> When the number of firms is excessively small, price is probably close to the monopoly price. ... In the Japanese steel and petrochemical industries, or in the integrated circuit industry where learning by doing was important, there were 10 to 15 firms (a relatively large number) engaged in vigorous competition, which we believe underlay the good performance of these oligopolistic markets. In this the large size of the domestic Japanese market played a very important role.[9]

This condition suggests that smaller countries may not be able to emulate Japan's tactics.

A "Sunset" Provision for Ending Protection

Once industries come close to reaching world prices, protection must end, as we discuss in detail immediately below.

Why the System Soured

Perhaps the greatest danger in industrial policy is not that aid is given to the wrong industries—although this is a big danger. The greatest danger is that the policy goes on far too long. Protection and aid must be ended once an industry is close to meeting world prices. Otherwise, it will simply be a permanent crutch. This is the heart of Japan's post-1973 problems.

This issue is illustrated in Figure A.2, where "C" industries are those with the potential to become exporters and "Not-C" are those industries whose costs never go low enough to meet world prices.

True infant industries, the "C" industries, have a "life cycle." From zero production to $x1$, they require shelter. As they get larger, costs go down until they finally go below world prices at $x1$. Then, from $x1$ to $x2$ they can succeed on their own on the basis of domestic sales without further protection and promotion. Then, from $x2$ to $x3$, they will become big exporters. After $x3$, as costs rise again to a point above world prices, they can no longer export successfully and the country will begin to import the product again. They have become "formerly competitive" industries. In the meantime, the country will have moved on to other industries in which it now has greater comparative advantage.

If, as in Japan, protection is applied to "senile industries, i.e., "C" industries after they pass $x3$ (as was the case of Japanese textiles, shipbuilding and steel, for example), this will be entirely counterproductive from the standpoint of the economy.

Figure A.2 **When Accelerationism Works and When It Doesn't**

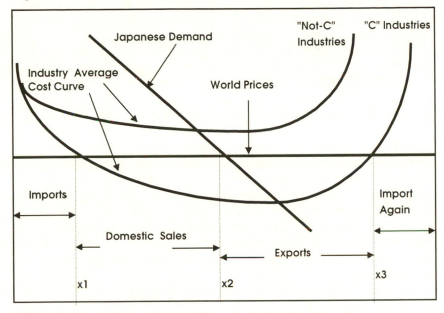

Source: Author's elaboration of chart by Itoh et. al. (1988), pg. 262
Note: This chart compares what happens when protectionism is applied to competitive
infant industries (C industries), and when it is applied to non-competitive ("Not-C"
industries). Costs in "Not-C" industries never meet world prices. For explanation, see
text. Vertical axis shows price/cost. Horizontal axis shows quantity.

In the "Not-C" industries, at no point do costs ever come down to world
prices. No matter how much aid these industries are given, they will never be
able to be competitive on their own. Such industries should never be given
protection because they would need to be permanent wards of the state at great
cost to the overall development of the economy. Yet, this is exactly what Japan
did, particularly in the post-1973 era.

Over time, the brunt of Japanese protectionism gradually switched. As we saw in
Figure 2.5, initially, the lion's share of protection went to "C" industries in their
infancy. But after 1973, industries that never had global competitiveness in the first
place—e.g., paper, glass, cement—or industries which lost it—e.g., textiles, shipbuilding and steel—continued to receive powerful protection with enormous
costs to Japan.

One does not even have to presume a change of operating procedure to see
how this shift could gradually occur. Imagine a situation in which all industries
operating above world prices, no matter what their future potential, receive
equivalent protection. Then, once they no longer need it, protection is lifted. In

such a case, some industries will become exporters and will be seen as stars. As protection of them is lifted, who will be left with protection? Precisely those industries that have not yet—and probably never will—meet world prices, as well as those that once met world prices but no longer do.

But in fact, as shown by the rebound in the co-efficient of variation in Figure A.3, it was not inertia, but active political intervention, that caused this shift from promoting winners to protecting losers.

Market-Conforming versus Market-Defying Industrial Policy

When neoclassical economists say the market allocates resources to their most efficient use, they mean that the marginal private return to the individual consumer or producer or investor equals the marginal return to society as a whole. If the conditions for competitive markets are met, this usually happens.

Market-conforming industrial policy addresses a problem of "market failure" where, for some reason, the private returns are greater than or less than social returns. We mentioned in the text the problem of insufficient R&D because the company doing the R&D can only capture a small part of the benefits. Market-conforming industrial policy, like an R&D tax credit, raises the private return to make it equal to the social return in order to generate enough R&D. Pollution is a case of private returns being too great relative to social returns. Fines lower the private returns and reduce pollution. Using subsidies and protection to overcome infant industry problems is also a case of raising private returns to match social returns so as to increase the desired activity. Society as a whole is better off.

Market-defying industrial policy, as in Japan's protection of inefficient industries, represents the opposite effect. In this case, protection and subsidies raise private returns *above* social returns. The result is too much of an undesirable activity. The effect is the same as if society rewarded pollution. The return to the economy as a whole is negative.

Figure A.3 **The Fall and Rise of Japanese Protectionism**

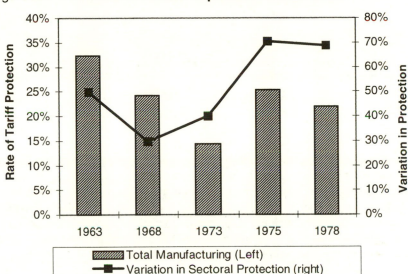

Source: Author calculations based on data in Itoh and Kiyono (1988), pg. 161

Note: In Figure A.3, the bar measures the effective rate of protection (ERP) for manufac-turing as a whole. The line labeled "Variation in Sectoral Protection" measures how much ERP rates vary from sector to sector using a statistical index called the co-efficient of variation. The higher the index, the more variation. In the early 1960s, the variation was relatively high as exporting sectors received a lot of protection. In 1968, it was lower as high tariffs in exporting sectors came down to match relatively lower tariffs elsewhere. In the 1970s, the variation rebounded to new heights as tariffs contin-ued to decline in exporting sectors, but were imposed again on import-competing sectors.

Appendix B

Controversy over Export-Led Industrialization

A lot of ink has been spilled in a controversy over whether or not Japan's industrial takeoff was export-led or domestic-led. This is a false dichotomy. Under conditions of economies of scale and inter-industry externalities, anything that promoted growth, whether exports or domestic demand, lowered costs, thereby leading to a further increase in demand, and still lower costs. Since exports helped the key exporting industries grow faster than they would have through domestic demand alone, exports played a vital role in Japan's industrial takeoff. Notably the industries that grew fastest through exports also grew fastest at home.

Krause and Sekiguchi disagree. Using an argument originated by Richard Caves, they argue that, for growth to be export-led, price and quantity should be *positively* correlated in the export goods, but in Japan, they were *negatively* correlated. The argument is that, if exports are growing because of higher foreign demand, price and quantity will be positively correlated. But if exports are growing because changes in the domestic economy lower the supply curve for exports, the price and quantity will be negatively correlated.[10]

But this argument ignores the issue of economies of scale. As Tsuru explains, expanding an industry through exports "make[s] full use of the economy of scale so that price and quantity changes become *negatively* correlated [emphasis added]."[11]

Masahiro Takemoto argues that the distinction between exporting and domestic sources of growth is a false one since both contributed to the business profits that perpetuated growth.[12]

Appendix C

Reading the Econometric Tables

The essential principle of econometrics is very basic. Economic theory tells us that, on average, countries that invest more grow faster. But how much more? Does a country that invests twice as much of its GDP as a neighbor grow twice as fast, 10 percent faster, or at some other rate? Similarly, if the price of cars rises by 5 percent, theory tells us that people will buy fewer of them. But 1 percent fewer or 10 percent fewer? Theory can't answer that. The statistical technique of econometric regressions can.

In order to answer these questions, we have to make sure that other factors aren't interfering. For example, theory tells us that middle-income countries, on average, grow faster than richer ones. So, if we want to see how much investment rates affect growth, we have to adjust for the different levels of income.

Once we consider the various factors that affect growth—e.g., level of income, educational attainment, investment rates, level of trade and so forth—we can estimate how fast a country is expected to grow at any given period of time. We can also tell whether it is getting the same growth rate from the various growth-promoting factors, like investment and education, as other countries.

The same techniques allow us to explore a whole range of issues, from how much a country trades relative to GDP, to how much a currency change affects import levels, to how much interest rates affect savings, or even how much nutrition affects childhood growth.

In Table D.2 on page 368, the dependent variable is the rate of growth in 1973–90. The independent variables (i.e., causative factors in growth) are GDP in 1973, investment:GDP ratio, population size, trade:GDP ratio and education attainment.

We use logarithms for the following reason. In the case of investment ratios, if we didn't use logarithms, then the equation would be assuming that the difference between a country investing 5 percent of GDP and one investing 10 percent of GDP is the same as the difference between one investing 25 percent and another investing 30 percent. Even though the absolute difference in both pairs is 5 percent of GDP, this distorts the picture. In the first pair, the latter country is investing at twice the rate as the first. In the second pair, the second country is investing only 20 percent more than the first. With logarithms, we are measuring what happens when a country increases its investment by 10 percent or 20 percent no matter what its starting level.

Now let's look at Table D.2. The first line gives the result. The intercept may for now be ignored. Ln 1973 and Ln 1973^2 means the GDP level in 1973 and the square of its level. The 11.6 for Ln 1973 and negative 0.7 for Ln 1973^2 means that, initially, as very poor countries get a little richer they grow faster. But after awhile, with diminishing returns, this effect tapers off. They reach their fastest rate of growth as middle-income newly industrializing countries. After that, the richer they get the more slowly they grow as indicated by the negative 0.7 for Ln 1973^2. This is exactly what we saw in the "arc of development" discussed in Chapter 6. The positive 2.5 for Ln I/Y (the investment rate) means that, once we adjust for the level of GDP per worker, the more a country invests the faster it will grow. Positive numbers for the other factors mean that the more populous a country is, the more it trades and the more its people are educated, the faster it will grow.

Under each of the numbers is a number in percentages. This percentage tells us how reliable—or, in technical terms "significant"—the result is. Specifically, it shows us the probability that the result is the product of pure coincidence. That is, does higher investment really raise growth or is the statistical correlation just a coincidence? In Table D.2, the 0.6 percent under investment rates tells us there is only a 0.6 percent chance that investment has no effect on growth rates. The 4.1 percent figure under trade tells us that there is just a 4 percent chance that trade has no effect. With low numbers like that, we can safely accept the notion that, once we hold other factors constant, nations that trade more grow faster.

The R^2 number tells us how much of the variation from country to country in growth rates is explained by the independent variables. In Table D.2, the Adjusted R^2 of 91 percent tells us that 91 percent of the difference in growth rates of Germany, Japan, the U.S. and all the other countries can be explained by the factors we have included. That is very high explanatory success.

Since, however, about 10 percent of the difference cannot be explained, there is some residual between the growth rate that the model predicts for a given country and its actual growth rate. The standard error term of 0.46 means that, on average, the actual growth of a country is 0.46 percent above or below what the model predicts. For example, in Equation 2 of Table D.1, under Japan prediction and residual, we see that Japan was predicted to grow 7.84 percent a year in 1960–70, whereas it actually grew 0.5 percent faster.

A "dummy" is used when the pattern in a country or group of countries is so far from the norm—i.e., it is an "outlier"—that the equation as a whole fits better if allowance is made for this. In this case, there is something special about that country that causes its growth to react differently to the factors we have used than most other countries. In Equation 1 of Table D.1, the "Japan dummy" is 1.4 percent, meaning that Japan, during 1960–70, grew 1.4 percent *faster* than the model predicted. In Table D.2, the "Japan dummy" is –1.31 percent meaning that Japan grew 1.3 percent more *slowly* than the model predicted.

How do we know when to use the "Japan dummy"? In Table D.2, the probability percentage tells us there is only a 6.2 percent chance of the result being pure coincidence. As a matter of convention, if this figure is below 10 percent, the result is accepted. So the regression tells us that something special about Japan made it grow more slowly during 1973–90 than the typical country with its attributes would have grown. In Table D.1, the chance of coincidence is 13 percent; 13 percent is pretty close to 10 percent, but it could be considered suggestive rather than conclusive. So, in Table D.1, which result is more accurate, that of Equation 1 with the "dummy" or Equation 2 without it? While the probability statistic does not quite reach the 10 percent threshold, the "standard error" is smaller in Equation 1 with the dummy than in Equation 2. So we judge that Equation 1 is probably a bit more accurate, although the true result may lie somewhere in between.

We will find throughout this appendix section that the use of a "Japan dummy" is justified. This indicates that, in many features of its economy, Japan's patterns lie far from the norm. It is an "outlier" in many respects.

Finally, the "F-test" tells us the odds that the entire equation is the result of coincidence. In Equation 1 of Table D.1, the chance of that is less than 1 percent. The result is 99.1 percent reliable. In Equation 2, the result is 99.5 percent reliable.

Appendix D

From Superstar to Laggard: The Growth Model

In Chapter 4, we argued that Japan's economic policies created a true economic miracle during the high-growth era of the 1950s and 1960s, but that these policies became counterproductive after 1973 and that, contrary to popular impression, Japanese growth started to become sub-par as early as the 1970s and 1980s. This assertion is confirmed by a cross-country regression based on the "conditional convergence" model developed by Robert Barro and Xavier Sala-i-Martin.[13] Japan performed *above* model projections in 1960–70, but *below* in 1973–90.

Before discussing the model results in detail, let us give the theoretical background for the "conditional convergence" growth model.

The conditional convergence model was developed as an answer to the well-known predictive flaws in the standard neoclassical model developed by Robert Solow. It is a modification of that model, and, unlike recent "endogenous growth" models, accepts the Solow model's fundamental premise of diminishing returns to capital.

In the Solow model, (top panel of Figure D.1), $Y/L = f(k)$, where Y/L is the output per worker and k is the capital–labor ratio. $S^1 * f(k)$ is the savings curve determined by a fixed savings:GDP ratio, e.g., 15 percent. $N + d$ equals the investment rate just high enough to cover population growth and depreciation and keep k steady. As long as $S > I$, k keeps rising and consequently, so does per worker income. The steady-state equilibrium is reached when $S = I$, i.e., $s^1 * f(k) = n + d$ at P1. Once it reaches this steady state, the only source of long-term growth is exogenous disembodied technological change.

In the transition to the steady-state, as seen in the bottom panel, the economy's growth rate $= [S*f(k)/k] - [n + d]$. The model is characterized by diminishing returns since, at all points, $f(k)$ grows more slowly than k. Hence, growth steadily declines with rising k, i.e., rising per worker GDP.

This model implies "absolute convergence." That is, relative growth is *solely* a function of relative k. Neither policies nor institutions, nor savings rates matter. All poorer nations, where k is lower, grow faster than all richer nations. Assuming a constant capital:labor share, then relative growth is solely a function of relative GDP per worker. Figure 4.2 is based on the absolute convergence hypothesis.

Figure D.1 **Absolute vs. Conditional Convergence**

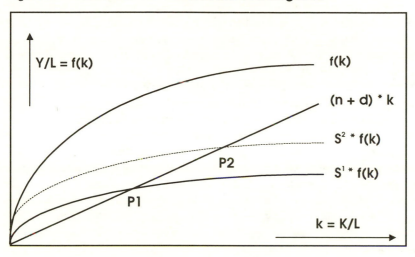

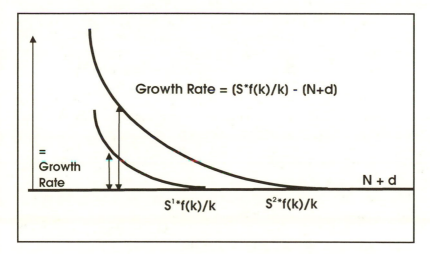

Source: Adapted by author from Barro and Sala-i-Martin (1995)

However, there is a fatal flaw in this hypothesis. Its predictions don't come true. If absolute convergence prevailed, Africa, not Asia, would be the world's fastest growing continent. A host of studies have refuted the absolute convergence prediction.

Quite a number of economists have tried to come up with solutions that correct the absolute convergence corollary of the neoclassical model without losing that model's virtues. We believe the effort by Robert Barro and Xavier Sala-i-Martin is the most convincing.[14]

As Barro and Sala-i-Martin point out, the implicit premise of absolute convergence is that all nations are converging on the same steady-state per worker income (an imputed, but never-reached moving target). Policies, institutions and so forth don't matter. The rationale is that, given mobility of capital, technology and education, all nations are on the same production function—just at different points on it. But, if we drop this assumption, then we can modify the model in such a way that it holds both theoretically and empirically.

For example, what happens if a nation increases its savings rate to 25 percent of GDP, i.e., $S^2f(k)$ in Figure D.1? Then the steady-state point is moved to P2, where both k and per worker income are higher than at P1. Moreover, immediately the distance between $S^*f(k)/k$ and n + d increases. Hence, growth accelerates.

In the absolute convergence hypothesis, the interpretation is that the increase in growth is simply "transitional." But, as Barro and Sala-i-Martin point out, the "transition" can take decades or even a century or more. Even after 40 years, stellar Korea has only cut the per worker income gap with the U.S. from 11 percent of U.S. levels to about 50 percent. Such a lengthy differential in growth rates cannot be discounted as transitional.

Even more important, Barro and Sala-i-Martin persuasively argue that nations are not all aiming for the same steady-state point. If a rich nation has a permanently higher savings rate than a poor one, and if the differential is sufficiently high, then $[S^*f(k)/k] - [n + d]$ would be bigger in the rich country. The rich nation will grow faster than the poor one indefinitely, despite a higher level of k. And so, the convergence is *conditional*. Africa grows more slowly than Asia because its steady-state target is lower. (In practice, S/Y tends to decrease once nations become rich. This, along with diminishing returns to k, is why growth invariably decelerates after the industrial takeoff is over.)

In addition, since about 80 percent of technological change is embodied in capital equipment, higher investment rates mean faster absorption of modern technology—and faster growth.

De Long and Summers estimate that each 3 percent increase in the ratio of investment in equipment to GDP raises GDP growth by 1 percent.[15]

The bottom line: whether, and how fast, a nation converges on the leader depends on several "conditional" variables, not just k.

The savings rate is only one factor in producing higher growth. Other "conditional variables" also affect growth. They do this by influencing A, the technological parameter in the neoclassical model. In the neoclassical model, long-term growth is solely a function of A, which equates to Total Factor Productivity (TFP). In the absolute convergence model, this is assumed to be a product of exogenous, disembodied technological change.

Barro and Sala-i-Martin, however, show that a number of conditional variables elevate A or TFP, including educational attainment levels, political and macroeconomic stability, and trade openness. By raising A, these variables can elevate long-run growth.

Figure D.2 **Trade Elevates the Production Function, Raises Growth**

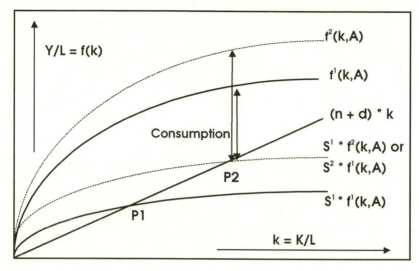

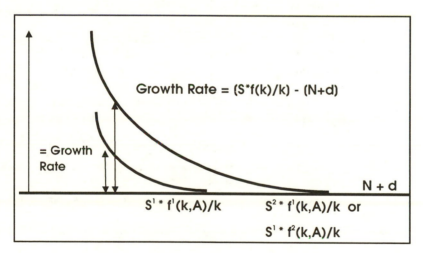

Source: Bottom panel adapted by author from Barro and Sala-i-Martin (1995)

In Figure D.2, suppose we keep the savings rate at its original 15 percent. Now, let us suppose that, through more education, more trade, and so forth, we raise the production function to $f^2(k,A)$. Let's make $f^2(k,A)$ high enough so that 15 percent of the higher GDP is the same as 25 percent of the original GDP. In other words, the new savings curve $S^1*f^2(k,A)$ coincides with $S^2*f^1(k,A)$. In this case, the steady-state would still move from P1 to P2. And the growth rate would still rise.

In fact, as the regressions in Table E.1 will confirm, the more a country trades, the less it has to invest to get the same amount of growth.

But, what a difference in terms of welfare. Consumption equals the distance between f(k,A) and s*f(k,A). At P2, consumption will be higher in the case of trade-led growth.

In the cross-country regressions shown in Table D.1, Table D.2, and Table D.3, we use this model to judge Japan's growth performance in the catch-up era and the 1973–90 period. In this estimation, we regressed growth in GDP per worker on five variables: initial GDP, population, the investment:GDP ratio, years of secondary education for all adults, and the trade:GDP ratio (all independent variables in log form).[16]

Growth was, as expected, negatively related to initial GDP and positively related to the investment rate (i.e., investment:GDP ratio).

(Some analysts, arguing from an absolute convergence standpoint, have argued that growth should not be regressed on the investment rate, but rather on the growth of capital stock. However, in the conditional convergence model, growth is regressed on the investment rate.)[17]

Growth was also positively related to population. Presumably larger populations provided economies of scale, while enhancing competition by decreasing industrial concentration.

In 1960–70, trade openness was positive for a subset of 10 countries with less than 20 million people, where trade averaged over 50 percent of GDP. But it was not significant for the whole group, where trade:GDP ratios were lower. Trade appears not to have been large enough relative to GDP in 1960–70 to show up as a significant factor in growth for big countries. By 1973–90, when trade averaged 55 percent for the group as a whole, it did become significant for the whole group.

The fact that both population and trade boost growth suggests that one of the reasons trade boosts growth is because it enlarges the effective economic population of a country. This is coherent with the well-known finding that less populous countries have higher trade:GDP ratios.

Education was not significant during 1960–70, but it was positive and significant in 1973–90.

During 1960–70, as we see in Equation 1 of Table D.1, *Japan's growth was 1.4 percent above model predictions.* Its GDP per worker rose 8.4 percent a year, compared to a projection of only 7.0 percent. Moreover, a dummy for Japan is both sizable and positive. At a 13 percent P-value, it almost reaches the 10 percent significance level, and the dummy lowers the standard error of the equation.

Even without using a Japan dummy, Japan's growth was still 0.5 percent above the model's 7.8 percent projection.

By contrast, *in 1973–90, Japan underperformed* (Table D.2). *It only grew 3.0 percent a year whereas the model projected 4.3 percent.* The dummy for Japan is significant at the 6 percent level.

As we discussed in Chapter 4, one of the most important reasons for Japan's

Table D.1

Growth Regressions, 1960–70 (Dependent variable = Annual growth in GDP per worker)

Eq.	Intercept	Ln 1960	Ln 1960^2	Ln I/Y	Ln I/Y^2	Ln pop	Ln pop^2	Japan prediction and resid.	Japan dummy	R^2	Standard error	F-test
1	−213 0.0%	18.7 1.0%	−1.21 0.4%	52.8 1.1%	−7.7 1.6%	11.6 3.4%	−0.57 3.9%		1.40 13.2%	0.90	0.53	26.9 0.009%
2	−199 0.0%	16.9 2.0%	−1.12 0.8%	62.9 0.3%	−9.2 0.5%	7.2 11.4%	−0.35 13.3%	7.84 0.50		0.89	0.56	27.8 0.005%
3	−159 0.1%	11.6 16.0%	−0.82 7.7%	76.4 0.3%	−11.5 0.4%			7.38 1.00		0.81	0.74	23.8 0.009%
4	−155 0.1%	12.5 11.7%	−0.86 5.6%	71.2 0.4%	−10.8 0.5%				1.38 11.8%	0.83	0.70	21.5 0.001%

Source: Author's calculation based on data from Summers and Heston (1995); Barro and Lee (1994)

Note: The variable labeled 1960 means GDP in year 1960. I/Y = investment/GDP ratio. Pop = Population. Ln = natural logarithm.

The percentage numbers underneath the coefficients are the probability values of the T–statistic numbers. Equations 1 and 2 leave out the U.S., Equations 3 and 4 contain the U.S., but leave out the population variable. For an explanation of this process, see footnote 16. Note that Equations 1 and 4 give similar results for the Japan dummy.

Table D.2

Growth Regressions, 1973–90 (Dependent variable = Annual growth in GDP per worker)

Intercept	Ln 1973	Ln 1973^2	Ln I/Y	Ln pop	Ln trade	Ln edu 75–85	Japan dummy	Adj. R^2	Standard error	F–Test
−56.2	11.6	−0.7	2.5	0.5	0.7	0.7	−1.31	0.91	0.46	34.2
1.3%	1.7%	0.6%	0.6%	0.2%	4.1%	0.5%	6.2%			0.0%

Source: Author's calculation based on data from Summers and Heston (1995); Barro and Lee (1994)

Note: The variable labeled 1973 means GDP in year 1973. I/Y = investment/GDP. Pop = Population. Edu = average years of secondary education for all adults. Trade = (exports + imports)/GDP ratio. Ln = natural logarithm.

The percentage numbers underneath the coefficients are the probability values of the T-statistic numbers.

Table D.3

Growth Regressions, 1986–90 (Dependent variable = Annual growth in GDP per worker)

	Intercept	Ln 1986 Y	Ln 1986²	Ln pop	Ln I/Y	Ln trade	Japan prediction and resid.	Japan dummy	Adj. R²	Standard error	F-test
1986–90	−96	18.7	−1.1	2.4	1.0	1.7	3.9		0.86	0.76	27.6
	11.6%	14.1%	9.1%	3.0%	0.0%	0.3%	−0.6				0.0%

Source: Author's calculation based on data from Summers and Heston (1995); Barro and Lee (1994)

Note: The variable labeled 1986 means GDP in year 1986. I/Y = investment/GDP ratio. Pop = Population. Trade = (exports + imports)/GDP ratio. Ln = natural logarithm. In 1986, the educational attainment variable was not significant and an equation with it produces almost identical results.

The percentage numbers underneath the coefficients are the probability values of the T–statistic numbers.

Table D.4

Growth Regressions, 1975-90 (Dependent variable = Annual growth in GDP per worker)

	Intercept	Ln 1975	Ln 1975^2	Ln pop	Ln I/Y	Ln trade	Ln edu 75-85	Japan prediction and resid	Japan dummy	Adj. R^2	Standard error	F-Test
Eq. 1	−79.1	16.9	−1.0	0.5	2.1	0.7	0.7		−1.1	0.88	0.53	24.9
	0.8%	0.9%	0.4%	0.4%	2.6%	7.5%	1.5%		15.6%			0.0%
Eq. 2	−65.0	14.1	−0.9	0.5	1.6	0.8	0.7	4.1		0.87	0.55	26.6
	2.0%	2.1%	0.9%	0.9%	6.6%	4.4%	2.5%	−0.6				0.0%

Source: Author's calculation based on data from Summers and Heston (1995); Barro and Lee (1994)

Note: The variable labeled 1975 means GDP in year 1975. I/Y = investment/GDP. Pop = Population. Trade = (exports + imports)/GDP. Edu = average years of secondary education for all adults. Ln = natural logarithm.

The percentage numbers underneath the coefficients are the probability values of the T-statistic numbers.

poor performance is its incredibly low productivity of capital. The regression reported in Table E.1 projects that Japan should have been able to achieve its 1973–90 growth with only 25 percent of GDP devoted to investment instead of 35 percent.

Since the onset of the laggard period coincides with the two oil shocks, we tested whether Japan's poor performance was simply the result of its special vulnerability to high oil prices.

First of all, we did a separate check for 1986–90, when oil prices had fallen back and when the "bubble" had raised Japanese growth. Once again, Japan showed a sub-par performance, 3.4 percent growth versus a forecast of 3.9 percent (Table D.3). Japan invested a lot, but got low returns. A dummy for Japan was not significant.

We also tested the period of 1975–90, instead of 1973–90 (Table D.4). The purpose of this was to eliminate the possibility that the results were skewed by the 1973–74 recession that followed the first oil shock. The results more or less conform to the results of the 1973–90 period as a whole. Japan's grew at 3.5 percent a year during that period. This was a full 1.1 percent *below* the model projection in Equation 1 for 1975–90. That's almost as large as the 1.3 percent shortfall shown from 1973–90 in Table D.2. At a P-value of 15 percent, the Japan dummy in this equation is suggestive, but not as conclusive as in the model run for 1973–90 as a whole. However, even if we don't use a dummy, the residual for Japan suggests that Japan's growth was still 0.6 percent a year below the projection.

It was not the oil shocks, but Japan's poor response, that caused the post-1973 malaise.[18]

As shown by the dummies for 1960–70 and 1973–90, "something special" made Japan a growth superstar in the industrialization era and a laggard after it reached maturity. We believe that, in both cases, part of that "something special" was Japan's trade patterns.

Appendix E

Trade and Growth

A host of studies, and our own regressions, have shown that countries which trade more grow faster. Suppose, for example, that in 1973–90, instead of the actual trade:GDP ratio of 23 percent, Japan's trade:GDP had reached what our trade regression in Table F.1 projects: 33 percent of GDP. If we plug that 33 percent level into our growth model (Equation 1 of Table D.2), then Japan's predicted growth would have been about 10 percent faster. Even with all its other problems, it still would have grown at 3.25 percent a year instead of its actual pace of 3.0 percent.[19]

Unfortunately, the notion that greater trade openness accelerates growth is theoretically difficult to justify in the dominant Heckscher–Olin–Samuelson (HOS) trade model. In that model, an increase in trade improves resource allocation, but this only raises the *level* of GDP on a one-shot basis, not its ongoing *growth rate*. Moreover, it is the *increase* in the trade:GDP ratio, say from 20 percent to 40 percent, that yields the gain. But the data show that growth is a function of the *level* of openness.

Finally, the *size* of the gain from trade within the HOS model is surprisingly small. For example, Sazanami et al. estimate that, even though protectionism lowers Japan's imports by 20 percent, the cost to Japan is only 0.6 percent of GDP—far less than our results show. If the cost of a closed market were really that small, free traders would find themselves hard put to justify putting a country through all the pain of transitional costs.[20]

We contend that the HOS model's difficulty in explaining growth lies in its fundamental premise that all nations use identical technology and have equal efficiencies in each industry. In this model, differences in comparative advantage, as well as gains from trade, arise solely from different factor endowments, i.e., Mexico and the U.S. gain from trade with each other because Mexico has little capital but lots of cheap labor, while the U.S. has the reverse. So Mexico exports labor-intensive goods and imports capital-intensive goods, while the U.S. does the reverse. Through this exchange, each country is richer than before the trade.

In fact, if the HOS model were a complete explanation of trade, it would predict that advanced nations' trade with each other would *diminish* as their factor endowments became more similar. In reality, the opposite is true.

But the HOS model is not the only model of comparative advantage. And, in an alternative model, the Modified Ricardian Model (MRM), the opposite is assumed: that technologies and efficiencies differ substantially even among countries with similar factor endowments.

Research by Dollar and Wolff shows that trade among advanced nations corresponds more closely to the MRM assumptions than the HOS premise. They find that advanced countries show *economy-wide* convergence of terms of capital–labor ratios and TFP, but much less convergence on an *industry* basis, and note how this contradicts HOS premises. They also find that one of the big reasons for the existence of trade is that these countries specialize according to differences in TFP by industry.[21]

In fact, we would argue that the very thing that the HOS model assumes to be true *prior* to trade is precisely what is achieved *by means* of trade: convergence in technology and productivity on an industry basis. And that is why trade enhances growth. That is why advanced nations continue to trade so much with each other. As Dollar and Wolff put it:

> [T]he manufacturing sector, which is the most open in trade and investment, consistently showed the least variation in productivity levels. . . . Dispersion in productivity level was particularly high in sectors that are insulated from international trade, such as utilities [and] services. . . . *The results support the argument that international trade plays a crucial role in the convergence process* [emphasis added].[22]

This explains why trade in *competing products* most enhances growth. It does this by forcing companies to converge upon the world's best practice upon pain of extinction. This suggests that, if our growth regressions had used trade in manufactured goods (as a proxy for trade in substitutes) instead of total trade, we might have found an even tighter connection between trade and growth than we did.[23]

Earlier (page 366), we argued that, according to the conditional convergence model, the more a country traded, the less it had to invest to achieve the same rate of growth. This is confirmed in Table E.1. Regressing investment on trade, holding growth and other factors constant, gives a negative co-efficient for trade.

Suppose during 1973–90, Japan's trade:GDP ratio had been 33 percent instead of 23 percent, as our trade regressions project. It would only have had to invest 33 percent of GDP instead of 35 percent to attain the same growth rate. *It could have raised consumption by 2 percent of GDP without sacrificing any growth.*

Moreover, Table E.1 also confirms Japan's extraordinarily low productivity of capital. As shown by the "Japan dummy" for investment, *Japan had to invest 35 percent of GDP to get the same growth that a typical country could have gained by investing only 25 percent of GDP.*

Whereas Japan tried—and failed—to achieve high growth by emphasizing investment, the Asian NICs relied more on trade (see Chapter 10).

Table E.1

To Get Growth, the More Trade the Less Investment (Dependent variable = Average investment/GDP during 1973–90)

	Intercept	Ln 1973	Ln 1973^2	Ln growth	Ln growth^2	Ln (pop)	Ln (trade)	Japan dummy	Japan forecast and resid.	Adj. R^2	Standard error	F-test
1	9.9 16.0%	-1.394 36.1%	0.089 30.1%	0.199 17.1%	0.097 21.4%	-0.116 0.9%	-0.159 9.7%	0.338 4.5%		0.43	0.124	3.375 2.3%
2	203.5 22.0%	2.344 25.5%	-36.938 31.0%	5.319 12.6%	2.248 22.7%	-2.962 0.6%	-4.141 7.2%	9.664 1.9%		0.50	2.936	4.126 1.0%
3	6.2 41.7%	0.046 63.0%	-0.590 72.8%	0.233 17.4%	0.092 31.3%	-0.105 3.4%	-0.206 8.3%		3.327 22.4%	0.27	0.142	2.304 8.9%

Source: Author's calculation based on data from Summers and Heston (1995); Barro and Lee (1994)
Eq. 1—The dependent variable is Ln I/Y. I/Y = investment/GDP. The dummy is equivalent to 10% of GDP
Eq. 2—The dependent variable is I/Y
Eq. 3—The dependent variable is Ln I/Y. There is no Japanese dummy. The residual is equivalent to 7% of GDP
The variable labeled 1973 means GDP in year 1973. The variable labeled growth means the rate of growth in real GDP per worker from 1973 to 1990. Pop = Population. Trade = (exports + imports)/GDP. Education was not significant. Ln = natural logarithm.
The percentage numbers underneath the co-efficients are the probability values of the T-statistic numbers.

The MRM model also sheds a lot of light on why Japanese trade policy became so pervasively and perversely protectionist in the 1970s-80s. As Sachs and Warner point out:

> [Under] the Ricardo-Viner theory [i.e., factor-specific MRM model] . . . when capital or labor cannot move between sectors, the immobile factors should tend to favor protectionism for their own sector. . . . Firms with sunk capital in the import-competing sector and workers with skills specific to that sector, should tend to favor protection of that sector.[24]

Since, in a world of intra-industry trade, so many sectors are potentially import-competing, factor immobility will produce widespread demands for protection. As we saw in Chapter 7, Japan suffered increasing factor immobility beginning in the 1970s. Thus, it is not surprising that demands for protection increased.

Moreover, the MRM model predicts precisely the economic consequences that we discussed in Chapter 3: a transfer of income from the exporting sectors to the import-competing sectors. As Peter Kenen points out, where factors are immobile, protectionism raises incomes of both capital and labor in the import-competing sectors and *lowers* returns to both capital and labor in the *export* sector.[25]

This economic logic suggests that Japan's exporting firms may eventually become a source for anti-protectionist politics, as they have in other countries. This is yet another area where the MRM and HOS models differ. According to the HOS model, ina mature country like Japan, free trade benefits all capitalists and hurts all workers, regardless of whether they are in a capital-intensive sector like autos or a labor-intensive one like apparel. Hence, capitalists should favor free trade and workers should favor protectionism, regardless of whether their sector is an exporting or import-competing or non-trading sector. In other words, attitudes toward free trade are a function of the productive *factor* (capital or labor), not the *sector*. In the MRM model, the opposite forecast is made. Free trade favors both capital and labor in the exporting sector and hurts both capital and labor in the import-competing sectors. Hence, both capital and labor in the computer industry should favor free trade while both capital and labor in textiles should favor protection. Protectionist attitudes are a function of the *sector* not the *factor*. Evidence from other countries suggests the MRM political forecast is more reliable, at least regarding the attitudes of companies. Since Japan's exporters are hurt so badly by Japan's protectionism, they have an interst in free trade—and may eventually come to see it that way.

Appendix F

Japan's Peculiar Trade

Sachs and Warner argue, "Open economies tend to converge; but closed ones do not."[26] If so, then it is very suggestive that Japan was far more open to trade during its high-growth period than during its laggard period (see Chapter 11).

Japan, virtually alone of all the major nations, trades less relative to GDP today than it did four decades ago. Considering the rise of the yen and the decline of import prices, this implies astoundingly low price and income elasticities. Petri reports the import price elasticity of manufactured imports at only −0.38 through 1985. It rose to 0.84 in the late 1980s due to the *endaka*. Even after all the supposed improvement in Japan's trade structure, its imports still consist mainly of price-insensitive complements rather than price-sensitive substitutes for domestic output.[27]

The issue of time is what is missing from much of the debate over whether or not Japan "under-imports." During the high-growth era, Japan's trade dependence was as high, or even higher, than other nations—based on its population, per worker GDP, and distance from major trading partners. But by 1990, Japan's trade was only a bit more than *half* of the prediction—21 percent actual versus 37 percent forecast (Figure F.1 and Table F.1).

In the regressions in Table F.1, trade is a function of population, distance from trading partners, and per capita GDP. The object was not to aim for the highest R^2, but rather to include only exogenous factors. Any differences in trade patterns could then be attributed to policies and economic structures. Although it is not shown in the table, we tried several other factors, like membership in the EU (European Union) and resource endowment (as measured by raw materials as a percentage of imports and exports) and found that this did not change the pattern significantly. It appears that the trade bloc issue was already covered by the distance factor. Resource endowment affected the composition of trade, but not the volume.

If Japan's trade is too low, there still remains the question of which is the cart and which is the horse. Do low imports cause low exports, or vice versa?

The argument is this: let's say Japan runs a current account surplus at 2 percent of GDP. It can do this with exports of 10 percent and imports of 8 percent, or with exports of 30 percent and imports of 28 percent. Clearly, Japan is doing the former, while Germany is closer to the latter.[28]

Figure F.1   **Japan Moves from "Excess Trade" to Too Little Trade**

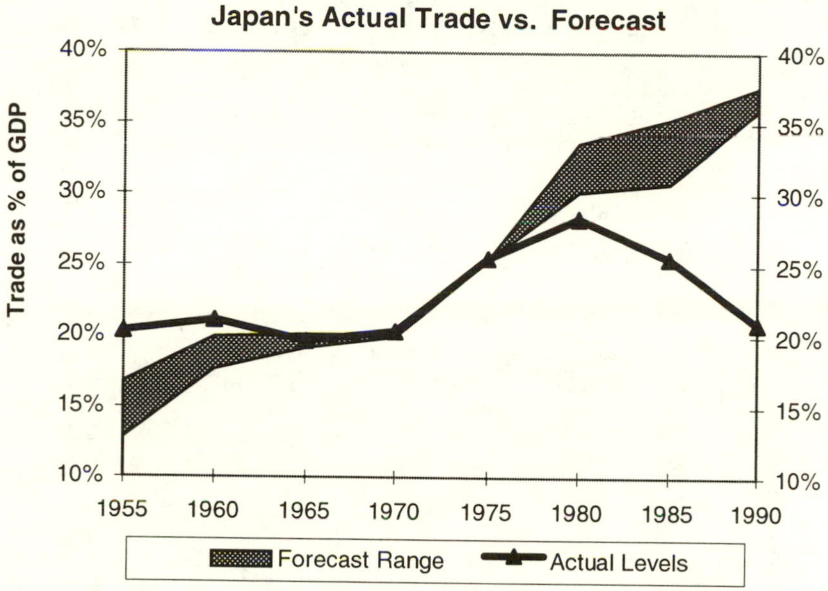

Japan's Actual Trade vs. Forecast

Source: Table F.1 plus regressions (not shown) that include dummies for East Asia

If the current account is limited by the domestic savings–investment imbalance, then anything that reduces imports must reduce exports by the same amount, and vice versa.[29]

There are some who suggest that the cause of Japan's low trade is not its own barriers to imports, but rather other countries' barriers to Japanese exports. The so-called Voluntary Restraint Agreement on Japanese auto shipments to the U.S. during the 1980s is cited as a typical example.

But this view does not cohere with the evidence. Back in the late 1950s and early 1960s, before Japan accepted OECD rules, barriers to Japan's exports—including its chief export, textiles—were far more extensive than any barriers remaining by 1990. Hence, if barriers to exports were the problem, Japan's trade dependence should have increased.

Prof. Motoshige Itoh also argues that limits on Japan's exports are the source of the problem. His argument is based, not on barriers, but on differing growth rates.[30] His argument is the following: If Japan's exports equal its imports, then Japan's imports from the rest of the world must equal the rest of the world's imports from Japan:

$$Mj = Mwj$$

Table F.1

Regressions on Trade:GDP, 1955–90 (Dependent variable = [Exports + Imports]/GDP)

	Intercept	Ln pop	Ln dist	Ln dist²	Ln Y	Ln Y²	Japan dummy	Japan forecast and resid.	Adj. R²	Standard error	F-test
1955	7.94	-0.34	-1.65	0.50				16.7	0.51	0.46	9.07
	0.0%	0.2%	8.6%	15.2%				3.6	0.054%		
1960	7.69	-0.32	-1.51	0.47				19.9	0.60	0.36	13.12
	0.0%	0.0%	4.4%	8.4%				1.2			0.005%
1965	-4.47	-0.32	-1.16	0.31	3.11	-0.20		20.1	0.75	0.29	15.60
	54.0%	0.0%	6.5%	17.4%	9.3%	8.7%		-0.5			0.000%
1970	9.52	-0.27	-1.34	0.35	-0.24			20.1	0.72	0.27	16.68
	0.0%	0.0%	2.0%	8.5%	1.7%			0.20			0.000%
1975	9.96	-0.21	-1.07	0.26	-0.35			25.3	0.67	0.26	12.92
	0.0%	0.1%	4.7%	17.9%	0.1%			0.20			0.002%
1980	-1.11	-0.20	-1.47	0.42	2.37	-0.16		33.5	0.67	0.26	10.60
	91.8%	0.3%	1.4%	4.6%	34.5%	27.2%		-5.2			0.006%
1985	-10.88	-0.19	-1.52	0.42	4.58	-0.29		31.4	0.73	0.25	14.30
	35.1%	0.2%	0.7%	3.5%	9.3%	7.0%		-5.9			0.001%
1990	-20.66	-0.15	-1.96	0.62	6.77	-0.41	-16.58	37.5	0.69	0.28	9.80
	18.5%	3.0%	0.4%	1.1%	5.9%	4.4%	10.4%	-16.6			0.007%

Source: Author's calculation based on data from Summers and Heston (1995); Barro and Lee (1994).

Note: The variable labeled dist means the weighted average distance of a country's capital from the capitals of its 20 largest trading partners. Y = Real GDP per worker. Pop = Population. Ln = natural logarithm. The percentage numbers underneath the coefficients are the probability values of the T-statistic numbers.

$$\frac{Mj}{Yj} * Yj = \frac{Mwj}{Yw} * Yw \qquad (1)$$

$$\frac{Mj}{Yj} = \frac{Mwj}{Yw} * \frac{Yw}{Yj} \qquad (2)$$

Equation 2 mandates that, if the GDP of Japan rises faster than the rest of the world, leading to a decline in $\frac{Yw}{Yj}$, then, as long as $\frac{Mwj}{Yw}$ remains constant, $\frac{Mj}{Yj}$ must fall. That, Prof. Itoh insisted, is why Japan's trade is so low.

But $\frac{Mwj}{Yw}$ is far from constant. On a global basis, import:GDP ratios have been rising rapidly. That is why other fast-growing countries like Korea experienced an explosion in trade. Moreover, during 1970–86, according to Paul Krugman, the income elasticity of import demand for Japanese exports among Japan's 14 largest trading partners was 1.65. This is more than twice Japan's own import elasticity of 0.80.[31]

There is a simple test we can use to judge Prof. Itoh's argument as well as those who point to foreign trade barriers: the changing rate of the yen.

If limits to exports were the problem, this would create a continual tendency for Japan to run a trade *deficit* as it grew. That, in turn, would require that the yen keep *declining* in real terms in order to correct that tendency. In fact, the opposite has been the case: Japan has had a continual tendency toward growing trade surpluses and the yen has had to appreciate in real terms to keep the surplus down.[32]

The yen test for the cause of Japan's low trade is illustrated in Figure F.2.

In this figure, the bold Export line **X** and the bold Import line **M** yield Japanese trade volumes at Point **P**. A leftward shift of world demand for Japanese exports (e.g., due to trade barriers like the auto Voluntary Restraint Agreement) is represented by X-1. A leftward shift of Japanese demand for imports, due to "invisible" barriers, is represented by M-1.

If the export curve had shifted, the new equilibrium would be at Point P-1B. If, on the other hand, insufficient Japanese demand for imports is the cause, equilibrium will be reached at Point P-2A. The volume of trade at P-2A and P-1B is exactly the same; the only difference is the value of the yen. It is higher at P-2A, where import barriers are the problem.

Suppose, over time, that the Japanese import demand curve never expands from M-1, but world demand for Japanese exports continues to grow year by year. In that case, *the volume of trade would slowly increase and the yen would continually rise* as equilibrium shifted from P-1A to P-2A to P-3A.

And yet, the volume of trade in year 2 at P-2A would not be as high as it would have been if both curves had moved rightward to produce equilibrium at P-2B.

Clearly, Japan's secularly rising real yen rate means import barriers are the culprit. For a given trade balance, the yen has to rise to restrain exports to the level mandated by low imports.

Figure F.2 **Rising Yen Shows Import Barriers Cause Low Trade**

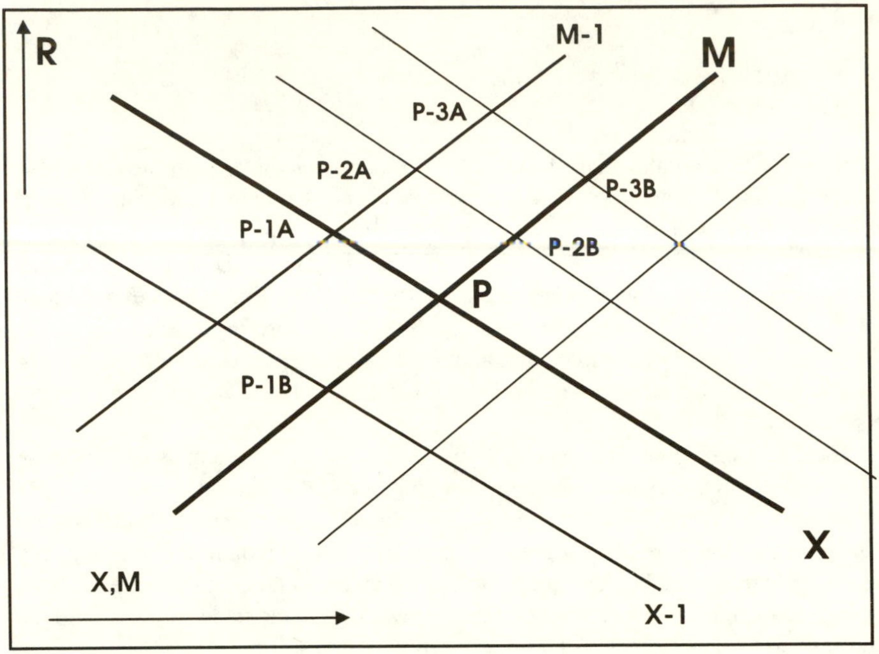

$X=Exports = F(R,Y_{row})$; $M=Imports = F(R,Y_{Japan})$, $R = \$/\yen$

During 1970–86, Japan's growth rate was 1.75 times that of its 14 major trading partners; hence, in order for the yen to remain stable in real terms, the foreign elasticity of demand for Japanese products had to be 1.75 times as high as Japan's import elasticity of demand. If the foreign demand were higher, the yen would have to appreciate to keep exports down; if it were lower, the yen would have to decline to keep imports down.

In reality, the ratio of foreign import elasticity for Japanese goods to Japanese import elasticity was significantly higher than 1.75; it was 2.06. And so the yen has had to appreciate.[33]

Keep in mind that this formula speaks only of the *ratio* of foreign import elasticities to Japanese import elasticities. It says nothing about their *absolute* value. The 1.75 ratio, for example, could be achieved with Japanese import elasticity at 0.50 and foreigners at 0.875 or with Japanese import elasticity at 2 and foreigners at 3.5.

In 1970–86, Japan's import elasticity of demand was 0.80, according to Krugman. In fact, Japan was the *only* country among the eight he studied with an import elasticity of less than 1. Moreover, when Krugman's estimates are compared to the famous Houthakker and Magee estimates for the 1950s-60s, Japan is the only country apart from the U.S. whose import elasticity in the 1970s-80s was *less* than in the 1950s-60s.[34]

The bottom line is this: as shown by the rising yen, *the greatest impediment to Japan's exports are its own barriers to imports*. Whether Japan's exporters recognize it or not, they have an interest in promoting trade reform.[35]

Appendix G

The "Overloan" System in Banking: Artificial Scarcity

During the high-growth era, Japan's monetary authorities perpetuated an artificial scarcity in capital that enabled them to have influence over the allocation of private credit. In essence it was rationing (see Chapters 5 and 6).

Capital was, of course, genuinely scarce in Japan. The need for capital was much greater than the supply. But in a market situation, the interest rate would have risen high enough to reduce demand for borrowing. Thus prices would "clear" the market. At the same time, if foreign capital were allowed in, that would have added to supply and also helped clear the market. But, to retain their leverage, the monetary authorities would not allow in foreign capital. At the same time, to subsidize modern industries, they dictated low interest rates—rates too low to clear the market. This created an artificial scarcity. More people wanted to borrow at those rates than there was money to lend. So, borrowers, in effect, stood in line just like people in the former Soviet Union stood in line at empty stores because low prices there created artificial scarcity. With borrowers standing in line, that allowed the banks to dictate who could, and could not, get funds (Figure G.1).

If borrowers stood in line at the banks, the banks stood in line at the Bank of Japan. As opposed to the U.S. system, where the Federal Reserve adds to money supply through "open market" operations, the BOJ expanded money supply by lending directly to the major city banks. Banks were often dependent on the BOJ for up to 10 percent of the funds they needed to expand lending. This gave the BOJ rationing power, issued through so-called window guidance. Banks generally followed the guidelines lest they be denied further BOJ funding.

Once Japan became capital-rich, this rationing was no longer possible.

Figure G.1 **Low Interest Rates Create Artificial Scarcity, Rationing**

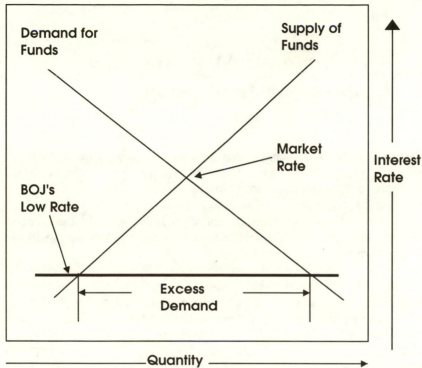

Appendix H

"Economic Anorexia" in a Developmental Perspective

The source of Japan's "economic anorexia" is not that consumption fell relative to GDP during the high-growth era. The problem is that consumption continued to lag even after the economy reached maturity.

The best way to examine this process is to start with the "dual economy" model of industrialization developed by Arthur Lewis. In this model, there are two sectors: a "traditional," mainly agricultural, sector and, a "modern" industrializing sector (see Chapter 8).

Subsistence wages in the traditional sector are above marginal productivity. So, labor can be withdrawn without lowering output. Hence, modern industry faces a perfectly elastic supply of labor for a while. It can hire all it wants without facing rising wages—until it runs out of surplus labor. Then, the wage curve—labeled W in Figure H.1—will start to turn up.

This was *not* true of Japan in this form. Surplus labor could be withdrawn from farming, not because wages were higher than marginal productivity, but because *labor productivity in farming rose so rapidly*.[36]

Nonetheless, the implications for modern industry—the ability to hire lots of labor without facing excessively rising wages—was essentially the same as seen in the Lewis model. During the high-growth era, surplus labor coming off the farms provided about 55 percent of the total growth in the labor force in the nonfarm sector.[37] Moreover, up until the early 1970s, wages in farming and other traditional sectors lagged far behind wages in modern industry. In this sense, farming and other traditional sectors are subsidizing industrialization.

Figure H.1 makes it clear why the labor share declines during industrialization. For any given supply of capital, industry will hire labor up to the point that marginal productivity equals the wage rate. In year 1, this is where the curve F(K1) meets the W curve at Point A. Total output equals the area under the curve F(K1). The labor share is the area OWAL1, labeled WAGES, and the capital share equals the area F(K1)WA labeled PROFITS. In year 2, output is higher, becoming the curve under F(K2). Absolute labor income is greater, now the area OWBL2, because there are more workers. However, the labor share of GDP has decreased. Meanwhile, the capital share of GDP has increased to the area F(K2)WB.

In this model, profits are the sole source of investable savings. So, the in-

Figure H.1 **Profits and Wages in the Lewis Model of Industrialization**

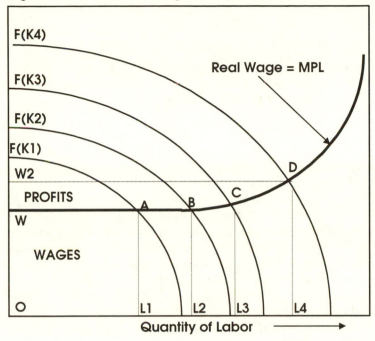

creased capital share translates into a higher capital formation rate and greater growth. Again, we see this in Japan where business, not households, provided the increased savings that fueled investment in the high-growth era.

This pattern continues until the surplus labor runs out and the labor supply curve (i.e., the wage curve) starts turning up, as we see after Point C. When that happens, then the relationship between the capital and labor shares changes radically. When we get to year 4, the wage rate has now risen to the dotted line D-W2. As a result, the labor share has now risen to the area OW2DL4. Consequently, the area WW2D has now shifted from capital to labor. At this point wages and consumption rise rapidly.

In Japan, the labor share fell and the capital share rose during the high-growth era, just as the Lewis model predicts. Then, in the early 1970s, as the flow of labor from farm to city slowed, the labor share and consumption *initially* rose, while the capital share fell, as the model predicts.

However, from the mid-1970s on, this process was aborted and reversed. The labor share and consumption once again started to fall back, while the capital share began to rebound. By 1990, the consumption share of GDP was all the way back down to its previous low of 1970.

High consumer prices, the mechanism of Japan's subsidy for the inefficient sectors, are responsible for this syndrome.

Appendix I

How Japan's Cartels Destroy Productivity

Factor Immobility Leads to Pervasive Protectionism

Throughout the 1970s, barriers to both exit and entry increasingly proliferated. These ranged from paternalistic government regulations, to legal and illegal cartels, to formal and informal import protection, to lifetime employment. To all of this was added poor mobility of capital due to the *keiretsu* system, and over-reliance on financing from "main banks" instead of the capital markets (see Chapter 7).

The slowdown in growth and in factor mobility reinforced each other. Slower growth provoked resistance from those worried about losing their jobs or investment. But the very effort to protect jobs through cartels made factor and price rigidity even worse, which *added to unemployment*.

Cartels were a cure that exacerbated the disease, as shown by Sekiguchi and Horiuchi.[38] To see how, consider Figure I.1. The price ratio between the output of Industry 1 and Industry 2 in a closed economy is given by the line labeled Price Ratio 1. This meets the production possibility curve at P-1,C-1 (i.e., Production 1 and Consumption 1, since in a closed economy, the two must be identical).

Now, suppose the economy opens up to trade and faces the new Price Ratio 2. Assuming that domestic prices and factors are not rigid, the economy will switch its production to P-2, the point on the production possibility curve that is tangent to Price Ratio 2. It will export Good 2 equal to A-P2 and it will import Good 1 equal to A-C2. It will consume at C-2, the point on the highest utility curve that is tangent to Price Ratio 2. Welfare has clearly increased since the consumption of both Good 1 and Good 2 is higher at C-2 than at C-1.

Suppose, however, that the economy is characterized by relative factor immobility and rigid prices, as in Japan.[39] In that case:

> *If prices are rigid, unemployment will result* as the reduction in resources used in the industry adversely affected by changes in product prices (Industry 1 in this instance) would not be completely absorbed in the industry affected favorably. In terms of [Figure I.1], this could be represented by a shift of the production point *within the short-run production frontier* [e.g., point P-R; emphasis added].[40]

Figure I.1 **Factor and Price Rigidity Creates Unemployed Resources**

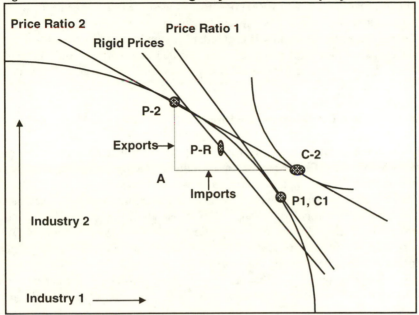

Source: Adapted by author from Sekiguchi and Horiuchi (1988), pg. 371

This is what Japan faced in the crisis of the 1970s. Barriers to exit as well as entry made it difficult to adjust. The situation was made worse when, in response to low demand and structural rigidities, government and business took steps to slow the process of change even further under the rubric of "structural adjustment" and "second-best solutions":

> Measures like intervention in the process of price formation in product markets to neutralize price changes (exigency import restrictions, etc.), provisions for discriminatory use of subsidies to productive factors among sectors, and so on could help in preventing unemployment of resources and facilitate factor movements. Subsidies to *contracting* sectors reduce unemployment of resources in these sectors, *thereby delaying resource transfers*. Subsidies to expanding sectors hasten the pace of the adjustment process [emphasis added].
>
> Rigidities in the price of a single factor (wages, for example) would facilitate a shift in the other factors (for example, capital). Now, if it is capital that is easy to shift, it would result in a large outflow of capital from the stagnating industry causing a steeper fall in the employment of labor and a higher rate of unemployment in this industry. Under these circumstances, if wage-adjustment cannot be optimized, *slowing down the reallocation of capital would become a second-best policy* [emphasis added].[41]

In Japan, both capital and labor were relatively immobile. According to the Modified Ricardian Model (MRM) of trade, as we noted in Appendix E, where factors are immobile, we should expect pervasive protectionism.

To be sure, some immobility is unavoidable in any country. Steel mills do not turn themselves into VCR assembly lines. Skilled autoworkers don't suddenly become adept software programmers. But, pervasive barriers to entry and exit, as in Japan, exacerbate these genuine obstacles.

Cartels: A Cure That Worsens the Disease

Japan's cartels actually lowered productivity in the protected sectors. To see how, consider the difference between an industry facing excess capacity in a normal market situation and one in a Japanese-style "recession cartel."

In Figure I.2, we start off with demand at D-1 and Supply at S-1. They meet at P-1, where demand is large enough to purchase all of the industry output at a price equal to marginal costs. Now, suppose that demand drops, moving to D-2, so that there is overcapacity. The only way to sell all the output is by steep price drops, so that the price initially plunges to P-2.

But, soon it becomes clear that the drop in demand to D-2 is permanent. In a market situation, the new equilibrium point where demand equals supply at a price equal to marginal cost is P-3A. Hence, all firms whose costs put them above the price at P-3A will drop out of the market, leaving only those firms that produce at or below the P-3A price. The supply curve (i.e., the industry marginal cost curve) remains the same. The price rebounds because all the output can now be sold at the equilibrium price. But it doesn't rebound all the way to the P-1 price, since demand has dropped.

Moreover, while the marginal cost *curve* remains the same, the *average* cost drops, i.e., *average* productivity rises, because the high-cost producers have dropped out.

In a Japanese-style recession cartel, the result is quite different. The capacity reduction is *not* done in accordance with marginal cost or efficiency. Rather, *all firms make pro rata cuts* according to their share of the market or share of capacity. Sometimes the bigger or stronger firms even have to take a bigger cut.

While each firm may cut its least efficient plants, inevitably many plants remain that are less efficient than those of other firms. Indeed, *even efficient producers are forced to make cuts* under penalty of fines, industry association boycotts, and other coercive action. Otherwise, the cartel wouldn't work.

The overall result of this system is *to shift the supply curve to the left* to S-2 (in Figure I.2), as each firm, efficient or not, makes a proportional cut. It now costs more to produce the item for any given level of output. As a result, the supply curve now meets the demand curve at P-3B, a higher price and with less volume than P-3A. *This means a drop in average productivity*.

But as we discussed in Chapter 7, the cartel system led companies to expand

Figure I.2 **Japan's Capacity-Reducing Cartels Reduce Productivity**

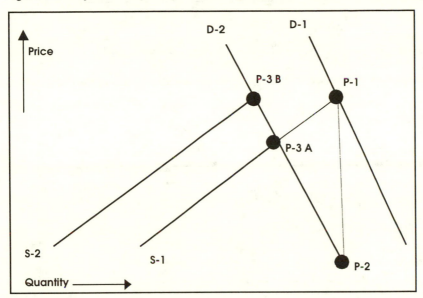

capacity during each upturn in preparation for the next downturn. In terms of Figure I.2, the cartel system produces a continuous *oscillation* of the supply curve and of prices.

And so the cartel system is both an *effect* of Japan's structural rigidities and a *cause* of them.

Barriers to Imports and "Price Destruction"

As with any cartel, this system requires barriers to imports. As Sekiguchi put it, "Joint reduction of production is not effective in raising prices if foreign supply is elastic."[42]

Even economists from Japan's own Finance Ministry have acknowledged that the very existence of the cartels was proof positive that Japan had no free market in imports in the cartelized sectors. In a 1989 article, Kazuyuki Matsumoto, then the chief researcher of the MOF's Institute for Monetary and Economic Studies, wrote:

> In domestic markets that are perfectly competitive, when the prices of imported products supplied by foreign competitors decline due to appreciation of the value of the yen, it becomes impossible for the Japanese firms to maintain high prices for their own products which they sell in Japan. However, observed facts show that this is possible.[43]

As we can see in Figure I.3, cartels allow domestic Japanese industries to charge monopolistic prices, which they could not do if imports were free to enter.

Figure I.3 **Cartels Protected from Imports Raise Prices Even More**

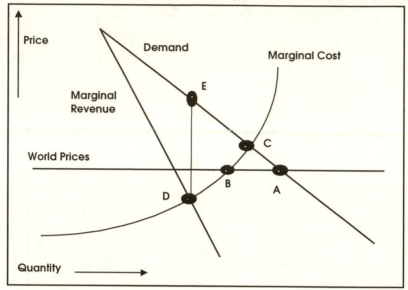

Normally, in a competitive market, the price is set where the industry supply curve (i.e., the industry marginal cost curve) meets the demand curve, i.e., Point C in Figure I.3. Since world prices are below Point C, under free trade, domestic prices would be the same as world prices. Domestic producers who could produce below that price would produce up to Point B, and Japan would import the quantity BA, until the world price met the domestic demand curve at Point A.

Suppose that, due to import restraints, no imports whatever come in. In that case, *if* Japan's internal market still functioned *competitively*, the equilibrium point would rise to C.

However, the absence of imports makes it possible for the industry to function as a cartel. In this case, the price it charges is much more akin to a monopoly situation. The maximum profits are made at the quantity where marginal costs meet marginal revenue, at Point D, and the price is on the demand curve for that quantity, Point E.

Point E is not only above Point C, but it is very far above Point A, the world price. This is what typically happens in a Japanese-style cartel.

Now, suppose that even a small amount of imports comes in, enough to destroy the monopoly power of the cartel. In such a case, prices will fall, heading toward C and beyond—*toward Point A.*

This is the reason "price destruction" has been so dramatic in cartelized industries even in cases where the penetration of imports has only been a few percent. Tuna prices, for example, dropped 63 percent during 1995, beer fell 32 percent, whiskey 17 percent, gasoline 25–30 percent.[44]

Since the whole purpose of the cartels was to raise prices, this makes it clear why keeping competitive imports out was absolutely indispensable for the cartels to function.

How Import Barriers Destroyed Productivity

From a technical standpoint, Japan's protectionism functioned more like a quota than a tariff. In other words, with very low price elasticities, no more than a certain amount of imports can get in no matter how big the price differential.[45]

This may sound like an arcane distinction, but it has enormous implications for productivity. Quotas are far more pernicious and corrosive than tariffs, which is why GATT has always insisted that the first step in trade liberalization be converting quotas to tariffs.

In case of a tariff, the impact of protection is limited. Consider Figure I.4. Under free trade, with world prices at World Price 1, and the domestic supply curve at S-1, domestic demand would cross the world price level at C. Domestic suppliers would produce up to Point D, and DC would be the level of imports. A tariff raises the price facing domestic customers to the dotted line above World Price 1. As a result, domestic suppliers can now supply up to Point B, and customers lower their demand to Point A. Imports are now reduced to the line BA. Finally, the deadweight loss to society (gain for producers minus loss to consumers) is the area DBAC.

What happens if world prices drop to World Price 2 because of improved productivity? With the tariff rate staying the same, the new price facing Japanese customers drops by the same amount as world prices, as we can see by the dotted line above World Price 2. Domestic producers must increase their productivity or else lose more market share. To keep the amount of imports (A'B') under World Price 2 the same as under World Price 1 (AB), the domestic supply curve would have to shift *downward* from S-1 to S-2.

Based on the assumption that Japanese protection operated in this manner, many economists have projected amazingly small losses to Japan from its pervasive protectionism. For example, Sazanami et al. suggested that, in 1989, the cost of Japanese protection to Japanese consumers was anywhere from ¥10 to ¥15 trillion (about $100 to $150 billion at the rate of ¥100 per dollar), or a maximum *3.8 percent of Japanese GDP or 6.6 percent of private consumption.* Of this amount, ¥7 to ¥9.6 was transferred to the producers of the protected products. As a result the net loss from all this protectionism to Japan as a whole was only *0.6 percent of Japanese GDP.*[46]

Of course, removing the protection under this analysis would result in a lot more Japanese imports, about a 20 percent increase, but most of that gain would go to foreigners, not to Japanese. With the gains from free trade so small, why should any Japanese politician rock the boat of powerful interests?

In reality, this is not the true impact of Japanese protection. Rather, protecting the weak sectors is a source of cumulative rot that, with ever-increasing severity,

Figure I.4 **Tariff Has Limited Impact on Productivity Over Time**

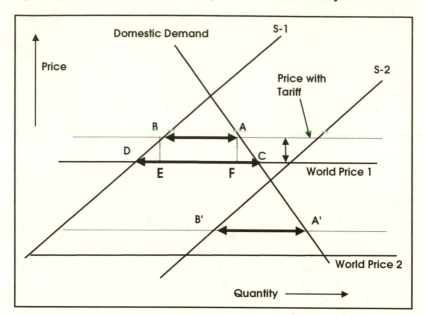

undermines Japanese productivity and growth potential. The reason is that Japan's barriers act not like tariffs, but like quotas.

To see the impact of quota-like barriers, particularly ones applied to an industry that does not export, let's examine Figure I.5. Here, the situation is entirely different over time. The quota creates a curve paralleling the domestic demand curve. Imports are constant at the distance from the domestic demand curve to the quota curve. At World Price 1 and domestic supply curve S-1, the equilibrium point is A.

For any given quota level, there is a corresponding tariff rate, and an equal "deadweight" loss to the economy. But that's where the resemblance ends.

Suppose world prices now drop due to an increase in productivity. Unlike with a tariff where hikes in world productivity would create pressure for comparable hikes in Japan, under a quota there is no such pressure. An increase in world productivity would have *zero* effect on the supply–demand equilibrium in Japan. The equilibrium point stays at Point A.

Therefore, as the world productivity changes but that in Japan does not, the gap between world prices and Japanese prices increases and the deadweight loss to the economy increases. It's as if the tariff rate were suddenly raised.

That's just the beginning. Suppose the productivity of Japanese industry actually drops. Under a tariff, the Japanese industry would lose business as imports flooded in. But, under a quota, not a single additional ton of foreign steel or yard of foreign cloth can get in. Instead, the Japanese domestic supply and demand

Figure I.5 **How Quotas Destroy Productivity**

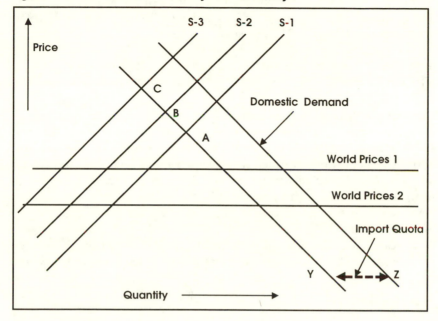

curves now meet at B instead of A. Even with another drop in productivity, they can meet at C, with no worry about losing the market to imports.

If Japan's barriers were like tariffs, the cartels would be self-defeating—a virtual invitation for foreign firms to come in and take over the market. It's only because the import barriers are quotas enforced by industry associations that the cartels work.

As this process continues, the losses to the economy in lowered or forgone productivity and lowered growth multiply. A constant quota acts like an ever-increasing tariff.

Under this circumstance, we should expect to see a continuous increase in the productivity gap between the sheltered Japanese industries and their global counterparts. And we do see that.

Japan's quota-like import barriers are the ultimate source of the dual economy. That's why trade opening is the key to busting up the power of the cartels and to overall economic reform.

A Rising Yen Busts Up the Cartels

Of course, the Japanese barriers are not true quotas. They are quota-like arrangements worked out as a mutual protection racket among industries, combined with government "guidance." At some price differential, the cartel finds it hard to hold together. That's why the skyrocketing of the yen has had some effect. Its effect is seen in the rise of Japan's price elasticity of imports from –0.38 before the late 1980s *endaka* to –0.84 afterward.[47]

Quota Rents Gained by Foreign Exporters Are an Import Barrier

When there are quotas, foreign companies can be induced to take an attitude of: "If you can't beat them, join them." They are urged to tacitly accept the quota since they can sell at the higher price and collect the "quota rents," i.e., the extra high price resulting from the cartel. As we can see from Figure I.5, when productivity drops to create an equilibrium at Point B, the foreign sellers get to sell the same amount at a much higher price.

And so the quota rent can act as an implicit bribe to foreigners to accept their low market share.

For years, American companies from Johnny Walker to GM accepted the myth from their Japanese agents that they should sell fewer products at higher price. In effect, they were being advised to accept the fact of the quota and enjoy the quota rents. When VW told its exclusive agent in Japan, Yanase, to lower the price, it refused. VW fired Yanase, lowered the price, and sold more.[48] Also, GE recently lowered its price on refrigerators and sold more. The same occurred with Compaq and PCs.

Of course, gaining volume through lower price only works if the company can reach the customer—or its distributor will agree to pass on price cuts, and if the customer will respond to lower prices. Petri has shown that Japanese individuals will buy imports if the price is lower, but that Japanese business, and especially the Japanese government, are far more reluctant to buy imports at any price. This is further evidence of the quota-like nature of Japan's barriers.[49]

Michael Knetter has shed light on this through his study of the pricing policy of German exporters. Looking at about three dozen products, he found that German exporters fairly consistently charged higher prices on shipments to Japan than to the U.S., Canada or UK.

Knetter reasoned that foreign exporters know they cannot gain more sales by lowering their price, because of the implicit quota. In effect, they face an inelastic demand curve. So, they are better off getting the highest price they can. In the U.S., UK and Canada, by contrast, they can get more sales by lowering price (i.e., they face an elastic demand curve) and so they do lower price:

> This empirical result is consistent with the view that higher levels of non-tariff barriers (NTBs) explain higher Japanese retail prices. It is not an indicator of higher distribution costs in the Japanese market.[50]

Knetter adds that this result is consistent with an assumption that "the impact of NTBs on price levels . . . is more similar to a quota than a tariff."[51]

How big are the quota rents? Noland examined data from the MITI-DOC price surveys showing that prices of goods made overseas are higher in Japan than in either the U.S. or third-country markets. His calculations suggested that, if Japan's formal barriers and the structural impediments created by *keiretsu* suddenly disappeared, "Japanese [retail] prices would fall by 41 percent."[52]

Appendix J

The Dual Economy and Hollowing Out

Japan's protection forces a transfer of income from the efficient to the inefficient, via the price mechanism (see Chapter 3).

Suppose we have a two-sector economy, with one progressive and one stagnant sector. Suppose that labor is the only input and that all workers, regardless of sector, get the same wage (Japan has a very egalitarian distribution of income). Suppose also that this wage is a constant function of the price of goods in the *stagnant* sector, so that:

$$W = K * P_s$$

With wages at a constant ratio of P_s, then profit in the stagnant sector is also at a constant rate since profit equals the price minus the wage bill.

Now, let's divide both sides of the above equation by the price of goods in the progressive sector, so that:

$$W/P_p = K * P_s/P_p$$

That means a rise in the price of goods by the stagnant sector will mean a rise in the wage bill, or input costs, in the progressive sector.

A rise in W/P_p means, of course, a cut in profits of the progressive sector. It also means a direct cut in the competitiveness of the progressive sector in the export market. We have seen how dependent the progressive sectors are on exports: every rise in the ratio of P_s to P_p is a further drag for Japanese exports. According to MITI, about 30 percent of input costs in Japanese manufacturing come from four highly regulated sectors where Japanese prices are far above world prices.

This is how, in the MRM model, income is transferred from export industries to import-competing industries.

This confirms what we have long known in other contexts: except under unusual "infant industry" circumstances, import protection equals export restriction.

In one sense, Japan has always had a dual economy. The difference is that, in the high-growth era, the traditional sectors subsidized the modern. Due to rising productivity, P_s (e.g., farm prices) *fell* relative to P_p. Today, the healthy are being bled to prop up the dying.

Appendix K

The Macroeconomics of the U.S.–Japan Trade Imbalance

Over the past two decades, opponents of reform in both Japan and the U.S. have used the bilateral trade imbalance to tell the other country to put its house in order.

Some Americans blame Japan's unfair trade practices for most of the bilateral trade imbalance, thereby relieving the U.S. of the need for budget cuts, increased savings, and other remedial measures.

Japanese opponents of internal reform have retorted that the U.S. trade deficit with Japan is almost entirely the result of internal U.S. mismanagement and has nothing to do with Japan. Nor, they say, does Japan need to reduce the trade surplus in its own interests. Besides, some contend, macroeconomic theory dictates that there are no policy measures Japan could take to reduce its trade surplus even if it wanted to.[53]

The American argument ignores the well-known formula that the internal investment–savings imbalance equals the current account imbalance. The Japanese argument misuses this truism.

If Y = GDP, C = consumption, I = Investment, S = Savings, G = Government spending, T = Taxes, X = exports and M = imports, then, in a closed economy where supply equals demand:

$$Y = C + I + G \qquad \text{(Eq.1)}$$

In an open economy, where imports can add to supply and exports add to demand:

$$M + Y = C + G + I + X \qquad \text{(Eq.2)}$$

$$(X - M) = Y - (C + G + I) \qquad \text{(Eq.3)}$$

Equation 3 tells us that, in a country like the U.S. that runs a trade deficit, domestic demand is greater than domestic supply. In a country like Japan that runs a trade surplus, domestic demand is less than domestic supply.

Now, since income can be spent, paid in taxes or saved:

$$Y = C + T + S \tag{Eq.4}$$

Hence, combining Eq. 3 and Eq. 4:

$$(X - M) = (C + T + S) - (C + G + I) \tag{Eq.5}$$

$$(X - M) = (S - I) + (T - G) \tag{Eq.6}$$

Equation 6 explains the well-known phenomenon of the "twin deficits" in the U.S., i.e., why the budget deficit expansion led to greater trade deficits. If the government budget deficit $(T - G)$ rises by 2 percent of GDP, and if $S - I$ doesn't change, then the trade deficit must also rise by 2 percent of GDP. On the other hand, if the budget deficit equals 2 percent of GDP, but private savings are so large that $S - I$ equals 4 percent of GDP, then the nation will run a 2 percent trade *surplus* despite its budget deficit. This describes Japan.[54]

The point we want to underline is that *the causality works in both directions.*

Suppose a nation's current account surplus (the broadest measure of trade) changes due to purely external events. Let's say a lowering of interest rates in Japan causes investors to move assets from Japan to the U.S. This will raise the value of the dollar, and thereby increase America's trade deficit.

Let's suppose this leads $X - M$ to grow to –2 percent of GDP (a negative number since this is deficit). In that case, the sum of $(S - I)$ and $(T - G)$ must also equal –2 percent of GDP.

How does this happen? The inflow of funds from Japan would lower U.S. interest rates and therefore the cost of investment. Investment would increase. Meanwhile domestic savings might even drop due to lower rates. Hence $(S - I)$ would turn further negative until it reached –2 percent of GDP.

To simplify things, $(X - M)$ = CA [for current account]; $(S - I)$ = IS [for investment–savings balance], and $(T - G)$ = BB [for budget balance]. In that case:

$$IS + BB = CA \tag{Eq. 7}$$

A country's current account balance (or external balance) must equal its internal balance, which is the sum of the private investment–savings balance and the government budget balance (deficit or surplus). In other words, if Japan's internal balance equals a $100 billion surplus, so must its current account surplus.

Now, for Japan to run a trade *surplus* of $100 billion, the entire Rest of the World (ROW) must run a combined *deficit* of $100 billion. In equation form this is:

$$CA_{(J)} = (-1)*CA_{(ROW)} \tag{Eq. 8}$$

Since the internal and external balances also must equal each other in other countries, we combine Equations 7 and 8 to get:

$$[IS + BB]_{(J)} = CA_{(J)} = (-1)*CA_{(ROW)} = (-1)*[IS + BB]_{(ROW)} \qquad \text{(Eq. 9)}$$

What happens if the combined internal deficit in the rest of the world declines from \$100 billion to \$80 billion, e.g., through budget cuts in the U.S.? Then if nothing else changes, the current account deficit of the rest of the world must also decline to \$80 billion. That means Japan's current account surplus must also fall to only \$80 billion. That, in turn, requires a decline in Japan's internal balance, through a decrease in private savings in Japan, an increase in investment, or an increase in the Japanese budget deficit. During the 1970s-90s, Japan's budget deficit has usually played the strongest swing role. In the bubble era, artificially stimulated private investment played this role.

What happens if Japan's internal balance dictates a current account surplus of \$100 billion while balances in the rest of the world allow it to run a deficit of only \$80 billion? Then, balances must meet somewhere in the middle. This is accomplished through an intricate and sometimes tumultuous dance of exchange rates, interest rates, prices and production levels until an equilibrium is once again established. Over the past two decades, the secularly rising yen has been the strongest force keeping Japan's trade surplus from growing above these macroeconomic constraints.

If we put into equation form what we just described about how changes elsewhere affect Japan, we get the following two equations, which derive directly from Equation 9.

$$CA_{(J)} = (-1)*[IS + BB]_{(ROW)} \qquad \text{(Eq. 10)}$$

$$[IS + BB]_{(J)} = (-1)*[IS + BB]_{(ROW)} \qquad \text{(Eq. 11)}$$

Over the past two decades, changes in the U.S. budget have had a particularly strong effect on Japan (see Chapter 8). We can see this by dividing the Rest of the World in Equations 8 and 9 into the U.S. and All Other Countries (AOC). That gives us:

$$CA_{(J)} = (-1)*[IS + BB]_{(U.S.)} + (-1)*[IS + BB]_{(AOC)} \qquad \text{(Eq. 12)}$$

$$[IS + BB]_{(J)} = (-1)*[IS + BB]_{(U.S.)} + (-1)*[IS + BB]_{(AOC)} \qquad \text{(Eq. 13)}$$

Of the four external elements on the right side of Equations 12 and 13 that work with internal forces to determine Japan's current account as well as Japan's internal balance, the strongest over the past 20 years has been the influence of the American budget deficit. Without even considering all the other factors, a regression tells us that we can reliably explain about two-thirds of the ups and downs of Japan's trade balance during 1974–94 just by looking at the U.S. budget a year earlier. According to the U.S. Federal Reserve, as of 1996, every time the U.S. cuts its fiscal stimulus by 1 percent of U.S. GDP, Japan's current account surplus drops by 0.3 percent of Japanese GDP.[55]

The only reason the Nakasone Administration was able to cut Japan's huge budget deficits in the early 1980s was that the Reagan Administration was simultaneously increasing America's budget deficit. That raised America's trade deficit, which raised Japan's trade surplus, thereby allowing Japan to lower its budget without causing a recession. The obverse is equally true. How was the Reagan Administration able to cut taxes so much without raising interest rates so high as to totally stifle private investment? The only reason was that Japan was running a huge trade surplus, thereby sending goods and capital to America. Once the U.S. budget deficit started coming down in the late 1980s, so did the Japanese trade surplus. (In the late 1990s, by the way, it has been America's private IS deficit rather than a government deficit that boosted America's trade deficit and thus Japan's trade surplus.)

This also explains why Japan cannot indefinitely export its way out of its economic problems. The bigger Japan's surplus, the bigger everyone else's deficits. In the 1980s, Japan could run a huge trade surplus, for years, hitting a peak above 4 percent of GDP in 1986, because of the Reagan–Volcker policy mix. If Japan were to try a similar feat today, who would run the corresponding deficits? The U.S.? Asia? Deputy Treasury Secretary Lawrence Summers has reportedly named 2.5 percent of GDP as the "line in the sand" for the maximum tolerable Japanese current account surplus. This is about half the peak that Japan achieved in the mid-1980s. The point is, even without a policy response, markets via the yen rate would have to limit the Japanese trade surplus to what foreign economies can absorb.

For years, apologists for Japan's neomercantilism have insisted that America's gigantic trade deficits were caused by the U.S. savings–investment gap and that nothing Japan could do would solve this problem. The U.S. should cut its budget deficit and stop complaining about Japan. This argument ignores the arithmetic reality that no country can run a surplus unless someone else runs a deficit. The arguments were voiced by economists in Japan who denied that Japan had an "excess savings" problem or a need to reform, and who opposed the Maekawa Commission proposals.[56]

Today, the U.S. still runs a big trade deficit even though the budget deficit has come down. That's because now private investment has risen, but private savings are still low. Nonetheless, relative to GDP the size of the goods and services trade deficit in 1997 was one-third the level of the 1986 peak.

Now that Japan can no longer export its way out of its troubles for more than a couple years, it is under much greater pressure to face its homegrown problems.

Appendix L

Trade, Capital Flows, and the Gyrations of the Yen

A rising yen is the ultimate macroeconomic corrective for the fact that Japan's internal tendencies push its trade surplus higher than the rest of the world can absorb. The yen has to rise to hold down exports. That has been the history of the past 25 years and nothing on the horizon yet seems likely to change that.

However, the yen has never risen in straight linear fashion. Instead there is a roller coaster effect. One reason is that the yen rate is not determined simply by trade flows. It is also determined by capital flows. Ultimately, the two forces have to match. But, they can be out of sync for quite a long time, even years. As a result, the yen lurches too high in one year and then too low a few years later. The farther away it is from an equilibrium rate—and the longer it stays away—the bigger the ultimate correction. This is what happened in the early and mid-1980s (Figure L.1).

There are those who see a parallel in the late 1990s.[57] With the yen at around 115 during much of 1997, down 30 percent from its 1995 peak strength, Japan's current account surplus rose from its low of about 1.5 percent of GDP in the second quarter of 1996 to 2.6 percent of GDP by the second quarter of 1997. The yen is kept weak by lack of confidence in Japanese finances as well as a huge gap between U.S. and Japanese interest rates, which lures money out of Japan and to the U.S. As long as the yen stays so weak, there is fear that the surplus could continue rising. Ultimately, there is a limit, of course. It is imposed by the absorption ability of other countries. But how far out of whack could the yen and the Japanese surplus get? That is determined by the interplay of trade flows and capital flows.

Let's say Japan has a current account surplus of $100 billion with the rest of the world. How does the world pay for the extra goods and services Japan is supplying it? It can only do so if Japan lends it the money. So, Japan's capital outflows (the capital account) must balance its current account.

Suppose the process starts from the other end. That is, suppose Japanese investors decide to invest $100 billion in overseas assets, from stocks, bonds and Treasury bills to factories and golf courses. From an economic standpoint, Japan has in effect transferred $100 billion in purchasing power. But that transfer is only real if it is backed up by a transfer of real goods and services. A capital outflow

Figure L.1 **The Yen's "Roller Coaster Path"**

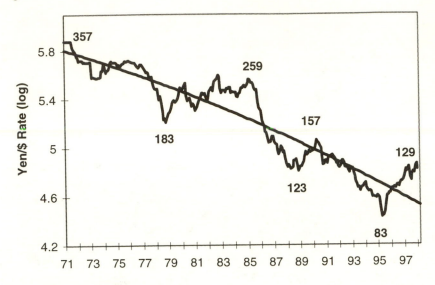

Source: Deutsche Morgan Grenfell
Note: Every few years the yen cycles between overshooting and undershooting its long-term trend toward greater strength. The chart is rendered in logarithm scale so that a 10% fall from 300 and a 10% fall from 100 are proportional.

of $100 billion must be backed up by a Japanese trade surplus of $100 billion.

So, whether the process starts from the side of goods and services or from the side of money transfers, *Japan's current account surplus and its capital account outflows must ultimately balance.* Neither can be more or less than the other.

Another way to look at it is that the Japanese current account surplus creates a *demand* for yen to pay for the surplus outflow of goods and services. Net capital outflows provide the supply of the needed yen. Supply and demand must equal.

But here's the rub. The mere fact that this process must ultimately occur does *not* mean that it occurs immediately or *automatically*. The companies that export Japanese cars and VCRs and the companies that invest in golf courses and Treasury bills are not the same. We can, and often do, have a situation like in the early 1990s. Japan's current account surpluses temporarily reached a peak of 3 percent of GDP in 1993. And yet, Japan's investors were reluctant to send money overseas. They had lost hundreds of billions of dollars on their foreign investments in the late 1980s as the dollar dropped, and they did not want to repeat the experience—especially since the new Clinton Administration was "talking down" the dollar.

And so, in 1993, Japan's current account surplus was ¥14 trillion, but its net capital outflows only ¥11.5 trillion. That's a shortfall of roughly $35 billion. Since the demand for yen (current surplus) was higher than the supply (capital outflow), the yen started to rise. As a result, the following year, Japan's current account surplus dropped a bit to ¥13.3 trillion. But, as the dollar dropped and investors feared more foreign exchange losses, Japan's net capital outflows dropped even more to ¥8.8 trillion. This sent the yen even higher. In the end, a rising yen brought the current account surplus down from 3 percent of GDP to 1.3 percent over three years.

What would happen in this situation if the Bank of Japan let nature take its course? The yen would keep on rising. Had the yen risen even higher, Japan's exports would have been hurt even more.

But the BOJ did not let nature take its course. It made up most of the shortfall between the current and capital accounts by buying dollars, i.e., supplying the deficient yen. This intervention is seen in the changes reported every month in the BOJ's foreign exchange reserves. A rise in those reserves means the BOJ is buying dollars (or other hard currency) with yen, which tends to raise the value of the dollar and lower the value of the yen compared to a free market level.

It's simply incorrect to say that central bank intervention is meaningless because the central banks have only billions while there are trillions of dollars of capital flows. What counts is the ratio of central bank action to *net* capital and current account flows—not to the gross trading.

The BOJ's intervention (as measured by the change in the BOJ's foreign exchange reserves) was equal to 20 percent of Japan's entire current account surplus in 1993–94, 52 percent in 1995, and 68 percent in the first three quarters of 1996. The peak came in the first quarter of 1996 at 116 percent of the current account surplus. Then it declined to 48 percent in the second quarter, and 30 percent in the third quarter.

Since the last few months of 1996, the BOJ has not had to artificially keep the yen down since it was depreciating on its own. Ever since the 1995 deal between the MOF's Eisuke Sakakibara and the Treasury's Lawrence Summers, U.S. Treasury Secretary Robert Rubin and the MOF have said they wanted a strong dollar. Finally, it became clear to the markets that they meant it.

Let's see what this near-guarantee looks like to investors. In 1997, anyone could earn 5 percent totally risk-free by investing in 3-month U.S. Treasury bills; he could earn only 0.5 percent by investing in equivalent yen assets. If investors can earn almost 5 percent more and there is no short-term foreign exchange risk, money is going to flood into the U.S. As it does, it pushes the dollar even higher, thereby becoming a self-fulfilling prophecy. And so Japanese investors get a double benefit: higher interest rates and a higher dollar. A Japanese investor who put ¥100 into T-bills a year ago would have gotten back ¥128 today. Those who left them in Japan got back ¥100.5.

On top of that, lack of confidence in Japanese banks and stocks has also sent money fleeing out of Japan. During 1997, there was a significant correlation between the rise and fall of bank shares on the Tokyo Stock Exchange and the rise and fall of the yen. As confidence in banks weakens and stock prices also weaken, investors take their money out of Japanese assets and invest them abroad instead, which also lowers the value of the yen vis-à-vis the dollar (see Figure 12.5).

For all these reasons, during 1997, net capital outflow from Japan (i.e., supply of yen) outdistanced the current account surplus (i.e., demand for yen)—the opposite of the situation in 1995. With supply of yen outstripping demand in 1997, the price of the yen did what prices always do when supply outstrips demand: the yen fell.

There has also been speculation that, when changes in regulations scheduled to come into force on April 1, 1998, make it easier for Japanese individuals to send their money out of the country in search of higher rates, outflows would increase still further.

Ultimately, however, what goes up too much must eventually come crashing down. The weak yen has sent Japan's current account back up again. By the third quarter of 1997 it was at 2.6 percent of GDP and still rising.

As has occurred so many times in the past, whenever the current account gets too big for foreigners to absorb, the yen eventually starts to rise.

So, as of late 1997, trade flows are signaling the yen to get weaker, but capital flows (the gap between U.S. and Japanese interest rates) are signaling it to get stronger. But, once investors feel the yen will get stronger (the dollar weaker) and foreign exchange losses become possible, then the attraction to weaken dollar assets will decline. As money flows to the U.S. slow down, that will make the dollar weaken in a self-fulfilling prophecy in the other direction. The rush to the exits, whenever it comes, could be sudden and massive.

Through this interplay of capital and trade flows—combined with the well-known tendency of currency traders to think "the trend is your friend"—for the past 25 years, the yen has lurched back and forth between overvaluation and undervaluation.

History has made one thing very clear: the weaker the yen gets and the longer it stays too weak, the higher it will eventually have to go.

Appendix M

Investment-Driven Growth Versus Productivity-Driven Growth

After 1973, Japan tried to make up for sagging productivity growth by pouring on tons of investment (Chapter 4). Ultimately, due to the law of diminishing returns, this proved a dead end.

In any economy, the growth of GDP is the sum of two factors: the growth of the labor force and the growth of labor productivity (GDP per worker). Labor productivity in turn is elevated by two factors: giving each worker more tools (i.e. a higher capital-labor ratio); and giving each worker more modern tools as well as increasing efficiency (i.e. higher Total Factor Productivity). In other words, as we see in Equation 1, spending more bucks and getting more bang for each buck (For Japan, see Table 6.3)

$$G(Y/L) = A*G(K/L) + G(TFP) \qquad \text{(Eq. 1)}$$

$G(Y/L)$ = growth of GDP per worker; A = the marginal productivity of capital = the capital share of national income; (K/L) = growth in capital stock per worker; $G(TFP)$ = the growth of Total Factor Productivity.

Due to the law of diminishing returns, *unless increases in K/L are accompanied by sufficient increases in TFP*, then increasing K/L by, say, 10 percent, will yield a hike in Y/L that is less than 10 percent . This has two results.

First, as Y grows more slowly than K, the rate of return on assets (ROA) for firms will decline (Eq. 2), making them less eager to invest.

$$ROA = (A*Y) / K \qquad \text{(Eq. 2)}$$

Secondly, because Y/L increases more slowly than K/L, the capital-output ratio, K/Y, must increase (Eq. 3).

$$\frac{K}{Y} = \frac{K/L}{Y/L} \qquad \text{(Eq. 3)}$$

If K/Y increases, then the savings/investment rate (I/Y) has to keep increasing just to sustain the same rate of growth (Eq. 4).

$$I/Y = K/Y * [G(Y) + D]$$ (Eq. 4)

For example, if K/Y = 2, and the depreciation rate on capital stock (D) = 5 percent, then for growth to equal 5 percent a year, society must save/invest 20 percent of GDP. If K/Y rises to 3, then to maintain 5 percent growth, I/Y has to rise to 30 percent. What happens if K/Y rises to 3 but society will only save 25 percent of GDP? Then, growth must fall to 3.3 percent.

Under these conditions, sustaining *steady* growth requires a continual *increase* in the savings/investment rate. But this is impossible. The decline in ROA makes firms less eager to invest. Moreover, in order to entice more household savings, firms would have to offer a higher return (e.g. a higher interest rate). But, with their own ROA falling, they cannot do this. Hence, growth must fall.

The *only* way to lessen this difficulty is by hiking TFP growth. (Diminishing returns cannot be entirely surmounted, which is why mature nations grow more slowly than NICs.) Market-oriented reforms would accelerate Japan's growth because, in the long run in a mature economy, maximizing profits and maximizing TFP are largely equivalent.

During Japan's high-growth era, not only was K/L rising at a rapid clip, but TFP grew so fast that K/Y actually *declined* for a while, and then it flattened out. After 1973, K/L kept rising, but TFP slowed even more sharply than the end of catch-up would have dictated. (Figures 4.12, 6.10). Hence, K/Y doubled from 0.8 in 1970 to 1.8 by 1990. Japan futilely tried to make up for faltering TFP by stoking up investment. Running on a treadmill that kept accelerating, it eventually fell off.

Notes

Notes to Chapter 1

1. Keynes (1964), pp. 383–384.
2. Murakami (1996), p. 226.
3. MITI (1995), pp. 2, 4. EPA (1996b), p. 1.
4. Fingleton (1995). *Why Japan Is Still on Track to Overtake the U.S. by the Year 2000* is the subtitle of Fingleton's book, *Blindside*.
5. MITI (1996).
6. The "capitalist developmental state" is a term introduced by Chalmers Johnson (1982) in his book on MITI. It refers to a panoply of policies that "late industrializers" like Japan used to accelerate industrialization, e.g., import restrictions; export and production subsidies; state-directed private credit and below-market government credit; and cartels for production, price controls, and exports. Japanese economist Yasusuke Murakami uses the term "developmentalism." While Murakami believes these policies work only in the "catch-up era," Johnson believes that Japan still benefits from its trade and industrial policies. A good collection of articles on industrial policy by Japanese sources is Komiya, et. al., (1988).
7. See Table 2.1.
8. This will be documented in Chapter 4. See Appendix E.
9. McKinsey (1996); Alexander (1997).
10. Normally, a stock price can be no higher than a certain ratio of corporate earnings, e.g., 15–25 times earnings in the U.S. In Japan, the Price-Earnings (PE) ratio hit 80–100 before the bubble popped.
11. Japan Securities Research Institute (1988).
12. Sakakibara (1993).
13. Fallows (1989, 1994). List himself regarded "developmental state" policies as a *temporary transition belt* to help Germany, the U.S. and other "late industrializers" catch up to England. Once they had done so, said List, universal free trade should rule. See the quotation from List at the opening of Chapter 7. Although Fallows does not mention it, this understanding was widely shared by List's admirers in Meiji Era Japan, none of whom Fallows discusses. See, for example, the quotation from List's Japanese translator, Sadamasu Oshima, in Chapter 13. See Roll (1938), pp. 230–231, Galbraith (1987), pp. 92–95, and Sugiyama (1994), pp. 11, 103. This issue will be discussed further in Chapter 13.

14. Thurow (1992).

15. Fallows (1989).

16. Summers (1989), p. 52.

17. Courtis (1997), p. 5. In 1991, bad loans in America amounted to less than 3 percent of GDP and were mostly concentrated in fringe banks. In early 1998, the MOF put the estimate of nonperforming loans at ¥26 trillion (about $200 billion), or 5 percent of GDP and the number of problematic loans as high as ¥79 trillion (or almost $600 billion), or 15 percent of GDP. Some private economists say the true number is probably closer to $800 billion. See Chapter 8 and Asher (1996a) for details.

18. The U.S. lost 3 million out of 21 million jobs in only four years, a loss of 17 percent. Japan's projected loss of 2.25 million jobs equals 14 percent of its 1992 manufacturing job level of 13 million.

19. Summers (1997). The point here is not to single out Summers. Quite the contrary, the fact that even as normally sensible an observer as Summers was taken in shows the pervasiveness of the hysteria.

20. MITI (1995), pp. 2, 4.

21. EPA (1996a). In EPA (1994), the EPA acknowledged that Japan's sky-high prices were caused, in part, by "import restrictions and other regulations, [that] resist the natural drive to lower prices . . . ."

22. Feldman (1996).

23. MITI (1996).

24. Courtis (1997).

25. Interview, 1994. Washington, DC.

26. On the bank–corporate relationship, see Courtis (1997). On corporate stock-holdings, including even ownership of competitors, see Caves and Uekasa (1976), p. 492, and Okimoto (1989), pp. 140, 149. This is discussed fully in Chapter 7.

27. See North (1990) on the role of institutions in economic performance.

28. EPA (1995b), pp. 1–2.

29. Hatoyama (1997).

30. Olson (1982).

31. Johnson (1996). Johnson was responding to Asher (1996a). Asher (1996b) is the reply.

32. Fingleton (1995). It should be noted that other revisionists, such as Clyde Prestowitz and Taggart Murphy, readily acknowledge Japan's current economic difficulties. This will be discussed in the last chapter.

33. Patrick (1977), p. 239. For government control of imports and of cartels, see Chapters 5 and 6.

34. Weinstein and Beason (1994), pp. 1, 17. Weinstein and Beason's statistical techniques don't take into account the "dualism" of the high-growth era, that government both promoted "strategic" sectors and "compensated" troubled sectors. But, on balance, as we will discuss in Chapter 6, industrial policy accelerated industrialization.

35. See Katz (1994b).

36. Lawrence (1991); Lincoln (1990). See Chapter 5 of Bergsten and Noland (1993), for a review of the literature.

37. Yamamura (1982) and Pepper, et. al. (1985), pp. 135–142.
38. Translated in Ueno (1980), p. 415.
39. Okubo (1996), pp. v-ix.

Notes to Chapter 2

1. Industries like shipbuilding, cement, steel, chemicals, and machinery formed cartels again and again under a series of laws for "structurally depressed industries" passed in the 1970s and 1980s. After the U.S. complained that the cartels restricted imports, Japan changed its laws in 1987. These days, "administrative guidance" and the power of industry associations produce the same results as formal cartels. This will be detailed in Chapter 7.
2. UNIDO (1995), p. 54.
3. McKinsey (1993), p. 5.
4. Patrick (1986), p. 22.
5. Under this law, which is still in force, MITI also administers the number of gas stations and licenses entry. Not surprisingly, price-fixing among competing gas stations is rampant. According to a former MITI official, 20 yen out of the 120 yen price in 1994 was due to the barriers to entry and price-fixing. So, when in 1994, a rice retailer opened a gas station without registering with MITI and announced he was going to charge only 100 yen, MITI acted to quell this mini-rebellion. It threatened fines and legal action. See also Tilton (1996), p. 197.
6. Kikkawa (1995), p. 92.
7. A former MITI official reported the secret cartel in a May 1997 interview in Tokyo.
8. Sakaiya (1993), p. 32.
9. The Price Structure Policy Committee (1994), p. R-11, reported that, in actual cases of U.S. vs. Japanese bids for the same civil engineering projects, the Japanese bids were 13–45 percent higher.
10. See Chapter 7.
11. McCormack (1996), p. 34. See also Schlesinger (1997).
12. Confidential interview in Tokyo, May 1997.
13. McKinsey (1992). NTT's monopoly has only recently been undermined by allowing new competitors.
14. USTR (1994), p. 142.
15. Asher (1996a).
16. Porter (1990a), p. 414.
17. The Goldman Sachs research is cited in "The Shock of the Yen." *Economist.* April 8, 1995, p. 33. See also Jorgenson (1995), pp. 412–413.
18. McKinsey (1993), pp. S1, S2. When McKinsey studied nine industries in the U.S., Germany and Japan, they found: "In five of the cases—autos, auto parts, metalworking, steel, and consumer electronics—labor productivity in Japan is significantly higher than in the U.S. (by 45 percent in steel in 1990). In the other four industries—computers, soap and detergent, beer and food processing—Japan is behind, by large

margins in beer and food processing. . . . Evidently, Japanese manufacturing exhibits the attributes of a 'dual economy.' . . . Our case studies suggest no such dual economy for manufacturing in Germany."

19. Tilton (1996).

20. Tilton (1996). See also Uriu (1996). For a Japanese presentation of the barriers, see Sekiguchi (1991).

21. Tilton (1996), pp. 82, 93, 100, 104–108.

22. Tilton (1996).

Notes to Chapter 3

1. Confidential interview with an executive of one of Japan's leading electronics firms, February 1995.

2. Katz (1997b). In May 1997, with the yen at 115, with Japan's electric rates for industry at an index of 100, the index in the U.S. was 73, with 77 for Germany and 79 for UK. Despite attempts to favor industry over consumers, the comparable indexes for the two sectors were not that much different. With Japan at 100 for consumers, the U.S. was 82, Germany was 79 and UK was 75. *Nikkei Weekly*, August 4, 1997, p. 2.

3. Interview with MITI official. Tokyo, May 1997.

4. The limits to the trade surplus are detailed in Chapter 8 and Appendix K. When the gap between rising exports and restricted imports leads to a trade surplus that bumps up against this elastic, but still very real, limit, exports have to be limited. The mechanism is the rising yen. When Japan imports, it *supplies* the world with yen to buy the products. When Japan exports, it creates a *demand* for yen as other countries have to change dollars into yen to buy the Japanese goods. When the trade surplus rises, the demand for yen grows much bigger than the supply of yen. As with any good, when demand outstrips supply, the price rises. And so the yen goes up. As the yen goes up, the prices of a Toyota Camry or Honda Accord go up, and people switch to the Ford Taurus.

5. Noguchi (1994), pp. 25–28.

6. EPA (1996a).

7. Under a 1986 law that expired in 1996, only Japan's refiners could import consumer-oriented petroleum products like gasoline and kerosene.

8. See Katz (1997b) and Government of Japan (1997).

9. Automakers even told officials at the U.S. Embassy of their plans to cut back, expecting the latter to be happy. Instead, Embassy officials replied, as they should, that Washington was not asking Japan to export less to the U.S. but to import more from the U.S. Confidential interview with Embassy official, 1997.

10. Interview in Tokyo, May 1997.

11. Asher (1996a), p. 14. Henry (1995), p. 3.

12. Henry (1995), pp. 2, 4.

13. Milner (1988), Keohane and Milner (1996).

14. There is some difference of opinion among analysts as to whether Japanese

multinationals, free from the political constraints binding them back home, act differently in Asia. David Asher (1996a), p. 14 and *Business Week* (1997), p. 28 suggest that Japanese multinationals appear to feel more free in Asia than at home to buy supplies based on market factors rather than outdated buyer-supplier ties. They suggest that Japanese affiliates are purchasing more from indigenous firms in Asia and less from either firms back home or Japanese transplants in Asia. Walter Hatch, co-author of Hatch and Yamamura (1996), in a letter to this author, disputes that contention. Just as Japan's own imports rose in 1995 as the yen soared and then retreated as the yen declined again, so, says Hatch, did the purchasing patterns of Japanese affiliates in Asia. "It is true that Japanese affiliates in Asia, and around the world, turned to foreign firms in panic in 1995. But Japanese firms went back to their old ways in 1996, after the yen returned to less stratospheric levels. Localization has been achieved almost entirely by relying on Japanese transplants. All of my plant tours in the region revealed that local suppliers played small or insignificant roles in Japanese procurement patterns." Whether this is just an artifact of the relative newness of Japanese firms or will continue to be the case remains to be seen, especially in the aftermath of the Asian financial turmoil. *Business Week* (1997) points to financial problems preventing many Japanese transplants from following their parents to Asia.

Notes to Chapter 4

1. Maddison is cited in Yoshikawa (1995).
2. Cited in Saxonhouse (1994), p. 11.
3. Cited in *Japan Weekly Monitor* (1996).
4. Feldman (1996).
5. Keep in mind that we are reporting the growth of GDP per worker, not total GDP. If GDP grows 9 percent and the labor force grows 3 percent, then GDP per worker grows 6 percent.
6. In this growth model, we took a sample of 23 North American, European and Asian countries that were on the catch-up path and used standard "econometric regressions" to calculate a country's expected growth for a particular period based on the following factors: the level of GDP per worker, investment:GDP ratio, educational attainment, population size, and trade:GDP ratio. These factors very reliably explain more than 90 percent of the variation in growth among the sample countries in both 1960–70 and 1973–90. This model will be explained in more detail in Appendix D.
7. Porter (1990), pp. 551, 555.
8. Some of the differences among rich countries in how much they have to invest in order to grow is not due to differences in efficiency, but to differences in industrial structure. A nation that concentrates on capital-intensive industries like steel and autos will show a very different pattern from one that focuses on finance and software.
9. McKinsey (1996).
10. Lau (1996), pp. 76–78.

Notes to Chapter 5

1. Sachs and Warner (1995), pp. 17–19.
2. Cited in Vestal (1993), p. 28.
3. Seki (1994), pp. 3, 34–35.
4. An American official, E. Peshine Smith, served as an adviser to the Japanese Foreign Ministry from 1871 to 1877 and helped it negotiate the regaining of its tariff autonomy. Smith was a disciple of the American protectionist economist Henry Carey, who was one of the first protectionists to be translated into Japanese. See Ennis and Katz (1994) and Sugiyama (1994).
5. The name arose because, ostensibly, the new leaders were restoring the power of Emperor Meiji versus the Tokugawa Shoguns.
6. Crawcour (1997), p. 41. On the role of the state in "late industrializers" see Gershenkron (1962). On the new class of business leaders' being former *samurai* rather than pre-Meiji merchants, see Horiye (1965), Hirschmeier (1965) and Yamamura (1997). By the nineteenth century, the *samurai* were no longer sword-wielding swashbucklers but educated nobility akin to the peerage of Europe. Ehrlich (1960), Chapter 12, contrasts Mitsui and Mitsubishi, with the latter, a post-Meiji creation, far more partial to the new manufacturing industries than was Mitsui, which favored trade, banking and mining.
7. Clark (1979), p. 258.
8. As late as 1976, LDP power broker Etsusaburo Shiina, an MITI veteran who earned his spurs in Manchuria as an associate of Kishi, wrote an article entitled: "Manchuria: the Great Proving Ground for Japanese Industry" (cited in Calder, 1993, p. 50). The role of MITI men in Manchuria is reported in Johnson (1982), Chapter 4.
9. Discussion in this and following paragraphs is based on Johnson (1982), Chapters 3 and 4.
10. Noguchi (1994).
11. Noguchi (1994).
12. Patrick (1977), p. 239.
13. Johnson (1982), p. 24.
14. Patrick, along with Philip Trezise and a few other contributors in the influential 1976 volume *Asia's New Giant* (Patrick and Rosovsky, 1976), were reacting to "Japan Inc." kinds of caricatures. Johnson, in turn, felt he was correcting Patrick and his co-thinkers.
15. Haley (1987). Throughout the 1970s and 1980s, scholars discussed this process, using such varied notions as "reciprocal consent" of Richard Samuels (1987) and "patterned pluralism" put forth by Michio Muramatsu and Ellis Krauss (1987).
16. Calder (1988), passim, and Calder (1993), pp. 232–233.
17. Calder (1988), Chapter 7, and Okimoto (1989), p. 187.
18. Calder (1988), Chapter 7, and Okimoto (1989), pp. 187–188. On tax evasion, see Ramseyer and Rosenbluth (1997), p. 54.
19. The 1973 Large-Scale Retail Store Law was a revision of previous laws. For details, see Upham (1993). On the pharmacy issue, see Sakaiya (1993), pp. 37–38.

20. Ramseyer and Rosenbluth (1997), pp. 56–57. Finally, in 1989, the LDP's Commerce and Industry Division (representing small business) and its Finance Division (representing the banks) hammered out a compromise.

21. Calder (1988), p. 345.

22. On farm income from subsidies, see Sakaiya (1993), p. 32. Calder (1988), pp. 125–126, 231. Importing more farm goods would tend to lower Japan's trade surplus, which in turn would lower the value of the yen, which in turn would allow Japanese industry to boost exports. At the end of the process, the trade surplus would go back to the original level, but with greater farm imports and more industrial exports.

23. Vestal (1993).

24. Ramseyer and Rosenbluth (1997), pp. 31–34, discuss the structure and role of PARC. Their interpretation of Japanese politics is a mirror image of Chalmers Johnson's unidirectional view of Japanese political power—but in the opposite direction. In their schema, voters direct the politicians and the latter run the bureaucrats. See Uriu (1996), pp. 256–257, for a similar evaluation of Ramseyer and Rosenbluth's work.

25. Calder (1993), p. 102. There was one exception in the past. The ship-building industry, under the purview of the Transport Ministry, had been competitive until the oil shock. Calder (1988) *Crisis and Compensation* focuses on the cyclical politics of the strategy–compensation trade-off. In *Strategic Capitalism*, Calder focuses on the regulatory side while downplaying the strategic side. See also Okimoto (1989), p. 5.

26. Calder (1993), p. 105. Vestal (1993), p. 150, adds that, in return for a loan, the JDB would "often place its own representative in management to make sure that plant and equipment investment was made according to plan."

27. Unless otherwise stated, this entire discussion of coal is documented in Samuels (1987), Chapter 3. On "reciprocal consent," see footnote 15.

28. Samuels (1987), pp. 112, 115, 123, 129.

29. Calder (1993), p. 106.

30. For oil and petrochemicals, see Kikkawa (1995). On machinery makers and steel, see Tilton (1996), Chapter 6.

31. This account of Kawasaki is based on Calder (1993), pp. 183–195. See also Johnson (1982), p. 218.

32. Vestal (1993), p. 100.

33. On the prewar centralization, see Calder (1993), pp. 26–30. On the negligible role of the stock market, see Zysman (1983), p. 245. On the "overloan," see Zysman (1983), pp. 245–251, as well as Calder (1993), p. 88, who reports that the banks depended on the BOJ for about 10 percent of their funding during the 1950s and 1960s.

34. Ueno (1980), p. 384.

35. Ueno (1980), pp. 402–403.

36. Calder (1993), p. 155. From the Meiji Era through World War II, reports Calder, pp. 152–154, the bankers associations acted to set interest rates and restrict new entrants. When in 1947 the Fair Trade Commission (JFTC) ruled that this practice violated the new American-sponsored Anti-Monopoly law, then for the first time, the MOF set interest rates directly.

37. For the BOJ–MITI fight over autos, see Mutoh (1988), p. 312. For a discus-

sion of the allocation of credit according to industrial policy guidelines, see Zysman (1983), pp. 244–251.

38. Haley (1987), p. 185.

39. Ueno (1980), pp. 402–403.

40. Caves and Uekasa (1976), pp. 293–494.

41. Tsuru (1993), pp. 87–89.

42. Vestal (1993), p. 100.

43. Morita (1986), pp. 65–66.

44. Boltho (1985), p. 191.

45. Yamamura and Vandenberg (1986), p. 250.

46. Hadley, cited in Boltho (1985), p. 191.

47. Murakami and Yamamura (1982), p. 116.

48. Caves and Uekasa (1976), pp. 493–494.

49. On Sanken, see Johnson (1982), pp. 277–279. Calder (1993), pp. 181, reports: In the auto parts sector, which was highly dependent on low-interest government loans, MITI pressured small companies to consolidate into three firms in each product line: a Toyota affiliate, a Nissan affiliate and an independent. Under this pressure, the three-firm concentration for various products steadily rose throughout the 1960s. In clutches, it rose from 79 percent in 1963 to 96 percent in 1968. In piston rings and spark plugs it hit a full 100 percent by the late 1960s, and similar increases came in radiators, carburetors, and other engine components as well. Lockwood (1965), p. 499, reports "a sharp rise in the number of mergers, evidently in response to the pressures of trade liberalization."

50. On shipping, see Lockwood (1965), p. 499.

51. Yamamura (1982), p. 80.

52. Yamamura (1982), p. 82 and Caves and Uekasa (1976), p. 486.

53. Yamamura and Vandenberg (1986), p. 243.

54. There is an 80 percent correlation between the most cartelized sectors of Table 5.2 and the price-controlled sectors of Table 5.3. For more on this, see Ueno (1980), pp. 423–430.

55. Caves and Uekasa (1976), p. 492. See also Okimoto (1989), pp. 140, 149.

56. Okimoto (1989), p. 39. We'll discuss this more in Chapter 6.

57. Yamawaki (1988), pp. 295–298. Each steel firm was allowed to sell only through one wholesaler for each product in a territory. The reason was to make it more difficult for members of the cartel to cheat by offering cheap prices to a competitor's wholesaler. But this rule enshrined a system that made it more difficult for newcomers, Japanese or foreign, to find wholesalers for their products.

58. For the Sumitomo story, see Johnson (1982), pp. 268–71. In light of the impending loss of MITI's power to allocate foreign exchange, a longer-term solution was needed. MITI and top business leaders promoted the 1970 merger of Yawata and Fuji to form Nippon Steel, which now controlled 30 percent of Japan's market. Yamakawi (1988), p. 302 reports that the merger made domestic prices higher than they otherwise would have been while export prices were lower. In other words, high domestic prices subsidized exports. Exporters, like carmakers, passed on the higher steel prices at home to subsidize lower car prices abroad.

59. Uriu (1996), p. 251.

60. Murakami and Yamamura (1982), pp. 116–117, also stress the importance of barriers to entry for the implementation of the cartel policy.

61. Ramseyer and Rosenbluth (1997), p. 132.

62. Ramseyer and Rosenbluth (1997), p. 132.

63. Okimoto (1989), pp. 145–149; JFTC (1993).

64. Johnson (1982), pp. 194–195.

65. Johnson (1982), p. 287.

66. Johnson (1995), pp. 216–217.

67. Schlesinger (1997).

68. Although the Liberals and Democrats first united in 1955 to form the LDP, their predecessors ruled for most of the period before that, mainly in the person of Liberal Party Prime Minister Shigeru Yoshida.

69. Ramseyer and Rosenbluth (1997), p. 61, say this voting system was imposed in 1900 by the unelected post-Meiji oligarchs, particularly General Aritomo Yamagata, as a way of keeping the parties divided and weak and parliament weak. The 1994 electoral reform did end the multi-seat district system but in a manner calculated to leave the LDP in power and the Opposition splintered. We'll discuss that in Chapter 14.

70. Schoppa (1997), p. 98.

71. Ramseyer and Rosenbluth (1997), p. 24.

72. Ramseyer and Rosenbluth (1997), p. 25.

73. Pempel (1987), p. 136.

74. Pempel (1987), p. 136.

75. Trezise and Suzuki (1976), p. 772. On Tanaka faction, interview in May 1997.

76. Ramseyer and Rosenbluth (1997), p. 18.

77. Interview in Tokyo. On Tanaka and BOJ's monetary policy, see Suzuki (1997).

78. We'll put the deficit into context in Chapter 8.

79. Ramseyer and Rosenbluth (1997), p. 52.

80. Interview. See also Pempel (1982). Initially, Japan's equal distribution of income was not only a fruit of growth; it helped growth. Murakami has persuasively argued that Japan's income equality was key in providing demand for a mass-market auto industry as in America rather than a luxury market as in early Europe. This mass market was key to the success of first the American and then the Japanese industry. The same applied to other mass-market consumer appliances.

81. Olson (1982).

Notes to Chapter 6

1. Fallows (1994), pp. 203–204.

2. However, there is room in the theory for redistributing income through progressive taxes and government spending.

3. Rubin (1998).

4. For a discussion of the history of the "compensation principle" in trade theory, see Irwin (1996) pp. 61, 183–188. According to orthodox microeconomics, the idea that the free market is the most efficient allocator of resources, and that it maximizes welfare, is based on the premise that all market solutions are "Pareto optimal." This means that, compared with a non-market situation, at least some people can be made better off without anyone's being made worse off. Clearly, a move to free trade violates this "Pareto optimal" principle since some people are made worse off: unskilled laborers in the U.S. and owners of capital in Mexico. Compensation restores "Pareto optimality," but it requires a non-market supplement to the market. Economists have debated whether, for free trade to be optimal, such compensation actually has to be paid, or whether it is sufficient that there is enough additional income for it to be paid if the politicians so desired. Most economists have taken the latter position. But if compensation is not paid, it cannot be said that free trade maximizes welfare, only that it maximizes GDP.

5. Cited in Irwin (1996), p. 128. Mill was often aghast at how his comments were misused by protectionists in various countries, including the U.S., to support permanent protection. Nonetheless, he never retracted the comment. He later came to believe that subsidies were a better instrument than tariffs, since subsidies are transparent and thus easier to remove. For a history of the "infant industry" argument and the "economies of scale" arguments for protection, including the roles of List and Mill, see Irwin (1996), Chapters 8 and 9.

6. Johnson (1982), pp. 132–133, reports that the 1936 Automobile Manufacture Industry Law (drafted by Nobosuke Kishi) required that automakers be licensed by the government. Only Toyota and Nissan were granted licenses. By 1939, Ford and GM were out of the country despite having had a sizable presence prior to the law.

7. Watanabe (1993), pp. 202, 212–213. The 30,000 figure compares to 2,000 before restrictions were lifted.

8. Mutoh (1988), p. 312. Also see Calder (1993), p. 110, and Ueno (1980), p. 382. Ultimately, the World Bank did provide some loans—guaranteed by the Japan Development Bank—to Japan's four top automakers. Contrary to the oft-repeated claims of American critics of industrial policy, it was not MITI that opposed the development of an auto industry, but economists waving the flag of "factor endowment" trade theory.

9. Calder (1993), p. 182.

10. Watanabe (1993), pp. 194–195.

11. Mutoh (1988), pp. 313–314, 323.

12. JETRO boasts that "the government [was] the main entity behind the promotion of synthetic fibers" (Onada, 1993, p. 39). While textiles were Japan's biggest export in the 1950s, in 1949 these exports were all in traditional materials rather than synthetics. In the early 1970s, exports accounted for a full third of all Japanese textile production. But, after the oil shock, both textiles and petrochemicals were in trouble and subject to "recession cartels."

13. See Kikkawa (1995). Japan's refiners are so inefficient that they have had to be protected by official import restrictions up through 1996!

14. Porter (1990), pp. 414–415.

15. Kosai (1997), pp. 173–174.

16. See Bronfenbrenner (1965). Japan could have boosted exports by keeping its wages low and devaluing its currency from time to time. However, when these methods become a country's major source of export gains, they lead to "immiserizing growth." For this reason, some economists pessimistic about Japan's export potential advocated "domestic development."

17. For goods whose prices are dropping, high price elasticity of demand boosts sales. But when prices are rising, high price elasticity causes sales to dry up.

18. Kanamori (1968), p. 313.

19. The "Income Doubling Plan" of 1960 is excerpted in Pempel (1982), pp. 71–78. See also Itoh, Okuno, Kiyono, and Suzumura (1988), pp. 257–258, and Shinohara (1991).

20. Yonezawa (1988), p. 428.

21. Vestal (1993), p. 127. See also Yamawaki (1988), pp. 284, 290.

22. Vestal (1993), p. 127. Blumenthal (1972), p. 621, points out that such cross-industry "ripple effects" were stronger in exporting industries than in domestic industries.

23. This quotation is from Hugh Patrick (1977), p. 239.

24. Yamawaki (1988), p. 285; Yonezawa (1988), p. 432.

25. Johnson (1982), p. 211; Yonezawa (1988), p. 435.

26. Ogura and Yoshino (1988), pp. 128–129; Itoh and Kiyono (1988), pp. 171–173, and Yamawaki (1988), p. 287. See footnote 62.

27. Trezise and Suzuki (1976), p. 795.

28. Yonezawa (1988), p. 426; Uriu (1996), p. 190.

29. Krugman (1995), p. 45. See Bronfenbrenner (1965) regarding Shimamura.

30. Krause and Sekiguchi (1976), p. 423. Only half of Japan's growth in exports during the 1960s arose because its customers had grown larger and could afford to buy more. Increasing price competitiveness supplied a meager 12 percent of the export growth.

31. Kanamori (1968), p. 313.

32. Calder (1993), p. 106; Vestal (1993), pp. 83, 94, 192, 205.

33. Murakami (1996), p. 191.

34. Ito (1993), p. 199.

35. Lau (1996), pp. 76–78.

36. Ueno (1980), pp. 411–415, 423.

37. Murakami (1996), pp. 191, 226.

38. Ueno (1980), pp. 411–415, 423, 430. See also Tables 5.2 and 5.3.

39. Porter (1990), p. 551.

40. Porter (1990), p. 555.

41. Normally, returns to investment are measured by the incremental output–capital ratio, as we discussed in Chapter 4, that is, how much additional GDP is obtained from a given increase in the capital stock. Due to lack of data, we are instead measuring how much growth a country devises from its annual investment:GDP ratio. Following Minami (1994), p. 143, we define the marginal productivity of investment, or the growth return to investment, by dividing the growth rate by the investment rate. This calculation is based on the assumption that the investment rate times the marginal productivity of investment = the growth rate.

42. EPA (1995a). These figures are measured in 1990 dollars.

43. Tsuru (1993), p. 88; Kosai (1997), p. 168.

44. Johnson (1982), p. 31. See also Itoh and Kiyono (1988), pp. 156–157; Minami (1994), p. 100.

45. Denison and Chung (1976), p. 140.

46. World Bank (1993), p. 56. During 1960–89, Japan's TFP growth was the highest in the world except for Hong Kong and Taiwan. Considering the high-growth period alone, Japan's TFP growth was the highest.

47. Jorgenson (1995), p. 378. His data are for 1960–79.

48. Minami (1994), pp. 217–219.

49. Denison and Chung (1976), p. 100.

50. Peck and Tamura (1976).

51. World Bank (1993), p. 32.

52. Vestal (1993), pp. 90–93; Minami (1994), p. 60.

53. Minami (1994), pp. 60, 76.

54. Yoshikawa (1995a), p. 216.

55. Tsuru (1993), p. 84; and EPA NIPA Tables.

56. Mutoh (1988), p. 319.

57. EPA NIPA Tables.

58. In 1996, Japan exported $32 billion in semiconductors compared to $40 billion for passenger cars. These two products combined accounted for a sixth of Japan's total exports of $411 billion (JEI, 1997), p. 11.

59. The performance of chemicals in 1970–87 does not reflect competitiveness but rather its protection in a MITI-authorized "recession cartel."

60. Blumenthal (1972), p. 622.

61. Tsuru (1993) pp. 87–89; Calder (1993), p. 32.

62. Kanamori (1968). There is a controversy over the role of exports in Japan's takeoff. See Appendix B.

63. Dollar and Wolff (1993), pp. 190–191.

64. Tsuru (1993), p. 79.

65. Ogura and Yoshino (1988), pp. 128–129; Itoh and Kiyono (1988), pp. 171–173, and Yamawaki (1988), p. 287. From the 1950s through the early 1970s, Japan used successive systems of special depreciation allowances to promote investment in designated machinery by designated industries. The biggest beneficiaries of this scheme were: shipbuilding, (15 percent above normal depreciation), autos (13 percent), iron and steel (12 percent), general machinery (12 percent) and synthetic textiles (10 percent). Some economists contend that these tax breaks were not important because their size was relatively low compared to sales volume. However, just as the R&D tax credit in the U.S. rewards *increments* to R&D, so did the Japanese system. This marginal system provides the most incentive at the least cost to the government's treasury.

66. Itoh and Kiyono (1988), p. 171; Patrick and Rosovsky (1976), p. 23. For more details on government guidance of private banking, see Chapter 5 and Appendix G.

67. Itoh and Kiyono (1988), p. 158.

68. Itoh and Kiyono (1988), p. 179.

69. Lawrence (1991a), p. 20.

70. Tsuru (1993), p. 79.

71. Itoh and Kiyono (1988), pp. 159–160.

72. Itoh and Kiyono (1988), p. 161.

73. Johnson (1982), pp. 255–260.

74. Vestal (1993), p. 53.

75. Lawrence (1991b).

76. Aoki (1987), pp. 279–282.

77. Created in 1967, this committee worked with the Finance Ministry's Foreign Capital Council to hammer out a snail's pace schedule for liberalizing industries. Liberalization of the least competitive, or most strategic, or politically connected—like semiconductors and film—was held off until the 1970s (Johnson, 1982, p. 278).

78. For figures on cross-shareholding, see Koll (1997b). Both Japanese government officials and Japanese lawyers, after seeking confidentiality, have confirmed that stopping foreign takeovers was the purpose of this change. See Vestal (1993), p. 53.

79. Lawrence (1991b).

80. Ueno (1980). This is cited in Tables 5.1 and 5.3. See also Yamamura (1975).

81. Lawrence (1991b).

82. Krause and Sekiguchi (1976), pp. 419–420 report: "It is also noteworthy that the export prices of these critical industries declined more than their domestic wholesale prices."

83. Millstein (1983), pp. 279–280.

84. Millstein (1983), pp. 279–280.

85. Millstein (1983), pp. 107, 127.

86. Yamamura (1982), p. 81. The U.S.-created Anti-Monopoly Act was eviscerated by amendments soon after the American Occupation ended in 1952.

87. Yamamura and Vandenberg (1986), pp. 255–256, 259, 261.

88. Yamamura and Vandenberg (1986), pp. 255–256, 259, 261.

89. Yamamura and Vandenberg (1986), p. 257.

90. Yamamura and Vandenberg (1986), p. 248, comment: "A protected home market is a prerequisite to dumping."

91. Komiya (1988), p. 8. For the protection given to sewing machines and machine tools, see pp. 155–156 in this book.

92. See Komiya and Itoh (1988), pp. 209–210.

93. Katz (1988).

Notes to Chapter 7

1. List in the *National System of Political Economy* as cited in Hudson (1992), p. 247. For more on List see Chapter 13 of this book. See also Irwin (1996), Chapter 8.

2. Yoshikawa (1995a, 1995b).

3. See Figure 4.4b in Chapter 4.

4. Maddison is cited in Yoshikawa (1995b), p. 226. For a contrary view, see Jorgenson (1995), pp. 377–385. Yoshikawa (1995b) replies to Dale Jorgenson.

5. Cited in Saxonhouse (1994), p. 11.

6. Denison and Chung (1976), pp. 139–151; Patrick (1977), p. 238.

7. See Appendix A.

8. Calder (1993), p. 106. However, an examination of the loan portfolio of the Japan Development Bank by Vestal (1993), passim, shows a high degree of change.

9. Uriu (1996).

10. Uekasa (1988), p. 93.

11. Calder (1993), p. 148; Okimoto (1989), pp. 5–6.

12. Katz (1996a, 1996b), Lincoln (1988), p. 39. There is big difference between growth that is propelled by trade (exports plus imports), which raises productivity and investment, and growth inordinately dependent upon a trade *surplus* due to insufficient domestic demand. See Yoshikawa (1995b), pp. 82, 89; Horiye et al., (1987), p. 60; and Balassa and Noland (1988), p. 6.

13. Johnson (1982), p. 274.

14. We will discuss this situation in detail later in the chapter. Full descriptions are in Tilton (1996) and Sekiguchi (1991).

15. Tilton (1996), pp. 39–47.

16. These laws included the Depressed Industries Law (DIL) of 1978, then the Structurally Depressed Industries Law (SDIL) of 1983. When the U.S. complained that these laws impeded trade, MITI replaced them in 1987 with the Structural Conversion Facilitation Law (SCFL), which officially abolished cartels, but let MITI organize the same activities through negotiations with each firm. What was previously transparent now became opaque, but the pattern remained the same. On the prewar lineage of the Associations, see Noguchi (1994).

17. See footnote 22 and Appendix I.

18. Cited in Yamamura (1982), p. 97.

19. Sekiguchi (1991), pp. 430–431.

20. Tilton (1996), pp. 13, 100.

21. *Economist* (1995), p. 33.

22. Sekiguchi (1991), p. 432. For a more thorough explanation, see Appendix I.

23. Yamamura (1982), p. 96.

24. Yamamura (1982), p. 96.

25. Tilton (1996), p. 54.

26. Vestal (1993), pp. 200–201.

27. Sekiguchi (1991), p. 454.

28. Sekiguchi (1991), pp. 438, 454.

29. Yamazawa (1988), p. 417.

30. Tilton (1996), p. 7.

31. As Sekiguchi (1991), p. 428, put it in more technical terms, "Joint reduction of production is not effective in raising prices if foreign supply is elastic."

32. This is from a 1989 article by Kazuyuki Matsumoto, then the chief researcher of the MOF's Institute for Monetary and Economic studies, and two co-authors. It is cited in Yamamura (1990), p. 42.

33. *Economist* (1995).

34. Tilton (1996), p. 171.

35. Sekiguchi (1991), passim.

36. JFTC (1993), p. 15.

37. JFTC (1993), p. 23.

38. Confidential interview with JFTC official, New York, 1995. See also Wolff (1990).

39. Yamamura (1982), p. 88.

40. Except as otherwise noted, the facts in this account of cement are documented in Tilton (1996), pp. 80–121.

41. About half of cement costs were fixed and half variable. Companies felt that, if they could cover variable costs through exports, it was worth it to "dump." However, an export cartel was used to make sure that price wars in the export market did not push prices below even variable costs (Tilton, 1996, p. 103).

42. Tilton (1996), p. 82. Tilton adds (p. 100) that *Semento Nenkan* confirmed the "refusal to deal" policy with those buying imports.

43. Tilton (1996), pp. 104–108.

44. Tilton (1996), p. 107. Although Korean companies made complaints to the JFTC, the Japanese trucking firms refused to testify and the JFTC did nothing.

45. The Price Structure Policy Committee (1994), p. R-11, reported that, in actual cases of U.S. vs. Japanese bids for the same civil engineering construction projects, the Japanese bids for identical work were 13–45 percent higher.

46. Krauss and Coles (1990), pp. 340-341. See also Tilton (1996), p. 112.

47. See pp.171–172.

48. Ed Lincoln pointed out that these inflated costs must be taken into account when evaluating Japanese capital formation rates. Japanese may be spending a lot more of their GDP on plant and equipment investment than Americans, but, if that were deflated for exaggerated construction costs, some of the differential would disappear.

49. Tilton (1996), p. 91.

50. Unless otherwise noted, the facts in this section on steel are documented in Vestal (1993) pp. 114–144, and Tilton (1996), pp. 169–189.

51. Yamawaki (1988), p. 302; Yamakawi cited in Vestal (1993), p. 143.

52. Wolff (1990), p. 152.

53. Cited in Tilton (1996), p. 183.

54. See endnote 2 for Chapter 3.

55. For a discussion of the utilities, see Calder (1993), pp. 238, 254–255. See also Samuels (1987), pp. 161–167.

56. Wolff (1990), p. 152.

57. Unless otherwise noted, the facts in this section on petrochemicals are documented in Kikkawa (1995), pp. 89–109, Tilton (1996), pp. 122–168, and Uriu (1996), pp. 149–178.

58. Tilton (1996), p. 181. Some Japanese steel buyers may claim alleged quality differences but no one really doubts the quality of Pohang's steel since it is made with Mitsubishi technology.

59. Confidential interview, Tokyo, May 1997. An energy-intensive industry hard hit by the oil shocks, paper was one of the industries in MITI's recession cartels.

60. Tilton (1996), p. 183.

61. Tilton (1996), pp. 15, 131, 186.

62. Koll's comment came in a May 1997 interview. Unless otherwise noted, the facts in this discussion of aluminum are documented in Tanaka (1988), Tilton (1996), pp. 50–79, and Uriu (1996), pp. 178–185.

63. Tanaka (1988), p. 471.

64. Tilton (1996), pp. 59–60, 70.

65. Baumol, Blackman, and Wolff (1985); Baumol, Blackman, and Wolff (1989), Chapter 6.

66. Baumol, Blackman, and Wolff (1985), pp. 810–813.

67. Katz (1994a); Ennis and Katz (1994).

68. Dollar and Wolff (1993), p. 182.

Notes to Chapter 8

1. Yoshikawa, (1995a), pp. 82, 89. See also Horiye et al. (1987), Minami (1994), and Yamamura (1987), pp. 438–443. Some readers may wonder how this squares with our discussion of export-led industrialization. But, as Balassa and Noland (1988) note, there is a huge difference between growth led by exports, where exports provide demand for industrial output but are *matched* by imports, and growth led by trade *surpluses*.

2. See Yamamura (1987); also Komiya and Kazumoto (1990).

3. Former BOJ economist and current New Frontier Party Diet member Yoshio Suzuki (1997), p. 32, claims Finance Minister Kiichi Miyazawa ordered BOJ Governor Sumita to keep Japanese interest rates low after the February 1987 Louvre Accord in order to support the dollar. Even some foreign critics of the MOF, like Taggart Murphy, have claimed the bubble was launched to bail out America after the 1987 stock market crash. Murphy (1996), pp. 231–232, argues that the worst excesses of the bubble "all happened in 1988 and 1989 in large part because the MOF was trying to save the world from the consequences of American profligacy." This is particularly surprising on Murphy's part because much of his book focuses on the dilemmas created by Japan's deficient domestic demand.

4. EPA NIPA tables.

5. Fallows (1994), p. 8; also, Ennis and Katz (1994).

6. In some of the oldest suburbs of Tokyo, built hurriedly after the war, there are no underground gas lines or indoor flush toilets. People endure gas tanks and outhouses. Nonetheless, their cramped houses are full of TVs and microwaves and there are plenty of new cars parked outside. Not poverty, but the difficulty of digging up entire neighborhoods, is why some occasionally lack modern infrastructure.

7. Minami (1994), p. 221.

8. In most countries, investment is a *negative* function of capital stock, but in Japan during the high-growth era, some studies show it as a *positive* function of capital stock (Minami, 1994), p. 134; Yoshikawa (1995a), p. 89.

9. Yoshikawa (1995a), p. 89. Yoshikawa uses exports rather than net exports.

10. Yoshikawa (1995a), pp. 63–71. In essence, consumption rose as a *byproduct* of overall growth but anticipation of more consumption also stimulated growth. That is: $C = f(Y)$, while $Y = f(C, I, X-M)$, with I being the most important factor in the growth of Y. I, in turn, was a function of *anticipated* C and X.

11. Minami (1994), p. 221.

12. See Appendix H.

13. See Yamamura (1987) for a debate on the Maekawa thesis. See also Komiya and Kazumoto (1990).

14. EPA (1995a).

15. Sakakibara (1993).

16. The bank-centered system is not a permanent artifact of Japanese business culture. It was created after the 1927 financial crisis. Before that, the stock and bond markets in Japan functioned much as in the U.S. See Calder (1993), pp. 26–33.

17. Courtis (1997) pp. 6–7. He adds that this helps explain why these banks earn so little and provide such a low return to the savers. "In effect, Japan's financial institutions are owned by their largest borrowers. Clearly, these groups have very little interest in seeing a higher cost of borrowing. What these lose theoretically on their investment in the financial sector as a result of their lower returns, they more than make up for with the ultra low cost of their debt. In the past this was not an issue because the central focus of a younger society was creating jobs . . . [with aging] that is no longer the case and it will be less every day for the next twenty-five years."

18. Sakaiya (1993), p. 271. See also Dattel (1994), pp. 70–75.

19. Calder (1993), p. 213.

20. Japan Securities Research Institute (1988).

21. The figures and citation in the following section come from Katz (1995a).

22. In the U.S., the Resolution Trust Corporation (RTC) used taxpayers' money to buy bad assets from failed S&Ls and sell them off. In the process, many S&Ls were shut down, nearly 2,000 banker crooks went to jail, and real estate prices were allowed to hit bottom. The whole process was over in a few years and the economy barely gulped. In Japan, the MOF tried to sustain both stock and real estate prices at above-market levels. This is self-defeating, Bert Ely points out. Until buyers are sure prices have hit bottom, they won't come in; and until buyers come back, prices won't recover. As of mid-1997, seven years after the crash, stock prices were still less than half of 1990 levels. Real estate prices were less than a third of peak levels. For more on PKO, see Asher (1996a).

23. Telephone interview, February 1996. According to Balassa and Noland (1988), p. 152, back in the 1980s, when the U.S. share of Japan's trade surplus was higher, the BOJ estimated that a $40 billion cut in the U.S. budget deficit would cut the Japanese current account surplus by $22 billion a year later. The Fed found an impact about half as big.

24. Horiye et al. (1987). Japan's inordinate dependence on the U.S. is a product of its post-1973 distortions. Economist Hiroshi Yoshikawa (1995a), pp. 82, 89, stressed that "the correlation between the Japanese and U.S. business cycles is higher in the period of the 1970s and 1980s than it was in the previous period."

Notes to Chapter 9

1. From the *Communist Manifesto*. Cited in Sachs and Warner (1995), p. 5.

2. *Economist* (1996).

3. The classification of open versus closed countries in Sachs and Warner (1995) is based on factors like the prevalence of nontariff barriers, high tariffs, an overvalued currency, state control of exports, or a socialist economy. The *un*adjusted average trade:GDP ratio of the open countries was 66 percent and for the closed countries was 53 percent. However, the open countries averaged twice the population of the closed ones (29 million vs. 17 million). Since smaller countries trade far more than larger ones, we projected what the trade:GDP ratio of the closed countries would be if they had also averaged 29 million people. The result was 37 percent.

4. Sazanami, Urata and Kawai (1995) estimate that Japan's protection lowers its imports by 20 percent, but, because they limit themselves to the "resource allocation" benefits of trade, they put the cost of Japan's protection at a mere 0.6 percent of GDP. By contrast, our model, which emphasizes the competitive benefits of trade, puts the cost to Japan at a loss in growth amounting to 0.25 percent of GDP every year. After 25 years this would add up to a 10 percent smaller GDP. For more on this topic, see Appendix E.

5. Sachs and Warner (1995), p. 2.

6. Richardson (1989) focuses on the role of imports in promoting growth, as does Lee (1995). Feder (1983), pp. 59–73, reports that, in a sample of 19 semi-industrialized countries growing at 6.5–7.0 percent a year on average, export expansion contributed 2.2 percent in annual productivity gains. Half of this came because the export industries had better productivity than domestic industries. But the other half came as spillovers from the export industries, such as: competitive management, the introduction of improved production techniques, training of higher quality labor, steadier flow of imported inputs, and so forth.

7. *Nikkei Weekly*, August 4, 1997, p. 6, reports gasoline at ¥90 per liter in most metropolitan areas and the price is expected to head even lower if self-service gas stations are allowed.

8. McKinsey (1993), p. 5.

9. For documentation of this, see Appendix E.

10. This conclusion coheres with the finding of Fukuda and Toya (1995) that trade in manufactured goods alone is a much better predictor of growth than total trade.

Notes to Chapter 10

1. We deliberately left Hong Kong and Singapore out of the comparison since they are so unusual. They are cities with trade:GDP ratio in 1990 at 260 percent and 370 percent respectively.

2. World Bank (1993), pp. 54–58.

3. Krugman (1994) took Singapore's much higher dependence on investment and relatively low TFP and projected that onto all of Asia. See Katz (1995c). Even the investment-driven Asians may be doing better than the World Bank estimate if Lau (1996) is right that TFP may be underestimated in newly industrializing countries.

4. Katz (1997e).

5. Katz (1997e).

Notes to Chapter 11

1. See Appendix F.

2. To see how this squares with data showing that "outward-oriented countries" grow faster, see Appendix B. The short answer is that the key issue is not liberalism but the volume of trade.

3. The notion that Japan under-imports manufactured goods is now common-place. For a review of the literature, see Bergsten and Noland (1993), pp. 179–197. See also Lawrence (1991a, 1991b, 1993), Balassa and Noland (1988), Noland (1995a, 1995b), Petri (1991), and Knetter (1994). Bergsten and Noland (1993) cite a 1992 mimeo by James Harrigan that supports our view that both exports and imports are too low. Noland (1995a) also supports this conclusion. Also note Bergsten and Noland (1993), p. 184, where they report tariff-equivalent rates of protection due to nontariff barriers, including 70 percent for motor vehicles, 337 percent for communications equipment, 187 percent for apparel, and so forth. The main proponent of the view that Japan is not an outlier on trade is Gary Saxonhouse (1982, 1988, 1994). The proponents of the "Japan is an under-importer" view won an important victory when Bergsten gave much more credence to the view in Bergsten and Noland (1993) than he had in Bergsten and Cline (1987).

4. Tilton (1996), pp. 81, 123–124, 171.

5. Petri (1991), p. 71 ff.

6. Komiya and Itoh (1988), p. 209. See also Komiya and Kazumoto (1990) and Lincoln (1990), pp. 26, 27. These views are not so surprising in Komiya, who is well known for his opposition to reform. Moreover, as the Director-General of MITI's Research Institute of International Trade and Industry, Komiya would be expected to rationalize Japan's closed market. But it is more disappointing in Itoh, who is a proponent of reform. In a 1997 conversation, Prof. Itoh still insisted to the author that Japan's low level of trade was due to restraints on its exports rather than any closed market. On this, see Katz (1996d) and Appendix F. The trade issue seems to be a blind spot among many reformers. In a 1996 conversation with the author, Haruo Shimada, a prominent reform economist, strongly denied that Japan's market was in any way closed to imports. Its peculiar "input–output matrix" was responsible, he claimed.

7. Lincoln (1990), pp. 72–80.

8. Porter (1990), pp. 755, 758.

9. Back in 1971, when many overt restrictions on imports were just being lifted, Japan's ratio of manufactured goods to total imports was 29 percent. Using 1970 prices (to take account of oil price hikes) the ratio was still no higher than 44 percent in 1979, when the economy was supposedly liberalized. By comparison, the ratios of manufactured goods to total imports (in 1970 prices) was 74 percent for the U.S., 83 percent for Britain, 84 percent for Germany (another nation with no natural resources beyond coal), 82 percent for France, and 75 percent for Italy. In 1970, Japan's ratio of manufactured imports to total imports was 50 percent of the OECD average; by 1977 it was down to 37 percent. See Saxonhouse (1982), pp. 242–244. World Bank

figures (World Bank, 1997) show Japan at 59 percent of the OECD average in 1990 and 63 percent in 1993.

10. For more on this issue, see Katz (1996d), pp. 85–88.

11. Lawrence (1987), p. 519.

12. See Komiya and Kazumoto (1990) and Komiya and Itoh (1988).

13. Komiya and Itoh (1988), p. 209.

14. Krueger (1996), p. 194. One of the biggest drops in transport costs came in the nineteenth century when the defeat of piracy enabled commercial ships to dispense with heavy cannon, thus allowing them to devote more of their tonnage to freight.

15. Even if we combined population and distance together, they are less important. Back in 1960, the two factors combined could explain 60 percent of the difference in countries' trade levels. By 1990, they explained only 37 percent.

Notes to Chapter 12

1. See Tilton (1996), pp. 52–79; Tanaka (1988), pp. 451–471.

2. Feldman (1996b), p. 3.

3. Interview in Tokyo, May 1997.

4. *Economist* (1995).

5. *Economist* (1995); Noland (1995b).

6. Fujii (1996), pp. 5–6.

7. MITI (1996b). MITI changed its survey methods. In 1993, this survey covered firms in which the foreign share is at least one-third. In about 70 percent of the cases, the foreign share is 50 percent or more. The 1984 figures refer only to majority-owned foreign affiliates. Thus the decline in the majority-owned foreign affiliates' share is even greater than indicated by these numbers.

8. Krause and Sekiguchi (1976), p. 424. Of four classes of imports, only one, manufactured goods, had a price variable and its measured elasticity was less than one-half; i.e., for every 1 percent drop in import prices, imports increased 0.5 percent, a very low responsiveness.

9. Speech at New York Japan Society, February 7, 1994.

10. In most countries, prices affect imports in accordance with a relatively *static* parameter. E.g., the price elasticity of imports may be −1.2, so that a 1 percent decline in import prices creates a 1.2 percent rise in imports. In Japan, an abrupt appreciation of the yen has an impact because it *changes the parameter*. As we saw above, prior to the late 1980s rise of the yen, the price elasticity of imports was −0.3. After the *endaka* (rise of the yen) it moved to −0.9.

11. Sakakibara, now Vice Minister of the MOF for International Affairs, has been one of the powerful intellectual and bureaucratic opponents of reform. But he is also said to be a prime force behind Prime Minister Hashimoto's "Big Bang" reform in finance. See Sakakibara (1993).

Notes to Chapter 13

1. Choate (1990).

2. Lockwood (1965), p. 503.

3. Bronfenbrenner (1965), pp. 539–540.

4. Fairbank, Reischauer and Craig (1973), pp. 829–830.

5. Cited in Trezise and Suzuki (1976), p. 793.

6. Saxonhouse (1982), p. 244.

7. Saxonhouse (1982), p. 245.

8. Trezise cited in Livingston et al. (1973), p. 433.

9. Abegglen (1970). pp. 31–35.

10. Cited in Trezise and Suzuki (1976), p. 756.

11. Kaplan (1972).

12. Patrick and Rosovsky (1976), p. 916. During the heat of the 1980s, the charge arose that those who denied the importance of industrial policy in Japan were consciously skewing their views to the politics of trade. Andrea Boltho (1985), p. 187, wrote: "Admission that industrial policy is important carries with it, at least in American eyes, an admission that Japanese business–government relations are 'unfair' and, therefore, justify the imposition of protective measures. Hence, it is safer to claim that Japanese economic policy plays only a supportive rather than an initiating role." More likely, the pattern was more subtle. As Richardson (1997), p. 307, remarked on the Patrick–Trezise view, "Some studies in which the government role is downgraded also reflect normative preferences for free competition." Having been trained in the neoclassical paradigm, in which free markets almost always work better than government intervention in producing the highest growth, the orthodox economists were reluctant to admit of exceptions, out of fear of a "slippery slope." This is typical of all paradigms, even in the physical sciences. The instinctual impulse was to give greater credence to evidence that cast doubt on the importance and effectiveness of industrial policy.

13. Trezise and Suzuki (1976), p. 756; Patrick and Rosovsky (1976), pp. 899, 903.

14. Patrick and Rosovsky (1976), pp. 6, 20, 44–48, 57, 901–903; Trezise and Suzuki (1976), pp. 756–757, 808–811.

15. This quote is from Patrick (1977), p. 239, in which he summarizes and updates the findings of Asia's New Giant.

16. Patrick and Rosovsky (1976), pp. 47, 60.

17. Saxonhouse (1982).

18. On Saxonhouse and the rice issue, see Bergsten and Noland (1993), 180–181. Lawrence (1987) was quickly validated by Balassa and Noland (1988), Lincoln (1990), and Petri (1991), and further confirmed by Knetter (1994) and Noland (1995a and 1995b) and Sazanami, et al. (1995).

19. Bhagwati's letter was organized to criticize the Clinton Administration's trade tactics toward Japan. Even economists like Paul Krugman who knew Japan was closed felt compelled to sign, fearing that failure to do so would be misinterpreted as an endorsement of Clinton's policies. Apparently, it seemed too subtle for economic orthodoxy to say that Japan's market was closed but that Clinton's measures were a counterproductive response. See Katz (1994b).

20. Johnson (1982). See his Chapter 1 for Johnson's description of his relationship to other schools of thought.

21. The term "revisionism" was first used in a Japanese context by Business Week writers in 1989. See Neff et al. (1989).

22. Johnson (1982), p. 19. In this, Johnson was following the tradition of Alexander Gershenkron (1962) and others who posited a strong role for the state in late industrializers.

23. While the phrase "bureaucrats rule and politicians reign" is from Johnson, the "bureaucratic authoritarian" label appears to be a term invented not by Johnson himself, but by some of his followers. It is used extensively by Taggart Murphy (1996), p. 281, e.g., "What really drew brickbats, however, was the revisionists' portrayal of Japan's unchecked bureaucratic authoritarianism, which challenged [the notion] . . . that Japan was a functioning democracy."

24. Johnson (1982), pp. 24, 47–50, 274, 315–316.

25. Johnson (1982), pp. 315–316.

26. Prestowitz (1988), p. 6. When the paperback edition was published in 1989, just months before the bubble popped, the subtitle had escalated to: "How We Are Giving Our Future to Japan and How to Reclaim It."

27. Fallows (1989); Johnson (1996), pp. 432–433; Choate (1990). Eventually, the CIA was forced to disavow the *Japan 2000* report. Kent Harrington, National Intelligence Officer for Asia, disagreed with the White view. For background on the *Japan 2000* report and on debates within the CIA about Japan, see Katz (1993).

28. Fingleton (1995), p. 3. Without naming names, Murphy (1996), p. 262, wrote that, by 1992, "It was getting harder and harder to claim, as a few clued-in observers had done a year or two earlier, that this was all some kind of show staged by the authorities for the benefit of gullible foreigners." Patrick Smith (1997), p. 36, also without naming names, blames certain revisionists for spreading "paranoia," such as the view that: "Japan did not really enter a recession in the early 1990s: It was 'blindsiding' us, a sort of sneak attack, the better to achieve economic domination."

29. Fallows (1994), Chapter 4.

30. Sugiyama (1994).

31. List (1885), Chapter 15.

32. Oshima translated List's 1841 book, *National System of Political Economy* in 1889. This passage, which both represents Oshima's own view and summarizes List's views, comes from Oshima's 1891 book "On the Present Situation." It is cited in Sugiyama (1994), p. 103. This view was common among List's followers in Meiji era Japan and was enunciated by Japan's first post-Meiji leader Toshimichi Okubo, following the 1872 "Iwakura Mission," which took a tour of the U.S. and Europe.

33. While List has earned general respect among modern economists, even among those who disagree with him, Carey is usually disparaged. Even John Stuart Mill, who brought the "infant industry" argument into classical economics, disparaged Carey's tract on protection as "about the worst book on political economy I ever read" (cited in Irwin, 1996, p. 132). For more on List and Fallows, see Ennis and Katz (1994). On List and Japan, see Sugiyama (1994), pp. 11, 71, 102–103. On Carey and Japan, see Sugiyama (1994), pp. 8, 10, 71, 104. On List's ideas, see Irwin (1996), Chapter 8; Hudson (1992), Chapter 10; Roll (1938), pp. 230–231; Galbraith (1987), pp. 92–95.

34. Galbraith (1987), pp. 94–95.

35. See footnote 18 for sources. While Lawrence himself stuck to free trade

methods, not all those who cited his analysis did. In 1989, a report of the USTR's corporate-led Advisory Committee on Trade Policy and Negotiations (ACTPN, 1989), cited Lawrence to justify a policy of asking Japan to agree to numerical targets on imports, using the term "temporary quantitative indicators." Lawrence disagreed. See ACTPN (1989).

36. Yamamura (1982), p. 103.

37. Pepper et al. (1985), pp. 135–136, 138.

38. Pepper et al. (1985), pp. 140–142.

39. Hadley (1976), pp. 65–67, reviewing Caves and Uekasa (1976), commented: "Granted that it was business which accomplished the performance, yet in my view it was MITI, the Finance Ministry, and to a lesser extent the other ministries and agencies which importantly participated in the determination of the direction which the Japanese economy would take. . . . To imply . . . that Japan's steel industry, its automobile industry, its chemicals industry, its electronics industry were the product of market forces alone is to ask too much."

40. Hadley (1983), p. 5. As for the ripple effects, Hadley writes on p. 7, "Automobiles were selected as a target not only because demand was expected to rise with rising incomes . . . but for a number of other industries auto would stimulate—glass, rubber, road-building machinery, and so forth."

41. ACTPN (1989).

42. For discussion of the SII, including attitudes of Japanese toward it, see Janow (1994), p. 71, and Schoppa (1997), passim.

43. Janow (1994), pp. 62–64, 94–95.

44. Prestowitz (1993), p. 97. Schoppa (1997), pp. 3–4, notes that the revisionists were never clear how to enforce results if Japan simply refused.

45. ACTPN (1993). Janow (1994), p. 76. It was widely reported that President Clinton read the ACTPN report and told USTR Mickey Kantor that he agreed with it.

46. Confidential interview in Tokyo, February 1996.

47. Interviews with author, 1989. Henry Kissinger and Cyrus Vance took a similar tack in their famous 1989 piece in *Foreign Affairs*. These arguments also appealed to the present author during this period.

48. Interview with author.

49. Interview, January 1998.

50. Vestal (1993). See also Wood (1993) for a good journalistic account of why the miracle failed.

51. Asher (1996a), p. 19.

52. Hirsh and Henry (1997), p. 11.

53. Note to author, September 1997. See also Hatch and Yamamura (1996).

54. Murphy (1996).

55. Telephone interview, April 1997.

56. Okubo (1996), passim in Preface.

57. See Katz (1997b, 1997c).

58. Schoppa (1997).

59. Hirsh and Henry (1997), p. 15. We will discuss the issue of financial reform and the pension funds further in Chapter 14.

60. Milner (1988).
61. Confidential interview with U.S. businessman.

Notes to Chapter 14

1. Speech at New York Japan Society, December 5, 1995.
2. Patrick (1995), p. 15.
3. Interview with author.
4. Ennis (1997), p. 2.
5. TOE (1997), p. 12.
6. Katz (1997b).
7. Ikuta (1995), pp. xiv, 21.
8. Cited in Johnson (1995), p. 212.
9. Under the pressure of the LDP's farm base, Hata issued the now-notorious statement that the Japanese people could not eat U.S. beef due to their especially long intestines. He was reportedly extremely embarrassed by the statement. In 1994, after Hata became a reformer and Prime Minister, former U.S. Trade Representative Carla Hills who had dealt with Hata as Agriculture Minister said in a phone interview that the comments about intestines "don't characterize the man. I've read that statement in the newspaper. He's never made any such statement to me."
10. Ramseyer and Rosenbluth (1997), p. 196.
11. Hata began his career in the Diet in 1968 when his father, a Diet member, died and Kakuei Tanaka personally recruited Hata to take his father's place. In the same year, Tanaka did the same for Opposition leader Ichiro Ozawa when Ozawa's father died. Hashimoto, incidentally, was recruited to run for the Diet in 1963 when his Diet member father died. Hashimoto's recruiter was Prime Minister Eisaku Sato. Tanaka at the time was a leader in Sato's faction. In other words, both the Prime Minister and many of the Opposition leaders are ex-Tanaka faction members who inherited *koenkai*-based Diet seats from their fathers. See Ramseyer and Rosenbluth (1977), p. 69.
12. See Schlesinger (1997).
13. See Courtis (1997) for more on the background of the "Big Bang."
14. Koll (1997a), p. 5. Koll suggests that, if banks could keep up the operating profits they had in 1997, on *aggregate*, they could get out of the bad debt problem by around the year 2000. But at least half of the top 20 banks would need another few years to get out of trouble. There are also questions of whether 1997 operating profits can continue as budget cutting hurts the construction and real estate sectors that account for a quarter of bank assets. Moreover, since low interest rates help bank profits, if recovery takes off enough to raise raises from their ultra-low 1997 levels, bank operating profits could be cut.
15. *Institutional Investor* (1997), p. 115; Hamilton (1997), p. A11; Desmond (1997), p. 95.
16. Weinberg (1996).
17. Interview with author, 1997; Desmond (1997), p. 95.
18. Hamilton (1997), p. A11.

19. *Nikkei Weekly* (1997).
20. Katz (1997b).
21. Pempel (1997), p. 335.
22. Hiatt (1998).
23. Interview with author, Tokyo, May 1997.

Notes to the Appendices

1. Miyohei Shinohara, a prominent economist who later became a senior official of the Economic Planning Agency, recounts and responds to the "impossibility objections" in Shinohara (1991). Ryutaro Komiya (1988), pp. 6–7, 21, who labels Shinohara a "giant" of the "prehistoric era" of thinking about industrial policy, insists the economy developed on its own without much of a role for industrial policy. For those who see industrial policy as permanent, see Johnson (1982), Chapter 9.

2. Porter (1990), passim.

3. For the issue of industry-wide increasing returns and external economies, see Irwin (1996), Chapter 9. Irwin reports Edgeworth's view on page 146.

4. Itoh et al. (1988), pp. 261–262.

5. Itoh et al. (1988), pp. 261–262.

6. Cited in Edwards (1993), p. 1372.

7. Krugman (1990), pp. 185–186.

8. Eads and Yamamura (1987), p. 434.

9. Itoh et al. (1988), p. 264.

10. Krause and Sekiguchi (1976).

11. Tsuru (1993), p. 85. For other views in agreement with ours, see Blumenthal (1972) and Kuznets (1988) pp. S29–S31.

12. Cited in Krause and Sekiguchi (1976), p. 402.

13. Barro and Sala-i-Martin (1995).

14. Barro and Sala-i-Martin (1995), Chapter 1.

15. De Long and Summers (1991). Some economists, in accordance with the absolute convergence model, insist that it is high growth that causes high savings rates, not the other way around. For more on this debate, see Katz (1996d, pp. 77–80). Also see footnote 16 below.

16. Our base of comparison is a selection of 22 countries (23 for 1973–90). We wanted only countries that had at least several million people, and were either already rich, or were clearly heading that way. We excluded Latin America because of the "lost decade" of the 1980s; India and China because they were too populous; and Hong Kong and Singapore because they were gross outliers on trade. That left us with: the U.S., Japan, Canada, Australia, Switzerland, Sweden, The Netherlands, UK, Belgium, Norway, Denmark, West Germany, France, Finland, Italy, Austria, Spain, Greece, Malaysia, Taiwan, South Korea, and Thailand. In the post-1973 period, when Indonesia took off, it was added, in order to have a third populous country besides Japan and the U.S.

For 1960–70 we tried various combinations of variables. The fly in the ointment is the interaction of trade and population. While trade was not significant, simply taking out trade wreaks havoc with the population variable. One reason is that Japan and the U.S. are outliers on population and growth. We tried removing the U.S. and show results with and without the U.S. Note that in Table D.1 Equation 1 and Equation 4 give similar results for the Japan dummy.

17. Another contention is that to avoid a "simultaneity bias," an instrumental variable should be used. We did try an instrumental variable and it did not appreciably change the result. For more on this issue, see Katz (1996d, pp. 76–77).

18. Our view is supported by Yoshikawa (1995d), who cites the findings of growth expert Angus Maddison that high oil prices lowered Japan's growth by only 0.2 percent a year during 1973–84.

19. Feder (1983); Edwards (1993); Krueger (1996).

20. Sazanami et al. (1995).

21. Dollar and Wolff (1993), pp. 138–140.

22. Dollar and Wolff (1993), p. 178.

23. Richardson (1989) points out that, when key industries are characterized by imperfect competition, imports break down concentration of industry and oligopolistic market power. This argument coheres with the findings of Fukuda and Toya (1995) that trade in *manufactured goods* is especially stimulative.

24. Sachs and Warner (1995), p. 20. In the HOS model, the factor, not the sector, matters for protection.

25. Kenen (1994), p. 243.

26. Sachs and Warner (1995), p. 3.

27. Petri (1991).

28. Lawrence (1987), p. 519. In 1986, when both Japan and Germany ran similar surpluses in merchandise trade (4.3 percent and 5.8 percent of GDP respectively), Germany's merchandise exports amounted to 27 percent of GDP and imports added up to 21 percent of GDP. By contrast, Japan exported 10 percent of its GDP while importing only 6 percent. The trade balances were similar, but, at 48 percent, Germany's total trade was three times as high as Japan's 16 percent.

29. This is a simplifying assumption. Changes in the current account can lead to changes in the domestic savings–investment imbalance, within limits. See Balassa and Noland (1988).

30. Prof. Itoh presented this argument in a private conversation in New York City in 1997.

31. Krugman (1995), p. 55.

32. Growth-associated trade deficits were a problem in the 1950s and early 1960s, but not since then.

33. Krugman (1995).

34. Houthakker and Magee findings are cited in Krugman (1995). In the case of the U.S., import elasticities dropped from 1.5 to 1.3, still well above 1. In Japan's case, income elasticities dropped from 1.23 to 0.80. Japan's imports have always been much more a function of manufacturing output than GDP. Since manufacturing was growing much faster than GDP in the earlier period, the apparent elasticity relative to GDP was greater than 1. When manufacturing slowed down to a level closer to GDP growth, and when manufacturing became less raw material and energy-intensive, then income elasticities fell below 1.

35. See Milner (1988) and Keohane and Milner (1996) for arguments and case studies showing that, in most countries, exporting and multinational companies lead anti-protectionist politics.

36. Vestal (1993), pp. 90–93; Minami (1994), p. 60. See discussion of this issue in Chapter 6.

37. Minami (1994), p. 221.

38. Sekiguchi and Horiuchi (1988), p. 371.

39. Yamamura (1982), p. 88, writes: "Economists had no difficulty in showing that prices of products of highly oligopolistic markets had grown more rigid and less responsive to the supply and demand in many markets."

40. Sekiguchi and Horiuchi (1988), p. 371.

41. Sekiguchi and Horiuchi (1988), p. 372.

42. Sekiguchi (1991), p. 428.

43. Cited in Yamamura (1990), p. 42.

44. *Economist* (1995).

45. Knetter (1994) also argues that Japanese barriers act like quotas, using as evidence the fact that German exporters charge higher prices in Japan than the U.S. because they hope to capture some of the quota "rents." Petri (1991) shows that Japanese consumers do respond to import prices much more so than Japanese business and especially the government. By contrast, Lawrence (1987), pp. 539–543, argues that Japan's barriers are more like a tariff because, on the whole, Japan's imports have a price elasticity significantly greater than zero, –0.7, compared to –1.1 for the U.S. But Lawrence finds the highest import price elasticities are in Japan's export sectors. He finds low or negligible price elasticities in motor vehicles and in such areas of Japanese weakness as food, textiles, and basic metals.

46. Sazanami et al. (1995), pp. 29–45.

47. Petri (1991).

48. Katz (1995b) and Meyer (1992). Chrysler and Ford have also learned that, if they want to control their own pricing and sell more in Japan, they must control their distribution. GM, for now, is sticking with Yanase.

49. Petri (1991).

50. Knetter (1994), p. 3.

51. Knetter (1994), p. 7.

52. Noland (1995b), pp. 259–260.

53. See Komiya and Irie (1990) for a presentation of this view.

54. Supply-siders claim the budget deficit has no effect on the trade deficit since some nations running budget deficits have trade surpluses. But they are ignoring the key role of savings–investment balance.

55. Katz (1996c). Back in the 1980s, when more of Japan's trade surplus came from trade with the U.S., the impact was about twice as high. See Balassa and Noland (1988), p. 152, for a report on BOJ and Fed estimates.

56. See Komiya and Irie (1990) for a presentation of this view. See Yamamura (1990) for a discussion of Komiya's opposition to the Maekawa thesis. Economists Bela Balassa and Marcus Noland (1988), pp. 135–141, comment: "Recently, however, there has been a revival of an old view that regards the current account as

simply the balance between exogenously determined domestic saving and investment propensities. This position is controversial since *it implies that neither exchange rates nor trade policy have any effect on the current account* [emphasis added]." Ironically, this theory puts Komiya et al. in the same camp as the revisionists, who also assert incorrectly that changes in the yen have no effect on Japan's trade surplus. Balassa and Noland present regressions that refute this one-way-street causality theory.

57. At a panel discussion at the April 1997 conference of the Economic Strategy Institute, economists Richard Koo, David Hale, Robert Hormats, and Wayne Angell all expressed concern along these lines.

Bibliography

Abegglen, James. 1970. "The Economic Growth of Japan." *Scientific American* 222:3 (March 1970). Pp. 31–35.

ACTPN (Advisory Committee for Trade Policy and Negotiations). 1989. *Analysis of the U.S.-Japan Trade Problem.* Washington: ACTPN, February 1989.

———. 1993. *Major Findings and Recommendations on U.S.-Japan Trade Policy.* Washington: ACTPN, January 1993.

Alexander, Arthur. 1997. "U.S.-Japan Relations and the Japanese Economy." *JEI Report* No. 25A. July 4, 1997.

Aoki, Masahiho. 1987. "The Japanese Firm in Transition." In *The Political Economy of Japan: Volume 1: The Domestic Transformation.* Ed. Kozo Yamamura and Yasukichi Yasuba. Stanford: Stanford University Press.

Asher, David. 1996a. "Economic Myths Explained: What Became of the Japanese Miracle." *Orbis.* Spring 1996.

———. 1996b. "The Author Responds." *Orbis.* Summer 1996.

Balassa, Bela. 1978. "Exports and Economic Growth: Further Evidence." *Journal of Development Economics* 5. Pp. 181–189.

———. 1988a. "The Lessons of East Asian Development: An Overview." *Economic Development and Cultural Change* 36 (Supplement, April 1988). S274–S290.

Balassa, Bela, and Marcus Noland. 1988. *Japan in the World Economy.* Washington: Institute for Intenational Economics.

Barro, Robert, and Jong-Wha Lee. 1994. Data Set for a Panel of 138 Countries. Diskette.

Barro, Robert, and Xavier Sala-i-Martin. 1995. *Economic Growth.* New York: McGraw Hill.

Baumol, William, Sue Anne Batey Blackman and Edward Wolff. 1985. "Unbalanced Growth Revisited: Asymptotic Stagnancy and New Evidence." *American Economic Review* 75. (September 1985). Pp. 806–817.

———. 1989. *Productivity and American Leadership: The Long View.* Cambridge: MIT.

Bergsten, C. Fred, and William Cline. 1987. *The U.S.-Japan Economic Problem.* Washington: Institute for International Economics.

Bergsten, C. Fred, and Marcus Noland. 1993. *Reconcilable Differences? U.S.-Japan Economic Conflict.* Washington: Institute for International Economics.

Blumenthal, Tuvia. 1972. "Exports and Economic Growth: The Cast of Postwar Japan." *Quarterly Journal of Economics* (November 1972). Pp. 617–631.

Boltho, Andrea. 1985. "Was Japan's Industrial Policy Successful?" *Cambridge Journal of Economics* 9. Pp. 187–201.

Borrus, Michael. 1983. "The Politics of Competitive Erosion in the U.S. Steel Industry." In *American Industry in International Competition*. Eds. John Zysman and Laura Tyson. Ithaca: Cornell University Press.

Bosworth, Barry. 1993. *Saving and Investment in a Global Economy*. Washington: The Brookings Institution.

Bronfenbrenner, Martin. (1965). "Economic Miracles and Japan's Income-Doubling Plan." In *The State and Economic Enterprise*. Ed. William Lockwood. Princeton: Princeton University Press.

Bronfenbrenner, Martin, and Yasukichi Yasuba. 1987. "Economic Welfare." In *The Political Economy of Japan: Volume 1: The Domestic Transformation*. Eds. Kozo Yamamura and Yasukichi Yasuba. Stanford: Stanford University Press.

Business Week. "Two Japans." January 27, 1997.

Calder, Kent. 1988. *Crisis and Compensation: Public Policy and Political Stability in Japan*. Princeton: Princeton University Press.

————. 1993. *Strategic Capitalism*. Princeton: Princeton University Press.

Caves, Richard, and Masu Uekasa. 1976. "Industrial Organization." In *Asia's New Giant*. Eds. Hugh Patrick and Henry Rosovksy. Washington: The Brookings Institution.

Choate, Pat. 1990. *Agents of Influence: How Japan's Lobbyists in the United States Manipulate America's Political and Economic System*. New York: Alfred A. Knopf.

Clark, Rodney. 1979. *The Japanese Company*. New Haven: Yale University Press.

Courtis, Kenneth. 1997. "Japan: Big Bang or Wee Whimper." Tokyo: Deutsche Morgan Grenfell. August 1, 1997.

Crawcour, E. Sidney. 1997. "Economic Change in the Nineteenth Century." In *The Economic Emergence of Modern Japan*. Ed. Kozo Yamamura. Cambridge, UK: Cambridge University Press.

Dattel, Eugene. 1994. *The Sun That Never Rose: The Inside Story of Japan's Failed Attempt at Global Financial Dominance*. Chicago: Probus.

De Long, J. Bradford, and Lawrence Summers. 1991. "Equipment Investment and Economic Growth." *Quarterly Journal of Economics* (May 1991).

Denison, Edward, and William Chung. 1976. "Economic Growth and Its Sources." In *Asia's New Giant*. Ed. Hugh Patrick and Henry Rosovksy. Washington: The Brookings Institution.

Desmond, Charles. 1997. "The Bottom Line on Japan." *Fortune*. July 21, 1997. Pp. 92–96.

Dollar, David, and Edward Wolff. 1993. *Competitiveness, Convergence, and International Specialization*. Cambridge: MIT Press.

Eads, George, and Kozo Yamamura. 1987. "The Future of Industrial Policy." In *The Political Economy of Japan, Volume 1: The Domestic Transformation*. Eds. Kozo Yamamura and Yasukichi Yasuba. Stanford: Stanford University Press.

Economic Planning Agency (EPA), Government of Japan. 1995a. *Report on Revised National Accounts on the Basis of 1990*. Tokyo: Economic Planning Agency. (CD-ROM Version).

————. 1995b. *Social and Economic Plan for Structural Reforms towards a More Vigorous Economy and Secure Life.* (English summary). Tokyo: Economic Planning Agency.

————. 1996a. *Economic Survey of Japan, 1995–96: Reforms Usher in New Perspectives.* Tokyo: Economic Planning Agency.

————. 1996b. *Structural Reform in Six Areas: The Summary of the Recommendation of the Economic Council.* (English summary). Tokyo: Economic Planning Agency.

————. 1997. *Report on Revised National Accounts on the Basis of 1990.* Tokyo: Economic Planning Agency. (CD-ROM Version).

Economist. 1995. "The Shock of the Yen." *Economist.* April 8, 1995. Pp. 33.

————. 1996. "Economics Focus: Tigers or Tortoises." *Economist.* October 26, 1996.

Edwards, Sebastion. 1992. "Trade Orientation, Distortions, and Growth in Developing Countries." *Journal of Development Economics* 39. Pp. 31–57.

————. 1993. "Openness, Trade Liberalization, and Growth in Developing Countries." *Journal of Economic Literature* 31. Pp. 1358–93.

Ehrlich, Edna. 1960. "The Role of Banking in Japan's Economic Development." Ph.D. dissertation submitted June 1960 to the Faculty of the Political and Social Sciences of the New School for Social Research. Chapter 12.

Ennis, Peter. 1997. "Impasse, Inc." *Oriental Economist Report* 65: 10 (December 1997).

Ennis, Peter, and Richard Katz. 1994. "The System That Never Was." *Tokyo Business Today.* (November 1994). Pp. 28–31.

Fairbank, John, Edwin Reischauer, and Albert Craig. 1973. *East Asia: Tradition and Transformation.* Boston: Houghton Mifflin.

Fallows, James. 1989. "Containing Japan." *Atlantic Monthly* (May 1989).

————. 1994. *Looking At the Sun.* New York: Pantheon Books.

Feder, Gershon. 1983. "On Exports and Economic Growth." *Journal of Development Economics* 12 (February–April 1983). Pp. 59–73.

Feldman, Robert. 1996. *The Golden Goose and the Silver Fox: Productivity, Aging and Japan's Economic Future.* June 12, 1996. Tokyo: Salomon Brothers.

Fingleton, Eammon. 1995. *Blindside: Why Japan Is Still on Track to Overtake the U.S. by the Year 2000.* Boston: Houghton Mifflin.

Fujii, Tomoko. 1996. *Import Boom Over.* June 17, 1996. Tokyo: Salomon Brothers.

Fukuda, Shin-ichi, and Hideko Toya. 1995. "Conditional Convergence in East Asian Countries: The Role of Exports in Economic Growth." In *Growth Theories in Light of the East Asian Experience.* Eds. Takatoshi Ito and Anne Krueger. Chicago: University of Chicago Press.

Galbraith, John K. 1987. *Economics in Perspective: A Critical History.* Boston: Houghton, Mifflin Co.

Gerschenkron, Alexander. 1962. *Economic Backwardness in Historical Perspective.* New York: Praeger.

Government of Japan. 1997. *The Program for Economic Structure Reform* (English summary). Tokyo: Government of Japan. January 1997.

Hadley, Eleanor. 1976. " 'Industrial Organization' by Caves and Uekasa: A Review Essay." *Japanese Economic Studies* (Winter 1976–77). Pp. 64–81.

————. 1983. "The Secret of Japan's Success." *Challenge* (May–June 1983). Pp. 4–10.

Haley, John. 1987. "Governance by Negotiation: A Reappraisal of Bureaucratic Power in Japan." In *The Trade Crisis: How Will Japan Respond?* Seattle: Society for Japanese Studies.

Hamilton, David. 1997. "Japan's Slow-Motion Economic Revolution Takes Shape." *Wall Street Journal*. September 18, 1997. Pp. A11.

Hatch, Walter, and Kozo Yamamura. 1996. *Asia in Japan's Embrace: Building a Regional Production Alliance*. Cambridge, UK: Cambridge University Press.

Hatoyama, Yukio. 1997. "An Agenda for Empowerment: With a Conciliatory Spirit of *Yuai* and *Kyosei*." Speech at New York Japan Society. September 9, 1997.

Helliwell, John. 1992. *International Growth Linkages: Evidence from Asia and the OECD*. NBER Working Paper No. 4245. Cambridge: National Bureau of Economic Research.

Henry, E. Keith. 1995. "Regional Expansion Abroad and Domestic Restructuring at Home." *The MITI Japan Program Science, Technology and Management Report* Vol. 2, No. 2.

Hiatt, Fred. 1998. "In Japan, Scandal—and Opportunity." *Washington Post*. February 1, 1998. Pp. C9.

Hirschmeier, Johannes. 1965. "Shibusawa, Eiichi: Industrial Pioneer." In *The State and Economic Enterprise*. Ed. William Lockwood. Princeton: Princeton University Press.

Hirsh, Michael, and E. Keith Henry. 1997. "The Unraveling of Japan Inc." *Foreign Affairs* 76: 3 (March/April 1997).

Horiye, Yasuhiro, Sadao Naniwa and Suzu Ishihara. 1987. "The Changes of Japanese Business Cycles." *Bank of Japan Monetary and Economic Studies* 5 (December 1987). Pp. 49–100.

Horiye, Yasuzo. 1965. "Entrepreneurship in Meiji Japan." In *The State and Economic Enterprise*. Ed. William Lockwood. Princeton: Princeton University Press.

Howell, Thomas, Brent Bartlett and Warren Davis. 1992. *Creating Advantage: Semiconductors and Government Industrial Policy in the 1990s*. San Jose: Semiconductor Industry Association.

Hudson, Michael. 1992. *Trade, Development and Foreign Debt: Volume I: International Trade*. London: Pluto Press.

Ikuta, Tadahide. 1995. *Kanryo: Japan's Hidden Government*. Tokyo: NHK Publishing.

Imai, Ken-ichi. 1980. "Japan's Industrial Organization." In *Industry and Business in Japan*. Ed. Kazuo Sato. Armonk, NY: M.E. Sharpe.

————. 1982. "Japan's Changing Industrial Structure and U.S.-Japan Relations." In *Policy and Trade Issues of the Japanese Economy: American and Japanese Perspectives*. Ed. Kozo Yamamura. Seattle: University of Washington Press.

Institutional Investor. 1997. "Fidelity Takes on Japan." *Institutional Investor* 31: 2 (February 1997).

Irwin, Douglas. 1996. *Against the Tide: An Intellectual History of Free Trade*. Princeton: Princeton University Press.

Ito, Takatoshi. 1993. *The Japanese Economy*. Cambridge: MIT Press.

Itoh, Motoshige, and Kazuharo Kiyono. 1988. "Foreign Trade and Direct Investment." In *Industrial Policy of Japan*. Eds. Ryutaro Komiya, Masahiro Okuno, and Kotaro Suzumura. San Diego: Academic Press.

Itoh, Motoshige, Masahiro Okuno, Kazuharo Kiyono and Kotaro Suzumura. 1988. "Industry Promotion and Trade." In *Industrial Policy of Japan*. Ed. Ryutaro Komiya, Masahiro Okuno, and Kotaro Suzumura. San Diego: Academic Press.

Janow, Merit. 1994. "Trading with an Ally: Progress and Discontent in U.S.-Japan Trade Relations." In *The United States, Japan, and Asia*. Ed. Gerald Curtis. New York: Norton.

Japan Economic Institute (JEI). 1995. "Statistical Profile: International Transactions of Japan and the U.S. in 1995." *JEI Report* 45A (December 5, 1997).

Japan Fair Trade Commission (JFTC). 1993. "Executive Summary." In *A Fact Finding Survey of Industrial Sector Transactions in Regard to the Flow of Flat Glass*. Tokyo: Japan Fair Trade Commission.

Japan Securities Research Institute. 1988. *Report on Japan's Stock Price Level*. Tokyo: Japan Securities Research Institute.

Japan Tariff Association. 1995. *The Summary Report on Trade of Japan* (November 1995).

Japan Weekly Monitor, November 4, 1996.

Johnson, Chalmers. 1982. *MITI and the Japanese Miracle: The Growth of Industrial Policy, 1925–1975*. Stanford: Stanford University Press.

———. 1995. *Japan: Who Governs?* New York: Norton.

———. 1996. "Japan's 'Miracle' Economy." *Orbis*. Summer 1996.

Jorgenson, Dale. 1995. *Productivity: Volume 2: International Comparisons of Economic Growth*. Cambridge: MIT Press.

Kanamori, Hisao. 1968. "Economic Growth and Exports." In *Economic Growth: The Japanese Experience Since the Meiji Era*. Eds. Lawrence Klein and Kazushi Ohkawa. Homewood, IL: Richard D. Irwin.

Kaplan, Eugene. 1972. *Japan: The Government:Business Relationship (A Guide for the American Businessman)*. Washington: U.S. Department of Commerce.

Katz, Richard. 1993. "Japan 2000 Controversy Reveals CIA Debate on Japan." *Nikkei Weekly*. February 1993.

———. 1994a. "Japan's Shifts to the Slow Lane: A U.S. View." *Diamond Weekly*. May 1994.

———. 1994b. "Paul Krugman: Why I Reversed My Stance on Competitiveness." *Global Business*. Winter 1994.

———. 1995a. "Why Japan's Banking Crisis Is So Intractable." *Global Business*. Winter 1995.

———. 1995b. "This Time They're Really Coming: U.S. Automakers in Japan, Asia. *Diamond Weekly*. July 1995.

———. 1995c. "Asian Realities and Paul Krugman's Myths." *Global Business*. Spring 1995.

———. 1996a. "Budget-Cutting in America Will Worsen Fiscal Woes in Japan." *Diamond Weekly*. January 27, 1996.

————. 1996b. "Jolt of U.S. Budget Cuts Felt in Japan." *Nikkei Weekly*. March 25, 1996.

————. 1996c. "Reply to Ken Shiraishi." *Diamond Weekly*. March 1996.

————. 1996d. "From Growth Superstar to Economic Underachiever: The Role of Trade in Japan's Sagging Fortunes," and "Reply to Professor Kazuo Sato." *Japanese Economic Studies*. March 1996.

————. 1997a. "Japan's Self-Defeating Trade Policy: Mainframe Economics in a PC World." *Washington Quarterly*. March 1997. Washington: Center for Strategic and International Studies.

————. 1997b. "Emerging U.S. View Portrays Japan as System That Soured." *Nikkei Weekly*. April 7, 1997.

————. 1997c. "Beyond Revisionism: New Commerce Department Report Marks Shift in Washington's View of Japan." The *Oriental Economist Report*. April 1997.

————. 1997d. "Look Who's 'Hollowing Out' Now." *The Oriental Economist Report*. 65: 5 (July 1987).

————. 1997e. "East Asia To Recover Faster Than Japan." *The Oriental Economist Report*. Vol. 65, No. 10. December 1997.

————. 1998. "Kodak's Moment: Not A Pretty Picture." *The Oriental Economist Report*. Vol. 66, No. 1. January 1998.

Keizai Koho Center. 1997. *Japan 1997: An International Comparison*. Tokyo: Keizai Koho Center.

Kenen, Peter. 1994. *The International Economy*. (Third Edition). Cambridge, UK: Cambridge University Press.

Keohane, Robert, and Helen Milner, eds. 1996. *Internationalization and Domestic Politics*. Cambridge, UK: Cambridge University Press.

Keynes, John Maynard. 1964. *The General Theory of Employment, Interest and Money*. New York: Harcourt, Brace and World.

Kikkawa, Takeo. 1995. "Enterprise Groups, Industry Associations, and Government: The Case of the Petrochemical Industry in Japan." *Business History* 37: 3. Pp. 89–110.

Knetter, Michael. 1994. "Why Are Retail Prices in Japan So High? Evidence from German Export Prices." NBER Working Paper No. 4894. Cambridge, MA: National Bureau of Economic Research.

Kohama, Hirohisa, and Shujiro Urata. 1993. In *Industrial Policy in East Asia*. Eds. Ryuichiro Inoue, Hirohisa Kohama and Shujiro Urata. Tokyo: Japan External Trade Organization (JETRO).

Koll, Jesper. 1997a. "The Endgame Has Started for Japan's Banks." Tokyo: J.P. Morgan. April 18, 1997.

————. 1997b. "Japan Economic Overview—From Global Player to Leading and Mature Player." Tokyo: J.P. Morgan. May 12, 1997.

Komiya, Ryutaro. 1988. "Introduction." In *Industrial Policy of Japan*. Eds. Ryutaro Komiya, Masahiro Okuno and Kotaro Suzumura. San Diego: Academic Press.

Komiya, Ryutaro, and Motoshige Itoh. 1988. "Japan's International Trade and Trade Policy, 1955–84." In *The Political Economy of Japan: Volume 2: The Changing*

International Context. Ed. Takashi Inoguchi and Daniel Okimoto. Stanford: Stanford University Press.

Komiya, Ryutaro, Masahiro Okuno and Kotaro Suzumura, Eds. 1988. *Industrial Policy of Japan.* San Diego: Academic Press.

Komiya, Ryutaro, and Kazumoto, Irie. 1990. "The U.S.-Japan Trade Problem: An Economic Analysis from a Japanese Viewpoint." In *Japan's Economic Structure: Should It Change?* Ed. Kozo Yamamura. Seattle, WA: Society for Japanese Studies.

Kosai, Yutaka. 1997. "The Postwar Japanese Economy, 1945–1973." In *The Economic Emergence of Modern Japan.* Ed. Kozo Yamamura. Cambridge, UK: Cambridge University Press.

Krause, Lawrence, and Sueo Sekiguchi. 1976. "Japan and the World Economy." In *Asia's New Giant.* Eds. Hugh Patrick and Henry Rosovksy. Washington: The Brookings Institution.

Krauss, Ellis, and Isobel Coles. 1990. "Built-In Impediments: The Political Economy of the U.S.-Japan Construction Dispute." In *Japan's Economic Structure: Should It Change?* Ed. Kozo Yamamura. Seattle, WA: Society for Japanese Studies.

Krueger, Anne. 1990. "Asian Trade and Growth Lessons." *American Economic Review* 80. Pp. 108–12.

———. 1996. "Threats to 21st Century Growth: The Challenge of the International Trading System." In *The Mosaic of Economic Growth.* Ed. Ralph Landau, Timothy Taylor and Gavin Wright. Stanford: Stanford University Press.

Krugman, Paul. 1981. "Trade, Accumulation, and Uneven Development." *Journal of Development Economics* 8. Pp. 149–161.

———. 1990. "Import Protection as Export Promotion: International Competition in the Presence of Oligopoly and Economies of Scale." In *Rethinking International Trade.* Cambridge: MIT.

———. 1994. "The Myth of the Asian Miracle." *Foreign Affairs.* November–December 1994.

———. 1995. "Differences in Income Elasticities and Trends in Real Exchange Rates. In *Currencies and Crises.* Cambridge: MIT Press.

Krugman, Paul, and Richard Baldwin. 1990. "Market Access and International Competition: A Simulation Study of 16K Random Access Memories." In *Rethinking International Trade.* Ed. Paul Krugman. Cambridge: MIT.

Kuznets, Paul. 1988. "An East Asian Model of Economic Development: Japan, Taiwan and South Korea." *Economic Development and Cultural Change* 36 (Supplement, April 1988). S11–S43.

Kuznets, Simon. 1968. "Notes on Japan's Economic Growth." In *Economic Growth: The Japanese Experience Since the Meiji Era.* Eds. Lawrence Klein and Kazushi Ohkawa. Homewood, IL: Richard D. Irwin.

Lau, Lawrence. 1996. "Sources of Long-Term Economic Growth." In *The Mosaic of Economic Growth.* Ed. Ralph Landau, Timothy Taylor and Gavin Wright. Stanford: Stanford University Press.

Lawrence, Robert. 1987. "Imports in Japan: Closed Markets or Minds?" In *Brookings Papers on Economic Activity* 2 (1987). Washington: The Brookings Institution.

———. 1991a. "How Open Is Japan?" In *Trade with Japan: Has the Door Opened*

Wider? Ed. Paul Krugman. Chicago: University of Chicago Press.

————. 1991b. "Efficient or Exclusionist? The Import Behavior of Japanese Corporate Groups." *Brookings Papers on Economic Activity* 1 (Summer 1991). Washington: The Brookings Institution.

————. 1993. "Japan's Different Trade Regimes: An Analysis with Particular Reference to *Keiretsu.*" *Journal of Economic Perspectives* 7: 3 (Summer 1993). Pp. 3–19.

Leamer, Edward. 1992. "Testing Trade Theory." NBER Working Paper No. 3957. Cambridge: National Bureau of Economic Research.

Lee, Jong-Wha. 1995. "Capital Goods Imports and Long-Run Growth." *Journal of Development Economics* 48. Pp. 91–110.

Lincoln, Edward. 1988. *Japan: Facing Economic Maturity.* Washington: The Brookings Institution.

————. 1990. *Japan's Unequal Trade.* Washington: The Brookings Institution.

List, Friedrich. 1885. *The National System of Political Economy.* Translated by Sampson S. Lloyd, 1885. Text reproduced on the Internet. At http://socserv2.soc sci.mcmaster.ca/econ/ugcm/3ll3/list/

Livingston, Jon, Joe Moore and Felicia Oldfather. 1973. *The Japan Reader 2: Postwar Japan: 1945 to the Present.* New York: Pantheon Books.

Lockwood, William. 1965. "Japan's 'New Capitalism.' " In *The State and Economic Enterprise in Japan.* Ed. William Lockwood, Princeton: Princeton University Press.

McCormack, Gavan. 1996. *The Emptiness of Japanese Affluence.* Armonk, NY: M.E. Sharpe.

McKinsey Global Institute. 1992. *Service Sector Productivity.* Washington: McKinsey Global Institute.

————. 1993. *Manufacturing Productivity.* Washington: McKinsey Global Institute.

————. 1996. *Capital Productivity.* Washington: McKinsey Global Institute.

Meyer, Richard. 1992. "Hari-Kiri: How Yanase & Co. Protects the Domestic Japanese Car Market." *Financial World.* (September 29, 1992). Pp. 24–26.

Millstein, James. 1983. "Decline in an Expanding Industry: Japanese Competition in Color Television." In *American Industry in International Competition.* Eds. John Zysman and Laura Tyson. Ithaca: Cornell University Press.

Milner, Helen. 1988. *Resisting Protectionism: Global Industries and the Politics of International Trade.* Princeton: Princeton University Press.

Minami, Ryoshin. 1994. *The Economic Development of Japan: A Quantitative Study.* New York: St. Martin's Press.

Ministry of International Trade and Industry (MITI). 1994a. White Paper on International Trade (English summary). Tokyo: MITI.

————. 1994b. "Survey of Trends in Overseas Business Activities of Japanese Companies." (English summary). Tokyo: MITI.

————. 1995. *Regarding the Report of the Subcommittee for Long-Range Issues of the Industrial Structure Council.* Tokyo: MITI. October 1995.

————. 1996a. *Outline of the Interim Report of the Subcommittee for Long-Range Issues of the Industrial Structure Council.* Tokyo: MITI. November 1996.

————. 1996b. "The 28th Survey of Trends in Business Activities of Foreign Affiliates." Tokyo: MITI. February 1996.

Mitsuhiro, Seki. 1993. *Beyond the Full-Set Industrial Structure*. Tokyo: Long-Term Credit Bank International Library Foundation.

Miyazaki, Isamu. 1990. *The Japanese Economy: What Makes It Tick*. Tokyo: Simul Press.

Morita, Akio. 1986. *Made in Japan*. New York: E. P. Dutton.

Murakami, Yasusuke. 1996. *An Anti-Classical Political-Economic Analysis: A Vision for the Next Century*. Stanford: Stanford University Press.

Murakami, Yasusuke, and Kozo Yamamura. 1982. "A Technical Note on Japanese Firm Behavior and Economic Policy." In *Policy and Trade Issues of the Japanese Economy: American and Japanese Perspectives*. Ed. Kozo Yamamura. Seattle: University of Washington Press.

Muramatsu, Michio, and Ellis Krauss. 1987. "The Conservative Policy Line and the Development of Patterned Pluralism." In *The Political Economy of Japan: Volume 1: The Domestic Transformation*. Eds. Kozo Yamamura and Yasukichi Yasuba. Stanford: Stanford University Press.

Murphy, R. Taggart. 1996. *The Weight of the Yen*. New York: Norton.

Mutoh, Hiromichi. 1988. "The Automotive Industry." In *Industrial Policy of Japan*. Eds. Ryutaro Komiya, Masahiro Okuno and Kotaro Suzumura. San Diego: Academic Press.

Nakajima, Makoto. 1996. *Industrial Policy for the Future*. Conference paper. September 2, 1996. Tokyo: MITI.

Neff, Robert, Paul Magnusson and William Holstein. 1989. "Rethinking Japan: The New Harder Line Toward Tokyo." *Business Week*. August 7, 1989. Pp. 44–52.

Nikkei Weekly. 1996a. "Food Producers Keep the Pasta Coming." May 27, 1996. P. 2.

————. 1996b. "Imports Change Fabric of Japan's Industry." June 3, 1996. P. 18.

————. 1996c. "Imports of Computers, Related Equipment Rise 61%." June 3, 1996. P. 7.

————. 1997. "Foreign Firms Take Head Start on 'Big Bang.' " July 28, 1997. P. 1.

Noguchi, Yukio. 1994. "Dismantle the 1940 Setup to Restructure the Economy." *Economic Eye*. Autumn. Pp. 25–28.

Noland, Marcus. 1995a. "Public Policy, Private Preferences, and the Japanese Trade Pattern." Draft paper to be published in forthcoming *Review of Economics and Statistics*. Washington: Institute for International Economics.

————. 1995b. "Why Are Prices in Japan So High?" *Japan and the World Economy* 7. Pp. 225–261.

North, Douglass. 1990. *Institutions, Institutional Change, and Economic Performance*. Cambridge, UK: Cambridge University Press.

Ogura, Seiritsu, and Naoyoki Yoshino. 1988. "The Tax System and the Fiscal Investment and Loan Program." In *Industrial Policy of Japan*. Ed. Ryutaro Komiya, Masahiro Okuno and Kotaro Suzumura. San Diego: Academic Press.

Ohkawa, Kazushi, and Henry Rosovsky. 1973. *Japanese Economic Growth: Trend Acceleration in the Twentieth Century*. Stanford: Stanford University Press.

Okimoto, Daniel. 1989. *Between MITI and the Marketplace: Japanese Industrial*

Policy for High Technology. Stanford: Stanford University Press.

Okubo, Sumiye. 1996. *Prospects for Growth in Japan in the 21st Century*. Washington: Department of Commerce.

Olson, Mancur. 1982. *The Rise and Decline of Nations: Economic Growth, Stagflation and Social Rigidities*. New Haven: Yale University Press.

Onada, Kinya. 1993. "Japan's Synthetic Fiber Industry: From Development to Industrial Adjustment." In *Industrial Policy in East Asia*. Eds. Ryuichiro Inoue, Hirohisa Kohama and Shujiro Urata. Tokyo: Japan External Trade Organization (JETRO).

Patrick, Hugh. 1977. "The Future of the Japanese Economy: Output and Labor Productivity." *Journal of Japanese Studies* 3 (Summer 1977).

———. 1986. "Japanese High Technology Industrial Policy in Comparative Context." In *Japan's High Technology Industries: Lessons and Limitations of Industrial Policy*. Eds. Hugh Patrick with Larry Meissner. Seattle: University of Washington Press.

———. 1991. "Concepts, Issues and Selected Findings." In *Pacific Basin Industries in Distress: Structural Adjustment and Trade Policy in Nine Industrialized Economies*. Ed. Hugh Patrick. New York: Columbia University Press.

———. 1995. "Crumbling or Transforming: Japan's Economic Success and the Postwar Economic Institutions." Columbia University Center on Japanese Economy and Business. Working Paper No. 98.

Patrick, Hugh, and Henry Rosovsky. 1976. "Japan's Economic Performance: An Overview" and "Prospects for the Future and Some Other Implications." In *Asia's New Giant*. Ed. Hugh Patrick and Henry Rosovsky. Washington: The Brookings Institution.

Peck, Merton, with the collaboration of Shuji Tamura. 1976. "Technology." In *Asia's New Giant*. Eds. Hugh Patrick and Henry Rosovsky. Washington: The Brookings Institution.

Pempel, T.J. 1982. *Policy and Politics in Japan: Creative Conservatism*. Philadelphia: Temple University Press.

———. 1987. The Unbundling of "Japan, Inc.": The Changing Dynamics of Japanese Policy Formation." In *The Trade Crisis: How Will Japan Respond?* Seattle: Society for Japanese Studies.

———. 1997. "Regime Shift: Japanese Politics in a Changing World Economy." *Journal of Japanese Studies*. Pp. 333–361. Volume 23, Number 2. Spring 1997.

Pepper, Thomas, Merit Janow and Jimmy Wheeler. 1985. *The Competition: Dealing with Japan*. New York: Praeger.

Petri, Peter. 1991. "Market Structure, Comparative Advantage, and Japanese Trade under the Strong Yen." In *Trade With Japan: Has the Door Opened Wider?* Ed. Paul Krugman. Chicago: University of Chicago Press.

Porter, Michael. 1990. *The Competitive Advantage of Nations*. New York: The Free Press.

Prestowitz, Clyde. 1988. *Trading Places: How We Allowed Japan to Take the Lead*. New York: Basic Books.

————. 1993. "Japan and the United States: Twins or Opposites." In *Harness the Rising Sun*. Lanham, MD: University Press of America.

Price Structure Policy Committee. 1994. *Interim Report on Deliberations of Price Structure Policy Committee*. (English summary). Tokyo: Economic Planning Agency.

Ramseyer, J. Mark, and Frances McCall Rosenbluth. 1997. *Japan's Political Marketplace*. Cambridge, MA: Harvard University Press.

Richardson, Bradley. 1997. *Japanese Democracy: Power, Coordination and Performance*. New Haven: Yale University Press.

Richardson, J. David. 1989. "Trade Liberalization with Imperfect Competition: A Survey. *OECD Economic Studies No. 12*. (Spring 1989). Pp. 7–50.

Roll, Eric. 1938. *A History of Economic Thought*. London: Faber & Faber.

Rubin, Robert. 1998. Speech at Georgetown University, January 21, 1998.

Sachs, Jeffrey, and Andrew Warner. 1995. *Economic Reform and the Process of Global Integration*. Reprint No. 2002. Cambridge: National Bureau of Economic Research.

Sakaiya, Taichi. 1993. *What Is Japan? Contradictions and Transformations*. New York: Kodansha International.

Sakakibara, Eisuke. 1993. *Beyond Capitalism: The Japanese Model of Market Economics*. Lanham, MD: University Press of America.

Samuels, Richard. 1987. *The Business of the Japanese State: Energy Markets in Comparative and Historical Perspective*. Ithaca: Cornell University Press.

Saxonhouse, Gary. 1979. "Industrial Restructuring in Japan." *Journal of Japanese Studies 5*.

————. 1982. "Evolving Comparative Advantage and Japan's Imports of Manufactures." In *Policy and Trade Issues of the Japanese Economy: American and Japanese Perspectives*. Ed. Kozo Yamamura. Seattle: University of Washington Press.

————. 1988. "Comparative Advantage, Structural Adaptation, and Japanese Performance." In *The Political Economy of Japan: Volume 2: The Changing International Context*. Eds. Takashi Inoguchi and Daniel Okimoto. Stanford: Stanford University Press.

————. 1994. "Japan: Growing Old Gracefully?" In *International Economic Insights*. January–February 1994. Pp. 11–14.

Sazanami, Yoko, Shujiro Urata and Hiroki Kawai. 1995. *Measuring the Costs of Protection in Japan*. Washington: Institute for International Economics.

Schlesinger, Jacob. 1997. *Shadow Shoguns: The Rise and Fall of Japan's Postwar Political Machine*. New York: Simon and Schuster.

Schoppa, Leonard. 1997. *Bargaining with Japan: What American Pressure Can and Cannot Do*. New York: Columbia University Press.

Seki, Mitsuhiro. 1994. *Beyond the Full-Set Industrial Structure: Japanese Industry in the New Age of East Asia*. Tokyo: LTCB International Library Foundation.

Sekiguchi, Sueo. 1991. "Japan: A Plethora of Programs." In *Pacific Basin Industries in Distress: Structural Adjustment and Trade Policy in Nine Industrialized Economies*. Ed. Hugh Patrick. New York: Columbia University Press.

Sekiguchi, Sueo, and Toshihiro Horiuchi. 1988. "Trade and Adjustment Assistance."

In *Industrial Policy of Japan*. Eds. Ryutaro Komiya, Masahiro Okuno and Kotaro Suzumura. San Diego: Academic Press.

Shinohara, Miyohei. 1968. "Patterns and Some Structural Changes in Japan's Postwar Industrial Growth." In *Economic Growth: The Japanese Experience Since the Meiji Era*. Ed. Lawrence Klein and Kazushi Ohkawa. Homewood, IL: Richard D. Irwin.

————. "The Japanese View." 1991. An excerpt from Miyohei Shinohara, *Industrial Growth, Trade and Dynamic Patterns in the Japanese Economy*. In *Powernomics: Economics and Strategy After the Cold War*. Eds. Clyde Prestowitz, Ronald Morse and Alan Tonelson. Washington: Madison Books.

Shiraishi, Ken. 1996. "Will Budget-Cutting in America Worsen Fiscal Woes in Japan?" *Diamond Weekly*. February 1996.

Smith, Patrick. 1997. *Japan: A Reinterpretation*. New York: Pantheon Books.

Sugiyama, Chuhei. 1994. *Origins of Economic Thought in Modern Japan*. London: Routledge.

Summers, Lawrence. 1989. "The Ishihara-Morita Brouhaha." In *The International Economy*. December 1989.

————. 1997. "U.S. Economic Policy toward Japan in the Second Clinton Administration." Speech before the Japan-America Society of Washington. February 28, 1997.

Summers, Robert, and Alan Heston. 1995. *Penn World Tables, Mark 5.6a*. Diskette version from National Bureau of Economic Research in Cambridge, MA.

Suzuki, Yoshio. 1997. "Bankers Ours." In *The International Economy*. July/August 1997.

Tanaka, Naoki. 1988. "Aluminum Refining Industry." In *Industrial Policy of Japan*. Eds. Ryutaro Komiya, Masahiro Okuno and Kotaro Suzumura. San Diego: Academic Press.

Thurow, Lester. 1992. *Head to Head: The Coming Economic Battle among Japan, Europe, and America*. New York: William Morrow.

Tilton, Mark. 1996. *Restrained Trade: Cartels in Japan's Basic Materials Industries*. Ithaca: Cornell University Press.

TOE (The Oriental Economist Report). 1997. "Crumbling Foundation: Construction Companies in Trouble." July 1997.

Trezise, Philip, and Yukio Suzuki. 1976. "Politics, Government and Economic Growth in Japan." In *Asia's New Giant*. Eds. Hugh Patrick and Henry Rosovsky. Washington: The Brookings Institution.

Tsuru, Shigeto. 1993. *Japan's Capitalism: Creative Defeat and Beyond*. Cambridge, UK: Cambridge University Press.

Uekasa, Masu. 1988. "The Oil Crisis and After." In *Industrial Policy of Japan*. Eds. Ryutaro Komiya, Masahiro Okuno and Kotaro Suzumura. San Diego: Academic Press.

Ueno, Hiroya. 1980. "Conception and Evaluation of Industrial Policy." In *Industry and Business in Japan*. Ed. Kazuo Sato. Armonk, NY: M.E. Sharpe.

United Nations Industrial Development Organization (UNIDO). 1995. *Industrial Development: Global Report, 1995*. New York: Oxford University Press.

United States Trade Representative (USTR). 1994. *Foreign Trade Barriers*. Washington: USTR.

Upham, Frank. 1993. "Privatizing Regulation: The Implementation of the Large-Scale Retail Stores Law." In *Political Dynamics in Contemporary Japan*. Eds. Gary Allison and Yasunori Sone. Ithaca: Cornell University Press.

Uriu, Robert. 1996. *Troubled Industries: Confronting Economic Change in Japan*. Ithaca: Cornell University Press.

van Ark, Bart. 1995. "Manufacturing Prices, Productivity and Labor Costs in Economies." *Monthly Labor Review* (July). Pp. 56–73.

van Ark, Bart and Dirk Pilat. 1993. "Productivity Levels in Germany, Japan, and the United States: Differences and Causes." In *Brookings Papers on Economic Activity, Microeconomics 2*. Reprint. Washington: The Brookings Institution.

van Wolferen, Karel. 1989. *The Enigma of Japanese Power*. New York: Alfred A. Knopf.

Vestal, James. 1993. *Planning for Change: Industrial Policy and Japanese Economic Development: 1945–90*. New York: Oxford University Press.

Watanabe, Machiko. 1993. In *Industrial Policy in East Asia*. Eds. Ryuichiro Inoue, Hirohisa Kohama and Shujiro Urata. Tokyo: Japan External Trade Organization (JETRO).

Weinberg, Neil. 1996. "Shortchanged Investors." *Forbes*. July 15, 1996. Pp. 54.

Weinstein, David, and Richard Beason. 1994. "Growth, Economies of Scale, and Targeting in Japan (1955–1990). Manuscript prepared for *Review of Economics and Statistics*.

Wolff, Alan. 1990. "U.S.-Japan Relations and the Rule of Law: The Nature of the Trade Conflict and the American Response." In *Japan's Economic Structure: Should it Change?* Ed. Kozo Yamamura. Seattle, WA: Society for Japanese Studies.

Wood, Christopher. 1994. *The End of Japan Inc.: And How the New Japan Will Look*. New York: Simon & Schuster.

World Bank. 1993. *The East Asian Miracle: Economic Growth and Public Policy*. Washington: World Bank.

———. 1995. *World Development Indicators, 1995* (CD-ROM). Washington: World Bank.

———. 1997. *World Development Indicators, 1997* (CD-ROM). Washington: World Bank.

Yamamura, Kozo. 1975. "Structure Is Behavior: An Appraisal of Japanese Economic Policy, 1960 to 1972." In *The Japanese Economy in International Perspective*. Ed. Isaiah Frank. Baltimore: Johns Hopkins University Press.

———. 1982. "Success That Soured: Administrative Cartels in Japan." In *Policy and Trade Issues of the Japanese Economy: American and Japanese Perspectives*. Ed. Kozo Yamamura. Seattle: University of Washington Press.

———. 1987. "Shedding the Shackles of Success: Saving Less for Japan's Future." In *Journal of Japanese Studies* (Spring 1987). Pps. 429–457.

———. 1990. "Introduction" and "Will Japan's Economic Structure Change? Confessions of a Former Optimist." In *Japan's Economic Structure: Should It Change?* Ed. Kozo Yamamura. Seattle, WA: Society for Japanese Studies.

————. 1997. "Entrepreneurship, Ownership and Management in Japan." In *The Economic Emergence of Modern Japan*. Ed. Kozo Yamamura. Cambridge, UK: Cambridge University Press.

Yamamura, Kozo, and Jan Vandenberg. 1986. "Japan's Rapid-Growth Policy on Trial: The Television Case." In *Law and Trade Issues of the Japanese Economy: American and Japanese Perspectives*. Eds. Gary Saxonhouse and Kozo Yamamura. Seattle: University of Washington Press.

Yamawaki, Hideki. 1988. "The Steel Industry." In *Industrial Policy of Japan*. Eds. Ryutaro Komiya, Masahiro Okuno and Kotaro Suzumura. San Diego: Academic Press.

Yamazawa, Ippa. 1988. "The Textile Industry." In *Industrial Policy of Japan*. Eds. Ryutaro Komiya, Masahiro Okuno and Kotaro Suzumura. San Diego: Academic Press.

Yonezawa, Yoshie. 1988. "The Shipbuilding Industry." In *Industrial Policy of Japan*. Eds. Ryutaro Komiya, Masahiro Okuno and Kotaro Suzumura. San Diego: Academic Press.

Yoshikawa, Hiroshi. 1995a. *Macroeconomics and the Japanese Economy*. New York: Oxford University Press.

————. 1995b. "High Economic Growth and Its End in Japan: An Explanation by a Model of Demand-Led Growth." In *The Structure of the Japanese Economy: Changes on the Domestic and International Fronts*. Ed. Mitsuaki Okabe. New York: St. Martin's Press.

Zysman, John. 1983. *Governments, Markets and Growth: Financial Systems and the Politics of Industrial Change*. Ithaca: Cornell University Press.

Index

About the Author

Richard Katz is Senior Editor at *The Oriental Economist Report*, a monthly English-language newsletter about Japan. He has reported on Japan-related issues for the past two decades in both American and Japanese publications. A Visiting Lecturer in Economics at the State University of New York (SUNY) at Stony Brook, he teaches a course on the postwar Japanese economy.